FORECASTING VOLATILITY IN THE FINANCIAL MARKETS

FORECASTING VOLATILITY IN THE FINANCIAL MARKETS

Edited by

John Knight

Stephen Satchell

OXFORD   AUCKLAND   BOSTON   JOHANNESBURG   MELBOURNE   NEW DELHI

Butterworth-Heinemann
Linacre House, Jordan Hill, Oxford OX2 8DP
225 Wildwood Avenue, Woburn, MA 01801-2041
A division of Reed Educational and Professional Publishing Ltd

A member of the Reed Elsevier plc group

First published 1998

British Library Cataloguing in Publication Data
A catalogue record for this book is available from the British Library

Library of Congress Cataloguing in Publication Data
A catalogue record for this book is available from the Library of Congress

ISBN 0 7506 4081 2

Typeset by Laser Words, Madras, India
Printed and bound in Great Britain by
Biddles Ltd, Guildford and King's Lynn.

Contents

Contributors

E. Acar
Dresdner Kleinwort Benson, UK

A.B. Aydemir
Department of Economics, University of Western Ontario, Canada

B. Bahra
Bank of England, UK

S. Bond
Hughes Hall, Cambridge, UK

G.A. Christodoulakis
Department of Economics, Birkbeck College, UK

A.C. Harvey
Faculty of Economics, University of Cambridge, UK

S. Hwang
Faculty of Economics, University of Cambridge, UK

G.J. Jiang
Department of Econometrics, University of Groningen, The Netherlands

J.L. Knight
Department of Economics, University of Western Ontario, Canada

P. Lequeux
Banque Nationale de Paris plc, UK

G. Perez-Quiros
Federal Reserve Bank of New York, USA

E. Petitdidier
BAREP, Société Générale, France

L.C.G. Rogers
Department of Mathematics, University of Bath, UK

S.E. Satchell
Faculty of Economics, Trinity College and University of Cambridge, UK

A. Timmermann
Department of Economics, University of California, San Diego, USA

Introduction

This book presents recent research on volatility in financial markets with a special emphasis on forecasting. This literature has grown at a frightening rate in recent years and would-be readers may feel daunted by the prospect of learning hundreds of new acronyms, prior to grappling with the ideas they represent. To reduce the entry costs of our readers we present two summary chapters in the first section, a chapter on volatility in finance by A.B. Aydemir and a survey of applications of stochastic volatility models to option pricing problems by G.J. Jiang. This is an area of some importance as one of the sources of data in the study of volatility is the implied volatility series derived from option prices.

These summaries are followed by a section of two practitioner chapters, namely one by E. Acar and E. Petitdidier and one by P. Lequeux. These are followed by a chapter by a monetary economist, B. Bahra. All three chapters focus on practical issues concerning the use of volatilities; the first two examine high-frequency data, the third considers how risk-neutral probability measurement can be put into a forecasting framework.

The following four chapters concentrate on direct forecasting using GARCH, forecasting implied volatility and looking at tick-by-tick data. These chapters concentrate much more on theoretical issues in volatility and risk modelling. S. Bond considers dynamic models of semi-variance, a measure of downside risk. G. Perez-Quiros and A. Timmermann examine connections between volatility of stock markets and business cycle turning points A. Harvey examines long memory stochastic volatility. J. Knight and S. Satchell examine some exact properties of conditional heteroscedasticity models.

Taken together these chapters reflect the extraordinary diversity of procedures now available for forecasting volatility. It seems likely that many of these can be incorporated into trading strategies or built into investment technology products. The editors have put the book together with the twin goals of encouraging both researchers and practitioners. We hope that this book is useful to both audiences.

Chapter 1

Volatility modelling in finance[*]

ABDURRAHMAN BEKIR AYDEMIR[†]

1.1 INTRODUCTION

Volatility modelling has been a very active area of research in recent years. This interest is largely motivated by the importance of volatility in financial markets. Volatility estimates are widely used as simple risk measures in many asset pricing models. Also volatility enters option pricing formulas derived from models such as the famous Black–Scholes model and its various extensions. For hedging against risk, portfolio management, reliable volatility estimates are crucial.

This very active area of research resulted in the development of several types of models. These alternative models try to account for different stylized facts documented in the literature. Autoregressive Moving Average (ARMA) models, Autoregressive Conditional Heteroscedasticity (ARCH) models, Stochastic Volatility (SV) models, Regime Switching models and Threshold models are the most well-known ones in the literature.

For ARCH-type models several excellent reviews are available including those by Bera and Higgins (1995), Bollerslev, Chou and Kroner (1992), Bollerslev, Engle and Nelson (1994) and Diebold and Lopez (1995). Ghysels, Harvey and Renault (1996) provide a very nice survey of SV models.

The above review papers focus on a single class of models; however, this study presents all available techniques for modelling volatility and tries to highlight the similarities and differences between them. The emphasis in this chapter is on applications in finance. Due to the space limitations we do not cover the details of several issues, such as estimation and testing in ARCH-type and SV models, as these are covered in detail by previous studies. However, for the

---

[*] I am grateful to the editors of this volume for their helpful comments. The usual disclaimer applies.
[†] The University of Western Ontario, Department of Economics, SSC, London, ON, Canada, N6A 5C2, e-mail: aydemir@sscl.uwo.ca

regime switching and threshold models we deviate from this since these models are relatively new in the literature and surveys are not readily available.

The next section starts with ARMA-type models and discusses their limitations for modelling volatility. Section 1.3 highlights the stylized facts in the data about volatility while section 1.4 presents ARCH-type models. SV models are discussed in section 1.5. Section 1.6 considers models that allow for structural breaks in the underlying process, the regime switching models and the threshold models. The last section concludes.

1.2 AUTOREGRESSIVE MOVING AVERAGE MODELS

Linear Gaussian models have been the most frequently used models in time series analysis for the past five decades. The general representation for these models is:

$$X_t = \alpha_0 + \sum_{j=1}^{p} \alpha_j X_{t-j} + \sum_{j=0}^{q} \beta_j \varepsilon_{t-j} \tag{1.1}$$

where α_j and β_j are real constants, $\alpha_p \neq 0$, $\beta_q \neq 0$ and ε_t are zero-mean uncorrelated random variables, called white noise (WN),[1] with a common variance, $\sigma^2(<\infty)$. The above model is called an *autoregressive moving average model* or an ARMA(p,q) model. An ARMA(0,q) model is referred to as the *moving average* model of order q, and denoted by MA(q); whereas an ARMA(p,0) model is an *autoregressive* model of order p, denoted by AR(p).

Several advantages and limitations of these models are discussed in the literature (Tong, 1990). The advantages of these models include the following. First, for linear difference equations there is a complete theory available. Since the theory of Gaussian models is well understood, there is a well-developed theory of statistical inference (assuming normality for ε_t). Second, in terms of computation, modelling data with ARMA structure is easy and there are several statistical packages available for this purpose. Third, this class of models enjoyed a reasonable level of success in analysis of data, forecasting and control.

ARMA-type models are widely used in the finance literature. A stationary AR(1) process is used for modelling volatility of monthly returns on the Standard & Poor's (S&P) composite index by Poterba and Summers (1986). The logarithm of the volatility of S&P monthly returns is modelled by a nonstationary ARIMA(0,1,3) model by French, Schwert and Stambaugh (1987) and the model is reported to work reasonably well. Schwert (1990) and Schwert and Seguin (1990) use an AR(12) model for monthly volatility process. ARMA-type models work well as first-order approximations to many processes.

In many time series data we observe asymmetries, sudden bursts at irregular time intervals, periods of high and low volatility. Exchange rate data is an example of this kind of behaviour. Also, cyclicality and time irreversibility is reported by several practitioners using different data sets. Linear Gaussian models have definite limitations in mimicking these properties.

One of the important shortcomings of the ARMA-type models is the assumption of constant variance. Most financial data exhibit changes in volatility and this feature of the data cannot be captured due to the above assumption.

Tong (1990) criticizes linear Gaussian models, noting that if ε_t is set equal to a constant for all t, equation (1.1) becomes a deterministic linear difference equation in X_t. X_t will have a 'stable limit point', as X_t always tends to a unique finite constant, independent of the initial value. The symmetric joint distribution of the stationary Gaussian ARMA models does not fit data with strong asymmetry as well. Due to the assumption of normality, it is more suitable to use these models with data that have only negligible probability of sudden bursts of very large amplitude at irregular time epochs.

For data exhibiting strong cyclicality, the autocorrelation function is also strongly cyclical. Since the joint normality assumption implies the regression function at lag (j), $E(X_t \mid X_{t-j})$, $(j \in Z)$, to be linear for ARMA models; at those lags for which the autocorrelation function is quite small in modulus, a linear approximation may not be appropriate. Finally, ARMA models are not well suited for data exhibiting time irreversibility.

The above limitations of ARMA models lead us to models where we either retain the general ARMA framework and allow the WN to be non-Gaussian, or abandon the linearity assumption.

1.3   CHANGES IN VOLATILITY

In many time series models we observe changes in volatility which is the main topic of interest for this chapter. ARMA models assume a constant variance for ε_t, hence they cannot account for the observed changes in volatility especially in financial data such as exchange rate data and data on stock returns. Before presenting different methods of volatility modelling, stylized facts about volatility are presented in the next section.

1.3.1   Stylized facts about volatility in financial time series

Financial time series such as stock returns, exchange rates etc. exhibit certain patterns which are crucial for correct model specification, estimation and forecasting.

Fat tails
When the distribution of financial time series such as stock returns are compared with the normal distribution, fatter tails are observed. This observation is also

referred to as excess kurtosis. The standardized fourth moment for a normal distribution is 3 whereas for many financial time series a value well above 3 is observed (Mandelbrot (1963) and Fama (1963, 1965) are the first studies to report this feature). For modelling excess kurtosis, distributions that have fatter tails than normal are proposed in the literature such as Paretian and Levy.

Volatility clustering
The second stylized fact is periods of volatility clustering which refer to the observation of large movements being followed by large movements. This is an indication of persistence in shocks. Correlograms and corresponding Box–Ljung statistics show significant correlations which exist at extended lag lengths.

Leverage effects
This refers to the idea that price movements are negatively correlated with volatility. It was first suggested by Black (1976) for stock returns. Black argued, however, that the measured effect of stock price changes on volatility was too large to be explained solely by leverage effects. Empirical evidence on leverage effects can be found in Nelson (1991), Gallant, Rossi and Tauchen (1992, 1993), Campbell and Kyle (1993) and Engle and Ng (1993).

Long memory
Especially for high-frequency data volatility is highly persistent and there exists evidence of near unit root behaviour of the conditional variance process. This observation led to two propositions for modelling persistence: unit root or long memory process. The Autoregressive Conditional Heteroscedasticity (ARCH) and Stochastic Volatility (SV) models use the second idea for modelling persistence.

Co-movements in volatility
When we look at financial time series across different markets, such as looking at exchange rate returns for different currencies, we observe big movements in one currency being matched by big movements in another. This suggests the importance of multivariate models in modelling cross-correlations in different markets.

These observations about volatility led many researchers to focus on the cause of these stylized facts. Information arrivals was a prominent one in the literature where many studies link the asset returns to the information flow. Asset returns are observed and measured at fixed time intervals such as daily, weekly or monthly. Much more frequent observations such as tick-by-tick data are also available. The rate of information arrival is non-uniform and not directly observable. Mandelbrot and Taylor (1967) use the idea of time deformation to explain the observed fat tails in the data. The same idea is used by Clark (1973) to explain volatility. Easley and O'Hara (1992) try to link market volatility with the trading volume, quote arrivals, forecastable events such as dividend announcements, and market closures.

To get reliable forecasts of future volatilities it is crucial to account for the stylized facts. There are various approaches in the literature for volatility modelling that try to capture these stylized facts which we will discuss in the following sections.

1.3.2   The basic set-up

The basic set-up for modelling the changes in variance is to regard the innovations in the mean as being a sequence of independent and identically distributed random variables, z_t, with zero mean and unit variance, multiplied by a factor σ_t, the standard deviation, that is,

$$\varepsilon_t = \sigma_t z_t, \quad z_t \sim \text{iid}(0, 1) \tag{1.2}$$

For modelling of σ_t the first alternative is the *stochastic volatility* models where σ_t is modelled by a stochastic process, such as an autoregression. Alternatively, the variance is modelled in terms of past observations which is known as *autoregressive conditional heteroscedasticity* or ARCH models. In either case the observations in (1.2) form a martingale difference[2] (MD) sequence although they are not independent.

In many applications ε_t corresponds to the innovation in the mean for some other stochastic process denoted by $\{y_t\}$ where

$$y_t = f(x_{t-1}; b) + \varepsilon_t \tag{1.3}$$

Above, $f(x_{t-1}; b)$ is a function of x_{t-1} which is in the $t-1$ information set, b corresponds to the parameter vector.

The next section starts with ARCH models for modelling volatility.

1.4   ARCH MODELS

The important property of ARCH models is their ability to capture the tendency for volatility clustering in financial data, i.e. a tendency for large (small) swings in prices to be followed by large (small) swings of random direction.

In ARCH framework σ_t is a time-varying, positive and measurable function of the time $t-1$ information set. Engle (1982) proposed that the variance in (1.2) be modelled in terms of past observations. The simplest possibility is to let:

$$\sigma_t^2 = \alpha + \beta \varepsilon_{t-1}^2, \quad \alpha > 0, \quad \beta \geq 0 \tag{1.4}$$

We need the constraints in (1.4) to ensure that variance remains positive. If z_t is Gaussian, so that (1.2) becomes

$$\varepsilon_t = \sigma_t z_t, \quad z_t \sim \text{NID}(0, 1) \tag{1.5}$$

the model itself is conditionally Gaussian (NID denotes above normally and independently distributed). We could write $\varepsilon_t \mid \varepsilon_{t-1} \sim N(0, \sigma_t^2)$. ε_{t-1} is the set of observations up to time $t - 1$ and the model's density is that of a one-step-ahead forecast density (Shephard, 1996).

This specification allows today's variance to depend on the variability of recent observations. Conditional normality of ε_t means ε_t is an MD, and so its unconditional mean is zero and is serially uncorrelated. Under strict stationarity[3] it has a symmetric unconditional density. The conditional variance of ε_t equals σ_t^2, which may be changing through time.

If $3\beta^2 < 1$, the kurtosis is greater than 3 for β positive, so the ARCH model yields observations with heavier tails than those of a normal distribution. If $\beta < 1$, ε_t is WN while ε_t^2 follows an autoregressive process, yielding volatility clustering. This does not imply covariance stationarity since the variance of ε_t^2 will be finite only if $3\beta^2 < 1$ (Shephard, 1996).

Shephard (1996) discusses advantages of building models out of explicit one-step-ahead forecast densities. First, a combination of these densities delivers the likelihood via prediction decomposition which makes estimation and testing straightforward. Second, finance theory is often specified using one-step-ahead moments. Third, this specification parallels the successful AR and MA models which found wide applications for modelling changes in means. Therefore, techniques developed for AR and MA models are applicable to ARCH models.

1.4.1   Generalized ARCH

In the above representation of the ARCH model, conditional variance depends on only a single observation. It is desirable to spread the memory of the process over a number of past observations by including more lags. This enables modelling the change in variance to occur more slowly. This leads to the following identification:

$$\sigma_t^2 = \alpha + \beta_1 \varepsilon_{t-1}^2 + \cdots + \beta_p \varepsilon_{t-p}^2 \tag{1.6}$$

which is denoted by ARCH(p) where $\alpha > 0$ and $\beta_i \geq 0$. An *ad hoc* linearly declining lag structure is often imposed that ensures a monotonic declining effect of more distant shocks, such as $\beta_i = \beta(q + 1 - i)/(q(q + 1))$ (see Engle, 1982, 1983). Including the lagged values of σ_t^2, we obtain the so-called *generalized* ARCH model:

$$\sigma_t^2 = \alpha + \beta_1 \varepsilon_{t-1}^2 + \cdots + \beta_p \varepsilon_{t-p}^2 + \gamma_1 \sigma_{t-1}^2 + \cdots + \gamma_q \sigma_{t-q}^2 \tag{1.7}$$

This model was first suggested by Bollerslev (1986) and Taylor (1986), and is termed GARCH(p,q). All GARCH models are MDs. If the sum of β_i's and γ_i's is less than one, the model has constant variance and so is WN (Harvey, 1981, pp. 276–279). In most of the empirical implementations, the values ($p \leq 2, q \leq 2$) are sufficient to model the volatility which provides a sufficient trade-off between flexibility and parsimony.

ARCH effects are documented in the finance literature by Akgiray (1989) for index returns, Schwert (1990) for futures markets, and Engle and Mustafa (1992) for individual stock returns. Using semiparametric methods Gallant and Tauchen (1989) explore the daily NYSE value-weighted index for two periods, 1959–1978, and 1954–1984, and find significant evidence of ARCH-type conditional heteroscedasticity and conditional non-normality. Hsieh (1988) finds ARCH effects in five different nominal US dollar rates where the conditional distributions of the daily nominal returns are changing through time. However, an interesting observation reported by Diebold (1988), Baillie and Bollerslev (1989), and Drost and Nijman (1993) is that ARCH effects which are highly significant with daily and weekly data weaken as the frequency of data decreases. Diebold and Nerlove (1989) and Gallant, Hsieh and Tauchen (1991) try to explain the existence of ARCH effects in the high-frequency data due to the amount of information or the quality of the information reaching the markets in clusters, or the time between information arrival and the processing of the information by market participants. Engle, Ito and Lin (1990) also suggest the information processing as the source of volatility clustering.

Nelson (1990) shows that the discrete time GARCH(1,1) model converges to a continuous time diffusion model as the sampling interval gets arbitrarily small. Even when misspecified, appropriately defined sequences of ARCH models may still serve as consistent estimators for the volatility of the true underlying diffusion, in the sense that the difference between the true instantaneous volatility and the ARCH estimates converges to zero in probability as the length of the sampling frequency diminishes. This important result bridges the gap between the finance theory which uses continuous time stochastic differential equations and the discrete nature of the all financial time series available. A related result is given by Nelson (1992) who shows that if the true model is a diffusion model with no jumps, then the discrete time variances are consistently estimated by a weighted average of past residuals as in the GARCH(1,1) formulation. Finally, Brock, Hsieh and LeBaron (1991) show that if ε_t^2 is linear in the sense of Priestley (1980), the GARCH(p,q) representation may be seen as a parsimonious approximation to the possibly infinite Wold representation for ε_t^2.

In modelling the above functional forms, normal conditional densities are generally used. However, the normality assumption cannot adequately account for the observed fat tails in the unconditional price and return distributions

(Fama, 1965). McCurdy and Morgan (1987), Milhoj (1987c), Hsieh (1989) and Baillie and Bollerslev (1989) give evidence of uncaptured excess kurtosis in daily or weekly exchange rate data under the assumption of conditional normality. This led to the departures from the normality assumption. Weiss (1984, 1986) derives asymptotic standard errors for the parameters in the conditional mean and variance functions under non-normality. Parametric densities other than normal that are used include Student-t distribution (Bollerslev, 1987; Hsieh, 1989), normal-Poisson mixture distribution (Jorion, 1988), the normal-lognormal mixture distribution (Hsieh, 1989), the power exponential distribution (Baillie and Bollerslev, 1989) and the generalized exponential distribution (Nelson, 1990). Baillie and DeGennaro (1990) show that failure to model the fat-tailed property can lead to spurious results in terms of the estimated risk-return trade-off where they assume that errors are conditionally t-distributed.

There are also semiparametric approaches which provide more efficient estimates for markedly skewed distributions; see Gallant, Hsieh and Tauchen (1991), and Gallant, Rossi and Tauchen (1992) for applications. Engle and Gonzalez-Rivera (1991) explore stock returns for small firms using a non-parametric method and draw the attention to the importance of both the skewness and kurtosis in conditional density function of returns.

Before proceeding with other types of ARCH specifications a few points about GARCH models are worth noting.

The most crucial property of the GARCH models is linearity. GARCH models of the type introduced by Engle (1982) and Bollerslev (1986) imply an ARMA equation for the squared innovation process ε^2. This allows for a complete study of the distributional properties of (ε_t) and also makes the statistical inference (parameter estimation, test for homoscedasticity) easier.

As a result of the choice of quadratic form for the conditional variance, the time paths are characterized by periods of high volatility and other periods where it is low. The impact of past values of innovation on the current volatility is only a function of their magnitude. But this is not generally true in financial data. Several authors such as Campbell and Hentschel (1990), Christie (1982), and Nelson (1990, 1991) pointed out the asymmetry where volatility tends to be higher after a decrease than after an equal increase. The choice of quadratic form for the conditional variance is a symmetric one and prevents modelling of such phenomena.

Non-negativity constraint on coefficients in GARCH models is only a sufficient condition and may be weakened in certain cases (Nelson and Cao, 1992). As noted by Rabemananjara and Zakoian (1993), non-negativity constraints may be a source of important difficulties in running the estimation procedures. With the non-negativity constraint, a shock in the past regardless of the sign always has a positive effect on the current volatility: the impact increases with the magnitude of the shock. Therefore, cyclical or any non-linear behaviour in volatility cannot be taken into account.

In empirical work it seems difficult to consider a large number of lags p and q. Several authors have found it necessary to impose an *ad hoc* structure to the coefficients in these models (Bollersev, 1986; Engle and Granger, 1987).

1.4.2 Integrated ARCH

If $\beta + \gamma = 1$ in the GARCH(1,1) model, we lose weak stationarity since it does not have finite variance. Using squared observations and specification of variance leads to the expression:

$$\varepsilon_t^2 = \alpha + \varepsilon_{t-1}^2 + v_t + \theta v_{t-1} \tag{1.8}$$

where $\theta = -\gamma = 1 - \beta$ and $v_t = \sigma_t^2 (z_t^2 - 1)$. Rearranging (1.8):

$$\Delta \varepsilon_t^2 = \alpha + v_t + \theta v_{t-1} \tag{1.9}$$

This leads to an analogy with ARIMA(0,1,1) in terms of defining an autocorrelation function (ACF) of squared observations. This model is called *integrated GARCH* since the squared observations are stationary in first differences, but it does not follow that ε_t^2 will behave like an integrated process. IGARCH is still an MD process. We require $\alpha > 0$, otherwise, independent of the starting point, σ_t^2 drops to zero almost surely, meaning that the series disappears.

In the IGARCH model current information remains important for forecasts of the conditional variance for all horizons. This property can account for the observed persistence implied by the estimates of the conditional variance in the high-frequency financial data.

The null hypothesis of a unit root in variance is not rejected by several authors using different sets of stock market data (French, Schwert and Stambaugh, 1987; Chou, 1988; Pagan and Schwert, 1990). Volatility persistence in interest rates also has been documented by many studies using data on bond yields, returns on Treasury Bills etc. (see Weiss, 1984; Hong, 1988). On the other hand, Engle and Bollerslev (1986), Bollerslev (1987), and McCurdy and Morgan (1987, 1988), among other studies, report persistence of volatility shocks in the foreign exchange market.

Although it is possible to observe persistence of the variance in the univariate time series representations to be common over different series, certain linear combinations of the variables may show no persistence. These variables are called co-persistent in variance (Bollerslev and Engle, 1993). In many asset pricing relationships this is crucial for the construction of optimal long-term forecasts for the conditional variances and covariances. Schwert and Seguin (1990) investigate the disaggregated stock portfolios where they find evidence for common source of time-varying volatility across the stocks, suggesting the portfolios might be co-persistent. Bollerslev and Engle (1993) also present evidence on the presence of the co-persistence among the variances across the exchange rates. Co-persistence is modelled by multivariate ARCH formulations which will be discussed later.

1.4.3 Exponential ARCH

A number of drawbacks of GARCH models are reported by Harvey (1981). First, the conditional variance is unable to respond asymmetrically to rises and falls in ε_t, and such effects are believed to be important in the behaviour of stock returns. In the linear GARCH(p,q) model the conditional variance is a function of past conditional variances and squared innovations; therefore, sign of returns cannot affect the volatilities. Therefore, GARCH models cannot account for the leverage effects observed in stock returns. Second, estimated coefficients often violate the parameter constraints. Moreover, these constraints may excessively restrict the dynamics of the conditional variance process. Third, assessment of whether shocks to conditional variance are 'persistent' is difficult because of the somewhat paradoxical behaviour noted earlier for IGARCH.

Nelson (1991) introduced EGARCH models, where conditional variance is constrained to be non-negative by assuming the logarithm of σ_t^2 is a function of the past z_t's:

$$\log \sigma_t^2 = \alpha + \sum_{i=1}^{\infty} \beta_i g(z_{t-i}), \quad \beta_1 = 1 \tag{1.10}$$

$$g(z_t) = wz_t + \lambda[|z_t| - E|z_t|] \tag{1.11}$$

where w and λ are real numbers. This specification enables σ_t^2 to respond asymmetrically to rises and falls in ε_t, as for $z_t > 0$ and $z_t < 0$, $g(z_t)$ will have different slopes ($w + \lambda$ and $w - \lambda$, respectively). The asymmetry of information is potentially useful since it allows the variance to respond more rapidly to falls in a market than to corresponding rises. This is a stylized fact for many assets reported by Black (1976), Schwert (1989), Sentana (1995) and Campbell and Hentschel (1992). Nelson (1989, 1990) provides empirical support for the EGARCH specification[4] (for equation (1.12) see Notes at end of chapter).

1.4.4 ARCH-M model

The trade-off between the risk and the expected return inherent in many finance theories can be modelled by the ARCH-in-Mean model introduced by Engle, Lilien and Robins (1987):

$$y_t = f(x_{t-1}, \sigma_t^2; b) + \varepsilon_t$$

A specific case of the above general expression is:

$$y_t = f(\sigma_t^2, b) + \varepsilon_t \sigma_t, \quad \sigma_t^2 = \alpha_0 + \alpha_1 \{y_{t-1} - f(\sigma_{t-1}^2, b)\}^2$$

A linear parametrization is commonly used in the literature:

$$f(\sigma_t^2, b) = \mu_0 + \mu_1 \sigma_t^2$$

Hong (1991) discusses the statistical properties of the above specification.

The ARCH-M model was used in asset pricing theories of CAPM, consumption-based CAPM and the asset pricing theory of Ross (1976). Depending on the functional form, conditional mean increases or decreases with an increase in the conditional variance. Mostly linear and logarithmic functions of σ_t^2 or σ_t are used in the functional form. In the linear specifications the parameter measuring the effect of the conditional variance on the excess return is interpreted as the coefficient of relative risk aversion.

In the linear specification a constant effect of conditional variance on the expected return is hypothesized. Harvey (1989), however, reports the coefficient to be varying over time depending on the phase of the business cycle. There is further empirical evidence against the time-invariant relationship in Chou, Engle and Kane (1992).

Engle, Lilien and Robins (1987) use the ARCH-M model with interest rate data where the conditional variance proxies for the time-varying risk premium and find that this leads to a good fit to the data. Correct model specification is required for consistent parameter estimation as in the EGARCH model. Chou (1988), Attanasio and Wadhwani (1989) and Campbell and Shiller (1989), among others, apply the ARCH-M model to different stock index returns. The ARCH-M model is used in exchange rate data as well. Conditional distribution of spot exchange rates varies over time leading to a time-varying risk premium. To proxy for the risk premium different functional forms that depend on the conditional variance of the spot rate are employed in the empirical literature. Some studies support a mean-variance trade-off (e.g. Kendall and McDonald, 1989), whereas some reach the opposite conclusion (Kendall, 1989).

Baillie and DeGennaro (1990) make a sensitivity analysis of the parameter estimates for the ARCH-M model for different model specifications under parametric specifications; Gallant, Rossi and Tauchen (1992) do a similar exercise under semiparametric specifications.

The use of the ARCH-M model for measuring risk has been criticized in the literature. Backus, Gregory and Zin (1989) and Backus and Gregory (1993) challenge ARCH-M modelling theoretically. Backus and Gregory (1993) show that there does not necessarily exist any relationship between the risk premium and conditional variances in their theoretical economy. Despite the above criticisms, ARCH-M models found their applications in many financial data.

1.4.5 Fractionally integrated ARCH

Ding, Granger and Engle (1993) discuss that volatility tends to change quite
slowly, with the effect of shocks taking a considerable time to decay. The
formulation based on this idea is the fractionally integrated ARCH (FIARCH)
model represented in its simplest form by:

$$\sigma_t^2 = \alpha_0 + \{1 - (1 - L)^d\}\varepsilon_t^2 = \alpha_0 + \alpha(L)\varepsilon_{t-1}^2$$

where $\alpha(L)$ is a polynomial in L that decays hyperbolically in lag length,
rather than geometrically. Baillie, Bollerslev and Mikkelsen (1996) introduce
the generalizations of this model which are straightforward transformations of
fractionally integrated ARMA (ARFIMA) models of Granger and Joyeux (1980)
and Hosking (1981) into long memory models of variance.

1.4.6 Other univariate ARCH formulations

Other parametric models suggested in the literature include the Augmented
ARCH model of Bera, Lee and Higgins (1990), the Asymmetric ARCH model
of Engle (1990), the Modified ARCH model of Friedman and Laibson (1989),
the Qualitative ARCH model of Gouriéroux and Monfort (1992), the Structural
ARCH model of Harvey, Ruiz and Sentana (1992) and the Threshold ARCH
model of Zakoian (1994),[5] the Absolute Residuals ARCH model of Taylor
(1986) and Schwert (1989), the Nonlinear ARCH (NARCH) model of Engle
and Bollerslev (1986) and Higgins and Bera (1992), and the Quadratic ARCH
(QARCH) model of Sentana (1995).

In the Structural ARCH model, ARCH disturbances appear in both the state
and updating equations.

The Absolute Residuals model suggests

$$\sigma_t = \alpha_0 + \beta_1 |\varepsilon_{t-1}|$$

whereas the NARCH model is similar to Box–Cox generalization:

$$\sigma_t^2 = \alpha_0 + \beta_1 |\varepsilon_{t-1}|^\gamma$$

or a non-symmetric version:

$$\sigma_t^2 = \alpha_0 + \beta_1 |\varepsilon_{t-1} - k|^\gamma$$

The Quadratic ARCH model captures asymmetry and has the form:

$$\sigma_t^2 = \alpha_0 + \beta_1 \varepsilon_{t-1}^2 + \beta_2 \varepsilon_{t-1}$$

with the appropriate constraints on the parameters to ensure positivity of σ_t^2.

There are also non-parametric alternatives suggested in the literature. One line of research uses Kernel methods where σ_t^2 is estimated as a weighted average of ε_t^2, $t = 1, 2, \ldots, T$. Amongst the several weighting schemes proposed, the most popular has been the Gaussian kernels. Pagan and Ullah (1988), Robinson (1988), and Whistler (1988) are a few of the existing works in this area. Another non-parametric approach is introduced by Gallant (1981) where σ_t^2 is approximated by a function of polynomial and trigonometric terms in lagged values of ε_t. Gallant and Nychka (1987) propose a semi-non-parametric approach where the normal density used in the MLE estimation of the ARCH model is multiplied by a polynomial expansion. Estimators obtained for high orders of this expansion has the same properties as non-parametric estimates.

1.4.7 Multivariate ARCH models

Dependence among asset prices, common volatility clustering across different assets and portfolio allocation decisions led researchers to multivariate ARCH specifications. There are different approaches in modelling the covariance matrix Ω_t in a multivariate ARCH model represented by:

$$\varepsilon_t = z_t \Omega_t^{1/2}$$

$$z_t \text{ iid } E(z_t) = 0, \quad \text{Var}(z_t) = I$$

Amongst the alternative specifications, there is the multivariate linear ARCH(q) model of Kraft and Engle (1983), the multivariate latent factor ARCH model of Diebold and Nerlove (1989) and the constant conditional correlation model of Bollerslev (1990). The applications of the multivariate ARCH model include modelling the return and volatility relation in domestic and international equity markets (e.g. Bodurtha and Mark, 1991; Giovanni and Jorion, 1989); studies of the links between international stock markets (e.g. King, Sentana and Wadhwani, 1990); effects of volatility in one market on the other markets (e.g. Chan, Chan and Karolyi, 1992). The weakness of the univariate ARCH-M specification for modelling the risk-return trade-off in foreign exchange rate markets led to multivariate specifications. The possible dependence across currencies through cross-country conditional covariances may explain the time-varying risk premia better than the univariate specifications (Lee, 1988; Baillie and Bollerslev, 1990). Although, generally significant cross-correlations and better fits to the data are obtained in multivariate specifications, the improvements for forecasts are only slight. The biggest challenge in the multivariate ARCH framework is the computational difficulties that arise in various applications.

1.5　STOCHASTIC VARIANCE MODELS

Stochastic variance or stochastic volatility models treat σ_t as an unobserved variable which is assumed to follow a certain stochastic process. These models are able to overcome some of the drawbacks of GARCH models noted earlier and this modelling effort led to generalizations of the well-known Black–Scholes results in finance theory along many other applications.

The specification is:

$$\varepsilon_t = \sigma_t z_t, \quad \sigma_t^2 = \exp(h_t), \quad t = 1, \ldots, T \tag{1.13}$$

and let h_t, for example, be an AR(1) process:

$$h_t = \alpha + \beta h_{t-1} + \eta_t, \quad \eta_t \sim \text{NID}(0, \sigma_\eta^2) \tag{1.14}$$

η_t may or may not be independent of z_t.[6,7]

In this specification σ_t is a function of some unobserved or latent component, h_t. The log-volatility h_t is unobserved but can be estimated using the past observations. As opposed to standard GARCH models, h_t is not deterministic conditional on the $t - 1$ information set. The specification in (1.1) is that of a first-order autoregressive process where η_t is an innovation. The constraints on σ_t being positive are satisfied using the idea of EGARCH. The exponential specification ensures that the conditional variance remains positive.

Assuming η_t and z_t are independent, we will list some properties of this class of models. The details and some proofs can be found in Harvey (1981):

(1) If $|\beta| < 1$, h_t is strictly stationary and ε_t, being the product of two strictly stationary processes, is strictly stationary.
(2) ε_t is WN, which follows from the independence of z_t and η_t.
(3) If η_t is Gaussian, h_t is a standard Gaussian autoregression with mean and variance given by (for all $|\beta| < 1$):

$$\mu_h = E(h_t) = \frac{\alpha}{1 - \beta}$$

$$\sigma_h^2 = \text{Var}(h_t) = \frac{\sigma_\eta^2}{1 - \beta^2}$$

Under normality of η_t, using the properties of a lognormal distribution, it can be shown that $E[\exp(ah_t)] = \exp(a^2 \sigma_h^2 / 2)$, where a is a constant. Therefore, if z_t has a finite variance σ_z^2, then the variance of $\varepsilon_t (= \sigma_t z_t)$ can be computed as:

$$\text{Var}(\varepsilon_t) = \sigma_z^2 \exp(\sigma_h^2 / 2)$$

(4) The kurtosis of ε_t is $K \exp(\sigma_h^2)$ where K is the kurtosis of z_t (if the fourth moment exists). In particular, if z_t is Gaussian, the kurtosis

of ε_t is $3\exp(\sigma_h^2)$, which is greater than 3. Thus the model exhibits excess kurtosis compared with a normal distribution. SV models can be regarded as the continuous-time limit of discrete-time EGARCH models. They inherit the fat tails property of EGARCH models and produce the required leptokurtic effect noticed in financial data.

(5)   Various generalizations of the model are possible such as assuming that h_t follows any stationary ARMA process, or letting z_t have a Student-t distribution.

There are several advantages of SV models. Their properties can be found and manipulated much easier. Also multivariate extensions are easier. They possess simpler analogous continuous-time representations and this makes bridging to finance theory, which employs continuous time models, easier.

As noted above, SV models can mimic the fat tail property observed in the data. An important stylized fact in option prices is the so-called smile effect: implied volatilities from observed option prices are U-shaped as a function of the exercise price of the option. For a large class of valuation rules induced by the absence of arbitrage argument, Renault and Tovzi (1996) proved that the smile effect is a natural consequence of stochastic volatility.

Another advantage of SV models is that they induce incomplete markets. An important problem that emerges as a consequence of the complete market assumption is that contingent claims appear as redundant assets and therefore the trading in contingent claims is not justified from an economic viewpoint. SV models are not subject to such criticisms (Ghysels, Harvey and Renault, 1996).

1.5.1   From continuous time financial models to discrete time SV models

In above expression (1.13), the ε_t term can be regarded as the stochastic component of a return process denoted by Y_t:

$$Y_t = \log(S_t/S_{t-1}) = \mu + \varepsilon_t$$

$$\varepsilon_t = \log(S_t/S_{t-1}) - \mu \qquad\qquad (1.15)$$

where, for example, S_t is the stock price at time t and μ is the time-invariant average return for this stock.

The more general continuous time analogue of the above return process can be obtained from the following stock price dynamics:

$$dS_t = \mu_t S_t\, dt + \sigma_t S_t\, dW_t \qquad\qquad (1.16)$$

where W_t is a standard Brownian motion.

The famous Black and Scholes (1973) option-pricing formula is obtained when

$$\mu_t = \mu \quad \text{and} \quad \sigma_t = \sigma$$

are constants for all t. Then the asset price is a geometric Brownian motion. In a risk-neutral world, by equating the average rate of return to the riskless instantaneous interest rate, expression (1.16) becomes:

$$dS_t/S_t = r_t\, dt + \sigma_t\, dW_t \tag{1.17}$$

The Black and Scholes formula for a call option price obtained using the above assumptions is widely used by practitioners. Due to difficulties associated with the estimation, empirical applications of SV models have been limited. This led many researchers to use the Black and Scholes (BS) formulation and another concept called the Black and Scholes implied volatility developed by Latane and Rendlemen (1976).

BS formulation relies, however, on very strong assumptions. Especially, the assumption of a constant variance is known to be violated in real life. This leads to an option pricing model introduced by Hull and White (1987). In this model the volatility is time-variant, governed by a stochastic process:

$$dS_t/S_t = r_t\, dt + \sigma_t\, dW_t \tag{1.18}$$

where σ_t and W_t are independent Markovian.

Expression (1.15) above, where average return is assumed to be constant, is the discrete time analogue of (1.18). In the discrete time specification (1.13), above, $\varepsilon_t(=\sigma_t z_t)$ corresponds to the second term on the right-hand side of the equality in (1.18). The analogue of the process dW_t in the discrete time specification is z_t in (1.13).

1.5.2   Persistence and the SV model

In SV models persistence in volatilities can be captured by specifying a Random Walk (RW) process for the h_t process. Squaring the expression in (1.13) and taking the logarithms of both sides we obtain:

$$\log \varepsilon_t^2 = \log \sigma_t^2 + \log z_t^2$$
$$= h_t + \log z_t^2 \tag{1.19}$$

The process in (1.19) is not stationary but first differencing yields a stationary process.

This specification is analogous to the IGARCH specification in the ARCH-type models where $\alpha + \beta = 1$. In that specification, as well, squared observations are stationary in first-differences and the current information remains important for forecasts of conditional variance over all horizons.

Above, other non-stationary specifications can be used instead of the RW specification. A doubly integrated RW where Δh_t^2 is white noise is one of the possibilities, along with other possible non-stationarities such as seasonal and intradaily components. The specification is the same as in the corresponding levels models discussed in Harvey (1989) and Harvey and Koopman (1993) (Ghysels, Harvey and Renault, 1996).

1.5.3 Long memory SV models

In order to account for the long memory property observed in the data the process h_t can be modelled as a fractional process. This class of models is similar to the Fractionally Integrated GARCH and Fractionally Integrated EGARCH models. They have been introduced to the SV context by Breidt, Crato and deLima (1993) and Harvey (1993). The specification is as follows:

$$h_t = \eta_t / (1 - L)^d, \quad \eta_t \sim \text{NID}(0, \sigma_\eta^2), \quad 0 \le d \le 1 \qquad (1.20)$$

In the above specification when $d = 1$ the process is an RW and when $d = 0$ it is WN. Covariance stationarity is obtained when $d < 0.5$. Harvey (1993) compares two cases, one where h_t follows a long memory process and another where the process is an AR(1). He shows a much slower rate of decline in the autocorrelation function (ACF) for the long memory process.

The ACF for a GARCH model decays geometrically, hence called a short memory process. In contrast to a GARCH model, a long memory SV model has a hyperbolic decay (Breidt, Crato and deLima, 1993). Ding, Granger and Engle (1993) discuss the decay of the autocorrelations of fractional moments of return series using the Standard & Poor's 500 daily closing price index. From the return series that they construct they find very slowly decaying autocorrelations. deLima and Crato (1994) reject the null hypothesis of short memory for the high-frequency daily series by applying long memory tests to the squared residuals of various filtered US stock returns indexes. Bollerslev and Mikkelsen (1996) also found evidence of slowly decaying autocorrelations for the absolute returns of the Standard & Poor's 500 index.

Breidt, Crato and deLima (1993) suggest the following specification to model long memory stochastic volatility:

$$\varepsilon_t = \sigma_t z_t, \quad \sigma_t = \sigma \exp(h_t/2)$$

where $\{h_t\}$ is independent of $\{z_t\}$, $\{z_t\}$ is iid with mean zero and variance one, and $\{h_t\}$ is a long memory process. The series is transformed into a stationary process as follows:

$$\varepsilon_t = \log \varepsilon_t^2$$
$$= \log \sigma^2 + E[\log z_t^2] + h_t + (\log z_t^2 - E[\log z_t^2])$$
$$= \mu + h_t + s_t$$

where $\{s_t\}$ is iid with mean zero and variance σ_s^2. The process ε_t is therefore a summation of a long memory process and the noise s_t. Breidt, Crato and deLima (1993) apply this model to the daily stock market returns and find that the long memory SV model provides an improved description of the volatility behaviour relative to GARCH, IGRACH and EGARCH models.

1.5.4   Leverage effects in SV models

The asymmetric behaviour in stock returns can be captured in SV models easily by letting $\text{Cov}(z_t, \eta_t) \neq 0$; letting $\text{Cov}(z_t, \eta_t) < 0$ picks up the leverage effects. This corresponds to the EGARCH model's ability to respond asymmetrically to shocks. The formulation was first suggested by Hull and White (1987). Hull and White deal with the pricing of a European call on an asset that has stochastic volatility. They consider a derivative asset f with a price that depends upon some security price, S, and its instantaneous variance σ^2 which are assumed to follow the following stochastic process:

$$dS_t = \mu S_t \, dt + \sigma_t S_t \, dW_t$$
$$d\sigma_t^2 = \lambda \sigma_t^2 \, dt + \theta \sigma_t^2 \, d\xi_t$$

Above, the variable μ is a parameter that may depend on S, σ and t. It is assumed that variables λ and θ depend on σ and t but are independent of S. In this continuous time representation the asymmetric behaviour is captured by allowing the processes dW_t and $d\xi_t$ to have correlation ρ. Hull and White determine the option price in series form for the case in which the stochastic volatility is independent of the stock price. Also, numerical solutions are produced for the case in which volatility is correlated with the stock price. They find that the BS price frequently overprices options and that the degree of overpricing increases with the time to maturity.

SV models with leverage effects are applied to exchange rate data as well. In a standard model for foreign currency options a lognormal probability distribution with constant variance is assumed. Melino and Turnbull (1991), however, find evidence that the volatility parameter is highly unstable over time using exchange rate data. Press (1968), McFarland, Petit and Jung (1982), and Engle (1982) show that finite but heteroscedastic variances can generate the fat tail property in exchange rate data which is also consistent with the limiting normal distribution reported by Boothe and Glassman (1987). Melino and Turnbull (1990), using an SV model where they allow for leverage effects, show that the assumption of lognormality along with a constant variance assumption are inappropriate and a hypothesis of volatility changing stochastically is more plausible. The SV specification provides a much closer fit to the empirical distribution of exchange rate changes than those produced by the lognormal model.

The SV formulation with leverage effects was also estimated by Scott (1991) using GMM, Harvey, and Shephard (1993) by the Quasi Likelihood method, and Jacquier, Polson and Rossi (1995) by an extension of the Markov Chain Monte Carlo method.

1.5.5 Risk-return trade-off in SV models

The trade-off between risk and return which is captured by ARCH-M models in the ARCH framework can be captured in the SV framework by the following specification:

$$\varepsilon_t = \alpha + \beta \exp(h_t) + z_t \exp(h_t/2)$$

This specification allows ε_t to be moderately serially correlated. Several properties of this specification are analysed by Pitt and Shephard (1995). A similar type of formulation has been produced by French, Schwert and Stambaugh (1987), and Harvey and Shephard (1996).

1.5.6 Multivariate SV models

Extension of SV models to a multivariate framework adopts the following specification:

$$\varepsilon_{it} = \exp(h_{it}/2)z_{it}, \quad i = 1, 2, \ldots, N \tag{1.21}$$

$$h_{t+1} = \Phi h_t + \eta_t$$

where

$$z_t = (z_{1t}, \ldots, z_{Nt})' \sim \text{iid}(0, \Sigma_z)$$

$$\eta_t = (\eta_{1t}, \ldots, \eta_{Nt})' \sim \text{iid}(0, \Sigma_\eta)$$

The covariance (correlation) matrix for z_t is Σ_z and the covariance (correlation) matrix for η_t is Σ_η. In this specification, Σ_η allows for the movements in volatility to be correlated across different series. The effect of different series on each other can be captured by non-zero off-diagonal entries in Φ.

Harvey, Ruiz and Shephard (1994) allow h_t to follow a multivariate random walk. This simple non-stationary model is obtained when $\Phi = I$. They use a linearization of the form:

$$\log \varepsilon_{it}^2 = h_{it} + \log z_{it}^2$$

If Σ_η is singular of rank $K < N$, then there are K components in volatility, and each h_{it} in (1.21) is a linear combination of $K < N$ common trends:

$$h_t = \theta h_t^+ + \overline{h}$$

where h_t^+ is the $Kx1$ vector of common RW volatilities, $\overline{h}$ is a vector of constants and θ is an NxK matrix of factor loadings. Under certain restrictions θ and $\overline{h}$ can be identified (see Harvey, Ruiz and Shephard, 1994).

In the above specification the logarithms of the squared observations are 'co-integrated' in the sense of Engle and Granger (1987). There are $N - K$ linear combinations which are WN and therefore stationary. If two series of returns exhibit stochastic volatility and this volatility is the same with $\theta' = (1, 1)$, this implies that the ratio of two series will have no stochastic volatility. This concept is similar to the 'co-persistence' we discussed earlier.

Harvey, Ruiz and Shephard (1994) apply the non-stationary model to four exchange rates and find just two common factors driving volatility. Another application is by Mahieu and Schotman (1994a, b). Jacquier, Polson and Rossi (1995) use a Markov Chain Monte Carlo (MCMC) sampler on this model.

Compared with the multivariate GARCH model, the multivariate SV model is much simpler. This specification allows common trends and cycles in volatility. However, the model allows for changing variances but constant correlation similar to the work of Bollerslev (1990).

1.5.7   Estimation of SV models

Compared with ARCH-type models, statistical aspects of SV models are much harder. The main disadvantage of these models is the difficulty of writing exact likelihood function. The likelihood function is only available in the form of a multiple integral since the variance is an unobserved component. Most of the SV models do not have one-step-ahead densities and the distribution of $\varepsilon_t \mid \varepsilon_{t-1}$ is an implicit one (Shephard, 1996).

Estimation and prediction can be done through filtering or smoothing. A filtered estimate is based on all the observations up to, and possibly including, the one at time t. A smoothed estimate, on the other hand, is based on all the observations in the sample, including those after time t.

Ghysels, Harvey and Renault (1996) remark that, unlike the linear and Gaussian time series models where the state space form can be used as the basis for filtering and smoothing algorithms, the SV model is non-linear. They list the three resulting possibilities for estimation as:

(1) Compute inefficient estimates based on a linear state space model;
(2) Estimate the optimal filter to a desired level of accuracy using computer intensive techniques;
(3) Approximate the optimal filter using an (unspecified) ARCH model.

The first method is an approximation to computing optimal filters. It is well known that obtaining an optimal filter is computer intensive and sometimes the required computing time makes it impractical.

ARCH models are also regarded as a device which can be used to perform filtering and smoothing estimation of unobserved volatilities in SV models. Nelson and Foster (1994) point out that in ARCH models the assumption of conditional variance to be a function of past observations is *ad hoc* on both economic and statistical grounds. Nelson (1992) and Nelson and Foster (1994), therefore, regard the ARCH estimates as filters which produce estimates of the conditional variance. Nelson and Foster derive an ARCH model that will give the closest approximation to the continuous time SV formulation which is close to an EGARCH model. Filtering theory for discrete time SV models, however, is not as extensively developed (Ghysels, Harvey and Renault, 1996).

Other alternative estimation techniques used in the literature include Generalized Method-of-Moments (GMM), Quasi Maximum Likelihood (QML) estimation, Bayesian approaches such as Markov Chain Monte Carlo, etc. Shephard (1996) discusses various alternatives for estimation of the SV models.

The QML method is relatively easy to apply and distributional assumptions on z_t are not required. However, Jacquier, Polson and Rossi (1994) and Andersen (1994) show that QML and method-of-moments estimators are not very reliable. Mahieu and Schotman (1994a) consider four different estimators (Quasi Maximum Likelihood, two different simulated EM techniques, and a Bayesian method based on the Gibbs sampler) for the exchange rate data. From the estimation of the time series of volatilities they find that different smoothing algorithms produce very different estimates, even if the parameters of the underlying process are the same. They report that differences are caused by the explicit consideration of the measurement error density in the state space model for log volatility. A disturbing result is that even the most efficient simulation smoothers produce very large standard errors for the volatility estimates.

ARCH-type models and SV models are compared by Jacquier, Polson and Rossi (1994). The most widely used form of GARCH models, the GARCH(1,1) model displays similar properties to the SV model when β is close to 1 in (1.13). Jacquier, Polson and Rossi plot a graph of the correlogram of the squared weekly returns of a portfolio on the New York Stock Exchange. They also plot the ACFs implied by a GARCH(1,1) and an SV model. They show that ACF implied by the SV model is closer to the sample values.

1.5.8 Structural breaks

In all the discussions so far about the ARCH-type models and the SV models, the implicit assumption is that there are no structural changes in the underlying process governing the volatility. Structural breaks in the underlying process, however, are an important possibility in many time series. In financial data sudden shifts at irregular time intervals are observed. These can be due to a government policy change, or to a financial panic etc. For example, the volatility may be following a different process during financial crises than a 'normal' trading day. If such shifts in the data exist then there will be sudden changes in moments of the time series. We already know from our discussions so far that in classical statistical models, such as an AR model, the mean of the process, autoregressive parameters and the variance of WN are assumed to be constant. Although ARCH, GARCH and the SV models will allow changes in volatility, they are not suitable for modelling data that have sudden bursts changing the moments of the time series.

Neglecting such structural breaks will clearly lead to a model misspec-ification. Therefore modelling the structural breaks is important for correct specification of the model, consistency of parameter estimates and forecasting. Whether or not taking into account the structural breaks will provide improvements in terms of forecast accuracy is a matter of how easily such structural breaks can be identified and the underlying parameters can be recovered from the data.

In such time series data, where the process undergoes fairly abrupt changes, an obvious and simple procedure which has been used in practice is to do segmentation by inspection of the raw data, so that segments are obtained with an approximate constant structure, then to fit separate models (e.g. an AR or ARCH) to each segment. However, this practice has several disadvantages. The absence of an explicit statistical model for the structural changes makes it difficult to investigate statistical properties of the model and to make forecasts. Also, a systematic algorithm for determining the points of structural change might be difficult to construct.

The discussion in the next section will focus on two modelling efforts that allow for structural changes, namely the regime switching model and the threshold model.

1.6 STRUCTURAL CHANGES IN THE UNDERLYING PROCESS

1.6.1 Regime switching models

A convenient assumption is to assume that sudden changes in parameters can be identified by a Markov chain. The series of models that use this idea are often referred to as 'regime switching models'. Hamilton (1988) proposed the Markov switching model first for capturing the effects of sudden dramatic political and economic events on the properties of financial and economic time series.

Tyssedal and Tjostheim (1988) state that empirical evidence for step changes has been provided by several investigators and detecting inhomogeneity for reasons of economic interpretation and for improving forecasts is important. Similar to the approach by Andel (1993), they utilize a Markov chain for modelling. The discrete Markov assumption implies that the parameter states will occur repeatedly over the available data, which makes the estimation more efficient since several data sections can be combined to yield the estimate of a given parameter value.

It is assumed that the observations are generated by a stochastic process $\{X_t\}$, which has an AR(1) structure:

$$X_t = \beta_t X_{t-1} + \varepsilon_t, \quad t = 0, \pm 1, \pm 2 \ldots \tag{1.22}$$

where $\{\beta_t\}$ is a Markov chain which is irreducible and aperiodic and has a finite state space consisting of k states (regimes) $s_1, \ldots, s_k$. $\{\varepsilon_t\}$ is a sequence of iid random variables with zero mean and variance σ^2. It is assumed that $\{\beta_t\}$ and $\{\varepsilon_t\}$ are independent. $Q(q_{ij})$ denotes the transition probability matrix for shifts between regimes where $q_{ij} = P(\beta_t = s_j \mid \beta_{t-1} = s_i)$, $i, j = 1 \ldots k$. For an irreducible and aperiodic Markov chain with a finite state space, there is a unique vector of stationary probabilities denoted by $\pi = [\pi_1, \ldots, \pi_k]$.

In this specification the variance of $\{\varepsilon_t\}$ is assumed to be constant in every regime but can vary across regimes. For example, if there are two regimes, a high volatility and a low volatility regime, and volatilities are approximately constant within these regimes, specification in (1.22) could be used to model the time series. Note that, in a more general setting, a higher order of AR for each regime could be allowed.

One advantage obtained by modelling the changes in terms of strictly stationary Markov chains as opposed to using a deterministic function is that $\{X_t\}$ may still under certain conditions be a strictly stationary and ergodic process, even though a particular realization of $\{X_t\}$ may have a very nonstationary outlook. Tjostheim (1986) discusses the stationarity problem in more detail. The properties of stationarity and ergodicity mean that the strong law of large numbers and central limit theorems are available in an asymptotic analysis, whereas working with deterministic changes will produce a nonstationary process $\{X_t\}$. The Markov property is also ideal for forecasting.

As the number of states increases from one to two or more, the difficulty of estimation increases by an order of magnitude. The unknown parameters in the model are Q, π, σ^2 and the process $\{\Delta_t\}$ which indicates at each time point which state the process $\{\beta_t\}$ is in. Two methods are used by Tyssedal and Tjostheim (1988) for estimation: method-of-moments and a least squares procedure.

In method-of-moments estimation, to be able to evaluate moments of $\{X_t\}$, $\{X_t\}$ must be stationary, and the moments of the desired order must exist. Identification of the process requires matching empirical moments with the theoretical ones. Even with the assumption of three regimes, the problem of estimating parameters becomes very complicated when Q is unknown, a case of practical interest. In general we need to evaluate higher order moments, to obtain a sufficient number of equations for evaluating the parameters of Q. For three regimes, an explicit evaluation of higher order moments is difficult to obtain. Simulation experiments show that for a case with two regimes where the only unknowns are $s_1 = s$ and σ^2 (s_2 is set to 0), very bad estimates of the state s can be produced for quite large sample sizes, whereas the estimates of σ^2 appear more well behaved. It is reported that for sample sizes of 100 and 200, where moment estimators for ordinary AR(1) models perform quite well, the standard errors of $\hat{s}$ in some cases are so large that they render the estimates virtually useless. Although method-of-moments produces consistent estimates, they may be of quite limited value in practice, since in some cases the sample size required to obtain small standard errors is very substantial.

Tyssedal and Tjostheim propose an iterative algorithm which minimizes either a local sum of squares criterion over a window or minimizes the global sum of squares criterion depending on the assumption of *a priori* information about P, k and Δ_t. They show that the least squares algorithm performs much better with less bias. If there are more frequent shifts, the performance of the algorithm deteriorates markedly.

Andel (1993) assumes that time series fluctuates about two states. The assumed process is:

$$X_t = \beta_t + \varepsilon_t, \quad \varepsilon_t \text{ is strict } WN, \beta_t \text{ a Markov chain}$$

The Markov chain is assumed to have two states s_1 and s_2, which are real numbers. ε_t is a random variable with zero mean and finite variance. Andel shows that there is a serious problem of existence of estimators using a method-of-moments estimation technique. Moreover, the estimates of σ^2 were very poor. He concludes that a modification of the least squares method used by Tyssedal and Tjostheim (1988) could give better results.

Hamilton (1994) discusses the estimation of parameters for regime switching models. Hamilton derives a system of non-linear equations that characterize the maximum likelihood estimates of the population parameters. However, solving these equations analytically is not possible. Therefore, estimation of the parameters in these models is either done using numerical methods or by using the EM algorithm.

The determination of the correct number of regimes, which is important for correct model specification, is discussed by Hamilton (1996) and Hansen (1992, 1996). A Markov chain specification is built on the presumption that the future will in some sense be like the past. There is a flexibility in these models where one can specify a probability law consistent with a broad range of different outcomes, and choose particular parameters within that class on the basis of data. The regime switching model was very successful for modelling short-term interest rates as documented by Hamilton (1988) and Driffill (1992). Further applications of this model include Hamilton's (1989) model of long-run trends in gross national product and the business cycle; the excess return and volatility model of Turner, Startz and Nelson (1989); an explanation of mean reversion in equilibrium asset prices by Ceccehetti, Lam and Mark (1990b); and the exchange rate dynamics model of Engle and Hamilton (1990). Garcia and Perron (1996), Ceccehetti, Lam and Mark (1990a) are other applications in finance. Schwert (1989b, 1990) uses the regime switching model to provide a useful descriptive summary of the financial panics during the past century. The regime switching model has also been used to model various macroeconomic time series such as the GNP series. Another application is for explaining business cycles where the recessions are treated as breaks in the time series process. Using the observed data, these models try to identify the dates of such breaks and describe their characteristic.

1.6.2 Extensions of the regime switching models

Cai (1994) develops a Markov model of switching regime ARCH. This model incorporates the features of both the switching regime model and the ARCH model to examine the issue of volatility persistence in the monthly excess returns of the three-month Treasury Bill. The model is able to retain the volatility clustering feature of the ARCH model and, in addition, capture the discrete shift in the intercept in the conditional variance that may cause spurious apparent persistence in the variance process. The switching-AR(K)-Markov-ARCH(G) model of Cai has the following specification:

$$X_t = \alpha_0 + \alpha_1 S_t + Y_t$$

$$Y_t = b_1 Y_{t-1} + \cdots + b_k Y_{t-k} + \varepsilon_t$$

$$\varepsilon_t = z_t \sigma_t \quad z_t \sim \mathrm{ii} \sim N(0, 1)$$

$$\sigma_t = (h_t)^{1/2}$$

$$h_t = \gamma(S_t) + \sum_{i=1}^{g} \alpha_i \varepsilon_{t-i}^2$$

where

$$\gamma(S_t) = \gamma_0 + \gamma_1 S_t, \quad \gamma_0 > 0, \quad \gamma_1 > 0$$

$S_t = 0$ or 1 denotes the unobserved state of the system. $c_0 + c_1 S_t$ is the regime mean and Y_t is the deviation from this mean. S_t is assumed to follow a first-order Markov process. Cai shows that once the discrete shifts in the asymptotic variance are considered ARCH coefficients are significantly reduced and the ARCH process is much less persistent. This is in contrast to previous studies which in general find the ARCH process to be highly persistent. Cai's model is successful in describing the dramatic change in interest rate volatility associated with the change in Federal Reserve operating procedures in the period 1979–1982.

Hamilton and Susmel (1994) propose another parametrization of the switching regime ARCH (SWARCH) model where changes in regime are modelled as changes in the scale of the ARCH process. For the weekly returns of the New York Stock Exchange value-weighted index, they find that SWARCH specification offers a better statistical fit to the data, better forecasts, and a better description of the October 1987 crash.

Gray (1996) develops a generalized regime switching model of the short-term interest rate that allows the short rate to exhibit both mean reversion and conditional heteroscedasticity and nests the GARCH and square root process specifications. Similarly Evans and Lewis (1995) estimate a regime switching model of exchange rates where they test the hypothesis that spot and forward rates move together one-for-one in the long run. They can't reject this hypothesis and note that a long-run relationship between spot and forward rates is likely to be biased when a sample contains infrequent shifts in regime.

It is also possible to extend these models so that the probability of a regime not only depends on the regime of the previous period but also on a vector of other observed variables. Several recent works have extended the Hamilton model by incorporating time-varying state transition probabilities. Diebold, Lee and Weinbach (1994) and Filardo (1992, 1993, 1994) allowed the state transition probabilities to evolve as logistic functions of observable economic fundamentals, whereas Ghysels (1994) conditioned on seasonal indicators. Durland and McCurdy (1993), (1994) extend the Hamilton model by allowing the state transition probabilities to be functions of both the inferred current state and the associated number of periods the system has been in the current state. For generalizations see Lam (1990), Durland and McCurdy (1992), and Diebold, Lee and Weinbach (1994).

1.7   THRESHOLD MODELS

The idea in the regime switching model is that the data which show changes in the regime will repeat themselves in the future, therefore we can predict the future states using the parameter estimates from the past observations. The shifts between the regimes are modelled through a Markov chain which implies an exogenous change between the regimes. The only information necessary to predict the future regimes or to forecast the observables is the current regime of the time series. In threshold models the shifts between the regimes are modelled explicitly in terms of the time series that is under consideration. That is, if we have a time series $\{X_t\}, t = 1, \ldots, T$, the switch between the regimes depends on either X_T or some other realization in the past, X_{T-d} (or it could depend on another time series which is assumed to determine the shifts in the time series of interest).

Tong (1990) discusses that, the basic idea of a 'threshold' is the local approximation over the states, i.e. the introduction of regimes via threshold. This idea is called the 'threshold principle' where a complex stochastic system is decomposed into simpler subsystems. Inherent in the threshold models is a feedback mechanism from the past observations to the parameters. Such a mechanism is lacking for the Markov chain-driven models, where the jumps are supposed to be driven by external events. In threshold models we have a piecewise linearization of non-linear models over the state space by the introduction of the thresholds. As a result we get locally linear models. Priestley (1965), Priestley and Tong (1973) and Ozaki and Tong (1975) use a similar idea in analysis of non-stationary time series and time dependent systems. Local stationarity in those papers is the analogue of local linearity in threshold models. Important features of the TAR models include their ability to give rise to limit cycles and time irreversibility (Tong, 1983).

For presentation of the threshold models in the following sections, we will follow the classification and the similar notation of Tong and Lim (1980) and Tong (1983, 1990).

1.7.1 Self-exciting threshold models

Let $\{X_t\}$ be a k-dimensional time series and, for each t, S_t be an observable (indicator) random variable, taking integer values $\{1, 2, \ldots, l\}$.

Definition: $\{X_t, S_t\}$ is said to be a general *threshold AR* (TAR) if

$$X_t = B^{(S_t)}X_t + A^{(S_t)}X_{t-1} + H^{(S_t)}\varepsilon_t^{(S_t)} + C^{(S_t)} \tag{1.23}$$

where, for $S_t = s$, $A^{(s)}$, $B^{(s)}$ and $H^{(s)}$ are $k \times k$ (non-random) matrix coefficients, $C^{(s)}$ is a $k \times 1$ vector of constants, and $\{\varepsilon_t^{(s)}\}$ is a k-dimensional strict WN sequence of independent random vectors with a diagonal covariance matrix. It is also assumed that $\{\varepsilon_t^{(s)}\}$ and $\{\varepsilon_t^{(s')}\}$ are independent for $s \neq s'$.

Let $r_0 < r_1 < \cdots < r_l$ be a subset of the real numbers, where r_0 and r_l are taken to be $-\infty$ and $+\infty$, respectively. They define a partition of the real line R, i.e.

$$R = R_1 \cup R_2 \cup \cdots \cup R_l, \quad \text{where } R_i = (r_{i-1}, r_i] \tag{1.24}$$

Denoting $\mathbf{X}_t = (X_t, X_{t-1}, \ldots, X_{t-k+1})^T$

$$\mathbf{A}^{(s)} = \begin{bmatrix} a_1^{(s)} a_2^{(s)} \cdots & a_{k-1}^{(s)} a_k^{(s)} \\ I_{k-1} & 0 \end{bmatrix}$$

$$\mathbf{B}^{(s)} = 0$$

$$\mathbf{H}^{(s)} = \begin{bmatrix} h_1^{(s)} & 0 \\ 0 & 0 \end{bmatrix}$$

$$\boldsymbol{\varepsilon}_t^{(s)} = (\varepsilon_t^{(s)}, 0, 0, \ldots, 0), \quad \mathbf{C}^{(s)} = (a_0^{(s)}, 0, \ldots, 0)$$

and $\mathbf{R}_s^k = R \times \cdots R \times R_s \times R \cdots \times R$

is the cylinder set in the Cartesian product of k real lines, on the interval R_s with dth co-ordinate space (d some fixed integer belonging to $\{1, 2, \ldots, k\}$), and setting $S_t = s$ if $X_{t-1} \in R_s^{(k)}$, we have

$$X_t = a_0^{(s)} + \sum_{i=1}^{k} a_i^{(s)} X_{t-i} + h_1^{(s)} \varepsilon_t^{(s)} \tag{1.25}$$

conditional on $X_{t-d} \in R_s$; $s = 1, 2, \ldots, l$. Since $\{S_t\}$ is now a function of $\{X_t\}$ itself, we call the univariate time series $\{X_t\}$ given by (1.25) a *self-exciting threshold autoregressive model* of order $(l; k, \ldots, k)$ or SETAR$(l; k, \ldots, k)$ where k is repeated l times. If, for $s = 1, 2, \ldots, l$,

$$a_i^{(s)} = 0 \text{ for } i = k_s + 1, k_s + 2, \ldots, k$$

then we call $\{X_t\}$ as SETAR$(l; k_1, k_2, \ldots, k_l) \cdot r_1, r_2, \ldots, r_{l-1}$ are called the thresholds. Note that a SETAR$(1; k)$ is just a linear AR model of order k.

Letting the first row of $H^{(s)}$ to be of the form $(h_1^{(s)}, h_2^{(s)}, \ldots, h_k^{(s)})$ where $h_k^{(s)} \neq 0$, $(s = 1, 2, \ldots, l)$, then we have the generalization of SETAR to a set of *self-exciting threshold autoregressive/moving average* models of order $(l; k, k, \ldots, k; k - 1, \ldots, k - 1)$. This model has the following form:

$$X_t = a_0^{(s)} + \sum_{i=1}^{k} a_i^{(s)} X_{t-i} + \sum_{i=0}^{k-1} h_i^{(s)} \varepsilon_{t-i} \tag{1.26}$$

conditional on $X_{t-d} \in R_s$, $s = 1, 2, \ldots, l$.

A more general form would be SETARMA$(l; k_1, \ldots, k_l; k_1', \ldots, k_l')$, where k_s and k_s' refer to AR order and MA order, respectively, conditional on $X_{t-d} \in R_s$.

1.7.2   Open loop threshold models

$\{X_t, Y_t\}$ is called an *open loop threshold autoregressive system*, where $\{X_t\}$ is the observable output and $\{Y_t\}$ is the observable input, if

$$X_t = a_0^{(s)} + \sum_{i=1}^{m_s} a_i^{(s)} X_{t-i} + \sum_{i=0}^{m_s'} b_i^{(s)} Y_{t-i} + \varepsilon_t^{(s)} \tag{1.27}$$

conditional on $Y_{t-d} \in R_s$; $(s = 1, \ldots, l)$, where $(\varepsilon_t^{(s)})$; $s = 1, 2, \ldots, l$, are strict WN sequences, with zero mean and finite variances and each are independent of $\{Y_t\}$. Also, WN sequences are assumed to be independent of each other. This system is denoted by TARSO$(l; (m_1, m_1'), \ldots, (m_l, m_l'))$. This model enables another time series to determine the regime shifts for the $\{X_t\}$ series. If we were to plot two time series and find out that the regime shifts in one time series are correlated to the level of the other series, then the above model could be an appropriate tool to model the data. The important assumption is that although $\{Y_t\}$ series affects $\{X_t\}$ series, the reverse is not necessarily true.

1.7.3   Closed loop threshold models

$\{X_t, Y_t\}$ is called a *closed loop threshold autoregressive system*, denoted by TARSC, if $\{X_t, Y_t\}$ are both TARSO. The assumption is that all WN sequences involved are independent of one another. This type of models allows both series to affect the corresponding regime in the other series.

1.7.4   Smooth threshold autoregressive models

Consider a SETAR$(2; k_1, k_2)$ model that has two regimes and represented as follows:

$$X_t = a_0 + \sum_{j=1}^{k_1} a_j X_{t-j} + \left(b_0 + \sum_{j=1}^{k_2} b_j X_{t-j} \right) I_s(X_{t-d}) + \varepsilon_t \tag{1.28}$$

For the SETAR model I_s is the indicator function where

$$I_s(x) = \left\{ \begin{matrix} 0 \text{ if } x \le r \\ 1 \text{ if } x > r \end{matrix} \right\} \tag{1.29}$$

and r is the threshold. If we choose the indicator function to be any 'smooth' function F where the only requirement on F is to be continuous and non-decreasing, we get a *smooth threshold autoregressive* (STAR) model. This allows for the regime change to be more smooth rather than having a jump in the process as in SETAR models.

1.7.5   Identification in SETAR models

Tong (1983) proposes an algorithm for the identification of the SETAR models. The assumption is that all WN sequences are Gaussian which enables us to write down a likelihood function and derive the maximum likelihood estimates of the unknown parameters as in AR models. Tsay (1989) proposes another procedure for estimation of TAR models. Using the concept of arranged autoregression and local estimation, a TAR model is transformed into a regular change point problem.

The procedures proposed in the literature are *ad hoc* and include several subjective choices. Identification is still a challenging issue in the research agenda.

Non-linear least-squares prediction may be easily obtained in the case of one-step-ahead. This reduces to that of a linear least-square prediction of one-step of the appropriate piecewise linear AR model. For more than one-step-ahead, a recursive prediction may be obtained successively taking conditional expectations.

For illustration, a TAR model due to Petrucelli and Woolford (1984) and a threshold MA model by Wecker (1981) will be discussed. These type of models are often used in the literature.

1.7.6   A threshold AR(1) model

Petrucelli and Woolford (1984) consider the following TAR model:

$$X_t = a_1 X_{t-1}^1 + a_2 X_{t-1}^2 + \varepsilon_t, \quad t = 1, 2, \ldots \tag{1.30}$$

where $X^1 = \text{Max}(X, 0)$ and $X^2 = \text{Min}(X, 0)$. This notation is equivalent to the notation we had earlier where we have two regimes and the threshold level $r = 0$. This is a SETAR(2; 1, 1) model since only 1 lag of X_t is included in (1.30) for each regime. This model could equivalently be written:

$$X_t = [a_1 I(X_{t-1} > 0) + a_2 I(X_{t-1} \le 0)] X_{t-1} + \varepsilon_t \tag{1.31}$$

where $I(A)$ is the indicator function for set A. a_1 and a_2 are taken to be real constants and it is assumed that $\{\varepsilon_t\}$ is a sequence of iid random variables with zero mean and constant variance. This model could be referred to as an asymmetric AR model. Analogous asymmetric MA models are considered by Wecker (1981) which will be discussed later.

Simulations of the model to determine the small-sample properties of the estimators yield the following results:

(1)   In general $\hat{a}_1$ and $\hat{a}_2$ exhibit better overall performance when a_1 and a_2 are negative.

(2) When a_1 and a_2 are close to the boundaries of the ergodic region, unstable estimates of a_1 and a_2 are obtained.
(3) On average, the expected standard error tends to underestimate the corresponding sample standard error, $SE(\cdot)$.
(4) Performance of $\hat{\sigma}$ is consistent throughout and does not seem to be affected by the performance of $\hat{a}_1$ and $\hat{a}_2$.

Chan *et al.* (1985) consider a multiple threshold AR(1) model where they assume that thresholds are known. They propose estimates for the model but the sampling properties of the estimates are unclear. Estimation of the thresholds remains an open question for that model. The model discussed above also does not deal with the estimation of the threshold but rather takes it as given. We will return to the estimation of thresholds later in the chapter.

Besides the threshold autoregressive models discussed so far, which are in discrete time, there are continuous time versions of these models as well. Often, continuous time modelling is easier for analysis and obtaining analytical solutions. We will refer to some of the related literature without discussing these models: Brockwell (1993), Brockwell and Hyndman (1992), Brockwell and Stramer (1992), Tong and Yeung (1991) and Tong (1992).

1.7.7   A threshold MA model

Wecker (1981) analyses the 'asymmetric inertia' in industrial price movements using the threshold idea. It is suggested that when market conditions change, price quotations are revised with a delay, the delay operating more strongly against reductions in price quotations than against increases.

An asymmetric moving average process of order one is proposed for modelling the time series:

$$X_t = \varepsilon_t + a_1 \varepsilon_{t-1}^{(1)} + a_2 \varepsilon_{t-1}^{(2)} \tag{1.32}$$

where ε_t is a sequence of iid random shocks,

$$\varepsilon_t^{(1)} = \text{Max}(\varepsilon_t, 0), \text{ the positive innovations}$$

$$\varepsilon_t^{(2)} = \text{Min}(\varepsilon_t, 0), \text{ the negative innovations}$$

a_1 and a_2 are fixed parameters of the model. As in the AR model of Petrucelli and Woolford (1984) discussed earlier, there are assumed to be two regimes in this model, namely positive innovations and negative innovations. When $a = a_1 = a_2$, this model reduces to the MA(1) process:

$$X_t = \varepsilon_t + a\varepsilon_{t-1} \tag{1.33}$$

The author calls the model characterized by equation (1.32) the asymmetric MA(1) and the model characterized by (1.33) the symmetric MA(1). Under the assumption that $\varepsilon_t \sim N(0, 1)$, it is shown that the asymmetric MA(1) will have a non-zero mean whereas the symmetric MA(1) will have a zero mean. The asymmetric MA(1), like the symmetric MA(1), is distinguished by zero autoco-variances at lags greater than one. A *t*-statistic is proposed for testing asymmetry.

For estimation of model parameters a_1, a_2, σ^2 where ε_t are assumed to be iid $N(0, \sigma^2)$, the joint density function of the data $\{X_1, X_2, \ldots, X_n\}$ and the (fixed) initial value of ε_0 is used. Maximization of the likelihood function is then equivalent to minimization of one-step-ahead forecast errors ε_t, which is achieved by finding the parameter values that minimize the within-sample forecasting variance, conditional on $\varepsilon_0 = 0$.

The concept of invertibility for non-linear time series models developed by Granger and Anderson (1978) specifies a time series as invertible if the effect of conditioning parameter estimates on an erroneous value of ε_0 becomes negligible in large samples. Wecker (1981) is able to prove that for the asymmetric MA(1) case, a time series is invertible over a wide range of parameter values. This model is later applied to returns on the market portfolio and industrial prices.

Cao and Tsay (1993) use a TAR model in describing monthly volatility series. They compare the TAR model with ARMA, GARCH and EGARCH models. Using mean square error and average absolute deviation as the criteria, out-of-sample forecasts are compared. The comparisons show that TAR models consistently outperform ARMA models in multi-step ahead forecasts for S&P and value-weighted composite portfolio excess returns. TAR models provide better forecasts than the GARCH and EGARCH models for the volatilities of the same stocks. The EGARCH model is the best in long-horizon volatility forecasts for equal-weighted composite portfolios.

1.7.8   Threshold models and asymmetries in volatility

In the threshold models discussed so far the variance of the error terms was assumed to be constant. As discussed earlier, changing volatility over time is an important characteristic of financial time series.

GARCH models due to their specification cannot take into account asymme-tries in volatility. The semi-parametric ARCH models of Engle and Gonzalez-Rivera (1989), which use a non-quadratic variance specification, and the log-GARCH models of Pantula (1986), are alternative parameterizations proposed in the literature. Zakoian (1994) introduced a different functional form to account for asymmetries in volatility. The model, called *threshold* GARCH (TGARCH), specifies the variance of the error term as:

$$\varepsilon_t = \sigma_t Z_t$$
$$\sigma_t = a_0 + a_1^{(1)}\varepsilon_{t-1}^{(1)} - a_1^{(2)}\varepsilon_{t-1}^{(2)} + \cdots + a_q^{(1)}\varepsilon_{t-q}^{(1)} - a_q^{(2)}\varepsilon_{t-q}^{(2)}$$
$$+ b_1\sigma_{t-1} + \cdots + b_p\sigma_{t-p} \tag{1.34}$$

(Z_t) iid with $E(Z_t) = 0$, $\mathrm{Var}(Z_t) = 1$, Z_t independent of (ε_{t-1})

where $\varepsilon_t^{(1)} = \text{Max}(\varepsilon_t, 0)$, and $\varepsilon_t^{(2)} = \text{Min}(\varepsilon_t, 0)$. Non-negativity constraints on the a_i and b_j, $i = 0, \ldots, q$, $j = 1, \ldots, p$ make σ_t the conditional standard deviation of the (ε_t) process. If the distribution (Z_t) is symmetric, the effect of a shock $\varepsilon_{t-k}(k \leq q)$ on the present volatility is proportional to the difference $a_k^{(1)} - a_k^{(2)}$, the sign of which can be either positive or negative. Non-negativity constraints on the parameters make the model linear and stationarity can be analysed. Also, they allow two-stage least-squares estimation methods and provide simple best statistics for (conditional) homoscedasticity. The qualitative threshold GARCH model by Gourieroux and Monfort (1992) has similar features where σ_t is a stepwise function of the past ε_t values.

Nelson (1991) proposed the exponential GARCH (EGARCH) model that we presented earlier. In this model, as in the TGARCH model, positive and negative innovations of equal size do not generate the same volatility. The difference from previous parameterization is the multiplicative modelling of volatility and the fact that shocks are measured relative to their standard deviation. The main advantage of the EGARCH model is that it is no longer necessary to restrict parameters to avoid negative variances. Since parameters can be of either sign, this allows cyclical behaviour. Rabemananjara and Zakoian (1993) note that compared with the TGARCH model, EGARCH has the limitation that the effects on volatility of positive innovations relative to negative ones remains fixed over time. We should note that the EGARCH process implies a linear MA equation on the $(\ln \sigma^2)$ process.

Tong's (1990) main criticism against linear time series models was that stochastic linear difference equations do not permit stable periodic solutions independent of the initial value. With the non-negativity constraint in the TGARCH model of Zakoian (1994), (1.34) can be rewritten with the following Markovian representation:

$$\varepsilon_t^{(1)} = \sigma_t Z_t^{(1)}, \quad \varepsilon_t^{(2)} = \sigma_t Z_t^{(2)}$$

$$\sigma_t = a_0 + A_1[Z_{t-1}]\sigma_{t-1} + \cdots + A_p[Z_{t-p}]\sigma_{t-p} \tag{1.35}$$

$$A_i[Z_{t-i}] = a_i^{(1)} Z_{t-i}^{(1)} - a_i^{(2)} Z_{t-i}^{(2)} + b_i$$

This is a linear dynamic equation in σ_t with independent non-negative random coefficients $A_i[Z_{t-i}]$. If we set (Z_t) to a constant for all t, equation (1.35) becomes a deterministic equation in σ with non-negative parameters, and under some well-known regularity conditions, σ will always tend to a unique constant, independent of initial values. This model can be viewed as a linear ARCH model. The earlier mentioned EGARCH model by Nelson is also linear and represents an ARMA process in $\ln \sigma^2$. Both of these models cannot respond to Tong's criticism, that is they do not provide cyclical behaviours.

Given the above criticisms, Rabemananjara and Zakoian (1993) propose an unconstrained TGARCH model (where we drop the non-negativity constraints on a_i and b_j's):

$$\varepsilon_t = \sigma_t Z_t$$

$$\sigma_t = a_0 + \sum_{i=1}^{q}(a_i^{(1)}\varepsilon_{t-i}^{(1)} - a_i^{(2)}\varepsilon_{t-i}^{(2)}) + \sum_{j=1}^{p}(b_j^{(1)}\sigma_{t-j}^{(1)} - b_j^{(2)}\sigma_{t-j}^{(2)}) \qquad (1.36)$$

(Z_t) iid with $E(Z_t) = 0$, $\text{Var}(Z_t) = 1$, Z_t independent of (ε_{t-1})

This model is closely related to the TAR model of Tong and Lim (1980) in that σ_t depends on its past values as well as past values of WN through a piecewise linear function. This type of model is able to catch non-linear cyclical patterns. Compared to the constrained TGARCH there is no Markovian representation for (1.36) and studying the distributional properties is very complex. Also, note that σ_t here is allowed to be negative. The authors look at the special case of one lag in all variables and compute the model of Tong and Lim (1980). For the special case of one lag, they get the following representation (for intermediate steps, see Rabemananjara and Zakoian (1993)):

$$E[\sigma_t \mid \sigma_{t-1}] = a_0 + EA_1^{(1)}[Z_{t-1}]\sigma_{t-1}^{(1)} + EA_1^{(2)}[Z_{t-1}]\sigma_{t-1}^{(2)}$$

$$A_i^{(1)}[Z_{t-i}] = a_i^{(1)}Z_{t-i}^{(1)} - a_i^{(2)}Z_{t-i}^{(2)} + b_i^{(1)} \qquad (1.37)$$

$$A_i^{(2)}[Z_{t-i}] = -a_i^{(2)}Z_{t-i}^{(1)} + a_i^{(1)}Z_{t-i}^{(2)} - b_i^{(1)}$$

Thus, σ_t has the AR representation:

$$\sigma_t = a_0 + a_1^{(1)}\sigma_{t-1}^{(1)} + a_1^{(2)}\sigma_{t-1}^{(2)} + u_t \qquad (1.38)$$

with $E[u_t \mid \sigma_{t-1}] = 0$, $a_1 = EA_1^{(1)}[Z_{t-1}]$, $a_1^{(2)} = EA_1^{(2)}[Z_{t-1}]$

In (1.38), we have a threshold equation with two regimes for σ_t. These models are especially useful for time series with 'non-linear' behaviour, mainly for limit cycles. Here, we can get much more complex patterns of volatility compared to linear specifications.

Asymptotics of ML estimation of TGARCH models have several difficulties as in the ARCH context. Also, lack of differentiability at the thresholds causes further difficulties in the TGARCH context. Estimation is carried out by assuming asymptotic normality of estimators and as in the GARCH context it results in a recursive relation in first-order conditions of ML function. Iterative procedures are used to obtain the MLE estimates of their standard errors.

The authors derive a Lagrange multiplier test for asymmetry in the data which under the null hypothesis of symmetry is asymptotically distributed as chi-squared. Simulation results show that for small-sample sizes the test has incorrect results but as the sample size increases (100 to 500 observations) results are satisfactory. TGARCH models are useful in situations where past positive and negative shocks on returns have different effects on volatility. TGARCH models provide a way of capturing such effects, while keeping the classical GARCH simplicity (linearity) when the data do not contain non-linearity.

1.7.9 Testing for non-linearity

Two natural questions that arise in this context are: 'How can we tell if a given time series is non-linear?' and 'How can we decide if it is worth trying to fit a non-linear model?' There are two obvious reasons for developing tests for non-linearity of time series data. First, the test will suggest when it might be useful to use non-linear predictors in preference to linear ones. Second, in terms of underlying process, there is a fundamentally different system of dynamics between a non-linear system and a linear one. Finally, the tests will give an idea about the incidence rate of non-linearity in real time series (Chan and Tong, 1986).

See Chan and Tong (1986), Tong (1990) and references in these papers for several tests proposed in the literature and performance of these tests. The general conclusion is in favour of running more than one test in any situation before the model specification since the performance of tests varies across different data. Tong (1990) also suggests making graphical analysis before using the tests.

1.7.10 Threshold estimation and prediction of TAR models

In the threshold AR model of Petrucelli and Woolford (1984), the threshold MA model of Wecker (1981) and the threshold GARCH model of Rabemanajara and Zakoian (1993) that we discussed in earlier sections, the authors hypothesize a threshold value. In many cases, however, determination of the thresholds from the data is necessary.

Most non-linear techniques, including TAR models, give good sample fit but they are poor when used for out-of-sample forecasting. Dacco' and Satchell (1995a, b) discuss this issue for the case of exchange rate data. They report that non-linear models are outperformed by random walks or random walk with drift when used for out-of-sample forecasting.

Dacco' and Satchell (1995a) conclude that it requires only a small misspecification when forecasting which regime the world will be in to lose any advantage from knowing the correct model specification. Aydemir (1997) shows in a Monte Carlo simulation framework that estimation of lag parameter and threshold value is crucial for forecast performance of TAR models. Also it is shown that long-run forecast performance results can be quite different than comparisons of alternative models based on a single data set. Depending on the measure used for comparisons (e.g. mean square error, mean absolute error etc.) the results can differ. Therefore, correct estimation of the number of regimes and corresponding thresholds is crucial for improvements in forecast performance over the other alternatives available in the literature. For a review of several issues in a threshold model context including estimation and testing, see Aydemir (1996).

1.8 CONCLUSION

The development of different models for volatility is guided by the stylized facts observed in the data. This leads to a large array of alternative models available to practitioners. However, alternative models should be considered as complements for each other rather than competitors. Although ARCH-type models and SV models were developed independently, the interpretation of ARCH models as approximate filters for SV models and Nelson's (1990) finding that GARCH models converge to a continuous time diffusion model bridges the gap between these two different approaches.

Inspection of the data and testing for stylized facts naturally appear to be important first steps for practitioners in order to determine which model is best suited for any given situation. Fitting more than one model for any given data set is not uncommon as it permits comparison of different models in terms of in-sample fit and out-of-sample forecast performance.

The most attractive class of models in application has been the ARCH-type models. Among the applications of SV models, although it is well known that several underlying assumptions are violated, formulas derived from Black–Scholes models and its various extensions have been the most widely used. Considering regime switching models and threshold models, their application to financial data has been quite limited. Clearly, the ease of implementation governs the applicability of the models to real data. Problems associated with estimation and testing, and unavailability of software largely prohibit the wide application of the latter models. Given the importance of the issues addressed in models that allow for structural breaks, future research is likely to focus on these models and develop new techniques that will make them more readily available to practitioners.

REFERENCES

Akgiray, V. (1989) Conditional heteroscedasticity in time series of stock returns: evidence and forecasts, *Journal of Business*, vol. 62, 55–80.
Andel, Jiri (1993) A time series model with suddenly changing parameters, *Journal of Time Series Analysis*, Vol. 14, No. 2.

Andersen, T.G. (1994) Stochastic autoregressive volatility: A framework for volatility modeling, *Mathematical Finance*, **4**, 75–102.

Attanasio, O.P. and Wadhwani, S. (1989) Risk and predictability of stock market returns, SCEPR, Discussion Paper no. 161, Department of Economics, Stanford University.

Aydemir, A.B. (1996) Threshold models in time series analysis with an application to US interest rates, unpublished manuscript, The University of Western Ontario, Department of Economics.

Aydemir, A.B. (1997) Forecast performance of threshold autoregressive models: a Monte Carlo study, unpublished manuscript, The University of Western Ontario, Department of Economics.

Backus, D.K. and Gregory, A.W. (1993) Theoretical relations between risk premiums and conditional variances, *Journal of Business and Economic Statistics*, **11**(2), 177–185.

Backus, D.K., Gregory, A.W. and Zin, S.E. (1989) Risk premiums in the term structure: evidence from artificial economics, *Journal of Monetary Economics*, vol. 24, 371–399.

Baillie, R.T. and Bollerslev, T. (1989) The message in daily exchange rates: a conditional variance tale, *Journal of Business and Economic Statistics*, vol. 7, 297–305.

Baillie, R.T. and Bollerslev, T. (1990) A multiplicative generalized ARCH approach to modeling risk premia in forward foreign rate markets, *Journal of International Money and Finance*, vol. 9, 309–324.

Baillie, R.T., Bollerslev, T. and Mikkelsen, H.O. (1996) Fractionally integrated generalized autoregressive conditional heteroscedasticity, *Journal of Econometrics*, **74**(1), 3–30.

Baillie, R.T. and DeGennaro, R.P. (1990) Stock returns and volatility, *Journal of Financial and Quantitative Analysis*, vol. 25, 203–214.

Bera, A.K. and Higgins, M.L. (1995) On ARCH models: properties, estimating and testing, in L. Exley, D. A. R. George, C. J. Roberts and S. Sawyer (eds), *Surveys in Econometrics*, Basil Blackwell: Oxford, reprinted from *Journal of Economic Surveys*.

Bera, A., Lee, S. and Higgins, M.L. (1990) On the formulation of a general structure for conditional heteroscedasticity, *University of California at San Diego, Dept. of Economics, WP 90-41*.

Black, F. (1976) Studies in stock price volatility changes, *Proceedings of the 1976 Business Meeting of the Business and Economics Statistics Section, American Statistical Association*, 177–181.

Black, F. and Scholes, M. (1973) The pricing of options and corporate liabilities, *Journal of Political Economy*, **81**, 637–654.

Bodurtha, J.N. and Mark, N.C. (1991) Testing the CAPM with time varying risks and returns, *Journal of Finance*, vol. 46, 1485–1505.

Bollerslev, T. (1986) Generalized autoregressive conditional heteroscedasticity, *Journal of Econometrics*, **31**, 307–327.

Bollerslev, T. (1987) A conditional heteroscedastic time series model for speculative prices and rates of return, *Review of Economics and Statistics*, vol. 69, 542–547.

Bollerslev, T. (1990) Modeling the coherence in short-run nominal exchange rates: a multivariate generalized ARCH approach, *Review of Economics and Statistics*, vol. 72, 498–505.

Bollerslev, T., Chou, R.Y. and Kroner, K.F. (1992) ARCH modeling in finance, a review of the theory and empirical evidence, *Journal of Econometrics*, vol. 52, 5–59.

Bollerslev, T. and Engle, R.F. (1993) Common persistence in conditional variances, *Econometrica*, **61**, 166–187.

Bollerslev, T., Engle, R. and Nelson, D. (1994) ARCH models, in R. F. Engle and D. MacFadden (eds), *Handbook of Econometrics*, vol. IV, North-Holland, Amsterdam.

Bollerslev, T. and Mikkelsen, H.O.A. (1996) Modelling and pricing long-memory in stock market volatility, *Journal of Econometrics*, **73**(1), 151–184.

Boothe, P. and Glassman, D. (1987) The statistical distribution of exchange rates, *Journal of International Economics*, **22**, 297–319.

Breidt, F.J., Crato, N. and deLima, P. (1993) Modelling long memory stochastic volatility, *Johns Hopkins University*, Dept. of Political Economy, WP 323.

Brock, W.A., Hsieh, D.A. and LeBaron, B. (1991) *Nonlinear Dynamics, Chaos, and Instability: Statistical Thoery and Economic Evidence*, Cambridge, MIT Press.

Brockwell, P.J. (1993) Threshold ARMA processes in continuous time, in H. Tong (ed.), *Dimension Estimation and Models*, Non-Linear Time Series and Chaos, Vol. 1, World Scientific.

Brockwell, P.J. and Hyndman, R.J. (1992) On continuous time threshold autoregression, *International Journal of Forecasting*, **8**, 157–173.

Brockwell, P.J. and Stramer, O. (1992) On the convergence of a class of continuous time threshold ARMA processes, *Technical Report, Department of Statistics, Colorado State University*.

Cai, J. (1994) A markov model of switching-regime ARCH, *Journal of Business and Economic Statistics*, vol. 12, no. 3, 309–316.

Campbell, J.Y. and Hentschel, L. (1992) No news is good news: an asymmetric model of changing volatility in stock returns, *Journal of Financial Economics*, **31**, 281–318.

Campbell, J.Y. and Kyle, A.S. (1993) Smart money, noise trading and stock price behaviour, *Review of Economic Studies*, **60**, 1–34.

Campbell, J.Y. and Shiller, R.J. (1989) The dividend price-ratio and expectations of future dividends and discount factors, *Review of Financial Studies*, vol. 1, 175–228.

Cao, C.Q. and Tsay, R.T. (1993) Nonlinear time series analysis of stock volatilities, in M.H. Pesaran and S.M. Potters (eds), *Nonlinear Dynamics, Chaos and Econometrics*, J. Wiley & Sons, Chichester 157–177.

Cecchetti, S.G., Lam, P.S. and Mark, N.C. (1990a) Evaluating empirical tests of asset pricing models: alternative interpretations, *AER*, **80**, 41–51.

Cecchetti, S.G., Lam, P.S. and Mark, N.C. (1990b) Mean reversion in equilibrium asset prices, *AER*, **80**, 398–418.

Chan, K.S., Petrucelli, J.D., Tong, H., and Woodford, S.W. (1985) A multiple threshold AR(1) model, *Journal of Applied Probability*, **22**, 267–279.

Chan, K.S. and Tong, H. (1986) On tests for non-linearity in time series analysis, *Journal Forecasting*, **5**, 217–228.

Chan, K., Chan, K.C. and Karolyi, G.A. (1992) Intraday volatility in the stock index and stock index futures markets, *Review of Financial Studies*, 4(4), 657–684.

Chou, R.Y. (1988) Volatility persistence and stock valuations: some empirical evidence using GARCH, *Journal of Applied Econometrics*, vol. 3, 279–294.

Chou, R.Y., Engle, R.F. and Kane, A. (1992) Estimating risk aversion with a time-varying price of volatility, *Journal of Econometrics*, vol. 52.

Christie, A. (1982) The stochastic behaviour of common stock variances: value, leverage and interest rate effects, *Journal of Financial Economics*, vol. 10, 407–432.

Clark, P.K. (1973) A subordinated stochastic process model with finite variance for speculative prices, *Econometrica*, **41**, 135–156.

Crato, N. and deLima, P.J.F. (July 1994) Long range dependence in the conditional variance of stock returns, *Economics Letters*, **45**(3), 281–5.

Dacco', R. and Satchell, S.E. (1995a) Why do regime switching models forecast so badly? *Discussion Paper in Financial Economics, FE-7/95*, Birkbeck College, University of London.

Dacco', R. and Satchell, S.E. (1995b) SETAR forecasting: an application to the exchange market, mimeo, Birkbeck College, University of London.

DeLima, P.J.F. and Crato, N. (1994) Long-range dependence in the conditional variance of stock returns, *Economics Letters*, **45**(3), 281–285.

Diebold, F.X. (1988) *Empirical Modeling of Exchange Rate Dynamics*, Springer Verlag, New York.

Diebold, F.X. and Nerlove, M. (1989) The dynamics of exchange rate volatility: a multivariate latent factor ARCH model, *Journal of Applied Econometrics*, vol. 4, 1–21.

Diebold, F., Lee, J. and Weinbach, G. (1994) Regime switching with time varying transition probabilities, in (C. Hargreaves (ed.), *Non-Stationary Time Series Analysis and Cointegration*, Oxford: Oxford University Press, 283–302.

Diebold, F. and Lopez, J.A. (1995) Modelling volatility dynamics, in K. Hoover (ed.), *Macroeconometrics: Developments, Tensions and Prospects*, 427–466.

Ding, Z., Granger, C.W.J. and Engle, R.F. (1993) A long memory property of stock market returns and a new model, *Journal of Empirical Finance*, **1**, 83–106.

Driffill, J. (1992) Changes in regime and the term structure: a note, *Journal of Economic Dynamics and Control*, **16**, 165–173.

Drost, F.C. and Nijman, T.E. (1993) Temporal aggregation of GARCH processes, *Econometrica*, **61**, 909–927.

Durland, J.M. and McCurdy, T.H. (1993) Duration dependence and transitions in a Markov model of US GNP data using restricted semi-Markov process, mimeo Queens University, Kingston, Ontario.

Durland, J.M. and McCurdy, T.H. (1994) Duration-dependent transitions in a Markov model of U.S. GNP growth, *Journal of Business and Economic Statistics*, vol. 12, no. 3, 279–289.

Easley, D. and O'Hara, M. (1992) Time and the process of security price adjustment, *Journal of Finance*, **47**, 577–605.

Engle, R.F. (1982) Autoregressive conditional heteroscedasticity with estimates of variance of U.K. inflation, *Econometrica*, **50**, 987–1008.

Engle, R.F. (1983) Estimates of the variance of US inflation based on the ARCH model, *Journal of Money, Credit and Banking*, vol. 15, 286–301.

Engle, R.F. (1990) Discussion: stock volatility and the crash of '87, *Review of Financial Studies*, **3**, 103–106.

Engle, R.F. and Bollerslev, T. (1986) Modeling the persistence of conditional variances, *Econometric Reviews*, vol. 5, 1–50, 81–87.

Engle, R.F. and Gonzalez-Rivera, G. (1991) Semi-parametric ARCH models, *Journal of Business and Economic Statistics*, vol. 9, 345–360.

Engle, R.F. and Granger, C.W.J. (1987) Co-integration and error correction: representation, estimation and testing, *Econometrica*, **50**, 987–1007.

Engle, C. and Hamilton, J.D. (1990) Long swings in the dollar: are they in the data and do markets know it? *AER*, **80**, 689–713.

Engle, R.F., Ito, T. and Lin, W. (1990) Meteor showers or heat waves? heteroscedastic intradaily volatility in the foreign exchange market, *Econometrica*, vol. 58, 525–542.

Engle, R.F., Lilien, D. and Robins, R. (1987) Estimation of time varying risk premiums in the term structure, *Econometrica*, **55**, 391–408.

Engle, R.F. and Mustafa, C. (1992) Implied ARCH models from option prices, *Journal of Econometrics*, vol. 52, 289–311.

Engle, R.F. and Ng, V.K. (1993) Measuring and testing the impact of news on volatility, *Journal of Finance*, **48**, 1749–1801.

Evans, M.D. and Lewis, K. (1995) Do long-term swings in the dollar affect estimates of the risk premia? *Review of Financial Studies*, **8**(3), 709–742.

Fama, E.F. (1963) Mandelbrot and the stable paretian distribution, *Journal of Business*, **36**, 420–429.

Fama, E.F. (1965) The behavior of stock market prices, *Journal of Business*, vol. 38, 34–105.

Filardo, A. (1992) U.S.-Canadian business cycles: expansions, contractions, and their transitions, Unpublished manuscript, Federal Reserve Bank of Kansas City.

Filardo, A. (1993) The evolution of U.S. business cycle phases, *Federal Reserve Bank of Kansas City Research WP 93-17*.

French, K.R., Schwert, G.W. and Stambaugh, R.F. (1987) Expected stock returns and volatility, *Journal of Financial Econometrics*, vol. 19, 3–30.

Friedman, B. and Laibson, D. (1989) Economic implications of extraordinary movements in stock prices, *Brookings Papers on Economic Activity*, 137–172.

Gallant, A.R. (1981) On the bias in flexible functional forms and an essentially unbiased form: the fourier flexible form, *Journal of Econometrics*, **15**, 211–244.

Gallant, A.R., Hsieh, D.A. and Tauchen, G. (1991) On fitting a recalcitrant series: the pound/dollar exchange rate 1974–83, in W. A. Barnett, J. Powell and G. Tauchen (eds), *Nonparametric and Semiparametric Methods in Econometrics and Statistics: Proceedings of the Fifth International Symposium in Economic Theory and Econometrics*, 199–240, New York: Cambridge University Press.

Gallant, A.R. and Nychka, D.W. (1987) Seminonparametric maximum likelihood estimation, *Econometrica*, **55**, 363–390.

Gallant, A.R., Rossi, P.E. and Tauchen, G. (1992) Stock prices and volume, *Review of Financial Studies*, **5**, 199–242.

Gallant, A.R., Rossi, P.E. and Tauchen, G. (1993) Nonlinear dynamic structures, *Econometrica*, **61**, 871–907.

Gallant, A.R. and Tauchen, G. (1989) Semi non-parametric estimation of conditionally heterogenous processes: asset pricing applications, *Econometrica*, **57**, 1091–1120.

Garcia, R. and Perron, P. (1996) An analysis of the real interest rate under regime shifts, *Review of Economics and Statistics*, **78**(1), 111–125.

Ghysels, E. (1994) On the periodic structure of the business cycle, *Journal of Business and Economic Statistics*, **12**(3), 289–298.

Ghysels, E., Harvey, A.C. and Renault, E. (1996) Stochastic volatility, in G.S. Maddala and C.R. Rao (eds), *Statistical Methods in Finance*, 119–192 Amsterdam: Elsevier Science Publishers.

Giovanni, A. and Jorion, P. (1989) The time variation of risk and return in the foreign exchange and stock markets, *Journal of Finance*, **44**, 307–325.

Gouriéroux, C. and Monfort, A. (1992) Qualitative threshold ARCH models, *Journal of Econometrics*, **52**, 159–199.

Granger, C.W.J. and Anderson, A. (1978) *An Introduction to Bilinear Time Series Models*, Gottingen: Vandenhock and Ruprecht.

Granger, C.W.J. and Joyeux, R. (1980) An introduction to long memory time series models and fractional differencing, *Journal of Time Series Analysis*, **1**, 15–39.

Gray, S.F. (1996) Modelling the conditional distribution of interest rates as a regime switching process, *Journal of Financial Economics*, **42**(1), 27–62.

Hamilton, J.D. (1988) Rational-expectations econometric analysis of changes in regime: an investigation of the term structure of interest rates, *Journal of Economics Dynamics and Control*, vol. 12, no. 2/3, 385–423.

Hamilton, J.D. (1989) A new approach to the economic analysis of nonstationary time series and the business cycle, *Econometrica*, **57**, 357–384.

Hamilton, J.D. (1994) *Time Series Analysis*, Princeton, New Jersey: Princeton University Press.

Hamilton, J.D. (1996) Specification testing in Markov-switching time series models, *Journal of Econometrics*, **70**(1), 127–157.

Hamilton, J.D. and Susmel, R. (1994) Autoregressive conditional heteroscedasticity and changes in regime, *Journal of Econometrics*, **64**(1–2), 307–333.

Hansen, B.E. (1992) The likelihood ratio test under non-standard conditions: testing the Markov switching model of GNP, *Journal of Applied Econometrics*, **7**, 561–582.

Hansen, B.E. (1996) Inference when a nuisance parameter is not identified under null hypothesis, *Econometrica*, **64**(2), 413–430.

Harvey, A. (1981) *The econometric analysis of time series*, New York: Wiley.

Harvey, A. (1989) *Forecasting, Structural Time Series Models and the Kalman Filter*, Cambridge University Press.

Harvey, A. (1993) Long-memory in stochastic volatility, unpublished manuscript, London School of Economics.

Harvey, A. and Koopman, S.J. (1993) Forecasting hourly electricity demand using time-varying splines, *Journal of American Statistical Association*, **88**, 1228–1236.

Harvey, A., Ruiz, E. and Sentana, E. (1992) Unobserved component time series models with ARCH disturbances, *Journal of Econometrics*, **52**(1–2), 129–158.

Harvey, A., Ruiz, E. and Shephard, N. (1994) Multivariate stochastic variance models, *Review of Economic Studies*, **61**, 247–264.

Harvey, A. and Shephard, N. (1993) Estimation and testing of stochastic variance models, *SICERD, LSE, Discussion Paper no. EM/93/268.*

Harvey, A. and Shephard, N. (1996) The estimation of an asymmetric stochastic volatility model for asset returns, *Journal of Business and Economic Statistics*, **14**(4), 429–434.

Harvey, C. (1989) Is the expected compensation for market volatility constant through time? unpublished manuscript, Fuqua School of Business, Duke University.

Higgins, M.L. and Bera, A.K. (1992) A class of non-linear ARCH models, *International Economic Review*, **33**, 137–158.

Hong, C. (1988) The integrated generalized autoregressive conditional heteroscedastic model: the process, estimation and Monte Carlo experiments, unpublished manuscript, Dept. of Economics, University of California, San Diego, CA.

Hong, P.Y. (1991) The autocorrelation structure for the GARCH-M process, *Economic Letters*, **37**, 129–132.

Hosking, J.R.M (1981) Fractional differencing, *Biometrika*, **68**, 165–176.

Hsieh, D.A. (1988) The statistical properties of daily foreign exchange rates: 1974–1983, *Journal of International Economics*, **24**, 129–145.

Hsieh, D.A. (1989) Modeling heteroscedasticity in daily foreign exchange rates, *Journal of Business and Economic Statistics*, **7**, 307–317.

Hull, J and White, A. (1987) The pricing of options and assets with stochastic volatilities, *Journal of Finance*, **42**, 281–300.

Jacquier, E.N., Polson, N.G. and Rossi, P.E. (1994) Bayesian analysis of stochastic volatility models, *Journal of Business and Economic Statistics*, **12**, 371–417.

Jacquier, E.N., Polson, N.G. and Rossi, P.E. (1995) Models and prior distributions for multivariate stochastic volatility, unpublished manuscript, Graduate School of Business, University of Chicago.

Jones, D.A. (1978) Non-linear autoregressive processes, *Proceedings of Royal Statistical Society*, **A360**, 71–95.

Jorion, P. (1988) On jump processes in the foreign exchange and stock markets, *Review of Financial Studies*, **1**, 427–445.

Kendall, J.D. (1989) Role of exchange rate volatility in US import price pass-through relationships, unpublished Ph.D. dissertation, Dept. of Economics, University of California, Davis.

Kendall, J.D. and McDonald, A.D. (1989) Univariate GARCH-M and the risk premium in a foreign exchange market, unpublished manuscript, Dept. of Economics, University of Tasmania, Hobart.

King, M.A., Sentana E. and Wadhwani, S.B. (1990) A heteroscedastic factor model for asset returns and risk premia with time varying volatility: an application to sixteen world stock markets, unpublished manuscript, LSE, London.

Kraft, D.F. and Engle, R.F. (1983) Autoregressive conditional heteroscedasticity in multiple time series, unpublished manuscript, Dept. of Economics, University of California, San Diego.

Lam, P. (1990) The Hamilton base with a general autoregressive component: estimation and comparison with other models of economic time series, *Journal of Monetary Economics*, **26**, 409–432.

Latane, H. and Rendleman, R. Jr (1976) Standard deviations of stock price ratios implied in option prices, *Journal of Finance*, **31**, 369–381.

Lee, T.K. (1988) Does conditional covariance or conditional variance explain time varying risk premia in foreign exchange returns? *Economics Letters*, **27**, 371–373.

Mahieu, R. and Schotman, P. (1994a) Stochastic volatility and the distribution of exchange rate news, *Institute for Empirical Macroeconomics, Discussion Paper 96*, University of Minnesota.

Mahieu, R. and Schotman, P. (1994b), Neglected common factors in exchange rate volatility, *Journal of Empirical Finance*, **1**, 279–311.

Mandelbrot, B. (1963) The variation of certain speculative prices, *Journal of Business*, **36**, 394–416.

Mandelbrot, B. and Taylor, H. (1967) On the distribution of stock prices differences, *Operations Research*, **15**, 1057–1062.

McCurdy, T.H. and Morgan, I. (1987) Tests of the martingale hypothesis for foreign currency futures with time varying volatility, *International Journal of Forecasting*, **3**, 131–148.

McCurdy, T.H. and Morgan, I. (1988) Testing the martingale hypothesis in Deutsche Mark futures with models specifying the form of the heteroscedasticity, *Journal of Applied Econometrics*, **3**, 187–202.

McFarland, J.W., Pettit, R.R. and Sung, S.K. (1982) The distribution of foreign exchange price changes: trading day effects and risk measurement, *Journal of Finance*, **37**, 693–715.

Melino, A. and Turnbull, S.M. (1990) The pricing of foreign currency options with stochastic volatility, *Journal of Econometrics*, **45**, 239–265.

Melino, A. and Turnbull, S.M. (1991) The pricing of foreign currency options, *Canadian Journal of Economics*, **24**(2), 251–281.

Milhoj, A. (1987a), A multiplicative parametrization of ARCH models, unpublished manuscript, Dept. of Statistics, University of Copenhagen.

Milhoj, A. (1987b) Simulation and application of MARCH models, unpublished manuscript, Dept. of Statistics, University of Copenhagen.

Milhoj, A. (1987c) A conditional variance model for daily observations of an exchange rate, *Journal of Business and Economic Statistics*, **5**, 99–103.

Nelson, D.B. (1989) Modeling stock market volatility changes, *1989 Proceedings of the American Statistical Association*, Business and Economics Section, 93–98.

Nelson, D.B. (1990) ARCH models as diffusion approximations, *Journal of Econometrics*, **45**, 7–38.

Nelson, D.B. (1991) Conditional heteroscedasticity in asset returns: a new approach, *Econometrica*, **59**, 347–370.

Nelson, D.B. (1992) Filtering forecasting with misspecified ARCH models I: getting the right variance with the wrong model, *Journal of Econometrics*, **25**, 61–90.

Nelson, D.B. and Cao, C.Q. (1992) Inequality constraints in the univariate GARCH model, *Journal of Business and Economic Statistics*, **10**(2), 229–235.

Nelson, D.B. and Foster, D.P. (1994) Asymptotic filtering theory for univariate ARCH models, *Econometrica*, **62**, 1–41.

Ozaki, T. and Tong, H. (1975) On fitting of non-stationary autoregressive models in time series analysis, in *Proc. 8th Hawai Int. Conf. on System Sciences*, pp. 225–226, North Hollywood: Western Periodicals.

Pagan, A.R. and Ullah, A. (1988) The econometric analysis of models with risk terms, *Journal of Applied Econometrics*, **3**, 87–105.

Pagan, A.R. and Schwert, G.W. (1990), Alternative models for conditional stock volatility, *Journal of Econometrics*, **45**, 267–290.

Pantula, S.G. (1986) Modeling the persistence of conditional variances: a comment, *Econometric Reviews*, **5**, 71–73.

Petrucelli, J.D. and Woolford, S.W. (1984) A threshold AR(1) model, *Journal of Applied Probability*, **21**, 207–286.

Pitt, M. and Shephard, N. (1995) Parameter-driven exponential family models, Unpublished Manuscript, Nuffield College, Oxford.

Poterba, J. and Summers, L. (1986) The persistence of volatility and stock market fluctuations, *AER*, **76**, 1141–1151.

Press, S.J. (1968) A compound events model for security prices, *Journal of Business*, **40**, 317–335.

Priestley, M.B. (1965) Evolutionary spectra and non-stationary processes, *Journal of Royal Statistical Society*, **B27**, 204–237.

Priestley, M.B. (1980) State dependent models: a general approach to non-linear time series, *Journal of Time Series Analysis*, **1**, 47–71.

Priestly, M.B. and Tong, H. (1973) On the analysis of bivariate non-stationary processes, *Journal of Royal Statistical Society*, **B35**, 153–166, 179–188.

Rabemananjara, R. and Zakoian, J.M. (1993) Threshold ARCH models and asymmetries in volatility, *Journal of Applied Econometrics*, vol. 8, no. 1.

Renault, E. and Tovzi, N. (1996), Option Hedging and Implied Volatilities in a stochastic volatility model, *Mathematical Finance*, **6**, 279–302.

Robinson, P.M. (1988) Semiparametric econometrics: a survey, *Journal of Applied Econometrics*, **3**, 35–51.

Ross, S.A. (1976) The arbitrage thoery of capital asset pricing, *Journal of Economic Theory*, **13**, 341–360.

Schwert, G.W. (1989a) Why does stock market volatility change over time? *Journal of Finance*, **44**, 1115–1153.

Schwert, G.W. (1989b) Business cycles, financial crises, and stock volatility, in K. Brunner and A. H. Meltzer (eds), IMF Policy Advice, Market Volatility, Commodity Price Rules, and Other Essays, *Carnegie-Rochester Series on Public Policy*, vol. 31, Autumn, 83–125.

Schwert, G.W. (1990) Stock volatility and the crash of 87, *Review of Financial Studies*, **3**, 77–102.

Schwert, G.W. and Seguin, P.J. (1990) Heteroscedasticity in stock returns, *Journal of Finance*, **45**, 1129–1155.

Scott, L. (1991) Random variance option pricing, *Advances in Futures and Options Research*, **5**, 113–135.

Sentana, E. (1995) Quadratic ARCH models, *Review of Economic Studies*, **62**(4), 639–661.

Shephard, N. (1996) Statistical aspects of ARCH and stochastic volatility, in D.R. Cox, D.V. Hinkley and O.E. Barndorff-Nielsen (eds), *Time Series Models in Econometrics, Finance and Other Fields*, London, New York: Chapman and Hall.

Subba Rao, T. and Gabr, M.M. (1980), A test for linearity of stationary time series, *Journal of Time Series Analysis*, **1**, 145–158.

Taylor, S.J. (1986) *Modelling Financial Times Series*, John Wiley, Chichester.

Tjostheim, D. (1986) Some doubly stochastic time series models, *Journal of Time Series Analysis*, **7**, 51–72.

Tong, H (1983) *Threshold Models in Non-Linear Time Series Analysis*, New York: Springer-Verlag.

Tong, H (1990) *Non-Linear Time Series*, Oxford: Oxford University Press.

Tong, H. (1992) Contrasting aspects of non-linear time series analysis, in Brillinger *et al.*, (eds), *New Directions in Time Series Analysis*, Part I, The IMA Volumes in Mathematics and Its Applications, vol. 45, New York: Springer-Verlag.

Tong, H. and Lim, K.S. (1980) Threshold autoregression, limit cycles and cyclical data, *Journal of Royal Statistical Society*, **B42**, 245–292.

Tong, H. and Yeung, I. (1991) Threshold autoregressive modeling in continuous time, *Statistica Sinica*, **1**, 411–430.

Tsay, R.S. (1989) Testing and modeling thresholds autoregressive processes, *Journal American Statistical Association*, **84**, 231–240.

Turner, C.M., Startz, R. and Nelson, C.R. (1989) A Markov model of heteroscedasticity, risk, and learning in the stock market, *Journal of Financial Economics*, **25**, 3–22.

Tyssedal, J.S. and Tjostheim, D. (1988) An autoregressive model with suddenly changing parameters and an application to stock market prices, *Applied Statistics*, vol. 37, no. 3, pp. 353–369.

Walsh, C.E. (1987) Testing for real effects of monetary policy regime shifts, *NBER Working Paper*, no. 2116.

Wecker, W.E. (1977) Asymmetric time series, *ASA Proc. Business and Economics Section*, 417–422.

Wecker, W.E.(1981) Asymmetric time series, *Journal of American Statistical Association*, vol. 76, no. 373, Applications Section.

Weiss, A. (1984) ARMA models with ARCH errors, *Journal of Time Series Analysis*, **5**, 129–143.

Weiss, A. (1986) Asymptotic theory for ARCH models: estimation and testing, *Econometric Theory*, **2**, 107–131.

Whistler, D. (1988) Semiparametric ARCH estimation of intradaily exchange rate volatility, unpublished manuscript, LSE, London.

Zakoian, J.M. (1994) Threshold heteroscedastic models, *Journal of Economic Dynamics and Control*, **18(5)**, 931–955.

NOTES

1. White noise property is characterized by $E(\varepsilon_t) = \mu$, $\text{Var}(\varepsilon_t) = \sigma^2$ and $\text{Cov}(\varepsilon_t, \varepsilon_{t+s}) = 0$ for all $s \neq 0$. Often μ is taken to be zero. If independence of ε_t's are assumed rather than being uncorrelated over time, this is called strong WN.

2. Martingale difference (MD) is characterized by $E|\varepsilon_t| < \infty$ and $E(\varepsilon_t \mid \varepsilon_{t-1}) = 0$. All MDs have zero means and are uncorrelated over time. The series is called white noise if the unconditional variance is constant over time.

3. The generalization of WN to allow autocovariance of the form $\text{Cov}(\varepsilon_t, \varepsilon_{t+s}) = \gamma(s)$ for all t leads to covariance stationarity. The autocorrelation function is denoted by $\text{Corr}(\varepsilon_t, \varepsilon_{t+s}) = \rho(s) = \gamma(s)/\sigma^2$. Strict stationarity implies

$$F(\varepsilon_{t+h}, \varepsilon_{t+h+1}, \ldots, \varepsilon_{t+h+p}) = F(\varepsilon_t, \varepsilon_{t+1}, \ldots, \varepsilon_{t+p}) \text{ for all } p \text{ and } h.$$

4. EGARCH model is closely related to the Multiplicative ARCH model suggested by Milhoj (1987a, b):

$$\log \sigma_t^2 = \alpha + \sum_{i=1}^{q} \beta_i \log z_{t-i}^2 + \sum_{i=1}^{p} \gamma_i (\log z_{t-i}^2 - \log \sigma_{t-i}^2) \qquad (1.12)$$

5. Threshold ARCH model will be discussed in the section where we introduce threshold models.

6. Another specification is:

$$\varepsilon_t = \sigma_t z_t = \sigma z_t \exp(h_t/2)$$

where

$$h_t = \beta h_{t-1} + \eta_t$$

In this specification, σ is a scale factor. This enables us to write the AR specification of h_t without an intercept term.

7. The specification in (1.13) and (1.14) is a special case of the Stochastic Autoregressive Variance Model (SARV) of Andersen (1994). In the SARV model σ_t is a polynomial function $g(K_t)$ of a Markovian process K_t with the dynamic specification of the following form:

$$K_t = \varpi + \beta K_{t-1} + [\gamma + \alpha K_{t-1}] u_t$$

In (1.14) $K_t = \log \sigma_t$, $\alpha = 0$, $\eta_t = \gamma u_t$.

   The Autoregressive Random Variance model of Taylor (1986) is also a special case of the SARV model.

Chapter 2

Stochastic volatility and option pricing

GEORGE J. JIANG*

SUMMARY

This chapter surveys the current literature on applications of stochastic volatility (SV) models in pricing options. We intend to cover the following subjects: (i) modelling of SV in both discrete time and continuous time and modelling of SV with jumps; (ii) option pricing under SV and implications of SV on option prices, as well as the interplay between SV and jumps; (iii) estimation of SV models with a focus on the simulation-based indirect inference as a generic approach and the efficient method-of-moments (EMM), a particular approach; and (iv) volatility forecasting based on standard volatility models and volatility forecasting using implied volatility from option prices.

2.1 INTRODUCTION

Acknowledging the fact that stochastic volatility is manifest in the time series of asset returns as well as in the empirical variances implied from observed market option prices through the Black–Scholes model, there have been numerous recent studies of option pricing based on stochastic volatility (SV) models. Examples of the continuous-time models include Hull and White (1987), Johnson and Shanno (1987), Wiggins (1987), Scott (1987, 1991, 1997), Bailey and Stulz (1989), Chesney and Scott (1989), Melino and Turnbull (1990), Stein and Stein (1991), Heston (1993), Bates (1996a,b), and Bakshi, Cao and Chen (1997), and examples of the discrete-time models include Taylor (1986, 1994), Amin and Ng (1993), Andersen (1994), and Kim, Shephard

* Department of Econometrics, University of Groningen, PO Box 800, 9700 AV Groningen, The Netherlands, phone +31 50 363 3711, fax, +31 50 363 3720, email: g.jiang@eco.rug.nl

and Chib (1996). Reviews of SV models are provided by Shephard (1996) which surveys the current literature on both ARCH/GARCH and SV models with a focus on the comparison of their statistical properties, and Ghysels, Harvey and Renault (1996) which surveys the current literature on SV models with a focus on statistical modelling and inference of stochastic volatility in financial markets.[1] This chapter extends the above surveys with a focus on the applications and implications of SV models in pricing asset options. We intend to cover the following subjects: (i) modelling of SV in both discrete time and continuous time and modelling of SV with jumps; (ii) option pricing under SV and implications of SV on option prices, as well as the interplay between SV and jumps; (iii) estimation of SV models with a focus on the simulation-based indirect inference as a generic approach and the efficient method-of-moments (EMM), a particular approach; and (iv) volatility forecasting based on standard volatility models and volatility forecasting using implied volatility from option prices.

2.2   THE STOCHASTIC VOLATILITY (SV) MODEL

2.2.1   The discrete-time stochastic autoregressive volatility model

Let S_t denote the asset price at time t and μ_t the conditional mean of the return process which is usually assumed to be a constant, i.e. $\mu_t = \mu$, then the demeaned or detrended return process y_t is defined as

$$y_t = \ln(S_t/S_{t-1}) - \mu_t \tag{2.1}$$

The discrete-time stochastic volatility (SV) model of the financial asset return may be written as

$$y_t = \sigma_t \varepsilon_t, \quad t = 1, 2, \ldots, T \tag{2.2}$$

or

$$y_t = \sigma \varepsilon_t \exp\{h_t/2\}, \quad t = 1, 2, \ldots, T \tag{2.3}$$

where ε_t is an iid random noise with a standard distribution, e.g. normal distribution or Student-t distribution. The most popular SV specification assumes that h_t follows an AR(1) process, as proposed by Taylor (1986), i.e.

$$h_{t+1} = \phi h_t + \eta_t, \quad |\phi| < 1 \tag{2.4}$$

which is a special case of the general stochastic autoregressive volatility (SARV) model defined in Andersen (1994), where $\eta_t \sim \text{iid}(0, \sigma_\eta^2)$ and the constant term is removed due to the introduction of the scale parameter σ in (2.3). When η_t is Gaussian, this model is called a lognormal SV model. One interpretation for the latent variable h_t is that it represents the random, uneven and yet autocorrelated flow of new information into financial markets (see earlier work by Clark, 1973, and Tauchen and Pitts, 1983), thus the volatility is time varying and sometimes clustered with bunching of high and low episodes. When ε_t and η_t are allowed to be correlated with each other, the above model can pick up the kind of asymmetric behaviour often observed in stock price movements, which is known as the *leverage effect* when the correlation is negative (see Black, 1976).

The statistical properties of the above SV model are discussed in Taylor (1986, 1994) and summarized in Shephard (1996) for the case that η_t is Gaussian and in Ghysels, Harvey and Renault (1997) for more general cases. Namely, (i) if η_t is Gaussian and $|\phi| < 1$, h_t is a standard stationary Gaussian autoregression, with $E[h_t] = 0$, Var $[h_t] = \sigma_h^2/(1 - \phi^2)$; (ii) y_t is a martingale difference as ε_t is iid, i.e. y_t has zeros mean and is uncorrelated over time. Furthermore, y_t is a white noise (WN) if $|\phi| < 1$; (iii) as ε_t is always stationary, y_t is stationary if and only if h_t is stationary; (iv) if η_t is normally distributed and h_t stationary and ε_t has finite moments, then all the moments of y_t exist and are given by

$$E[y_t^s] = \sigma^s E[\varepsilon_t^s] E[\exp\{sh_t/2\}] = \sigma^s E[\varepsilon_t^s] \exp\{s^2 \sigma_h^2/8\} \qquad (2.5)$$

when s is even and $E[y_t^s] = 0$ when s is odd if ε_t is symmetric. This suggests that

$$\text{Var}[y_t] = \sigma^2 \sigma_\varepsilon^2 \exp(\sigma_h^2/2) \qquad (2.6)$$

where σ_ε^2 is assumed known, e.g. $\sigma_\varepsilon^2 = 1$ if $\varepsilon_t \sim \text{iid} N(0, 1)$, $\sigma_\varepsilon^2 = v/(v - 2)$ if $\varepsilon_t \sim$ Student-t with $d.f. = v$. More interestingly, the kurtosis of y_t is $(E[\varepsilon_t^4]/\sigma_\varepsilon^4) \exp(\sigma_h^2)$ which is greater than $E[\varepsilon_t^4]/\sigma_\varepsilon^4$, the kurtosis of ε_t, as $\exp(\sigma_h^2) > 1$. When ε_t is also Gaussian, then $E[\varepsilon_t^4]/\sigma_\varepsilon^4 = 3$. In other words, the SV model has fatter tails than that of the corresponding noise disturbance of the return process. It is noted that the above properties of the SV model also hold true even if ε_t and η_t are contemporarily correlated. Harvey (1993) also derived moments of powers of absolute values for y_t under the assumption that η_t is normally distributed.

Dynamic properties of the SV model can be derived under the assumption that the disturbances ε_t and η_t are independent of each other. Squaring both sides of the SV process and then taking logarithms gives

$$\ln y_t^2 = \ln \sigma^2 + h_t + \ln \varepsilon_t^2 \qquad (2.7)$$

which is a linear process with the addition of the iid noise $\ln \varepsilon_t^2$ to the AR(1) process h_t. Thus, $\ln y_t^2 \sim \text{ARMA}(1,1)$. When ε_t is a standard normal distribution, then the mean and variance of $\ln \varepsilon_t^2$ are known to be -1.27 and $\pi^2/2$.

The distribution of $\ln y_t^2$ is far away from being normal, but with a very long left-hand tail. The autocorrelation function of order s for $\ln y_t^2$ is

$$\rho_{\ln y_t^2}(s) = \frac{\phi^s}{1 + \pi^2/2\,\text{Var}[h_t]} \tag{2.8}$$

Compared to the ARCH/GARCH models, proposed by Engle (1982), Bollerslev (1986) and Taylor (1986), the above SV process is also modelled in discrete time and shares similar properties. Unlike the ARCH/GARCH models whose conditional volatility σ_t^2 is driven by past known observations of y_t^2 and σ_t^2, the SV model assumes the conditional volatility driven by an extra random noise.[2] The major differences between ARCH/GARCH and SV models include: (i) the SV model displays excess kurtosis even if ϕ is zero since y_t is a mixture of disturbances (the parameter σ_h^2 governs the degree of mixing independently of the degree of smoothness of the variance evolution), while for a GARCH model the degree of kurtosis is tied to the roots of the variance equation. Hence it is often necessary to use a non-Gaussian model to capture the high kurtosis typically found in financial time series; (ii) the SV model can capture the asymmetric behaviour or *leverage effect* through contemporarily correlated disturbances, while a GARCH model has to modify the variance equation to handle asymmetry. For instance, the EGARCH model in Nelson (1991) assumes $\ln \sigma_t^2$ as a function of past squares and absolute values of the observations. Taylor (1994) believes that an understanding of both ARCH/GARCH and SV models for volatility is more beneficial than the knowledge of only one way to model volatility.

2.2.2   The continuous-time stochastic volatility model

The continuous-time SV model was first introduced by Hull and White (1987), Johnson and Shanno (1987), Scott (1987), and Wiggins (1987), Bailey and Stulz (1989) to price options where the underlying asset price volatility is believed also to be stochastic. A general representation of the continuous-time SV model may be written as

$$dS_t/S_t = \mu_t\,dt + \sigma_t(h_t)\,dW_t$$

$$dh_t = \gamma_t\,dt + \delta_t\,dW_t^h$$

$$dW_t\,dW_t^h = \rho_t\,dt, \quad t \in [0, T] \tag{2.9}$$

where h_t is an unobserved latent state variable governing the volatility of asset returns and itself also follows a diffusion process, W_t and W_t^h are Wiener processes or standard Brownian motion processes with $\text{cov}(dW_t, dW_t^h) = \rho_t dt$; let $\mathcal{I}_t$ be the natural filtration of the stochastic process which represents all the information available at time t (see Duffie (1988) for relevant concepts and definitions), we assume that all the coefficient functions μ_t, σ_t, γ_t, δ_t and ρ_t are adapted to $\mathcal{I}_t$. Same as in the discrete-time SV model, the volatility state variable h_t is also stochastic and evolves according to its own differential equation. Hull and White (1987) assume a geometric Brownian motion process for the volatility state variable as in (2.9) and in particular consider the case that $\rho_t = 0$.

A common specification of the continuous-time SV model resembles that in discrete time, i.e. the logarithmic instantaneous conditional volatility follows an Ornstein-Uhlenbeck process, used in, e.g. Wiggins (1987), Chesney and Scott (1989), and Melino and Turnbull (1990),[3] i.e.

$$\sigma_t(h_t) = \sigma \exp\{h_t/2\}$$
$$dh_t = -\beta h_t \, dt + \sigma_h \, dW_t^h \tag{2.10}$$

where $\beta > 0$ and the exponential functional specification guarantees the non-negativeness of volatility. Similar to the discrete-time autoregressive SV model, h_t is also an AR(1) process as

$$h_t = e^{-\beta} h_{t-1} + \int_{t-1}^{t} \sigma_h e^{-\beta(t-\tau)} \, dW_\tau^h$$

where $\int_{t-1}^{t} e^{-\beta(t-\tau)} \, dW_\tau^h \sim N\left(0, \frac{\sigma_h^2}{2\beta}(1 - e^{-2\beta})\right)$. When $\beta > 0$, h_t is stationary with mean zero and variance $\sigma_h^2/2\beta$.

Another specification which also guarantees the non-negativeness of the volatility is the model proposed by Cox, Ingersoll and Ross (1985) for nominal interest rates, used in, e.g. Bailey and Stulz (1989) and Heston (1993), i.e.

$$\sigma_t(h_t) = \sigma h_t^{1/2}$$
$$dh_t = (\alpha - \beta h_t) \, dt + \sigma_h h_t^{1/2} \, dW_t^h \tag{2.11}$$

The process has a reflecting barrier at zero which is attainable when $2\alpha < \sigma_h^2$. Similar to the Ornstein–Uhlenbeck specification, the Cox, Ingersoll and Ross specification also assumes that the underlying state variable is stationary with $E[h_t] = \alpha/\beta$, $\text{Var}[h_t] = \sigma_h^2\alpha/2\beta^2$. While the Ornstein–Uhlenbeck process assumes the underlying state variable follows a Gaussian distribution, the Cox, Ingersoll and Ross process assumes the underlying state variable follows a Gamma distribution.

While the continuous-time SV models can be viewed as the limit of discrete-time SV models, its ability to internalize enough short-term kurtosis may be limited due to the fact that its sampling path is essentially continuous. Meddahi and Renault (1995) studied the temporal aggregation of SV models and derived the conditions under which a class of discrete-time SV models are closed under temporal aggregation. For instance, when $\mu_t = 0$, $\sigma_t(h_t) = h_t^{1/2}$, and

$$dh_t = (\theta - \beta h_t)\,dt + \delta h_t^\gamma\,dW_t^h \tag{2.12}$$

which assumes the state variable h_t follows a CEV process (i.e. a constant elasticity of variance process due to Cox (1975) and Cox and Ross (1976)),[4] where 2γ is the elasticity of the instantaneous volatility and $\gamma \geq 1/2$ ensures that h_t is a stationary process with non-negative values, the CEV process defined in (2.12) implies an autoregressive model in discrete time for h_t, namely,

$$h_t = \theta(1 - e^{-\beta}) + e^{-\beta}h_{t-1} + \int_{t-1}^{t} e^{-\beta(t-\tau)}\delta h_\tau^\gamma\,dW_\tau^h \tag{2.13}$$

Meddahi and Renault (1995) show that the discrete-time process given by the above stochastic volatility satisfies certain restrictions. Thus, from the continuous-time SV model (2.12), we obtain a class of discrete-time SV models which is closed under temporal aggregation. More specifically, we have

$$y_{t+1} = \ln(S_{t+1}/S_t) = h_t^{1/2}\varepsilon_{t+1}$$

$$h_t = \omega + \phi h_{t-1} + \eta_t \tag{2.14}$$

where $\omega = \theta(1 - e^{-\beta})$, $\phi = e^{-\beta}$ and $\eta_t = \int_{t-1}^{t} e^{-\beta(t-\tau)}\delta h_\tau^\gamma\,dW_\tau^h$.

2.2.3   The jump-diffusion model with stochastic volatility

The jump-diffusion model with stochastic volatility proposed to model asset returns, as a mixture of continuous diffusion and discontinuous jump, can be written as

$$dS_t/S_t = (\mu_t - \lambda\mu_0)\,dt + \sigma_t(h_t)\,dW_t + (Y_t - 1)\,dq_t(\lambda)$$

$$dh_t = \gamma_t\,dt + \delta_t\,dW_t^h$$

$$dW_t\,dW_t^h = \rho_t\,dt, \quad t \in [0, T] \tag{2.15}$$

where

μ_t — the instantaneous expected return on the asset;

$\sigma_t^2(h_t)$ — the instantaneous volatility of the asset's return conditional on no arrivals of important new information (i.e. the Poisson jump event does not occur), h_t is a state variable governing the conditional volatility;

$q_t(\lambda)$ — a Poisson counting process which is assumed to be iid over time, λ is the mean number of jumps per unit of time, i.e. the intensity parameter of the Poisson distribution with Prob(dq_t $(\lambda) = 1) = \lambda\,dt$, Prob($dq_t(\lambda) = 0) = 1 - \lambda\,dt$;

$Y_t - 1$ — the random jump size ($Y_t \geq 0$) representing the random variable percentage change in the underlying asset price if the Poisson event occurs, $\int_0^t (Y_\tau - 1) \, dq_\tau(\lambda)$ is a compound Poisson process, and μ_0 is the expectation of the relative jump size, i.e. $\mu_0 = E[Y_t - 1]$;

$dq_t(\lambda)$ — assumed to be statistically independent of dW_t, dW_t^h;

dW_t, dW_t^h — the innovations of Wiener processes which are possibly correlated.

This general specification nests many models as special cases, such as the constant elasticity of variance (CEV) process when $\sigma_t(h_t) = h_t S_t^{\gamma-1}$ where $2(\gamma - 1)$ is the elasticity of instantaneous variance (0 for geometric Brownian motion); the stochastic volatility model without jumps when $\lambda = 0$ as discussed in section 2.2.2, and the jump-diffusion model without SV when $\sigma_t(\cdot) = \sigma$. Exceptions are option pricing models with jumps in the underlying volatility, e.g. the regime switching model of Naik (1993).

Discontinuous sample path models have been studied by Press (1967), Cox and Ross (1976), and Merton (1976a) among others. Motivations of using the jump-diffusion process to model stock returns were clearly stated in Merton (1976a) in which he distinguishes two types of changes in the stock price: the 'normal' vibrations in price due to, for example, a temporary supply and demand imbalance, changes in capitalization rates or in the economic outlook, or other information that causes only marginal changes in the stock's value; and the 'abnormal' vibrations in price due to random arrivals of important new information about the stock that has more than a marginal effect on prices. The first type of price change can be modelled by a stochastic process with continuous sampling path, e.g. a Wiener process, and the second type of price change can be modelled by a process which explicitly allows for jumps, e.g. a 'Poisson-driven' process.[5]

Since the early 1960s it was observed, notably by Mandelbrot (1963) and Fama (1963, 1965) among others, that asset returns have leptokurtic distributions. The jump-diffusion model can offer a formal link between the description of dynamic path behaviour and explanation of steady state leptokurtic distributions. Merton's (1976a) model is a special case of (2.15) with $\sigma_t(\cdot) = \sigma$, i.e.

$$dS_t/S_t = (\mu_t - \lambda\mu_0)\, dt + \sigma \, dW_t + (Y_t - 1)\, dq_t(\lambda) \tag{2.16}$$

Alternatively, it can be rewritten in terms of the logarithmic asset prices, i.e. $s_t = \ln S_t$, as:

$$ds_t = \alpha_t \, dt + \sigma \, dW_t + \ln Y_t \, dq_t(\lambda) \tag{2.17}$$

where $\alpha_t = \mu_t - \lambda\mu_0 - \frac{1}{2}\sigma^2$. When $\mu_t = \mu$ or $\alpha_t = \alpha$ and Y_t is assumed to be iid lognormal, i.e. $\ln Y_t \sim$ iid $N(\alpha_0, \nu^2)$, the above process is a well-defined

Markov process with discrete parameter space and continuous state space and the SDE (2.17) has an explicit solution.[6] The major properties of this process include: (i) it is a non-stationary compounding Poisson process; (ii) however, the first difference of $\ln S_t$ or s_t over τ (>0)-period or the τ-period return of asset, $y_t(\tau) = \ln(S_t/S_{t-\tau}) = \Delta_\tau s_t = s_t - s_{t-\tau}$ is a stationary process, with density given by

$$f(y_t(\tau) = y) = \sum_{n=0}^{\infty} \frac{e^{-\lambda\tau}(\lambda\tau)^n}{n!} \phi(y; \alpha\tau + n\alpha_0, \sigma^2\tau + nv^2) \tag{2.18}$$

which has an infinite series representation, where $\phi(x; \mu, \sigma)$ is the pdf of a standard normal distribution of $(x - \mu)/\sigma$. Let $\varphi_{y_t(\tau)}(u)$ denote the characteristic function of the asset return $y_t(\tau)$, then $\ln \varphi_{y_t(\tau)}(u) = \alpha\tau ui - \frac{1}{2}\sigma^2\tau u^2 + \lambda\tau(\exp(\alpha_0 ui - \frac{1}{2}v^2 u^2) - 1)$. It is easy to derive that

$$E[y_t(\tau)] = (\alpha + \lambda\alpha_0)\tau, \quad \mathrm{Var}[y_t(\tau)] = (\sigma^2 + \lambda(\alpha_0^2 + v^2))\tau,$$

$$E[(y_t(\tau) - E[y_t(\tau)])^3] = \lambda\tau\alpha_0(\alpha_0^2 + 3v^2),$$

$$E[(y_t(\tau) - E[y_t(\tau)])^4] = 3\,\mathrm{Var}[y_t(\tau)]^2 + \phi_0$$

where $\phi_0 = \lambda\tau\alpha_0^4 + 6\lambda\tau v^2\alpha_0^2 + 3\lambda\tau v^4$. That is, the distribution of $y_t(\tau)$ is leptokurtic, more peaked in the vicinity of its mean than the distribution of a comparable normal random variable, asymmetric if $\alpha_0 \neq 0$, and the skewness has the same sign as that of α_0. These features are more consistent with the empirical findings on the unconditional distributions of many financial asset returns. Special cases of the above model include: Press (1967) with $\alpha = 0$, Beckers (1981) and Ball and Torous (1985) with $\alpha_0 = 0$, and Lo (1988) with $\ln Y_t = \kappa(s_t)$, i.e. the jump size is also determined by the process itself.

2.3   OPTION PRICING UNDER STOCHASTIC VOLATILITY

Option pricing under stochastic volatility has received considerable attention, see, for example, Merton (1973), Cox (1975), Hull and White (1987), Johnson and Shanno (1987), Scott (1987), and Wiggins (1987). In this chapter we focus on those models which assume that the stochastic volatility is driven by a different noise to that of the return process. Unlike the situation where the stochastic volatility is driven by the same noise as that of the asset return, holding the stock now involves two sources of risk, the stock return risk and the volatility risk. Constructing a perfectly hedged portfolio is now more difficult since there are two different sources of uncertainty, namely $\{dW_t, dW_t^h\}$ in continuous time or $\{\varepsilon_t, \eta_t\}$ in discrete time, and only two securities, the stock and the call option, to hedge these risks. Throughout the section, we will intentionally review different methodologies in deriving various option pricing formulas, namely the partial differential equation (PDE) approach by Black–Scholes (1973) and Merton (1973, 1976a), the risk-neutral approach by Cox and Ross (1976) and Harrison and Kreps (1979), and the state price density (SPD) approach by Constantinides (1992) and Amin and Ng (1993). We adopt the following notation: $C(S_t, t)$ denotes the price of a European call option at time t with underlying asset price S_t, the subscript refers to the specific option pricing formula, K the strike price, T the maturity date, r the constant risk-free rate, and r_t the stochastic risk-free rate.

2.3.1 Pricing options under SV and jump: closed form solutions

A. The Hull–White option pricing formula

Hull and White (1987) was one of the first papers to derive an option pricing formula for a European call option on an asset whose price movements have stochastic volatility. The model specified in Hull and White (1987) is a special case of (2.9) with $\sigma_t(h_t) = h_t^{1/2}$ and

$$dh_t/h_t = \gamma_t \, dt + \delta_t \, dW_t^h \tag{2.19}$$

where the coefficients γ_t and δ_t do not depend on S_t. When both γ_t and δ_t are constant, the state variable h_t follows a geometric Brownian motion process, i.e. h_t has a lognormal distribution and is restricted to be positive. Let V_t be the value at time t of the portfolio involving the stock and the call option, define the function $\lambda_t(S_t, \sigma_t) \, dt = E_t[dV_t/V_t] - r \, dt$ as the excess expected return (per unit time) on this partially hedged portfolio. Using the argument that the return of the partially hedged portfolio equals the risk-free rate of return r plus the excess expected return, it can be shown that the call option price satisfies the following PDE:

$$\frac{1}{2}\sigma_t^2 S_t^2 \frac{\partial^2 C(S_t, t)}{\partial S_t^2} + (\lambda_t(S_t, \sigma_t) + r)S_t \frac{\partial C(S_t, t)}{\partial S_t}$$

$$+ \rho_t \delta_t \sigma_t S_t \frac{\partial^2 C(S_t, t)}{\partial S_t \partial \sigma_t} + \frac{1}{2}\delta_t^2 \frac{\partial^2 C(S_t, t)}{\partial \sigma_t^2} + \gamma_t \frac{\partial C(S_t, t)}{\partial \sigma_t}$$

$$+ \frac{\partial C(S_t, t)}{\partial t} - (\lambda_t(S_t, \sigma_t) + r)C(S_t, t) = 0 \tag{2.20}$$

subject to $C(S_T, T) = \text{Max}(S_T - K, 0)$, where $\sigma_t = h_t^{1/2}$. To solve this PDE, one needs to specify the explicit functional forms of γ_t, δ_t and $\lambda_t(S_t, \sigma_t)$, which implies that certain restrictions are imposed on investor preferences since $\lambda_t(S_t, \sigma_t)$ is an equilibrium determined function. Two approaches have been employed in the literature. The first approach assumes that the volatility risk is diversifiable and receives zero excess expected return, i.e. $\lambda_t(S_t, \sigma_t) = 0$

in, for example, Hull and White (1987) and Johnson and Shanno (1987). The second approach assumes a specific class of preferences, and explicitly solves for $\lambda_t(S_t, \sigma_t)$ in, for example, Wiggins (1987).

Hull and White (1987) further assume that $\rho_t = 0$, i.e. the conditional volatility is uncorrelated with the stock price. Thanks to the independence, as a solution of the above PDE (2.20) or based on a risk-neutral probability, the so-called Hull–White option pricing formula can be derived as

$$C_{HW}(S_t, t; K, T, r, V_t^T) = E_t[S_t \Phi(d_{1t}) - Ke^{-r(T-t)} \Phi(d_{2t})] \tag{2.21}$$

where

$$d_{1t} \equiv \frac{\ln(S_t/K) + \left(r + \frac{1}{2}V_t^T\right)(T - t)}{\sqrt{V_t^T(T - t)}}, \quad d_{2t} \equiv d_{1t} - \sqrt{V_t^T(T - t)},$$

$$V_t^T \equiv \frac{1}{T - t} \int_t^T \sigma_\tau^2 d\tau$$

and $\Phi(\cdot)$ is the cumulative distribution function (CDF) of standard normal distribution. When $\sigma_t = \sigma$, i.e. the conditional volatility is constant, the above pricing PDE reduces to the Black–Scholes equation and its solution for the option price formula is given by:

$$C_{BS}(S_t, t; K, T, r, \sigma^2) = S_t \Phi(d_1) - Ke^{-r(T-t)} \Phi(d_2) \tag{2.22}$$

where

$$d_1 \equiv \frac{\ln(S_t/K) + \left(r + \frac{1}{2}\sigma^2\right)(T - t)}{\sigma\sqrt{T - t}}, \quad d_2 \equiv d_1 - \sigma\sqrt{T - t}$$

B. The Amin-Ng option pricing formula

The uncertainty in the economy presented in Amin and Ng (1993), in the line of Rubinstein (1976), Brennan (1979) and Stapleton and Subrahmanyam (1984), is driven by the realization of a set of random variables at each discrete date. Among them are a random shock to consumption process $\{\varepsilon_{ct}, t = 0, 1, 2, \ldots, T\}$, a random shock to the individual stock price process $\{\varepsilon_{st}, t = 0, 1, 2, \ldots, T\}$, a set of systematic state variables $\{Y_t, t = 0, 1, 2, \ldots, T\}$ that determine the consumption process and stock returns, and finally a set of stock-specific state variables $\{U_t, t = 0, 1, 2, \ldots, T\}$ that determine the idiosyncratic part of the stock return volatility. The investors' information set at time t is represented by the σ-algebra $F_t \equiv \sigma(\{\varepsilon_{c\tau}, \varepsilon_{s\tau}, Y_\tau, U_\tau\}; \tau = 0, 1, \ldots, t)$ which consists of all available information up to t. Thus the consumption process is driven by, in addition to a random noise, the systematic state variables, and the stock price process is driven by, in addition to a random noise, both the systematic state variables and idiosyncratic state variables. In other words, the stock return variance can have a systematic component that is correlated and changes with the consumption variance. The joint evolution of the stock price and aggregate consumption can be expressed as

$$\ln(S_t/S_{t-1}) = \mu_{st} - \tfrac{1}{2}h_{st} + \varepsilon_{st}$$

$$\ln(C_t/C_{t-1}) = \mu_{ct} - \tfrac{1}{2}h_{ct} + \varepsilon_{ct} \tag{2.23}$$

where $\mu_{ct} = \mu_c(Y_\tau; \tau \le t)$, $\mu_{st} = \mu_s(Y_\tau, U_\tau; \tau \le t)$, conditional on $F_{t-1} \cup \sigma(Y_t, U_t)$, $(\varepsilon_{st}, \varepsilon_{ct})$ follows a bivariate normal distribution with $\mathrm{Var}[\varepsilon_{st}] = h_{st}(Y_\tau, U_\tau; \tau \le t)$, $\mathrm{Var}[\varepsilon_{ct}] = h_{ct}(Y_\tau; \tau \le t)$, $\mathrm{Cov}[\varepsilon_{ct}, \varepsilon_{st}] = \sigma_{cst}(Y_\tau, U_\tau; \tau \le t)$, and conditional on $\sigma(Y_\tau, U_\tau; \tau \le t)$, $(\varepsilon_{ct}, \varepsilon_{st})$ is independent of $\{Y_\tau, U_\tau; \tau > t\}$.

An important relationship derived under the equilibrium is that the variance of consumption growth h_{ct} is negatively related to the interest rate r_{t-1}. Therefore a larger proportion of systematic volatility implies a stronger negative relationship between the individual stock return variance and interest rate. Given that the variance and the interest rate are two important inputs in the determination of option prices and that they have the opposite effects on call option values, the correlation between the variance and interest rate will therefore be important in determining the net effect of the two inputs. Furthermore, the model is naturally extended to allow for stochastic interest rates.[7]

The closed form solution of the option prices is available and preference free under quite general conditions, i.e. the stochastic mean of the stock return process μ_{st}, the stochastic mean and variance of the consumption process μ_{ct} and h_{ct}, as well as the covariance between the changes of stock returns and consumptions σ_{cst} are predictable.[8] To price options, one can use the fact that the existence of a state price density (SPD) is equivalent to the absence of arbitrage as shown in Dalang, Morton and Willinger (1989). However, due to the incompleteness of the market, such SPD is not unique. By assuming the following functional form for the SPD

$$\xi_t = \exp\left\{-\sum_{\tau=1}^{t} r_\tau - \sum_{\tau=1}^{t}\left(\lambda_\tau \varepsilon_{c\tau}/h_{c\tau}^{1/2} + \tfrac{1}{2}\lambda_\tau^2\right)\right\} \tag{2.24}$$

with an F_{t-1}-measurable finite random variable $\lambda_t = (\mu_{ct} - r_t)/h_{ct}^{1/2}$, it leads to the Amin and Ng (1993) option pricing formula

$$C_{AN}(S_t, t) = E_t\left[S_t \cdot \Phi(d_{1t}) - K \exp\left(-\sum_{\tau=t}^{T-1} r_\tau\right)\Phi(d_{2t})\right] \tag{2.25}$$

where

$$
d_{1t} = \frac{\ln\left(S_t \middle/ \left(K \exp\left(\sum_{\tau=t}^{T-1} r_\tau\right)\right)\right) + \frac{1}{2}\sum_{\tau=t+1}^{T} h_{s\tau}}{\left(\sum_{\tau=t+1}^{T} h_{s\tau}\right)^{1/2}}, \quad d_{2t} = d_{1t} - \sum_{\tau=t+1}^{T} h_{s\tau}
$$

where the expectation is taken wrt the risk-neutral probability and can be calculated from simulations. As Amin and Ng (1993) point out, several option-pricing formulas in the available literature are special cases of the above option formula. They include the Black–Scholes (1973) formula, the Hull–White (1987) stochastic volatility option pricing formula, the Bailey–Stulz (1989) stochastic volatility index option pricing formula, and the Merton (1973), Amin and Jarrow (1992), and Turnbull and Milne (1991) stochastic interest rate option pricing formulas.

C. The Merton option pricing formula

Similar to the presence of stochastic volatility, in the Merton (1976a) jump-diffusion model it is impossible to construct a riskless portfolio of underlying asset and options due to the presence of 'jumps'. Under the assumption that the jump component represents only non-systematic risk, or the jump risk is diversifiable,[9] Merton (1976a) derives the call option pricing formula following along the line of the original Black–Scholes derivation which assumes that the CAPM is a valid description of equilibrium asset returns. Alternatively, using the equivalent martingale measure approach of Cox and Ross (1976) and Harrison and Kreps (1979) as in Aase (1988) and Bardhan and Chao (1993) for general random, marked point process, or Jeanblanc-Picque and Pontier (1990) for non-homogeneous Poisson jumps, or using a general equilibrium argument as in Bates (1988), it can be shown that the call option price satisfies the following integro-differential-difference equation

$$
\frac{1}{2}\sigma^2 S_t^2 \frac{\partial^2 C(S_t, t)}{\partial S_t^2} + (r - \lambda\alpha_0)S_t \frac{\partial C(S_t, t)}{\partial S_t} + \frac{\partial C(S_t, t)}{\partial t} - rC(S_t, t)
$$

$$
+ \lambda E_Y[C(S_t Y_t, t) - C(S_t, t)] = 0 \tag{2.26}
$$

subject to the boundary conditions $C(0, t) = 0$, $C(S_T, T) = \mathrm{Max}(0, S_T - K)$. If $\lambda = 0$, i.e. there is no jump, the above pricing PDE reduces to the Black–Scholes equation and its solution for the option price formula is given by (2.22). Let $C_M(S_t, t; K, T, r, \sigma^2)$ be the price of a European call option at time t for the jump-diffusion model with asset price S_t, expiration date T, exercise price K, the instantaneous riskless rate r, and the constant non-jump instantaneous volatility

σ^2, Merton (1976a) showed that the solution of call option price with jumps can be written as:

$$C_M(S_t, t; K, T, r, \sigma^2) = \sum_{n=0}^{\infty} \frac{e^{-\lambda\tau}(\lambda\tau)^n}{n!}$$

$$\times E_{Y(n)}[C_{BS}(S_t Y(n) e^{-\lambda\mu_0\tau}, t; K, T, r, \sigma^2)] \quad (2.27)$$

where $Y(n) = 1$ for $n = 0$, $Y(n) = \Pi_{i=1}^{n} Y_i$, for $n \geq 1$, Y_i, $i = 1, 2, \ldots, n$, are iid n jumps. Under further condition that Y follows a lognormal distribution as assumed by Press (1967), i.e. $\ln Y \sim$ iid $N(\ln(1 + \mu_0) - \frac{1}{2}v^2, v^2)$, thus $Y(n)$ has a lognormal distribution with the variance of logarithm of $Y(n)$, $\text{Var}[\ln Y(n)] = v^2 n$, and $E_{Y(n)}[Y(n)] = (1 + \mu_0)^n$, a closed-form solution is given by,

$$C_M(S_t, t; K, T, r, \sigma^2) = \sum_{n=0}^{\infty} \frac{e^{-\lambda'\tau}(\lambda'\tau)^n}{n!} C_{BS}(S_t, t; K, T, \gamma_n, v_n^2) \quad (2.28)$$

where $\lambda' = \lambda(1 + \mu_0)$, $v_n^2 = \sigma^2 + nv^2/\tau$ and $\gamma_n = r - \lambda\mu_0 + n\ln(1 + \mu_0)/\tau$. The option price is simply the weighted sum of the price conditional on knowing that exactly n Poisson jumps will occur during the life of the option with each weight being the probability that a Poisson random variable with intensity $\lambda'\tau$ will take on the value n.

D. The general option pricing formula for jump-diffusion with SV and stochastic interest rates

More recent Fourier inversion techniques proposed by Heston (1993) allow for a closed-form solution of European option prices even when there are non-zero correlations between the conditional volatility and the underlying asset price and the interest rate is also stochastic. That is, the joint evolution of asset price, conditional volatility, and interest rates are specified as

$$dS_t/S_t = (\mu_t - \lambda\mu_0) dt + \sigma_t(h_t) \ dW_t + (Y_t - 1) dq_t(\lambda)$$

$$dh_t = \gamma_t dt + \delta_t dW_t^h$$

$$dr_t = \kappa_t dt + v_t dW_t^r$$

$$dW_t dW_t^h = \rho_t dt, \quad t \in [0, T] \quad (2.29)$$

where $q_t(\lambda)$ is uncorrelated with Y_t, dW_t, dW_t^h and dW_t^r, and dW_t^r is uncorrelated with Y_t, dW_t and dW_t^h. In a general equilibrium framework, Bates (1988, 1991) shows that the 'risk-neutral' specification corresponding to the model defined in (2.29) under certain restrictions is given as

$$dS_t/S_t = (r_t - \tilde{\lambda}\tilde{\mu}_0) dt + \sigma_t(h_t) d\tilde{W}_t + (\tilde{Y}_t - 1) d\tilde{q}_t(\tilde{\lambda})$$

$$dh_t = (\gamma_t dt + \Phi_h) + \delta_t d\tilde{W}_t^h$$

$$dr_t = (\kappa_t\, dt + \Phi_r) + v_t d\tilde{W}_t^r$$

$$d\tilde{W}_t d\tilde{W}_t^h = \rho_t\, dt, \quad t \in [0, T] \tag{2.30}$$

where $\Phi_h = \mathrm{Cov}(dh_t, dJ_w/J_w), \Phi_r = \mathrm{Cov}(dr_t, dJ_w/J_w), \tilde{\lambda} = \lambda E(1 + \Delta J_w/J_w),$ $\tilde{\mu}_0 = \mu_0 + (\mathrm{Cov}(\mu_0, \Delta J_w/J_w)/E[1 + \Delta J_w/J_w]),$ and $\tilde{q}_t(\tilde{\lambda})$ is a Poisson counting process with intensity $\tilde{\lambda}$, J_w is the marginal utility of nominal wealth of the representative investor, $\Delta J_w/J_w$ is the random percentage jump conditional on a jump occurring; and dJ_w/J_w is the percentage shock in the absence of jumps. The correlations between innovations in risk-neutral Wiener processes $\tilde{W}_t$, $\tilde{W}_t^h$ and $\tilde{W}_t^r$ are the same as between innovations in the actual processes. That is, in the 'risk-neutral' specification, all the systematic asset, volatility, interest rate, and jump risk are appropriately compensated. Standard approaches for pricing systematic volatility risk, interest rate risk, and jump risk have typically involved either assuming the risk is non-systematic and therefore has zero price ($\Phi_\sigma = \Phi_r = 0; \tilde{\lambda} = \lambda, \tilde{\mu}_0 = \mu_0$), or by imposing a tractable functional form on the risk premium (e.g. $\Phi_r = \xi v_t$) with extra (free) parameters to be estimated from observed options prices.

Closed-form solutions for European call option prices are available with the following particular specification of the stochastic process of the state variables in the 'risk-neutral' measure

$$dS_t/S_t = (r_t - \tilde{\lambda}\tilde{\mu}_0)\, dt + \sqrt{\sigma_t}\, d\tilde{W}_t + (\tilde{Y}_t - 1)\, d\tilde{q}_t(\tilde{\lambda})$$

$$d\sigma_t = (\theta_\sigma - \kappa_\sigma \sigma_t)\, dt + v_\sigma \sqrt{\sigma_t}\, d\tilde{W}_t^\sigma$$

$$dr_t = (\theta_r - \kappa_r r_t)\, dt + v_r \sqrt{r_t}\, d\tilde{W}_t^r$$

$$d\tilde{W}_t^\sigma\, d\tilde{W}_t = \rho\, dt, \quad t \in [0, T] \tag{2.31}$$

where $\ln \tilde{Y}_t \sim N(\ln(1 + \tilde{\mu}_0) - \frac{1}{2}v^2, v^2)$ and $\tilde{q}_t(\tilde{\lambda})$ is uncorrelated over time or with $\tilde{W}_t$, $\tilde{W}_t^\sigma$, and $\tilde{W}_t^r$ is uncorrelated with any process in the economy. By a standard argument, it can be shown that $C(S_t, t)$ satisfies

$$\frac{1}{2}\sigma_t S_t^2 \frac{\partial^2 C(S_t, t)}{\partial S_t^2} + (r_t - \tilde{\lambda}\tilde{\mu}_0)S_t \frac{\partial C(S_t, t)}{\partial S_t} + \rho v_\sigma \sigma_t S_t \frac{\partial^2 C(S_t, t)}{\partial S_t \partial \sigma_t}$$

$$+ \frac{1}{2}v_\sigma^2 \sigma_t \frac{\partial^2 C(S_t, t)}{\partial \sigma_t^2} + (\theta_\sigma - \kappa_\sigma \sigma_t)\frac{\partial C(S_t, t)}{\partial \sigma_t} + \frac{1}{2}v_r^2 r_t \frac{\partial^2 C(S_t, t)}{\partial r_t^2}$$

$$+ (\theta_r - \kappa_r r_t)\frac{\partial C(S_t, t)}{\partial r_t} + \frac{\partial C(S_t, t)}{\partial t} - r_t C(S_t, t)$$

$$+ \tilde{\lambda} E[C(S_t \tilde{Y}_t, t) - C(S_t, t)] = 0 \tag{2.32}$$

subject to $C(S_T, T) = \max(S_T - K, 0)$. It can be shown that (see the derivation in appendix for illustration)

$$C(S_t, t) = S_t \Pi_1(S_t, t; K, T, r_t, \sigma_t) - KB(t, \tau)\Pi_2(S_t, t; K, T, r_t, \sigma_t) \quad (2.33)$$

where $B(t, \tau)$ is the current price of a zero coupon bond that pays \$1 in $\tau = T - t$ periods from time t, and the risk-neutral probabilities, Π_1 and Π_2, are recovered from inverting the respective characteristic functions (see, for example, Bates (1996a,b), Heston (1993), Scott (1997), and Bakshi, Cao and Chen (1997) for the methodology) as given by

$$\Pi_j(S_t, t; K, T, r_t, \sigma_t)$$
$$= \frac{1}{2} + \frac{1}{\pi} \int_0^\infty Re\left[\frac{\exp\{i\phi \ln K\}f_j(t, \tau, S_t, r_t, \sigma_t; \phi)}{i\phi}\right] d\phi$$

for $j = 1, 2$, with the characteristic functions f_j given in the appendix.

2.3.2 Pricing options under SV and jump: Monte Carlo simulation

As Bates (1996a) points out, to price asset options based on time series models specified in the objective measure, it is important to identify the relationship between the actual process followed by the underlying state variables and the 'risk-neutral' processes implicit in option prices. Representative agent equilibrium models such as Cox, Ingersoll and Ross (1985), Ahn and Thompson (1988), and Bates (1988, 1991) indicate that European options that pay off only at maturity are priced as if investors priced options at their expected discounted payoffs under an equivalent 'risk-neutral' representation that incorporates the appropriate compensation for systematic asset, volatility, interest rate, and jump risk. For instance, a European option on a non-dividend paying stock that pays off $F(S_T, T)$ at maturity T is priced at time t as

$$C(S_t, t) = E_t^*[e^{-\int_t^T r_t\, dt} F(S_T, T)] \quad (2.34)$$

where E_t^* is the expectation under the 'risk-neutral' specification of the state variables. Such an expectation is not always readily to be computed due to the complexity of payoff function, but has to rely on standard Monte Carlo simulation techniques, i.e.

$$C(S_t, t) = \frac{1}{N}\sum_{h=1}^N e^{-\int_t^T \tilde{r}_t^h\, dt} F(\tilde{S}_T^h, T) \quad (2.35)$$

where $\tilde{r}_t^h, \tilde{S}_t^h, h = 1, 2, \ldots, N$ are simulated sampling paths of the interest rate and stock price in the 'risk-neutral' probability measure. Furthermore, the integration $\int_t^T \tilde{r}_t^h\, dt$ also has to be approximated by discrete summation.

Simulation of the exact dynamic sampling path of the continuous-time SV model is in general impossible unless its transition density functions are explicitly known. Hence in general we can only simulate the approximated sampling path of the SV model. We illustrate the simulation of continuous-time diffusion processes using the following general jump-diffusion process

$$ds_t = \mu(s_t, t; \theta) \, dt + \sigma(s_t, t; \theta) \, dW_t + \ln Y_t \, dq_t(\lambda) \qquad (2.36)$$

where $\ln Y_t \sim$ iid $N(\alpha_0, v^2)$. First, we divide the time interval $[t_i, t_{i+1})$ further into small subintervals, i.e $[t_i + k\Delta_i/n, t_i + (k+1)\Delta_i/n)$, where $k = 0, 1, \ldots, n-1; i = 0, 1, \ldots, M-1$ and n is a large number with $t_0 = t, t_M = T$. Then we construct step functions of the coefficient functions as $\mu^n(s_t, t) = \mu(s_{t_i+k\Delta_i/n}, t_i + k\Delta_i/n), \sigma^n(s_t, t) = \sigma(s_{t_i+k\Delta_i/n}, t_i + k\Delta_i/n)$, for $t_i + k\Delta_i/n \leq t < t_i + (k+1)\Delta_i/n$. It leads to the following simulation model:

$$d\tilde{s}_t = \mu^n(\tilde{s}_t, t; \theta) \, dt + \sigma^n(\tilde{s}_t, t; \theta) \, dW_t + \ln Y_t \, dq_t(\lambda) \qquad (2.37)$$

or

$$\tilde{s}_{t_i+(k+1)\Delta_i/n} = \tilde{s}_{t_i+k\Delta_i/n} + \mu(\tilde{s}_{t_i+k\Delta_i/n}, t_i + k\Delta_i/n; \theta)\Delta_i/n$$
$$+ \sigma(\tilde{s}_{t_i+k\Delta_i/n}, t_i + k\Delta_i/n; \theta)(\Delta_i/n)^{1/2}\varepsilon^0_{t_{ik}} + \sum_{j=1}^{N_{\Delta_i/n}} (\alpha_0 + v\varepsilon^j_{t_{ik}}) \qquad (2.38)$$

where $\Delta_i = t_{i+1} - t_i$, $\varepsilon^j_{t_{ik}} \sim$ iid $N(0, 1)$, $j \geq 0, k = 0, 1, \ldots, n-1, i = 0, 1, \ldots, M-1$, and $N_{\Delta_i/n} \sim$ Poisson distribution with intensity $\lambda\Delta_i/n$. Discretization of the process described in the above is called the Euler scheme. As $n \to \infty$, it can be shown that the simulated path $\tilde{s}_t$ converges to the paths of s_t uniformly in probability on compact sets, i.e. $sup_{0 \leq t \leq T} |\tilde{s}(t) - s(t)|$ converges to zero in probability. Alternatively, the Milshtein scheme can be used for the continuous part of the process by adding one more term $\frac{1}{2}\sigma^2(\tilde{s}_{t_i+k\Delta_i/n}, t_i + k\Delta_i/n; \theta)(\Delta_i/n)^{1/2}(\varepsilon^0_{t_{ik}}2 - 1)$ as it has a better convergence rate than the Euler scheme for the convergence in $L^p(\Omega)$ and the almost sure convergence (see Talay, 1996).

Two points regarding the dynamic path simulation are noted here. First, the Monte Carlo solution is one of the often used approaches to solving the PDE such as the one defined in (2.20) when other methods are relatively difficult to implement; second, to reduce the computational burden and at the same time to achieve a high level of accuracy, a variety of variance reduction techniques have been proposed for random number simulation, such as control variates, antithetic variates, stratified sampling, importance sampling, and quasi-random number generator (see Boyle, Broadie and Glasserman, 1996).

2.3.3 Implications of stochastic volatility and jumps on option prices

A. Implications of SV on option prices

The relationship between option prices and underlying asset return dynamics offers a guidance in searching alternative option pricing models that have the 'right' distribution as implied from option prices. The SV model has a flexible distributional structure in which the correlation between volatility and asset returns serves to control the level of asymmetry and the volatility variation coefficient serves to control the level of kurtosis. It is obvious that implications of SV on option prices depend critically on the specification of the SV processes. Based on the SV model specified in (2.19), Hull and White (1987) show that when the volatility is uncorrelated with the stock price, the Black–Scholes model underprices the in-the-money (ITM) and out-of-the-money (OTM) options and overprices the at-the-money (ATM) options. The largest absolute price differences occur at or near the money. The actual magnitude of the pricing error, however, is quite small in general. When the volatility is correlated with the stock price, this ATM overprice continues on to ITM options for positive correlation and to OTM options for negative correlation. In particular, when the volatility is positively correlated with the stock price, the bias of the Black–Scholes model tends to decline as the stock price increases. OTM options are underpriced by the Black–Scholes model, while ITM options are overpriced by the Black–Scholes model. The crossing point is slightly OTM. When the volatility is negatively correlated with the stock price, the reverse is true. OTM options are overpriced by the Black–Scholes model, while ITM options are underpriced by the Black–Scholes model. The crossing point is slightly ITM. The intuitive explanation of the above effects offered by Hull and White (1987) is the impact of SV and the correlation between stock price and volatility on the terminal distribution of stock prices. For instance, when the volatility is negatively correlated, which is often observed in the stock price movements known as the 'leverage effect', high stock prices are associated with lower volatility and low stock prices are associated with higher volatility. High stock prices become more like absorbing states, so that a very low price becomes less likely than when the volatility is fixed. The net effect is that the terminal stock price distribution is more peaked and may be more negatively skewed than the lognormal distribution associated with the constant volatility.

Stein and Stein (1991) specify an Ornstein–Uhlenbeck process for the stochastic volatility $\sigma_t(h_t)$ with zero correlation between stock price and conditional volatility. Their results suggest that SV has an upward influence on option prices and SV is 'more important' for OTM options than ATM options in the sense that the implied volatility corresponding to the SV prices exhibits a U-shaped curve as the strike price is varied. Implied volatility is lowest for ATM options and rises as the strike price moves in either direction. Johnson and

Shanno (1987) specify a CEV-type SV process and investigate the implications of correlation coefficient ρ between stock price and volatility based on Monte Carlo simulations. They show that, when ρ changes from negative to positive, the call prices increase for OTM options, decrease for ITM options, but are rather insensitive for ATM options. Heston (1993) specifies a squared root SV process and assumes a non-zero correlation between volatility and asset prices. Using the underlying probability density function of spot asset returns, Heston shows that the SV model can induce almost any type of bias to option prices. In particular, the SV model links these biases to the dynamics of the spot asset prices and the distribution of spot asset returns.

Various empirical studies on the applications of SV models in pricing options have been conducted based on observed asset returns and/or observed market option prices. Scott (1987) used both the SV model and the Black–Scholes model to compute call option prices on Digital Equipment Co. (DEC) for the period July 1982 to June 1983. On each day of the sample, the volatility estimate is backed out from the ATM call option prices and used to compute all option prices. The empirical results suggest that the SV model marginally outperforms the Black–Scholes model with daily adjusted volatility, the mean squared error for the SV model is 8.7% less than that of the Black-Scholes model. The Black–Scholes model with constant volatility performs quite poorly in comparison with the SV model and the Black–Scholes model with daily adjusted volatility. Based on the models estimated for stock indices and individual stocks, Wiggins (1987) found that the SV option values do not differ dramatically from the Black–Scholes values in most cases, although there is some evidence that for longer maturity options, the Black-Scholes model overvalues OTM calls relative to ITM calls. But he did not compare the model prices with observed market prices. Chesney and Scott (1989) used the modified Black–Scholes model and the SV model to price calls and puts on the US $/Swiss franc exchange rate and compare the model prices to bid–ask quotes for European calls and puts with fixed maturity dates traded in Switzerland. They assume the volatility risk is proportional to the volatility of the stochastic volatility process. Similar to Scott (1987), the volatility estimate on each day of the sample is backed out from ATM option prices and then used to price all the calls and puts on that day. They found that the actual prices on calls and puts confirm more closely to the Black–Scholes model with daily revised volatility input, while the Black–Scholes model with constant volatility performs very poorly. They also show that even though a hedged trading strategy with stochastic volatility generates statistically and economically significant profits, the gains are small as these profits are more than offset by the bid–ask spread. Melino and Turnbull (1990) investigate the consequence of SV for pricing spot foreign currency options using the daily spot Canadian $/US $ exchange rate over the period 2 January 1975 to 10 December 1986. Similarly, they assume a constant price for volatility risk and examine the impact of different values for volatility risk price on option prices. Their results indicate that, with negative prices of risk, the SV models yield significantly better predictions than the standard non-stochastic volatility models. Bakshi, Cao and Chen (1997) examine the option pricing model with jumps and stochastic volatility as well as stochastic interest rates using S&P 500 options. Instead of estimating the underlying asset return process, they calibrate the option pricing model in a risk-neutral specification using observed market option prices and gauge each model's empirical performance based on both in-sample and out-of-sample fitting. Their results indicate that, overall, SV and jumps are important for reducing option pricing errors, while the stochastic interest rate is relatively less important. Jiang and van der Sluis (1998) estimated a multivariate SV process for the joint dynamics of stock returns and interest rates based on the observations of underlying state variables. They found a strongly significant negative correlation between stock price and volatility, confirming the leverage effect. While the SV can improve the option pricing performance over the Black–Scholes model, the stochastic interest rate has minimal effect on option prices. Similar to Melino and Turnbull (1990), they also found that with a negative market price of risk for the stochastic volatility and the implied volatility from market option prices, the SV models can significantly reduce the option pricing errors.

B. Systematic SV and stochastic interest rates

Empirical evidence shows that the volatility of stock returns is not only stochastic, but that it is also highly correlated with the volatility of the market as a whole. That is, in addition to an idiosyncratic volatility for the returns of individual stock, there is also a systematic component that is related to the market volatility (see, for example, Black, 1975; Conrad, Kaul and Gultekin, 1991; Jarrow and Rosenfeld, 1984; Jorion, 1988; Ng, Engle, and Rothschild, 1992). The empirical evidence also shows that the biases inherent in the Black–Scholes option prices are different for options on high and low risk stocks (see, for example, Black and Scholes, 1972; Gultekin, Rogalski and Tinic, 1982; Whaley, 1982). Since the variance of consumption growth is negatively related to the interest rate in equilibrium models such as Amin and Ng (1993), the dynamics of the consumption process relevant to option valuation are embodied in the interest rate process. The Amin and Ng (1993) model allows the study of the simultaneous effects of both stochastic interest rates and a stochastic stock return's volatility on the valuation of options. It is documented in the literature that when the interest rate is stochastic the Black–Scholes option pricing formula tends to underprice the European call options (Merton, 1973), while in the case that the stock return's volatility is stochastic, the Black–Scholes option pricing formula tends to overprice the at-the-money European call options (Hull and White, 1987). The combined effect of both factors depends on the relative variability of the two processes. Based on simulation, Amin and Ng (1993) show that stochastic interest rates cause option values to decrease if each of these effects acts by itself. However, this combined effect should depend on the relative importance (variability) of each of these two processes. In details, presence of mean reversion in only the idiosyncratic part of the stock return variance can cause the Black–Scholes formula to change from overpricing to underpricing the options, while mean reversion in the systematic variance alone causes the Black–Scholes overpricing to be even more significant. For significant mean reversion in both the systematic and idiosyncratic variance components which reduce the effect of the stochastic nature of both these inputs, the Black–Scholes biases are quite small. When the systematic component of the stock variance is large, the combined effect of the stochastic variance and the stochastic interest rate is more complicated since the two are now highly correlated.

Bailey and Stulz (1989) analyse the pricing of stock index options by assuming that both the volatility of the stock index and the spot rate of interest are driven by the same state variable. That is, the stock index return volatility is systematic or correlated with the market. In particular, the volatility of the stock index is proportional to the positive state variable, while the instantaneous interest rate is a decreasing linear function of the state variable. Thus, an increase in the volatility of the index does not necessarily increase the value of the option. For instance, for short-term maturity options, an increase in the index volatility brings about a decrease in interest rate, which reduces the value of the option and offsets the effect of volatility increase, while for long-term maturity options, the effect of an increase in the index volatility on interest rate becomes negligible, the value of the option tends to increase with the volatility. Bailey and Stulz (1989) further investigate the implications of the correlation coefficient between the state variable and the index, a positive correlation between the state variable and the index implies a positive correlation between the stochastic conditional volatility and the index but a negative correlation between the interest rate and the index. Their simulation results show that the SV call option values increase as the correlation between the index and the state variable increases. When a negative correlation between index and interest rate is observed, the Black–Scholes model tends to underprice the index options. Especially, if the index volatility is high, such biases can become extremely substantial for deep ITM options.

Even though systematic volatility proves to be important for option pricing, the empirical evidence in Jiang and van der Sluis (1998) suggest that interest rate fails to be a good proxy of the systematic factor. Empirical results in

Bakshi, Cao and Chen (1997) and Jiang and ver der Sluis (1998) also suggest that stochastic interest rate has minimal impact on option prices.

C. Implications of jump on option prices and its interplay with SV

The jump-diffusion option pricing model proposed by Merton (1976a) is an important alternative to and extension of the Black and Scholes (1973) option pricing model. Merton (1976a) suggested that distributions with fatter tails than the lognormal in Black–Scholes might explain the tendency for deep ITM, deep OTM, and short maturity options to sell for more than their Black––Scholes values, and the tendency of near-the-money and longer-maturity options to sell for less. The question raised in Merton (1976a) and answered in detail in Merton (1976b) is: suppose an investor believes that the stock price dynamics follows a continuous sample-path process with a constant variance per unit time and therefore uses the standard Black–Scholes formula to evaluate the options when the true process for the underlying stock price is described by the jump-diffusion process (2.16) with constant drift, how will the investor's appraised value based on a misspecified process for the stock compare with the true value based on the correct process?

To make the comparison feasible and straightforward, Merton (1976b) assumed that $\ln Y_t \sim \text{iid} N(-\frac{1}{2}v^2, v^2)$, or $\mu_0 = E[Y_t - 1] = 0$. Let $V = \sigma^2\tau + Nv^2$ be the random volatility of the true jump-diffusion process for the τ-period return, i.e. N is a Poisson-distributed random variable with intensity parameter $\lambda\tau$. So the true volatility observed over τ-period is

$$V_n = \sigma^2\tau + nv^2 \qquad (2.39)$$

when $N = n$. From Merton's jump-diffusion option price formula, we have the true option price given by (2.28) as $C_M = E_n[C_{BS}(S_t, t; K, T, r, V_n/\tau)]$. Based on a sufficiently long time series of data, the investor can obtain a true unconditional volatility for τ-period stock return, i.e.

$$V_{BS} = E[V] = (\sigma^2 + \lambda v^2)\tau \qquad (2.40)$$

and the incorrect price of the option based on the Black–Scholes model is given by (2.22) as $C_{BS} = C_{BS}(S_t, t; K, T, r, V_{BS}/\tau)$. It remains to compare the values between C_M and C_{BS}. The exact magnitude of the difference depends very much on the values of parameters. Merton (1976b) used the following four parameters to gauge the specific patterns of Black-Scholes model biases: (i) $X_t = S_t/Ke^{-r(T-t)}$, i.e. the measure of moneyness; (ii) $V = (\sigma^2 + \lambda v^2)(T - t)$, the expected variance, or total volatility, of the logarithmic return on the stock over the life of the option; (iii) $\gamma = \lambda v^2/(\sigma^2 + \lambda v^2)$, the fraction of the total expected variance in the stock's return caused by the jump component which measures the significance of the jump factor in the process and therefore reflects the degree of misspecification of the Black–Scholes model; (iv) $\omega = \lambda(T - t)/V$, the ratio of the expected number of jumps over the life of the option to the expected variance of the stock's return which is also a measure of the degree of misspecification. For given values of the above four parameters, Merton (1976b) showed that: (a) the Black–Scholes model tends to undervalue deep ITM and OTM options, while overvalues the near-the-money options; (b) in terms of percentage difference, there are two local extreme points: one is the largest percentage overvaluation of option price ATM, and the other is the largest percentage undervaluation for ITM options, there is no local maximum for the percentage undervaluation for OTM options, the error becomes larger and larger as the option becomes more OTM; and (c) the magnitude of the percentage error increases as either γ increases or ω decreases. In particular, suppose the value of total conditional volatility $\sigma^2 + \lambda v^2$ is fixed, an increase of λv^2 will have a larger impact on the option prices. Suppose λv^2 is fixed, when λ is relatively small, but v^2 is relatively large, then the difference between the Merton price and the Black–Scholes price will be relatively larger, especially for short-maturity and OTM options. Otherwise, if the jump frequency is very high while the variance of the jump becomes very small, applying the Central Limit Theorem (see, for example, Cox and Ross (1976) for this case), it can be shown that the compounding Poisson jump process approaches a continuous process with a corresponding normal distribution in the limit. Thus, the Merton jump-diffusion process and the Black–Scholes continuous sample process would not be distinguishable and hence the prices of options will not be largely different.

Since the introduction of the jump component and stochastic volatility into the underlying asset return process are both to feature the asymmetry and kurtosis of asset return distributions, it is not surprising to see that they have similar implications on option prices. Empirical results in Jiang (1997) show that with the introduction of stochastic volatility into the exchange rate jump-diffusion process, the jump frequency tends to decrease and the jump amplitude tends to increase. Thus it would be interesting to investigate the interplay between jump and stochastic volatility in pricing options. Intuitively, since the phenomenon of 'smile' and 'skewness' is more pronounced for the implied volatility of short-maturity options, inclusion of the jump component may be necessary in order to explain the short-term kurtosis and asymmetry in the underlying asset return distributions.

2.4   ESTIMATION OF STOCHASTIC VOLATILITY MODELS

Due to computationally intractable likelihood functions and hence the lack of readily available efficient estimation procedures, the general SV processes were viewed as an unattractive class of models in comparison to other models, such as ARCH/GARCH models. Standard Kalman filter techniques cannot be applied due to the fact that either the latent process is non-Gaussian or the resulting state-space form does not have a conjugate filter. Over the past few years, however, remarkable progress has been made in the field of statistics and econometrics regarding the estimation of non-linear latent variable models in general and SV models in particular. Various estimation methods have been proposed. For instance, the simple method-of-moment (MM) matching by Taylor (1986); the generalized method-of-moments (GMM) by Wiggins (1987), Scott (1987), Chesney and Scott (1987), Melino and Turnbull (1990), Andersen (1994), Andersen and Sørensen (1996), and Ho, Perraudin and Sørensen (1996); the Monte Carlo Maximum Likelihood by Sandmann and Koopman (1997); the Kalman filter techniques by Harvey, Ruiz and Shephard (1994), Harvey and Shephard (1996), Fridman and Harris (1996) and Sandmann and Koopman (1997); the Bayesian Markov chain Monte Carlo (MCMC) by Jacquier, Polson and Rossi (1994), Schotman and Mahieu (1994), and Kim, Shephard and Chib (1996); the simulation based MLE by Danielsson and Richard (1993), Danielsson (1993), Danielsson (1996), and Richard and Zhang (1995a,b); the simulation-based method-of-moments (SMM) by Duffie and Singleton (1993); the simulation-based indirect inference approach proposed by Gouriéroux, Monfort and Renault (1993); and the simulation-based efficient method-of-moments (EMM) by Gallant and Tauchen (1996) and Gallant, Hsieh and Tauchen (1994) with applications to SV models by Andersen and Lund (1996, 1997), Gallant and Long (1997) and Jiang and van der Sluis (1998). The Monte Carlo evidence in Jacquire, Polson and Rossi (1993) suggests that GMM and QML have poor finite sample performance in terms of bias and root-mean-square-error (RMSE) of the estimated parameters. Even though the results in Andersen and Sørensen (1996) suggest that the Jacquier, Polson and Rossi simulation results exaggerate the weakness of GMM due to the inclusion of an excessive number of sample moments and the choice of estimator of the GMM weighting matrix, the Bayesian MCMC still dominates the improved GMM procedure and the standard Kalman filter techniques in terms of RMSE. In this section, we focus on the relatively new estimation methods, namely the indirect inference method proposed by Gouriéroux, Monfort and Renault (1993) as a generic approach and the efficient method-of-moments (EMM) proposed by Gallant and Tauchen (1996) as a particularly efficient approach in estimating SV models.

2.4.1 Indirect inference: a general estimation approach

The SV models we consider in this chapter in both continuous time and discrete time can be thought as a special case of the dynamic model in Gouriéroux, Monfort and Renault (1993) or the model in case 2 of Gallant and Tauchen

(1996) in which there are no exogenous variables, i.e.

$$y_t = g(y_{t-1}, u_t; \theta)$$

$$u_t = \phi(u_{t-1}, \varepsilon_t, \theta), \quad \theta \in \Theta \tag{2.41}$$

where y_t is the observable stationary asset return process, ε_t is a white noise (WN) with known distribution G_0, and both u_t and ε_t are not observable. With starting values of u_t and y_t, denoted by $z_0 = (y_0, u_0)$, and the parameter value θ, the above process can be simulated by drawing random observations of $\tilde{\varepsilon}_t, t = 1, 2, \ldots, T$

$$\tilde{y}_0(\theta, z_0) = y_0$$

$$\tilde{y}_t(\theta, z_0) = g(\tilde{y}_{t-1}(\theta, z_0), \tilde{u}_t(\theta, u_0); \theta)$$

$$\tilde{u}_t(\theta, u_0) = \phi(\tilde{u}_{t-1}(\theta, u_0), \tilde{\varepsilon}_t, \theta) \tag{2.42}$$

given $\theta \in \Theta, z_0 = (y_0, u_0)$.

The sequence of conditional densities for the structural model can be denoted by

$$\{p_0(y_0|\theta), \{p_t(y_t|x_t, \theta)\}_{t=1}^{\infty}\} \tag{2.43}$$

where x_t is a vector of lagged y_t. The difficulty of the parameter estimation arises when the conditional density $p_t(\cdot|\cdot)$ is computationally intractable as in the case of SV models. The basic idea of the indirect inference, described in Gouriéroux, Monfort and Renault (1993), Gouriéroux and Monfort (1992), Gallant and Tauchen (1996), and Smith (1993), is to obtain a consistent estimator of θ in the structural model based on an 'incorrect' criterion. We explain the estimation procedure in the following two steps.

The first step involves the choice of an auxiliary or instrumental model with parameter $\beta \in B$ and an estimation criterion $Q_T(Y_T, \beta)$, such that based on the observations of $Y_T = (y_1, y_2, \ldots, y_T)$, the parameter β can be estimated through

$$\hat{\beta}_T = \text{Argmax}_{\beta \in B} Q_T(Y_T, \beta) \tag{2.44}$$

It is assumed that Q_T has an asymptotic non-stochastic limit, i.e. $\lim_{T \to \infty} Q_T(Y_T, \beta) = Q_\infty(G_0, \theta_0, \beta)$, where θ_0 is the true value of θ which generates the sample path Y_T. Following the results in Gallant and White (1988), if Q_∞ is continuous in β and has a unique maximum $\beta_0 = \text{Argmax}_{\beta \in B} Q_\infty(G_0, \theta_0, \beta)$, then $\hat{\beta}_T \to \beta_0$ in probability. A key concept of the indirect inference is the so-called *binding function*, defined as

$$b(G, \theta) = \text{Argmax}_{\beta \in B} Q_\infty(G, \theta, \beta) \tag{2.45}$$

which relates the parameter in the true structural model to that of the auxiliary model, i.e. $b(G_0, \cdot) : \theta \to b(G_0, \theta)$. Under the assumption that the binding function $b(G, \theta)$ is one-to-one and $\partial b / \partial \theta'(G_0, \theta_0)$ is of full-column rank, which implies that $\dim(\mathcal{B}) \geq \dim(\Theta)$, it is possible to identify θ from β. More specifically, we have

$$\hat{\theta}_T \longrightarrow \theta_0$$

in probability, where $\beta_0 = b(F_0, G_0, \theta_0)$ and $\hat{\beta}_T = b(F_0, G_0, \hat{\theta}_T)$.

The second step of the indirect inference is based on simulation to obtain a consistent estimator of the parameter θ. First, H sample paths of y_t, each has T observations, are simulated from the true structural model based on θ, z_0, i.e.

$$\tilde{Y}_T^h = \{\tilde{y}_t^h(\theta, z_0^h), \quad t = 0, 1, \ldots, T\}; \quad h = 1, 2, \ldots, H$$

or a long sample path with HT observations is simulated

$$\tilde{Y}_{HT} = \{\tilde{y}_t(\theta, z_0), \quad t = 0, 1, \ldots, T, T+1, \ldots, HT\}$$

Based on the simulated sampling paths, the parameter β of the auxiliary model can be estimated as

$$\hat{\beta}_T^h(\theta, z_0^h) = \text{Argmax}_{\beta \in \mathcal{B}} \, Q_T(\tilde{Y}_T^h, \beta)$$

from each of the H blocks of sampling paths, or

$$\hat{\beta}_{HT}(\theta, z_0) = \text{Argmax}_{\beta \in \mathcal{B}} \, Q_T(\tilde{Y}_{HT}, \beta)$$

from the single long sampling path.

Various indirect estimators are defined. The first estimator minimizes the difference between the estimate $\hat{\beta}_T$ from the observed sample and the average estimates of $\hat{\beta}_T^h(\theta, z_0^h)$ from H different sample paths, i.e

$$\hat{\theta}_I = \text{Argmin}_{\theta \in \Theta} \left[\hat{\beta}_T - \frac{1}{H} \sum_{h=1}^{H} \hat{\beta}_T^h(\theta, z_0^h)\right]' \hat{\Omega}_T \left[\hat{\beta}_T - \frac{1}{H} \sum_{h=1}^{H} \hat{\beta}_T^h(\theta, z_0^h)\right] \quad (2.46)$$

where $\hat{\Omega}_T$ is a positive definite weighting matrix. This estimator is proposed in Gouriéroux, Monfort and Renault (1993) and also called the minimum χ^2 estimator. The second estimator is defined as minimizing the difference between the estimate $\hat{\beta}_T$ from the observed sample and the estimate of $\hat{\beta}_{HT}(\theta, z_0)$ from the single long sample path with HT observations, i.e.

$$\hat{\theta}_{II} = \text{Argmin}_{\theta \in \Theta} [\hat{\beta}_T - \hat{\beta}_{HT}(\theta, z_0)]' \hat{\Omega}_T [\hat{\beta}_T - \hat{\beta}_{HT}(\theta, z_0)] \quad (2.47)$$

which is also proposed in Gouriéroux, Monfort and Renault (1993), where $\hat{\Omega}_T$ is a positive definite weighting matrix. Compared to the first estimator, this estimator only involves one sample path simulation and one optimization for the parameter estimation for each updated parameter value. The third estimator, proposed by Gallant and Tauchen (1996), is to minimize the gradient of the estimation criterion function, i.e.

$$\hat{\theta}_{III} = \text{Argmin}_{\theta \in \Theta} \frac{\partial Q_T}{\partial \beta'}(\tilde{y}_{HT}, \hat{\beta}_T) \Sigma \frac{\partial Q_T}{\partial \beta'}(\tilde{y}_{HT}, \hat{\beta}_T) \qquad (2.48)$$

with the efficient method-of-moments (EMM) as a special case, which we will discuss in the next section.

It can be shown that when H is fixed and T goes to infinity (see Gouriéroux, Monfort and Renault, 1993; Gouriéroux and Monfort, 1996:

$$\sqrt{T}(\hat{\theta}_{II}(\Omega^*) - \theta) \xrightarrow{d} N(0, V(H, \Omega^*)) \qquad (2.49)$$

where $V(H, \Omega^*) = (1 + 1/H)[(\partial b'/\partial \theta)(\theta_0)\Omega^*(\partial b/\partial \theta)(\theta_0)]^{-1}$, and Ω^* is the optimal weighting matrix. It is also shown that the above three estimators are asymptotically equivalent, i.e.

(i) $\hat{\theta}_I(\Omega) \xleftrightarrow{\text{asy.}} \hat{\theta}_I(I), \hat{\theta}_{II}(\Omega) \xleftrightarrow{\text{asy.}} \hat{\theta}_{II}(I)$, independent of Ω;

(ii) $\hat{\theta}_{III}(\Sigma) \xleftrightarrow{\text{asy.}} \hat{\theta}_{III}(I)$, independent of Σ;

(iii) $\hat{\theta}_I(\Omega) \xleftrightarrow{\text{asy.}} \hat{\theta}_{II}(\Omega) \xleftrightarrow{\text{asy.}} \hat{\theta}_{III}(\Sigma)$, for sufficiently large T.

The above relations are exact if $\dim(\theta) = \dim(\mathcal{B})$. Since the model does not contain exogenous variables, the optimal choice of Ω and Σ are (see Gouriéroux, Monfort and Renault, 1993):

$$\Omega^* = \mathcal{J}_0 \mathcal{I}_0^{-1} \mathcal{J}_0$$
$$\Sigma^* = \mathcal{I}_0^{-1} \qquad (2.50)$$

where under standard regularity conditions,

$$\mathcal{I}_0 = \lim_{T \to \infty} V_0 \left[\sqrt{T} \frac{\partial Q_T}{\partial \beta} (\{\tilde{y}_t^h; \theta_0\}_{t=1}^{HT}; \beta_0) \right]$$

$$\mathcal{J}_0 = \text{plim}_{T \to \infty} - \frac{\partial^2 Q_T}{\partial \beta \partial \beta'} (\{\tilde{y}_t^h; \theta_0\}_{t=1}^{HT}; \beta_0)$$

where V_0 indicates variance w.r.t. the true distribution of the process y_t.

2.4.2   Efficient method-of-moments (EMM): an efficient estimation approach

The efficient method-of-moments (EMM) proposed by Gallant and Tauchen (1996) is a special case of the third estimator defined in the last section, with the estimation criterion chosen as the sequence of conditional densities of the auxiliary model, i.e.

$$\{f_0(y_0|\beta), \{f_t(y_t|w_t, \beta)\}_{t=1}^{\infty}\} \qquad (2.51)$$

where w_t is a vector of lagged y_t. This conditional density is also referred as the score generator by Gallant and Tauchen (1996). We consider the case that the condition density is time invariant as in case 2 of Gallant and Tauchen (1996). Under assumptions 1 and 2 from Gallant and Long (1997), the standard properties of quasi maximum likelihood (QML) estimators leads to

$$\hat{\beta}_T = \text{Argmax}_{\beta \in B} \frac{1}{T} \sum_{t=1}^{T} \ln f_t(y_t | w_t, \beta)$$

Based on the theory of misspecified models, see, for example, White (1994), one can prove the consistency and asymptotic normality of $\hat{\beta}_T$ under the assumptions posed in Gallant and Tauchen (1996) and Gallant and Long (1997), i.e.

$$\lim_{T \to \infty} (\hat{\beta}_T - \beta_0) = 0$$

almost surely and $\sqrt{T}(\hat{\beta}_T - \beta_0) \xrightarrow{d} N(0, \mathcal{J}_0^{-1} \mathcal{I}_0 \mathcal{J}_0^{-1})$. Here under standard regularity assumptions

$$\mathcal{I}_0 = \lim_{T \to \infty} V_0 \left[\frac{1}{\sqrt{T}} \sum_{t=1}^{T} \left(\frac{\partial}{\partial \beta} \ln f_t(\tilde{y}_t | \tilde{w}_t, \hat{\beta}_T) \right) \right]$$

$$\mathcal{J}_0 = \lim_{T \to \infty} -\frac{\partial}{\partial \beta} m_N'(\theta_0, \hat{\beta}_T)$$

Gallant and Tauchen (1996) define generalized methods of moments (GMM) conditions as the expected score of the auxiliary model under the dynamic model, i.e.

$$m(\theta, \hat{\beta}_T) = \int \int \frac{\partial}{\partial \beta} \ln f(y|w, \hat{\beta}_T) p(y|x, \theta) dy \, p(x|\theta) \, dx \qquad (2.52)$$

In general, the above expectation is not readily computed but often relies on the approximation using standard Monte Carlo techniques. The Monte Carlo simulation approach consists of calculating this function as

$$m_N(\theta, \hat{\beta}_T) = \frac{1}{N} \sum_{\tau=1}^{N} \frac{\partial}{\partial \beta} \ln f(\tilde{y}_\tau(\theta) | \tilde{w}_\tau(\theta), \hat{\beta}_T)$$

The EMM estimator is defined as

$$\hat{\theta}_T(\hat{\beta}_T, \Sigma_T) = \text{Argmin}_{\theta \in \Theta} m_N'(\theta, \hat{\beta}_T)(\Sigma_T)^{-1} m_N(\theta, \hat{\beta}_T) \qquad (2.53)$$

where Σ_T is a weighting matrix. Obviously, the optimal weighting matrix here is

$$\mathcal{I}_0 = \lim_{T \to \infty} V_0 \left[\frac{1}{\sqrt{T}} \sum_{t=1}^{T} \left\{ \frac{\partial}{\partial \beta} \ln f_t(y_t | w_t, \beta_0) \right\} \right]$$

where β_0 is a (pseudo) true value. Consistency and asymptotic normality of the estimator of the structural parameters $\hat{\theta}_T$ follow:

$$\sqrt{T}(\hat{\theta}_T(\mathcal{I}_0) - \theta_0) \xrightarrow{d} N(0, [\mathcal{M}'_0(\mathcal{I}_0)^{-1}\mathcal{M}_0]^{-1}) \tag{2.54}$$

where $\mathcal{M}_0 = \partial/\partial\theta' m(\theta_0, \beta_0)$.

In order to achieve maximum likelihood (ML) efficiency, it is required that the auxiliary model embeds the structural model in the following sense: the model $p_0(y_0|\theta)$, $\{p_t|x_t, \theta\}_{t=1}^{\infty}\}_{\theta\in\Theta}$ is said to be smoothly embedded within the score generator $f_0(y_0|\beta)$, $\{f_t|w_t, \beta\}_{t=1}^{\infty}\}_{\beta\in B}$ if for some open neighbourhood R of θ_0, there is a twice continuously differentiable mapping $q : \Theta \to B$, such that

$$p_t(y_t|x_t, \theta) = f_t(y_t|w_t, q(\theta)), t = 1, 2, \dots$$

for every $\theta \in R$ and $p_0(y_0|\theta) = f_0(y_0|q(\theta))$ for every $\theta \in R$. Gallant and Tauchen (1996) prove that embeddedness implies that the EMM estimator $\hat{\theta}_T$ is as efficient as the maximum likelihood (ML) estimator in the sense of first-order asymptotic efficiency.

To ensure embeddedness, Gallant and Tauchen (1996) and Gallant and Long (1997) suggest that a good choice of the score generator is the semi-non-parametric (SNP) density due to Gallant and Nycka (1987). This score generator is built on earlier work by Phillips (1983); for recent results on SNP density see also Fenton and Gallant (1996a,b). Let $y_t(\theta_0)$ be the process under investigation, the SNP score generator is constructed as follows. First, let $\mu_t(\beta_0) = E_{t-1}[y_t(\theta_0)]$ be the conditional mean of the auxiliary model, $\sigma_t^2(\beta_0) = \mathrm{Cov}_{t-1}[y_t(\theta_0) - \mu_t(\beta_0)]$ be the conditional variance matrix and $z_t(\beta_0) = R_t^{-1}(\theta)[y_t(\theta_0) - \mu_t(\beta_0)]$ be the standardized process. Here R_t will typically be a lower or upper triangular matrix. Then, the SNP density takes the following form

$$f(y_t; \theta) = \frac{1}{|\det(R_t)|} \frac{[P_K(z_t, x_t)]^2\phi(z_t)}{\int [P_K(u, x_t)]^2\phi(u)\, du} \tag{2.55}$$

where ϕ denotes the standard multinormal density, $x = (y_{t-1}, \dots, y_{t-L})$ and the polynomials

$$P_K(z, x_t) = \sum_{i=0}^{K_z} a_i(x_t)z^i = \sum_{i=0}^{K_z}\left[\sum_{j=0}^{K_x} a_{ij}x_t^j\right]z^i$$

We need to be careful about the notation of z^i when z is a vector. Define i as a multi-index, such that for the k-dimension vector $z = (z_1, \dots, z_k)'$ we have $z^i = z_1^{i_1} \cdot z_2^{i_2} \dots z_k^{i_k}$ under the condition that $\sum_{j=1}^{k} i_j = i$ and $i_j \geq 0$ for $j \in \{1, \dots, k\}$. A specific form for the polynomials is the orthogonal Hermite polynomials (see Gallant, Hsieh and Tauchen, 1997; Andersen and Lund, 1997), with $\sigma_t^2(\beta)$ and $\mu_t(\beta)$ chosen as leading terms in the Hermite expansion to relieve the expansion of some of its task, dramatically improving its small sample properties. It is noted that in the SV model estimation using EMM, the leading term in the SNP expansion is often chosen as the GARCH/EGARCH model, see, for example, Andersen and Lund (1997), and Jiang and van der Sluis (1998). The EGARCH model is often a convenient choice since (i) it is a good approximation to the stochastic volatility model, see Nelson and Foster (1994), and (ii) direct maximum likelihood techniques are admitted by this class of models.

Advantages of the EMM approach include: (i) if the gradient of the score functions also has a closed form, it has computational advantage because it necessitates only one optimization in θ; (ii) the practical advantage of this technique is its flexibility, i.e. once the moments are chosen one may estimate a whole class of SV models without changing much in the program; (iii) this method can be ML efficient. In a stochastic volatility context, recent Monte Carlo studies in Andersen, Chung and Sørensen (1997) and van der Sluis (1997) confirm this for sample sizes larger than 2000, which is rather reasonable for financial time series. For lower sample sizes there is a small loss in small sample efficiency compared to the likelihood-based techniques such as Kim, Shephard and Chib (1997), Sandmann and Koopman (1997) and Fridman and Harris (1996). This is mainly caused by the imprecise estimate of the weighting matrix for sample size smaller than 2000. The same phenomenon occurs in ordinary GMM estimation.

It is also noted that in the implementation of EMM, it is necessary that the dimension of the parameter space in the auxiliary model, i.e. dim($\mathcal{B}$), increases with the sample size T, which is conceptually different from GMM. When any of the following model specification criteria such as the Akaike Information Criterion (AIC, Akaike, 1973), the Schwarz Criterion (BIC, Schwarz, 1978) or the Hannan–Quinn Criterion (HQC, Hannan and Quinn, 1979; Quinn, 1980) is used, it automatically requires that dim($\mathcal{B}$) increases with T. The theory of model selection in the context of SNP models is not very well developed yet. Results in Eastwood (1991) may lead us to believe that AIC is optimal in this case. However, as for multivariate ARMA models, the AIC may overfit the model to noise in the data so we may be better off by following the BIC or HQC. The same findings were reported in Andersen and Lund (1997). In their paper Gallant and Tauchen (1996) rely on the BIC in their applications.

2.5 FORECASTING STOCHASTIC VOLATILITY

As volatility plays so important a role in financial theory and the financial market, accurate measure and good forecasts of future volatility are critical for the implementation of asset and derivative pricing theories as well as trading and hedging strategies. Empirical findings, dating back to Mandelbrot (1963) and Fama (1965), suggest that financial asset returns display pronounced volatility clustering. Various recent studies based on standard time series models, such as ARCH/GARCH and SV models, also reported results supporting a very high degree of intertemporal volatility persistence in financial time series, see, for example, Bollerslev, Chou and Kroner (1992), Bollerslev, Engle and Nelson (1994), Ghysels, Harvey and Renault (1996) and Shephard (1996) for surveys. Such high degree of volatility persistence, coupled with significant parameter estimates of the model, suggest that the underlying volatility of asset returns is highly predictable.

2.5.1 Underlying volatility and implied volatility

In this chapter, we distinguish two types of volatility: volatility estimated from asset returns, we call it the underlying or historical volatility, and volatility implied from observed option prices through certain option pricing formula, we call it the implicit or implied volatility. Since volatility is not directly observable, the exact measures of both underlying volatility and implied volatility are model dependent. For instance, when the underlying volatility is modelled using standard time series models, such as ARCH/GARCH or SV processes, the underlying volatility can be computed or reprojected based on estimated processes, see Gallant and Tauchen (1997) for the reprojection of stochastic volatility in an SV model framework. In this chapter, we refer to the implied volatility as the volatility implied from the Black–Scholes model unless defined otherwise.

However, to judge the forecasting performance of any volatility models, a common approach is to compare the predictions with the subsequent volatility realizations. Thus a model independent measure of the *ex-post* volatility is very important. Let the return innovation be written as (2.2), since

$$E_t(y_{t+1}^2) = E_t(\sigma_{t+1}^2 \varepsilon_{t+1}^2) = \sigma_{t+1}^2 \tag{2.56}$$

when $E_t[\varepsilon_{t+1}^2] = 1$, the squared return is an unbiased estimator of the future latent volatility factor. If the model for σ_t^2 is correctly specified then the squared return innovation over the relevant horizon can be used as a proxy for the *ex-post* volatility.

The implied or implicit volatility is defined in Bates (1996a) as 'the value for the annualized standard deviation of log-differenced asset prices that equates the theoretical option pricing formula premised on geometric Brownian motion with the observed option price.[10] Since there is a one-to-one relationship between the volatility and the option price, there is a unique implied volatility for each observed option price,[11] namely

$$\hat{C}_{\tau i} = C_{BS}(S_t, K_i, \tau, r, \sigma_{\tau i}^{imp}) \tag{2.57}$$

where $\hat{C}_{\tau i}$ is the observed option price at time t with maturity τ and strike price K_i. Since $\hat{C}_{\tau i}$ is a cross-section of option prices at time t for $\tau \in R_+$ and $i = 1, 2, \ldots, N$, there will be also a cross-section of implied volatility at time t, $\hat{\sigma}_{\tau i}^{imp}$, which is not necessarily constant. The Black–Scholes model imposes a flat term structure of volatility, i.e. the volatility is constant across both maturity and moneyness of options. If option prices in the market were confirmable with the Black–Scholes formula, all the Black–Scholes implied volatility corresponding to various options written on the same asset would coincide with the volatility parameter σ of the underlying asset. In reality this is not the case, and the Black–Scholes implied volatility heavily depends on the calendar time, the time to maturity, and the moneyness of the options.[12] Rubinstein (1985) used this approach to examine the cross-sectional pricing errors of the Black–Scholes model based on the implied volatility from observed option prices using (2.57). Empirical studies have found various patterns of the implied volatility across different strike prices and maturities. The price distortions, well known to practitioners, are usually documented in the empirical literature under the terminology of the *smile* effect, referring to the U-shaped pattern of implied volatilities across different strike prices. More specifically, the following stylized facts are extensively documented in the literature (see, for instance, Rubinstein, 1985; Clewlow and Xu, 1993; Taylor and Xu, 1993) for the implied Black–Scholes volatility: (i) The U-shaped pattern of implied volatility as a function of moneyness has its minimum centred at near-the-money options; (ii) the volatility smile is often but not always symmetric as a function of moneyness; and (iii) the amplitude of the smile increases quickly when time to maturity decreases. Indeed, for short maturities the smile effect is very pronounced while it almost completely disappears for longer maturities.

The problem with the computation of implied volatility is that even though the volatility may be varying over time, it has only a single value at each point of time. To back out this single volatility from many simultaneously observed option prices with various strikes and maturities, different weighting schemes are used. Bates (1996a) gave a comprehensive survey of these weighting schemes. In addition, Engle and Mustafa (1992) and Bates (1996b) propose a non-linear generalized least-squares methodology that allows the appropriate weights to be determined endogenously by the data.

2.5.2 Forecasting volatility based on standard volatility models

Standard volatility models such as ARCH/GARCH and SV processes have been applied with great success to the modelling of financial times series. The models have in general reported significant parameter estimates for in-sample fitting with desirable time series properties, e.g. covariance stationarity. It naturally leads people to believe that such models can provide good forecasts of future volatility. In fact, the motivation of an ARCH/GARCH model setup comes directly from forecasting. For instance in the following GARCH(1,1) model

$$\sigma_t^2 = \gamma + \alpha y_{t-1}^2 + \beta \sigma_{t-1}^2, \quad t = 1, 2, \ldots, T \tag{2.58}$$

which is an AR(1) model with independent disturbances. The optimal prediction of the volatility in the next period is a fraction of the current observed volatility, and in the ARCH(1) case (i.e. $\beta = 0$), it is a fraction of the current squared observation. The fundamental reason here is that the optimal forecast is constructed conditional on the current information. The general GARCH formulation introduces terms analogous to moving average terms in an ARMA model, thereby making forecasts a function as a distributed lag of past squared observations.

However, despite highly significant in-sample parameter estimates, many studies have reported that standard volatility models perform poorly in forecasting out-of-sample volatility. Similar to the common regression-procedure used in evaluating forecasts for the conditional mean, the volatility forecast evaluation in the literature typically relies on the following *ex-post* squared return-volatility regression

$$y_{t+1}^2 = a + b\hat{\sigma}_{t+1}^2 + u_{t+1} \tag{2.59}$$

where $t = 0, 1, \ldots, y_{t+1}^2$ is used as a proxy for the *ex-post* volatility as it is an unbiased estimator of σ_{t+1}^2 as shown in (2.56). The coefficient of multiple determination, or R^2, from the above regression provides a direct assessment of the variability in the *ex-post* squared returns that is explained by the particular estimates of σ_{t+1}^2. The R^2 is often interpreted as a simple gauge of the degree of predictability in the volatility process, and hence of the potential economic significance of the volatility forecasts.[13] Many empirical studies based on the above regression evaluation of the volatility forecast have universally reported disappointingly low R^2 for various speculative returns and sample periods. For instance, Day and Lewis (1992) reported $R^2 = 0.039$ for the predictive power of a GARCH(1,1) model of weekly returns on the S&P 100 stock index from 1983 to 1989; Pagan and Schwert (1990) reported $R^2 = 0.067$ for the predictive power of a GARCH(1,2) model of monthly aggregate US stock market returns from 1835 to 1925; Jorion (1996) reported $R^2 = 0.024$ for the predictive power of a GARCH(1,1) model of the daily DM–$ returns from 1985 to 1992; Cumby, Figlewski and Hasbrouck (1993) reported R^2's ranging from 0.003 to 0.106 for the predictive power of an EGARCH model of the weekly stock and bond market volatility in the US and Japan from 1977 to 1990; West and Cho (1995) reported R^2's ranging from 0.001 to 0.045 for the predictive power of a GARCH(1,1) model of five different weekly US dollar exchange rates from 1973 to 1989. These systematically low R^2's have led to the conclusion that standard ARCH/GARCH models provide poor volatility forecasts due to possible severe misspecification, and consequently are of limited practical use.

Andersen and Bollerslev (1997) argue that the documented poor performance of volatility forecasting is not due to the misspecification of standard volatility models but due to the measure of *ex-post* volatility. Even though the squared innovation provides an unbiased etiquette for the latent volatility factor, it may yield very noisy measurements due to the idiosyncratic error term ε_t^2. This component typically displays a large degree of observation-by-observation variation relative to σ_t^2. It is not surprising to see a low fraction of the squared return variation attributable to the volatility process. Consequently, the poor predictive power of volatility models, when using y_{t+1}^2 as a measure of *ex-post* volatility, is an inevitable consequence of the inherent noise in the return generating process. Andersen and Bollerslev (1997) found that based on an alternative *ex-post* volatility measure building on the continuous-time SV framework, the high-frequency data allow for the construction of vastly improved *ex-post* volatility measurements via cumulative squared intraday returns. The proposed volatility measures, based on high-frequency returns, provide a dramatic reduction in noise and a radical improvement in temporal stability relative to measures based on daily returns. Further, when evaluated against these improved volatility measurements, they found that daily GARCH models perform well, readily explaining about half of the variability in the volatility factor. That is, there is no contradiction between good volatility forecasts and poor predictive power for daily squared returns.

Let the instantaneous returns be generated by the continuous-time martingale

$$d \ln S_t = \sigma_t \, dW_t \qquad (2.60)$$

where W_t denotes a standard Brownian motion process. By Ito's lemma, the minimum MSE forecast for the conditional variance of the one-day returns, or $y_{t+1} = \ln(S_{t+1}/S_t)$ is expressed as

$$E_t[y_{t+1}^2] = E_t \left[\int_0^1 y_{t+\tau}^2 \, d\tau \right] = E_t \left[\int_0^1 \sigma_{t+\tau}^2 \, d\tau \right] \qquad (2.61)$$

Certainly, with time-varying volatility it is in general that the expectation of the squared return calculated in discrete time is different from the continuous-time conditional variance $\int_0^1 E_t[\sigma_{t+\tau}^2] \, d\tau$. It is evident that the relevant notion of daily volatility in this setting becomes $\int_0^1 \sigma_{t+\tau}^2 \, d\tau$ which constitutes an alternative measure of the volatility instead of squared returns. In the daily frequency, such a measure can be approximately calculated based on intradaily observations. The computation of daily return variance from high-frequency intraday returns parallels the use of daily returns in calculating monthly *ex-post* volatility, as in Schwert (1989, 1990a) and Schwert and Sequin (1990). The idea has previously been applied by, among others, Hsieh (1991) and Schwert (1990b) in measuring daily equity market volatility and by Fung and Hsieh (1991) in analysing daily sample standard deviations for bonds and currencies.

Andersen and Bollerslev (1997) based their empirical analysis on daily volatility forecasts for the Deutsche Mark–US dollar (DM–$) and Japanese yen–US dollar (yen–$) spot exchange rates. The model estimates are based on daily returns of the above two time series from 1 October 1987 to 30 September 1992. The empirical out-of-sample forecast analysis is based on the temporal aggregate of the five-minute returns for the same two exchange rates from 1 October 1992 to 30 September 1993. Based on these data, they confirm that the GARCH(1,1) volatility forecasts explain little of the *ex-post* variability of squared returns. The R^2's in the regression (2.59) using the one-step-ahead return volatility for the 260 weekday returns over 1 October 1992 to 30 September 1993 equal 0.047 and 0.026, respectively. The continuous-time model used in Andersen and Bollerslev (1997) is the diffusion limit of the GARCH(1,1) process developed in Nelson (1990). The diffusion parameter estimates are obtained from the estimated weak GARCH(1,1) model through the exact one-to-one relationship between the discrete-time weak GARCH(1,1) parameters and the continuous-time SV model parameters. Due to the measurement error of the daily squared return as the one-day-ahead latent volatility factor, they show that in the continuous-time SV model framework, the true GARCH(1,1) model only explains between 5 to 10% of the variation in daily squared returns. While when the volatility is measured by the more appropriate statistic computed from continuous sampling, the population R^2 increases to 50%. That is, the weak GARCH(1,1) model accounts for close to half of the variation in the one-day-ahead volatility factors. Replacing the squared daily returns on the left-hand side of equation (2.59) with the sum of the corresponding squared intraday returns, i.e.

$$\sum_{i=1}^{m}(p_{t+i/m} - p_{t+(i-1)/m})^2 = a + b\hat{\sigma}_{t+1}^2 + u_{t+1} \tag{2.62}$$

Andersen and Bollerslev (1997) show that the population R^2's increase monotonically with sampling frequency. For instance, using the cumulative hourly squared returns on the left-hand side of equation (2.62), for the implied continuous-time weak GARCH(1,1) model, the R^2's are equal to 0.383 and 0.419; using the cumulative five-minute returns results in R^2's of 0.483 and 0.488. These findings suggest the theoretical advantages associated with the use of high-frequency intraday returns in the construction of interdaily volatility forecast evaluation criteria. They further show that with the normal

GARCH(1,1) model, the R^2's are 0.331 and 0.237 with hourly sampling and 0.479 and 0.392 with the five-minute sampling interval, respectively.

2.5.3 Forecasting underlying volatility using implied volatility

Since option prices reflect market traders' forecast of underlying asset price movements, the volatility implied from option prices is widely believed to be informationally superior to historical underlying volatility. If option markets are efficient, implied volatility should be an efficient forecast of future volatility over the remaining life of the relevant options, i.e. implied volatility should subsume the information contained in other variables in explaining future volatility. If it were not, one could design a trading strategy that would theoretically generate profits by identifying misspecified options. It is a common practice for option traders to make trading and hedging decisions by picking a point forecast of volatility as the one implied from current option prices (with possible subjective adjustment) and then inserting this point estimate into the Black–Scholes or binomial model. For academics, the implied volatility from currently observed option prices is invariably used as a measure of the market's volatility expectation. The questions of whether implied volatility predicts future volatility, and whether it does so efficiently, are both empirically testable propositions and have been the subject of many papers. Due to lack of time series data, earlier papers on this topic, e.g. Latane and Rendleman (1976), Chiras and Manaster (1978), and Beckers (1981), focused on static cross-sectional tests rather than time series predictions. The results of these studies essentially document that stocks with higher implied volatility also tend to have higher *ex-post* realized volatility, and the Black–Scholes implied volatilities predict future volatilities better than do close-to-close historic volatilities. More recent studies have focused on the information content and predictive power of implied volatility in dynamic setting using the available longer time series data.[14] Such studies examine whether the implied volatility of an option predicts the *ex-post* realized volatility in the remaining life of the option. The time series literature has produced mixed results, as documented in Scott and Tucker (1989), Day and Lewis (1992), Lamoureux and Lastrapes (1993), Canina and Figlewski (1993), Jorion (1995), and Christensen and Prabhala (1997).

The evidence reported in the study by Canina and Figlewski (1993) is probably the strongest in rejecting the implied volatility as an efficient predictor of realized volatility. Based on S&P 100 index options (OEX), Canina and Figlewski (1993) found implied volatility to be a poor forecast of subsequent realized volatility. The data set used in their study is the closing prices of all call options on the OEX index from 15 March 1983 to 28 March 1987. Options with fewer than seven or more than 127 days to expiration and those with more than 20 points ITM or OTM are excluded. Since the OEX index stock portfolio contains mostly dividend-paying stocks, the options are essentially American type. Thus the implied volatilities are backed out using a binomial model that adjusts for dividends and captures the value of early exercises. To avoid using weighting schemes for simultaneously observed option prices in calculating the implied volatility, they divide the option price sample into 32 subsamples according to moneyness and maturity. To test whether implied volatility represents the market's forecast of future underlying volatility, the following regression is estimated

$$\sigma_t(\tau) = \alpha + \beta \sigma_t^{imp}(i) + u_{ti}, \quad i = 1, 2, \ldots, 32 \tag{2.63}$$

where $\sigma_t^{imp}(i)$ is the implied volatility computed at time t from the option prices in subgroup i, u_{ti} is the regression disturbance, and $\sigma_t(\tau)$ is the realized annual volatility of returns over the period between t and $t + \tau$ (the option's expiration date). In their test, the realized volatility $\sigma_t(\tau)$ is calculated over the remaining life of the option as the annualized sample standard derivation of log returns including cash dividends. The estimation results show that in only six out of 32 subsamples, the slope coefficient estimate is significantly different from zero at 5% critical level. The R^2's range from 0.000 to 0.070.

However, replacing σ_t^{imp} in the regression (2.63) by a historical measure of volatility σ_t^h using the annualized standard derivation of the log returns of the S&P 100 stock index portfolio over the 60-day period preceding the date of the implied volatility, for all dates t corresponding to implied volatility observations contained in subsample i. The estimation results indicate that all the estimated slope coefficients are positive and mostly significantly different from zero at the 5% critical level. The R^2's are greater than 0.10 in 24 out of the 32 subsamples, with the highest $R^2 = 0.286$. A joint test based on the following 'encompassing regression' is also undertaken

$$\sigma_t(\tau) = \alpha + \beta_1 \sigma_t^{imp}(i) + \beta_2 \sigma_t^h(i) + u_{ti} \tag{2.64}$$

Again, the estimate of β_2 is significantly different from zero in most of the regressions, while that of β_1 is nowhere significantly greater than zero and is negative for 28 out of the 32 subsamples. Overall, the results suggest that 'implied volatility has virtually no correlation with future return volatility … and does not incorporate information contained in currently observed volatility', far from demonstrating that implied volatility in OEX options is an unbiased and efficient forecast of subsequent realized volatility.

Lamoureux and Lastrapes (1993) focus on 10 individual stocks with publicly traded options on the Chicago Board of Option Exchange (CBOE). The data set covers the period from 19 April 1982 to 31 March 1984, consisting of simultaneously observed option price quotes and stock price quotes. The data set alleviates the problem of non-synchronous quotes. To further reduce the biases of the implied expected volatility due to the non-linearity of the Black–Scholes option pricing formula and the possible non-zero correlation between volatility and stock returns, they used only the near-the-money options to back out the expected volatility through the Hull–White option pricing formula. The forecast horizons are carefully matched between the implied volatility and underlying volatility. Their empirical results suggest that historical time series contain predictive information over and above that of implied volatilities. Based on both in-sample and out-of-sample tests, the hypothesis that the forecasting errors of the future returns volatility using volatility implied in option prices is orthogonal to all available information is rejected. Thus, implied volatility is an inefficient predictor of subsequent realized underlying volatility and past volatility contains predictive information beyond that contained in implied volatility.

The interpretation offered by Canina and Figlewski (1993) is that along with investor's volatility forecasts, an option market price also impounds the net effect of many other factors that influence option supply and demand but are not in the option pricing model, such as liquidity considerations, interaction between the OEX option and other index future contract, investor taste for particular payoff patterns. Lamoureux and Lastrapes (1993) view their results as a rejection of the joint hypotheses of market efficiency and of the Hull–White option pricing formula. Given informational efficiency, they argue that the results can be explained by the existence of a risk premium applied to the non-traded volatility process. In other words, the assumption in the Hull–White option pricing formula that volatility risk is unpriced is violated.

In contrast, studies by Scott and Tucker (1989), Day and Lewis (1992), Jorion (1993), and Christensen and Prabhala (1997) reported results favouring the hypothesis that implied volatility has predictive power for the future volatility. Scott and Tucker (1989) present one OLS regression with five currencies, three maturities and 13 different dates and reported some predictive ability in implied volatility measured from PHLX currency options. However, their methodology does not allow formal tests of the hypothesis due to the correlations across observations. Day and Lewis (1992) analyse options on the S&P 100 index using the option data from 1983 to 1989, and find that the implied volatility has significant information content for weekly volatility. However, the information content of implied volatility is not necessarily higher than that of standard time series models, such as GARCH/EGARCH. A difference between their approach and that of Canina and Figlewski (1993) is that they ignore the term structure of volatility so that the return horizon used in their test is not matched with the life of the option.

Jorion (1995) argues that previous work on informational content of implied volatility has paid little attention to the effect of measurement error in reported prices. Instead of using stock options or stock index options, Jorion focuses on options on foreign currency futures for Deutche Mark (DM), Japanese yen (JY) and Swiss franc (SF). They are actively traded contracts, with both the underlying asset and the options traded side by side on the CME and close at the same time. In addition, all CME closing quotes are carefully scrutinized by the exchange because they are used for daily settlement, and therefore less likely to suffer from clerical measurement errors. Implied volatility is derived using the Black (1976) model for European options on futures from only ATM call and put option prices during the period of January 1985 to February 1992 for the DM, July 1986 to February 1992 for the JY, and March 1985 to February 1992 for the SF. Similar to Day and Lewis (1992), Jorion tested the informational content of implied volatility and the results indicate that the implied volatility contains a substantial amount of information for currency movements in the following day. The predictive power hypothesis is tested using equation (2.63). The estimated coefficients are respectively 0.547, 0.496 and 0.520 for the DM, JY and SF, with all of them significantly different from zero at 5% level. R^2's are respectively 0.156, 0.097 and 0.145. When the implied volatility is replaced by the moving average estimate or GARCH forecast of the future volatility, the explanatory power is invariably reduced, with R^2's ranging from 0.022 to 0.058. The results based on the 'encompassing regression' in (2.64) are consistent with the above findings, i.e. the implied volatility dominates the moving averaging and GARCH models in forecasting future volatilities, although the implied volatility appears to be a biased volatility forecast. Based on simulations, Jorion suggests that the forecast bias is due to the fact that implied volatility from option prices is too variable relative to future volatility. A linear transformation of the implied volatility provides a superior forecast of the exchange rate volatility.

The evidence in a more recent paper by Christensen and Prabhala (1997) based on S&P 100 stock index options over the period from November 1983 to May 1995 suggests even stronger results. They found that implied volatility reacts to and efficiently aggregates information about future volatility and subsumes the information content of past realized volatility in some of the model specifications. In their study, the implied volatility is backed out from option prices using the Black–Scholes formula and the *ex-post* return volatility or realized volatility over each option's life is computed as the sample standard derivation of the daily index returns over the remaining life of the option. Running the regression (2.63), they obtain a coefficient estimate of $\hat{\beta} = 0.76$ with standard deviation 0.08 and $R^2 = 0.39$. This suggests that implied volatility does contain some information about future volatility. However, it appears to be a biased forecast of future volatility since the slope coefficient is reliably different from unit and the intercept is different from zero. Replacing the implied volatility by the one-period lagged volatility, the regression yields a coefficient estimate $\hat{\beta} = 0.57$ with standard deviation 0.07 and $R^2 = 0.32$. This suggests that past realized volatility also explains future volatility. Running the 'encompassing regression' (2.64) with both implied volatility and past volatility, the regression coefficient of past volatility drops from 0.57 to 0.23 with standard deviation 0.10 and the coefficient of implied volatility decreases from 0.76 to 0.56 with standard deviation 0.12, and R^2 increases to 0.41. This suggests that while the implied volatility dominates the past volatility in forecasting future volatility, it is an inefficient forecast of the future volatility.

An alternative specification in Christensen and Prabhala (1997) assumes that the implied volatility should be modelled as an endogenous function of past volatility, both implied volatility and historical volatility, i.e.

$$\sigma_t^{imp} = \alpha_0 + \beta_1 \sigma_{t-1}^{imp} + \beta_2 \sigma_{t-1}^h + u_t \qquad (2.65)$$

Such a specification is used for two purposes: first, it is used to correct for the possible errors-in-variable (EIV) in OEX implied volatility in an instrumental variables framework; second, it is used in conjunction with the traditional specification (2.63) and (2.64) to investigate causal relations between the two volatility series. Using the lagged implied volatility as instrumental variables (IV) in regression (2.63) and lagged implied volatility and historical volatility as IV in (2.64), the IV estimates of the implied volatility coefficients are respectively 0.97 and 1.04 with standard deviations 0.12 and 0.28, and $R^2 = 0.36$ and 0.34. In both cases, the coefficients of implied volatility are not significantly different from unit, which suggests that implied volatility is an unbiased estimator of the future volatility. In addition, the IV estimate of the historical volatility coefficient in the encompassing regression is -0.06 with standard deviation 0.18, which is not significantly different from zero. This indicates that the implied volatility is an efficient forecast of future volatility. In addition, the test based on VAR regression suggests that implied (realized) volatility Granger-causes realized (implied) volatility.

The above results are sharply different from those in previous studies. Christensen and Prabhala (1997) believe that the reasons for their results to be essentially different from previous studies such as in Canina and Figlewski (1993) are: first, their study is based on a longer time series data set they found that a regime switch around the October 1987 stock market crash explains why implied volatility was more biased in previous work, which focused on pre-crash data; second, their time series is sampled over a lower (monthly) frequency. This enables them to construct volatility series in a non-overlapping manner with one implied and one realized volatility covering each time period in the sample. They argue that the apparent inefficiency of implied volatility documented before is an artifact of the use of overlapping data.

2.6   CONCLUSION

This chapter surveys current literature on the applications of SV models in pricing asset options. While the SV model is relatively new, numerous studies in this area have been undertaken as evidenced in the long reference list of this survey. It is clear from the survey that the statistical theory of SV models in discrete time is relatively well established compared to that of continuous-time SV models. On the other hand, the option pricing theory for continuous-time SV models is relatively well established compared to the discrete-time SV models. Even though theoretically the jump-diffusion model with SV offers a flexible and powerful tool for modelling the dynamics of asset returns, its empirical applications in the area of asset and derivative pricing are yet to be fully explored. First of all, since financial time series data are essentially observed over discrete time and limited sampling periods, the estimation of a general jump-diffusion with SV remains a challenge. Second, while the stochastic volatility generalizations have been shown to improve the explanatory power compared to the Black–Scholes model, their implications on option pricing have not yet been adequately tested. How well can such generalizations help resolve well-known systematic empirical biases associated with the Black–Scholes model, such as the volatility smiles (e.g. Rubinstein, 1985), and asymmetry of such smiles (e.g. Stein, 1989; Clewlow and Xu, 1993; Taylor and Xu, 1993, 1994)? Is the gain, if any, from such generalizations substantial compared to relatively simpler models? Or, in other words, is the gain worth the additional complexity or implementational costs? Answers to these questions require further thorough investigation.

2.7   APPENDIX: DERIVATION OF OPTION PRICING FORMULA FOR GENERAL JUMP-DIFFUSION PROCESS WITH STOCHASTIC VOLATILITY AND STOCHASTIC INTEREST RATES

The derivation of the option pricing formula for the general jump-diffusion process with stochastic volatility and stochastic interest rates follows the techniques in Heston (1993), Scott (1997), and Bakshi, Cao and Chen (1997). Let $s_t = \ln S_t$ and transform the PDE (2.32) in terms of s_t, then insert the conjectured solution given by (2.33) and result in the PDEs for the risk-neutral probabilities Π_j for $j = 1, 2$. The resulting PDEs are the Fokker–Planck forward equations for probability functions. This implies that Π_1 and Π_2 are valid probability functions with values bounded between 0 and 1 and the PDEs must be solved separately subject to the terminal condition $\Pi_j(S_T, T) = 1_{S_T \geq K}$, $j = 1, 2$. The corresponding characteristic functions f_1 and f_2 for Π_1 and Π_2 also satisfy similar PDEs given by

$$\frac{1}{2}\sigma_t \frac{\partial^2 f_1}{\partial s_t^2} + \left(r_t - \tilde{\lambda}\tilde{\mu}_0 + \frac{1}{2}\sigma_t\right)\frac{\partial f_1}{\partial s_t} + \rho v_\sigma \sigma_t \frac{\partial^2 f_1}{\partial s_t \partial \sigma_t} + \frac{1}{2}v_\sigma^2 \sigma_t \frac{\partial^2 f_1}{\partial \sigma_t^2}$$

$$+ (\theta_\sigma - (\kappa_\sigma - \rho v - \sigma)\sigma_t)\frac{\partial f_1}{\partial \sigma_t} + \frac{1}{2}v_r^2 r_t \frac{\partial^2 f_1}{\partial r_t^2} + (\theta_r - \kappa_r r_t)\frac{\partial f_1}{\partial r_t}$$

$$+ \frac{\partial f_1}{\partial t} - \tilde{\lambda}\tilde{\mu}_0 f_1 + \tilde{\lambda}E[(1 + \ln \tilde{Y}_t)f_1(t, \tau; s_t + \ln \tilde{Y}_t, r_t, \sigma_t)$$

$$- f_1(t, \tau; s_t, r_t, \sigma_t)] = 0$$

and

$$\frac{1}{2}\sigma_t \frac{\partial^2 f_2}{\partial s_t^2} + \left(r_t - \tilde{\lambda}\tilde{\mu}_0 + \frac{1}{2}\sigma_t\right)\frac{\partial f_2}{\partial s_t} + \rho v_\sigma \sigma_t \frac{\partial^2 f_2}{\partial s_t \partial \sigma_t}$$

$$+ \frac{1}{2}v_\sigma^2 \sigma_t \frac{\partial^2 f_2}{\partial \sigma_t^2} + (\theta_\sigma - \kappa_\sigma \sigma_t)\frac{\partial f_2}{\partial \sigma_t} + \frac{1}{2}v_r^2 r_t \frac{\partial^2 f_2}{\partial r_t^2}$$

$$+ \left(\theta_r - \left(\kappa_r - \frac{v_r^2}{B(t, \tau)}\frac{\partial B(t, \tau)}{\partial r_t}\right)r_t\right)\frac{\partial f_2}{\partial r_t} + \frac{\partial f_2}{\partial t} - \tilde{\lambda}\tilde{\mu}_0 f_2$$

$$+ \tilde{\lambda}E[f_2(t, \tau; s_t + \ln \tilde{Y}_t, r_t, \sigma_t) - f_2(t, \tau; s_t, r_t, \sigma_t)] = 0$$

with boundary conditions $f_j(T, 0; \phi) = \exp\{i\phi s_T\}$, $j = 1, 2$. Conjecture that the solutions of f_1 and f_2 are respectively given by

$$f_1 = \exp\{u(\tau) + x_r(\tau)r_t + x_\sigma(\tau)\sigma_t + i\phi s_t\}$$

$$f_2 = \exp\{v(\tau) + y_r(\tau)r_t + y_\sigma(\tau)\sigma_t + i\phi s_t - \ln B(t, \tau)\}$$

with $u(0) = x_r(0) = x_\sigma(0) = 0$ and $v(0) = y_r(0) = y_\sigma(0) = 0$. Substitute in the conjectured solutions and solve the resulting systems of differential equations and note that $B(T, 0) = 1$, we have the following solutions

$$f_1(t, \tau) = \exp\left\{-\frac{\theta_r}{v_r^2}\left[2\ln\left(1 - \frac{(1 - e^{-\xi_r \tau})(\xi_r - \kappa_r)}{2\xi_r}\right) + (\xi_r - \kappa_r)\tau\right]\right.$$

$$-\frac{\theta_\sigma}{v_\sigma^2}\left[2\ln(1 - \frac{(1 - e^{-\xi_\sigma \tau})(\xi_\sigma - \kappa_\sigma + (1 + i\phi)\rho v_\sigma)}{2\xi_\sigma)}\right]$$

$$-\frac{\theta_\sigma}{v_\sigma^2}[\xi_\sigma - \kappa_\sigma + (1 + i\phi)\rho v_\sigma]\tau + i\phi s_t$$

$$+\frac{2i\phi(1 - e^{-\xi_r \tau})}{2\xi_r - (1 - e^{-\xi_r \tau})(\xi_r - \kappa_r)}r_t$$

$$+ \tilde{\lambda}\tau(1 + \tilde{\mu}_0)[(1 + \tilde{\mu}_0)^{i\phi} e^{i\phi(1+\phi)v^2/2} - 1] - \tilde{\lambda}i\phi\tilde{\mu}_0\tau$$

$$+ \frac{i\phi(i\phi + 1)(1 - e^{-\xi_\sigma \tau})}{2\xi_\sigma - (1 - e^{-\xi_\sigma \tau})(\xi_\sigma - \kappa_\sigma + (1 + i\phi)\rho v_\sigma)} \sigma_t \Bigg\}$$

and

$$f_2(t, \tau) = \exp\Bigg\{ -\frac{\theta_r}{v_r^2} \left[2\ln\left(1 - \frac{(1 - e^{-\xi_r^* \tau})(\xi_r^* - \kappa_r)}{2\xi_r^*}\right) + (\xi_r^* - \kappa_r)\tau \right] $$

$$- \frac{\theta_\sigma}{v_\sigma^2} \left[2\ln(1 - \frac{(1 - e^{-\xi_\sigma^* \tau})(\xi_\sigma^* - \kappa_\sigma + i\phi\rho v_\sigma)}{2\xi_\sigma^*)} \right]$$

$$- \frac{\theta_\sigma}{v_\sigma^2}[\xi_\sigma^* - \kappa_\sigma + i\phi\rho v_\sigma]\tau + i\phi s_t - \ln B(t, \tau)$$

$$+ \frac{2(i\phi - 1)(1 - e^{-\xi_r^* \tau})}{2\xi_r^* - (1 - e^{-\xi_r \tau})(\xi_r^* - \kappa_r)} r_t + \tilde{\lambda}\tau[(1 + \tilde{\mu}_0)^{i\phi} e^{i\phi(\phi-1)v^2/2} - 1]$$

$$- \tilde{\lambda}i\phi\tilde{\mu}_0\tau + \frac{i\phi(i\phi - 1)(1 - e^{-\xi_\sigma^* \tau})}{2\xi_\sigma^* - (1 - e^{-\xi_\sigma^* \tau})(\xi_\sigma^* - \kappa_\sigma + i\phi\rho v_\sigma)} \sigma_t \Bigg\}$$

where $\xi_r = \sqrt{\kappa_r^2 - 2v_r^2 i\phi}, \xi_\sigma = \sqrt{(\kappa_\sigma - (1 + i\phi)\rho v_\sigma)^2 - i\phi(1 + i\phi)v_\sigma^2}, \xi_r^* = \sqrt{\kappa_r^2 - 2v_r^2(i\phi - 1)}$ and $\xi_\sigma^* = \sqrt{(\kappa_\sigma - i\phi\rho v_\sigma)^2 - i\phi(i\phi - 1)v_\sigma^2}$.

REFERENCES

Aase, K.K. (1988) Contingent claims valuation when the security price is a combination of an Itô process and a random point process, *Stochastic Processes and Their Applications*, **28**, 185–220.

Ahn, C.M. and Thompson, H.E. (1988) Jump-diffusion processes and the term structure of interest rates, *Journal of Finance*, **43**, 155–174.

Akaike, H. (1973) Information theory and an extension of the maximum likelihood principle, *Second International Symposium on Information Theory*, 267–281.

Amin, K. and Jarrow, R. (1992) Pricing options on risky assets in a stochastic interest rate economy, *Mathematical Finance*, **2**, 217–237.

Amin, K. and Ng, V. (1993) Option valuation with systematic stochastic volatility, *Journal of Finance*, **48**, 881–910.

Andersen, T.G. (1992) Volatility, working paper No. 144, Northwestern University.

Andersen, T.G. (1994) Stochastic autoregressive volatility; a framework for volatility modeling, *Mathematical Finance*, **4**, 75–102.

Andersen, T.G. and Lund, J. (1996) Stochastic volatility and mean drift in the short rate diffusion: sources of steepness, level and curvature in the yield curve, working paper No. 214, Northwestern University.

Andersen, T.G. and Lund, J. (1997) Estimating continuous time stochastic volatility models of the short term interest rate, *Journal of Econometrics*, **77**, 343–377.

Andersen, T.G. and Sørensen, B.E. (1996) GMM estimation of a stochastic volatility model: a Monte Carlo study, *Journal of Business Economics and Statistics*, **14**, 328–352.

Andersen, T.G. and Bollerslev, T. (1997) Answering the skeptics: yes, standard volatility models do provide accurate forecasts, working paper No. 227, Department of Finance, J.L. Kellogg Graduate School of Management.

Bailey, W. and Stulz, E. (1989) The pricing of stock index options in a general equilibrium model, *Journal of Financial and Quantitative Analysis*, **24**, 1–12.

Bakshi, G., Cao, C. and Chen, Z. (1997) Empirical performance of alternative option pricing models (Forthcoming in *Journal of Finance*).

Bakshi, G. and Chen, Z. (1997a) An alternative valuation model for contingent claims (Forthcoming in *Journal of Financial Economics*).

Bakshi, G. and Chen, Z. (1997b) Equilibrium valuation of foreign exchange claims (Forthcoming in *Journal of Finance*).

Ball, C.A. and Roma, A. (1994) Stochastic volatility option pricing, *Journal of Financial and Quantitative Analysis*, **29**, 589–607.

Ball, C.A. and Torous, W.N. (1985) On jumps in common stock prices and their impact on call option pricing, *Journal of Finance*, **40**, 155–173.

Bardhan, I. and Chao, X. (1993) Pricing options on securities with discontinuous returns, *Stochastic Processes and Their Application*, **48**, 123–137.

Bates, D.S. (1988) Pricing options on jump-diffusion processes, working paper 37–88, Rodney L. White Center, Wharton School.

Bates, D.S. (1991) The crash of 87: Was it expected? the evidence from option markets, *Journal of Finance*, **46**, 1009–1044.

Bates, D.S. (1996a) Testing option pricing models, in G.S. Maddala and C.R. Rao eds, *Handbook of Statistics, v. 14: Statistical Methods in Finance*, Elsevier, Amsterdam, 567–611.

Bates, D.S. (1996b) Jumps and stochastic volatility: exchange rate processes implicit in PHLX Deutschmark options, *Review of Financial Studies*, **9**(1), 69–107.

Beckers, S. (1981) A note on estimating the parameters of the diffusion-jump model of stock returns, *Journal of Financial and Quantitative Analysis*, **16**(1), 127–140.

Black, F. (1975) Fact and fantasy in the use of options, *Financial Analysts Journal*, **31**, 36–72.

Black, F. (1976) Studies of stock price volatility changes, *Proceedings from the American Statistical Association, Business and Economic Statistics Section*, 177–181.

Black, F. and Scholes, M. (1972) The valuation of option contracts and a test of market efficiency, *Journal of Finance*, **27**, 399–418.

Black, F. and Scholes, M. (1973) The pricing of options and corporate liabilities, *Journal of Political Economy*, **81**, 637–654.

Bollerslev, T.R.Y., Engle, R. and Nelson, D. (1994) Arch models, in R.F. Engle and D. McFadden (eds), *Handbook of Econometrics*, Vol. 4, North-Holland, Amsterdam.

Bollerslev, T.R.Y. (1986) Generalized autoregressive conditional heteroscedasticity, *Journal of Econometrics*, **51**, 307–327.

Bollerslev, T.R.Y., Chou, R.Y. and Kroner, K.F. (1992) Arch modeling in finance: a review of the theory and empirical evidence, *Journal of Econometrics*, **52**, 1–131.

Boyle, P., Broadie, M. and Glasserman, P. (1996) Monte Carlo methods for security pricing (Forthcoming in *Journal of Economics Dynamics and Control*).

Brennan, M.J. (1979) The pricing of contingent claims in discrete time models, *Journal of Finance*, **34**, 53–68.

Canina, L. and Figlewski, S. (1993) The informational content of implied volatility, *Review of Financial Studies*, **6**, 659–681.

Chesney, M. and Scott, L.O. (1989) Pricing European currency options: a comparison of the modified Black–Scholes model and a random variance model, *Journal of Financial Quantitative Analysis*, **24**, 267–284.

Chiras, D. and Manaster, S. (1978) The information content of option prices and a test of market efficiency, *Journal of Financial Economics*, **10**, 29–58.

Christensen, B.J. and Prabhala, N.R. (1997) The relation between implied and realized volatility (Forthcoming in *Journal of Financial Economics*).

Clark, P.K. (1973) A subordinated stochastic process model with finite variance for speculative prices, *Econometrica*, **41**, 135–55.

Clewlow, L. and Xu, X. (1993) The dynamics of stochastic volatility, discussion paper, University of Warwick.

Conrad, J., Kaul, G. and Gultekin, M. (1991) Asymmetric predictability of conditional variances, *Review of Financial Studies*, **4**, 597–622.

Constantinides, G. (1992) A theory of the nominal term structure of interest rates, *Review of Financial Studies*, **5**, 531–552.

Cox, J.C. and Ross, S.A. (1976) The valuation of options for alternative stochastic processes, *Journal of Financial Economics*, **3**, 145–166.

Cox, J.C. (1975) Notes on option pricing I: constant elasticity of variance diffusions, discussion paper, Stanford University.

Cox, J.C., Ingersoll, J.E. and Ross, S.A. (1985) The theory of the term structure of interest rates, *Econometrica*, **53**, 363–384.

Cumby, R., Figlewski, S. and Hasbrouck, J. (1993) Forecasting volatility and correlations with EGARCH models, *Journal of Derivatives*, Winter, 51–63.

Dalang, R., Morton, A. and Willinger, W. (1989) Equivalent martingale measures and no arbitrage in stochastic security market models, *Stochastics and Stochastic Reports*, **29**, 185–202.

Danielsson, J. (1993) Multivariate stochastic volatility, working paper, University of Iceland.

Danielsson, J. (1994) Stochastic volatility in asset prices: estimation with simulated maximum likelihood, *Journal of Econometrics*, **61**, 375–400.

Danielsson, J. (1996) Estimation of stochastic volatility models by simulated maximum likelihood: C++ code, *Studies in Non-Linear Dynamics and Econometrics*, **1.1**.

Danielsson, J. and Richard, J.F. (1993) Accelerated Gaussian importance sampler with application to dynamic latent variable models, *Journal of Applied Econometrics*, **8**, S153–S174.

Day, T. and Lewis, C. (1992) Stock market volatility and the information content of stock index options, *Journal of Econometrics*, **52**, 267–287.

Duffie, D. (1988) *Security Markets: Stochastic Models*, Academic Press, Boston.

Duffie, D. and Singleton, K.J. (1993) Simulated moments estimation of Markov models of asset prices, *Econometrica*, **61**, 929–952.

Eastwood, B. (1991) Asymptotic normality and consistency of seminonparametric regression estimators using an upward f-test rule, *Journal of Econometrics*, **48**, 151–183.

Engle, R.F. (1982) Autoregressive conditional heteroscedasticity with estimates of the variance of U.K. inflation, *Econometrica*, **50**, 987–1008.

Engle, R.F. and Mustafa, C. (1992) Implied ARCH models from option prices, *Journal of Econometrics*, **52**, 289–311.

Fama, E.F. (1963) The stable paretian distribution, *Journal of Business*, **36**, 420–429.

Fama, E.F. (1965) The behavior of stock market prices, *Journal of Business*, **38**, 34–105.

Fenton, V.M. and Gallant, A.R. (1996) Convergence rates of SNP density estimators, *Econometrica*, **64**, 719–727.

Fenton, V.M. and Gallant, A.R. (1996) Qualitative and asymptotic performance of SNP density estimators, *Journal of Econometrics*, **74**, 77–118.

Fridman, M. and Harris, L. (1996) A maximum likelihood approach for stochastic volatility models (Forthcoming in Journal of Business Economics and Statistics.

Fung, W.K.H. and Hsieh, D.A. (1991) Empirical analysis of implied volatility: stocks, bonds and currencies, Department of Finance, Duke University.

Gallant, A.R., Hsieh, D.A. and Tauchen, G.E. (1997) Estimation of stochastic volatility models with diagnostics, *Journal of Econometrics*, **81**, 159–192.

Gallant, A.R. and Long, J.R. (1997) Estimating stochastic differential equations efficiently by minimum chi-square, *Biometrika*, **84**, 125–141.

Gallant, A.R. and Nychka, D.W. (1987) Semi-nonparametric maximum likelihood estimation, *Econometrica*, **55**, 363–390.

Gallant, A.R and Tauchen, G.E. (1996) Which moments to match? *Econometric Theory*, **12**, 657–681.

Gallant, A.R. and White, H. (1988) *Estimation and Inference for Nonlinear Dynamic Models*, Blackwell, New York.

Ghysels, E., Harvey, A. and Renault, E. (1996) Stochastic volatility, in G.S. Maddala and C.R. Rao (eds), *Handbook of Statistics, v. 14: Statistical Methods in Finance*, Elsevier, Amsterdam, 119–191.

Gouriéroux, C. and Monfort, A. (1996) *Simulation-Based Econometric Methods*, Oxford University Press, New York.

Gouriéroux, C., Monfort, A. and Renault, E. (1993) Indirect inference, *Journal of Applied Econometrics*, **8**, S85–S199.

Gultekin, N.B., Rogalski, S.M. and Tinic, R.J. (1982) Option pricing model estimates: some empirical results, *Financial Management*, Spring, 58–69.

Hannan, E.J. and Quinn, B.G. (1979) The determination of the order of an autoregression, *Journal of the Royal Statistical Society*, **B41**, 190–195.

Harrison, M. and Kreps, D. (1979) Martingale and arbitrage in multiperiod securities markets, *Journal of Economic Theory*, **20**, 381–408.

Harvey, A.C., Ruiz, E. and Shephard, N.G. (1994) Multivariate stochastic variance models, *Review of Economic Studies*, **61**, 247–264.

Harvey, A.C. and Shephard, N.G (1996) Estimation of an asymmetric stochastic volatility model for asset returns, *Journal of Business and Economic Statistics*, **14**, 429–434.

Harvey, A.C. (1993) Long memory in stochastic volatility, discussion paper, London School of Economics.

Heston, S.I. (1993) A closed form solution for options with stochastic volatility with applications to bond and currency options, *Review of Financial Studies*, **6**, 327–344.

Ho, M., Perraudin, W. and Sørensen, B. (1996) A continuous-time arbitrage-pricing model with stochastic volatility and jump, *Journal of Business and Economic Statistics*, **14**(1), 31–43.

Hsieh, D.A. (1991) Chaos and nonlinear dynamics: application to financial markets, *Journal of Finance*, **46**, 1839–1877.

Hull, J. and White, A. (1987) The pricing of options on assets with stochastic volatilities, *Journal of Finance*, **42**, 281–300.

Jacquier, E.N., Polson, N.G. and Rossi, P.E. (1994) Bayesian analysis of stochastic volatility models (with discussion), *Journal of Business and Economic Statistics*, **12**, 371–417.

Jarrow, R. and Rosenfeld, E. (1984) Jump risks and the intertemporal capital asset pricing model, *Journal of Business*, **57**, 337–351.

Jeanblanc-Picqué, M. and Pontier, M. (1990) Optimal portfolio for a small investor in a market with discontinuous prices, *Applied Mathematical Optimisation*, **22**, 287–310.

Jiang, G. (1997) Estimation of jump-diffusion processes based on indirect inference, manuscript, University of Groningen, The Netherlands.

Jiang, G. and van der Sluis, P. (1998) Pricing stock options under stochastic volatility and stochastic interest rates with efficient method-of-moments estimation, manuscript, University of Groningen, The Netherlands.

Johnson, H. and Shanno, D. (1987) Option pricing when the variance is changing, *Journal of Financial and Quantitative Analysis*, **22**, 143–152.

Jones, E.P. (1984) Option arbitrage and strategy with large price changes, *Journal of Financial Economics*, **13**, 91–133.

Jorion, P. (1988) On jump processes in the foreign exchange and stock markets, *Review of Financial Studies*, **1**, 427–445.

Jorion, P. (1995) Predicting volatility in the foreign exchange market, *Journal of Finance*, **50**, 507–528.

Jorion, P. (1996) Risk and turnover in the foreign exchange market, in J.A. Frankel, G. Galli, and A. Giovannini (eds), *The Microstructure of Foreign Exchange Markets*, Chicago: The University of Chicago Press.

Kim, S., Shephard, N.G. and Chib, S. (1996) Stochastic volatility: optimal likelihood inference and comparison with arch models (Forthcoming in Review of Economic Studies).

Lamoureux, C.G. and Lastrapes, W. (1993) Forecasting stock return variance: towards understanding stochastic implied volatility, *Review of Financial Studies*, **6**, 293–326.

Latané, H. and Rendleman, R.J. (1976) Standard derivations of stock price ratios implied in option prices, *Journal of Finance*, **31**, 369–381.

Lo, A. (1988) Maximum likelihood estimation of generalized Itô processes with discretely sampled data, *Econometric Theory*, **4**, 231–247.

Maddala, G.S. and Rao, C.R. (1996) *Handbook of Statistics, v. 14: Statistical Methods in Finance*, Elsevier, Amsterdam.

Mandelbrot, B.B. (1963) The variation of certain speculative prices, *Journal of Business*, **36**, 394–416.

Meddahi, N. and Renault, E. (1995) Aggregations and marginalisations of GARCH and stochastic volatility models, discussion paper, GREMAQ.

Melino, A. and Turnbull, S.M. (1990) Pricing foreign currency options with stochastic volatility, *Journal of Econometrics*, **45**, 239–265.

Merton, R.C. (1973) Theory of rational option pricing, *Bell Journal of Economics and Management Science*, **4**, 141–183.

Merton, R.C. (1976a) Option pricing when underlying stock returns are discontinuous, *Journal of Financial Economics*, **3**, 125–144.

Merton, R.C. (1976b) The impact on option pricing of specification error in the underlying stock price returns, *Journal of Finance*, **31**, 333–350.

Naik, V. (1993) Option valuation and hedging strategies with jumps in the volatility of asset returns, *Journal of Finance*, **48**, 1969–1984.

Naik, V. and Lee, M.H. (1990) General equilibrium pricing of options on the market portfolio with discontinuous returns, *Review of Financial Studies*, **3**, 493–522.

Nelson, D.B. (1990) Arch models as diffusion approximations, *Journal of Econometrics*, **45**, 7–39.

Nelson, D.B. (1991) Conditional heteroscedasticity in asset returns: a new approach, *Econometrica*, **59**, 347–370.

Nelson, D.B. and Foster, D.P. (1994) Asymptotic filtering theory for univariate arch models, *Econometrica*, **62**, 1–41.

Ng, V., Engle, R. and Rothschild, M. (1992) A multi-dynamic factor model for stock returns, *Journal of Econometrics*, **52**, 245–266.

Pagan, A.R. and Schwert, G.W. (1990) Alternative models for conditional stock volatility, *Journal of Econometrics*, **45**, 267–290.

Phillips, P.C.B. (1983) Era's: a new approach to small sample theory, *Econometrica*, **51**, 1505–1527.

Press, J. (1967) A compound events model for security prices, *Journal of Business*, **40**, 317–335.

Quinn, B.G. (1980) Order determination for a multivariate autoregression, *Journal of the Royal Statistical Society*, **B42**, 182–185.

Rabinovitch, R. (1989) Pricing stock and bond option prices when the default-free rate is stochastic, *Journal of Financial and Quantitative Analysis*, **24**, 447–457.

Richard, J.F. and Zhang, W. (1995a) Accelerated importance sampling, University of Pittsburgh.

Richard, J.F. and Zhang, W. (1995b) Accelerated Monte Carlo integration: an application to dynamic latent variable models, University of Pittsburgh.

Rubinstein, M. (1976) The valuation of uncertain income streams and the pricing of options, *Journal of Economics and Management Science*, 407–425.

Sandman, G. and Koopman, S.J. (1997) Maximum likelihood estimation of stochastic volatility models, working paper, London School of Economics.

Schotman, P. and Mahieu, R. (1994) Stochastic volatility and the distribution of exchange rate news, LIFE University of Maastricht, mimeo.

Schwarz, G. (1978) Estimating the dimension of a model, *Annals of Statistics*, **6**, 461–464.

Schwert, G.W. (1989) Why does stock market volatility change over time, *Journal of Finance*, **44**, 1115–1153.

Schwert, G.W. (1990a) Stock volatility and the crash of '87, *Review of Financial Studies*, **3**, 77–102.

Schwert, G.W. (1990b) Stock market volatility, *Financial Analysts Journal*, May-June, 23–34.

Schwert, G.W. and Sequin, P.J. (1990) Heteroscedasticity in stock returns, *Journal of Finance*, **45**, 1129–1155.

Scott, E. and Tucker, A. (1989) Predicting currency return volatility, *Journal of Banking and Finance*, **13**, 839–851.

Scott, L. (1987) Option pricing when the variance changes randomly: theory, estimators, and applications, *Journal of Financial and Quantitative Analysis*, **22**, 419–438.

Scott, L. (1991) Random variance option pricing, *Advances in Futures and Options Research*, **5**, 113–135.

Scott, L. (1997) Pricing stock options in a jump-diffusion model with stochastic volatility and interest rates: application of Fourier inversion methods (Forthcoming in *Mathematical Finance*).

Shephard, N.G. (1996) Statistical aspects of ARCH and stochastic volatility, in D.R. Cox, D.V. Hinkley and O.E. Barndorff-Nielsen (eds), *Time Series Models. Econometrics, Finance and Other Fields*, Chapman and Hall, London.

Smith, A.A. (1993) Estimating nonlinear time series models using vector autoregressions: two approaches, *Journal of Applied Econometrics*, **8**, S63–S84.

Stapleton, R. and Subrahmanyam, M. (1984) The valuation of multivariate contingent claims in discrete-time model, *Journal of Finance*, **39**, 207–228.

Stein, E.M. and Stein, J. (1991) Stock price distributions with stochastic volatility: an analytic approach, *Review of Financial Studies*, **4**, 727–752.

Talay, D. (1996) Probabilistic numerical methods for PDES: elements of analysis, in D. Talay and L. Tubaro (eds), *Probabilistic Methods for Nonlinear PDEs*, Berlin: Springer.

Tauchen, G. and Pitts, M. (1983) The price variability-volume relationship on speculative markets, *Econometrica*, **51**, 485–505.

Taylor, S.J. (1986) *Modelling Financial Time Series*, Wiley, Chichester.

Taylor, S.J. (1994) Modelling stochastic volatility: a review and comparative study, *Mathematical Finance*, **4**, 183–204.

Taylor, S.J. and Xu, X. (1993) The magnitude of implied volatility smiles: theory and empirical evidence for exchange rates, discussion paper, University of Warwick.

Turnbull, S. and Milne, F. (1991) A simple approach to interest-rate option pricing, *Review of Financial Studies*, **4**, 81–121.

van der Sluis, P.J. (1997) Computationally attractive stability tests for the efficient method-of-moments, Tinbergen Institute Discussion Paper TI97–087/4.

West, K.D. and Cho, D. (1995) The predictive ability of several models of exchange rate volatility, *Journal of Econometrics*, **69**, 367–391.

Whaley, R.E. (1982) Valuation of American call options on dividend-paying stocks, *Journal of Financial Economics*, **10**, 29–58.

White, H. (1994) *Estimation, Inference and Specification Analysis*, Cambridge University Press, Cambridge.

Wiggins, J.B. (1987) Option values under stochastic volatility: theory and empirical estimates, *Journal of Financial Economics*, **19**, 351–72.

NOTES

1. Also see Taylor (1994), Andersen (1992) and Andersen (1994) for review and discussion of SV models.
2. In this sense, the SV model includes ARCH/GARCH as a special case when the random noise is replaced by the past observation of y_t^2.
3. Scott (1987), Stein and Stein (1991), and Ball and Roma (1994) assume that $\sigma_t(h_t)$ follows an Ornstein–Uhlenbeck process which allows $\sigma_t(h_t)$ to be negative.
4. Johnson and Shanno (1987) assume a similar volatility process.
5. Press (1967) first proposed a jump-diffusion model for stock price changes which is different from the 'random walk model' originally proposed by Bachelier in 1900 and its modified versions. Press assumes that the changes of logarithmic stock prices follow the distribution of a Poisson mixture of normal distributions, that is, the combination of a Wiener process and a compound Poisson process. The model resembles earlier random walk models in that it is a discrete parameter, continuous state space Markov process. But the presence of the compound Poisson process produces a non-Gaussian and essentially discontinuous process.
6. When Y_t is assumed to be lognormally distributed with $\mu_0 = E[Y_t - 1]$ and $\alpha_0 = E[\ln Y_t]$, the relation between α_0 and μ_0 is $\alpha_0 = \ln(1 + \mu_0) - \frac{1}{2}v^2$, where $v^2 = \text{Var}[\ln Y_t]$.
7. Existing work of extending the Black–Scholes model has moved away from considering either stochastic volatility or stochastic interest rates (examples include Merton (1973), and Rabinovitch (1989)) but to considering both, examples include Bailey and Stulz (1989), Bakshi and Chen (1997a,b) and Scott (1997). Simulation results show that there could be a significant impact of stochastic interest rates on option prices (see, for example, Rabinovitch, 1989).
8. These conditions are automatically satisfied in the continuous-time diffusion models, but require slight constraint imposed on the model specification in the discrete time. Under the standard SV model specification for the variance processes and the symmetric condition, i.e. there is no correlation between stock return and conditional volatility, these conditions are satisfied. Unfortunately, the

GARCH and EGARCH specifications are not consistent with the assumptions imposed on the model in Amin and Ng (1993).

9. Subsequent research by Jones (1984), Naik and Lee (1990) and Bates (1991) shows that Merton's option pricing formulas with modified parameters are still relevant under non-diversifiable jump risk or more general distributional assumptions.

10. In time series literature, both standard derivation σ_t and variance σ_t^2 are often referred to as volatility.

11. For this reason, the volatility is often used to quote the value of an option.

12. This may produce various biases in option pricing or hedging when Black–Scholes implied volatilities are used to evaluate new options with different strike prices and maturities.

13. As Andersen and Bollerslev (1997) point out, it is not without problem to use R^2 as a guide of the accuracy of volatility forecasts since under this scenario the R^2 simply measures the extent of idiosyncratic noise in squared returns relative to the mean which is given by the (true) conditional return variance.

14. Strictly speaking, informational content of implied volatility is measured in terms of the ability of the explanatory variable to forecast one time-unit ahead volatility, while the test of predictive power of implied volatility focuses on forecasting future volatility over the remaining life of the option contract. Thus the test of informational content is based on the regression (2.63) with $\tau = 1$, while the test of predictive power sets τ equal to the term to expiration of the option contract.

Chapter 3

Modelling slippage: an application to the bund futures contract[1]

EMMANUEL ACAR* AND EDOUARD PETITDIDIER†

3.1 INTRODUCTION

The increasing availability of high-frequency data has made possible the detailed study of intraday statistics. The positive correlation between price volatility and volume is now both well known and well documented (see Karpoff, 1987 for a pioneering survey). A recent literature review by Daigler (1997) points out the existence of intraday U-shaped curves in volatility, volume and bid–ask spreads. This has generated several theories to explain these patterns as well as empirical evidence investigating various aspects of these U-shaped curves. Daigler (1997) sees at least five reasons for trading at the open and close. At the close, portfolio traders anticipate price behaviour changes overnight in ways that would alter investors' optimal overnight portfolios, creating higher volume and volatility and therefore larger spreads. Trading occurs at the open because information arrives over the closed period. In addition traders can have greater divergence of opinion at the beginning of the day creating greater volatility and the potential for larger volume. On the other hand, trading at the close is initiated by index mutual fund managers who need to make trades at the closing prices for fund purchases and redemptions, while short sellers frequently close out their positions at the end of the day and hedgers often hedge their overnight positions.

This pattern exists in different markets: for example, the New York, London and Tokyo stock exchanges and the Chicago futures exchanges. The best known stylized facts about intradaily statistical characteristics come from the NYSE, the most extensively studied asset market in the world. The two main features, the volume of deals and the volatility of equity prices, both broadly follow a U-shaped pattern (or to be more precise, a reverse J). Thus both variables are

---

* Dresdner Kleinwort Benson
† BAREP, Société Générale.

at the highest point at the opening, fall quite rapidly to lower levels during the mid-day, and then rise again towards the close. See, among others, Wood, Mcluish and Ord (1985), Amihud and Mendleson (1987), and Stoll and Whaley (1990). Chang, Jain and Locke (1995) examine the effects of the closing New York Stock Exchange on volatility and price changes in the Standard and Poor's futures market which trades for 15 more minutes each day. For the entire day they find two separate U-shaped patterns (or a W-shape). The first one closely resembles the pattern in the stock market during the day when the stock market is open, while the second one is observed from just before the close of the stock market to the end of trading in the futures market.

However, not all contracts exhibit the same familiar shape for volume and volatility. Buckle, Thomas and Woodlams (1995) find that in the LIFFE market, volatility follows a rough L-shaped pattern for all contracts. On the LSE, where SEAQ does not have a formal opening and closing, the pattern of volatility remains U-shaped, whereas volume has a two-hump-shape rather than a U-shape over the day (Kleidon and Werner, 1996).

Until now, research has mainly focused on the analysis of intraday volatility and volume. The issues of intraday volatility and volume, although useful, might, however, not be sufficient for trading purposes. Market participants wish to execute larger and larger quantities without moving the market. Consequently, the questions of liquidity, market deepness and transaction costs have become increasingly relevant. Transaction costs might be inversely related to trading volume. When transaction costs are high, market makers have less opportunity to make profitable trades. Furthermore, market participants will search for alternative trading vehicles with lower transaction costs. All of these will lead to a decrease in volume.

A few studies have tried to establish intraday transaction costs. However, they have defined transaction costs as the bid–ask spread and concentrated on the cash markets. The fact is, in the futures markets there is no bid–ask spread. Consequently, transaction costs have to be otherwise defined. The goal of this study is to propose a new statistic; volume-weighted returns, which might overcome previous shortcomings while relating transaction costs to market liquidity. Any study involving transaction costs requires tick-by-tick data. To be reliable, every single transaction needs to be recorded with an accurate timestamp. This is achieved by electronic markets, which is why this chapter analyses the issue of slippage in the electronic DTB market.

More specifically, this chapter is organized as follows. Section 3.2 describes our data set. This presents basic statistics of intraday volume, volatility, kurtosis and skewness of underlying returns. Section 3.3 describes our methodology to include the effect of size in trading: volume-weighted rates of return. Section 3.4 attempts to relate slippage to intraday volume and volatility.

3.2 DATA DESCRIPTION

One of the problems of continuous time series is that high-frequency observations are subject to a wide range of idiosyncratic factors such as measurement errors due to bid–ask spreads, or reporting difficulties. Indicative quotes have existed for many years, they have been collected by the electronic news purveyors, e.g. Reuters, Telerates, Knight Ridder etc. Quotes are indicative in the sense that the participant posting such prices is not committed to trade at them. Nevertheless, transaction data is available for a few specific markets, especially the futures markets.

Our analysis concerns the Bund futures contract. The Bund futures contract is an agreement between buyer and seller to exchange a notional 6% German Government Bond (DM 250 000 face value) at a fixed date, for cash on delivery four times a year. Since September 1988, Bund futures have been traded at the London International Financial Futures Exchange (LIFFE). In November 1990 trading in Bund futures was introduced at the Deutsche TerminBörse (DTB) in Frankfurt. On the one hand, the Deutsche TerminBörse is one of the exchanges providing the price and number of contracts in each trade. Being an electronic exchange, the DTB keeps an audit trail of every single transaction, therefore the data set is not only accurate (no bid–ask spreads or reporting errors) but exhaustive as well. On the other hand, for LIFFE, intraday data on the size of each transaction are not available. The reader should refer for interesting discussions between the LIFFE and DTB Bund futures contracts to Hans Franses *et al.* (1994), Pirrong (1996) and Breedon and Holland (1997).

Since the primary goal of this study is to define and observe slippage in the futures markets, accurate volume statistics must be used. This is why this chapter collects data only from Frankfurt. The data set 'time and sales' tape[2] obtained from the DTB comes in the form of a file for each trading month of the year. Each transaction record contains time (day, hour, minutes, seconds, centiseconds, nanoseconds), volume, price and delivery date. However, it must be noted that trades are not signed. This means that we cannot tell directly whether a trade is a buy or a sell. The data are transactions data encompassing 68 months from December 1991 to the end of July 1997. In the life of the Bund contract, there have been two changes of timetable. From November 1990 to November 1991, the trading session used to be from 8:00 to 17:00. But from the 2 December the closing time was changed to 17:30. Again, another modification of timetable occurred on 1 August 1997, when the end of the session was postponed to 19:00. Changing opening and closing times drastically affects intraday patterns of volume and volatility. This is why our study only includes a period of constant trading session, 08:00 to 17:30 local time to make results comparable.

A decision also had to be made as to the length over which we would study the returns. It was decided that this should be at least 30 minutes as this was the minimum length of time that would include a 'reasonable' number of observations especially in the early years of the contract.

As we are using more than a year of intraday data in the analysis, there can be up to three contracts of the same type but different maturity being traded simultaneously. As we require a continuous series for the analysis, a decision had to be made concerning which contract we should examine at any one time. For the Bund contract, the heaviest trading occurs in the front month contract up to three days before expiration. There is no rollover problem since the study does not consider overnight returns between contracts of two different maturities, but only intraday returns involving the same maturity contract.

The 30-minute frequency exhibits interesting, although atypical, particularities (Figure 3.1). Volume and volatility curves are not following a U-shape. Volume and volatility, although positively correlated, do not exhibit any pronounced shape. This is notable given that in many futures markets volatility follows a U-shape or at the very least an L-shape. Surprisingly, the first and last 30 minutes are neither especially volatile nor liquid. Volume during the first 30 minutes is twice as small as during the next 30 minutes. This may be due to the interference with the LIFFE market. Trading on Bund starts slightly later on LIFFE (8:30 Frankfurt time) which might explain the increased volume and volatility at that time. Again at 17:15, LIFFE closes for 5 minutes, changing to the APT system. This might explain the lower levels of volume and volatility during the last 30 minutes on DTB. The peak at 14:30 corresponds to the release of US statistics.

At that time, we notice the biggest turnover for the all-day and high volatility. This result is not confined to the Bund futures markets. It merely highlights the importance of public information and might even lag what happens in the US bond markets. Indeed Daigler (1997) similarly observes higher volatility in T-bond futures prices after the governmental announcements.

Higher moments have been established to denote departures from the normal assumption. Positive skewness means that the upper tail of the curve is longer than the lower tail. Thirty-minute returns can be positively or negatively skewed (Figure 3.2). There are no clear, consistent patterns across different times of the day. Overall the skewness amount is rather low and insignificant, meaning that returns are fairly symmetrical. However, all returns distributions are massively leptokurtic. Positive kurtosis indicates that the curve is steep at the centre and has fat tails. This is a feature of high-frequency data (Müller *et al.*, 1990). They include many zero returns, no price change, and a few large moves.

It has been claimed by academics that when volume statistics are unavailable, such as in the foreign exchange markets, the number of quotes could be used

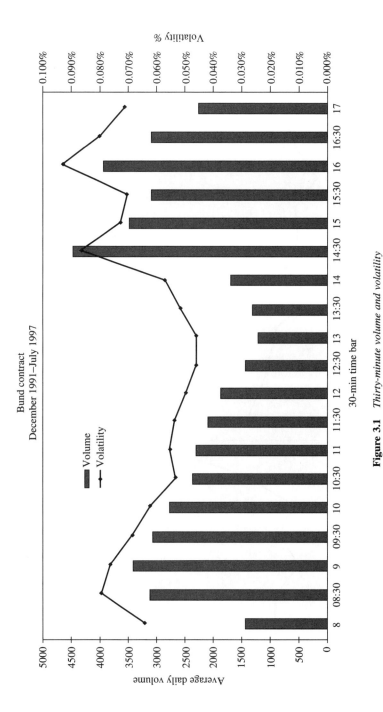

Figure 3.1 *Thirty-minute volume and volatility*

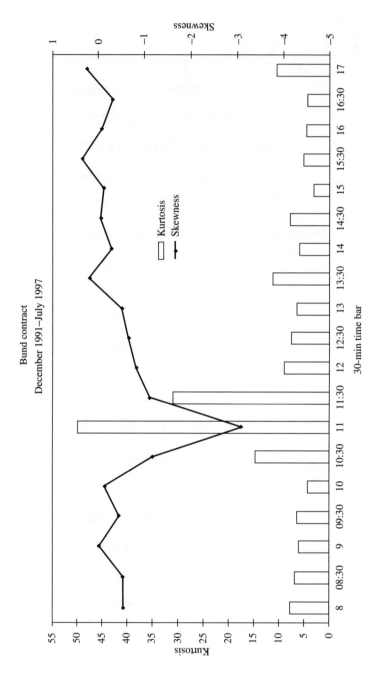

Figure 3.2 *Thirty-minute kurtosis and skewness*

instead. Figure 3.3 shows the number of trades is highly correlated with volume. This is not surprising given that Pirrong (1996) finds that tests of market depth employing the number of trades in fact give the same results as tests employing the number of contracts. Harris (1987) shows that 'tick volume' (number of price changes) for stocks is highly correlated with volume for NYSE data. Moreover, Karpoff (1986) argues that the tick volume within a given time period is superior to volume as a measure of price information.

Previous research using daily data has shown the average size of trade on the DTB to be roughly equal to 22 contracts. Using different time periods, Kofman and Moser (1995) find the average trade size to be equal to 23 contracts against 20 contracts for Breedon and Holland (1997). Our study confirms these finding using intraday transaction records. A more remarkable observation is that the ticket size or volume per trade is amazingly stable throughout the day. It stays around 22 lots during the full day.

With the availability of transaction-by-transaction data for high-frequency markets such as the NYSE, the time between trades has become another statistic for the empiricist. Engle and Russell (1998) model durations between trades for IBM, revealing significant autocorrelation or clumping of orders. If the factors which determine the timing of trades or price changes are related to the distribution of information amongst market traders, then forecasts of the time between market events may give added insight into the behaviour of liquidity. Here we can deduce the average time between trades from the volume and the number of trades during a 30-minute interval. This statistic has some importance for trading purpose since it should be part of a liquidity definition. Dealers consider that a market is liquid only and only if large sizes can be transacted in the quickest time. Entry and exit times are therefore determinant factors of a liquid market. A transaction for an identical number of contracts takes three times as long when done at lunch time between 13:00 and 13:30 as when US figures are released between 14:30 and 15:00.

3.3 SLIPPAGE

The discussion that follows looks at only one aspect of costs, slippage, which is a variable trading cost and gives an indication of relative liquidity. On the open outcry futures exchange, customer orders may be broken into smaller increments (to a minimum size of one contract) at the discretion of the floor broker. Thus if broker A is holding a customer order to buy 10 contracts at the market price and broker B is offering to sell six contracts, then broker A will buy six from broker B, and then perhaps buy four more from four separate floor traders trading for their own account, either at the same price or not. On electronic markets, broken execution is not uncommon either. By trading a small number of contracts at once, traders hope not to move the market against

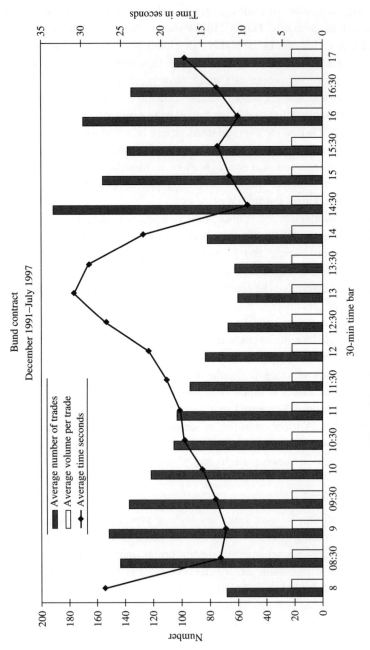

Figure 3.3 *Thirty-minute complementary statistics*

them. Surprisingly, the effect of broken execution on trading costs has not yet been quantified. Establishing time series of volume-weighted prices may be the way to measure the impact of size on trading.

More specifically, this article considers the execution of 1 to 350 lots at four different times of the day: 8:00, 11:00, 14:30 and 16:00. These times of the day have been chosen since they display interesting peculiarities. 8:00 is the opening of the market. 11:00 exhibits slightly below average volume and volatility. 14:30 is the most liquid and volatile time of the day. 16:00 displays slightly above average volume and volatility. The 'one-lot' study corresponds to the execution of one lot starting at 8:00, 11:00 and so on. Given the high volume of trades, the one-lot order is executed in the very first minute of each period. Then prices are linearly weighted per constant number of lots. The 'one-hundred-lots' study corresponds to the execution of one hundred lots starting at 08:00, 11:00 and so on.

There are two points to make. First, the duration of the fill can vary from a couple of seconds to more than 50 minutes depending not only on the size of the trade, but also on the particular day and time. Not to create spurious dependencies, starting times have been largely spaced and volumes have been aggregated up to 350 lots. Orders of more than 300 lots exist but are rather rare at the time of writing (1998) and were almost non-existent in 1991. For the period under scrutiny, this is still a large order amounting to almost 16 times the average trade size (22 lots).

Second, we have assumed that once an order was triggered, all the forthcoming lots traded on the exchange would be dedicated to fill this order. In practice, it is very difficult to assess how many 'parasite' orders would have occurred simultaneously, therefore postponing the total duration of the trade. In summary, if spurious dependencies are to be avoided, the sampling frequency must be low enough to include sufficient minimum volume.

Thompson and Waller (1988) estimate the bid–ask spread as the average absolute tick-to-tick price change over a time interval. Formally, if during an observation interval t there are n price changes observed, the estimated spread over this interval is:

$$S_{t-n} = \sum_{i=1}^{n} |P_{i-1} - P_i|$$

The primary limitation of this measure is that transactions price changes may be due to changes in the equilibrium price, rather than to movements between the bid and ask prices. This biases the spread estimate upwards. Here we propose a new spread measure which might be less biased. Let us note n the number of lots to trade and P_i the price at time t. We now assume that a trade of n lots has to be executed in the market. The average price at which the order will be executed is:

$$P_{t-n} = \frac{1}{n} \sum_{j=1}^{n} n_j P_{t_j}$$

where t is the time at which the order is triggered ($8:00, 11:00, \ldots, 16:00$), t_j the time at which a trade of size n_j has been done, and k the number of trades required to meet the trade size equal to $n = \sum_{j=1}^{k} n_j$.

Slippage has been defined as the difference between executing one and n lots. This difference can be negative when prices go down. To be realistic, we assume that a trader can only pay slippage on average. He cannot receive it. Basically when prices are going down overall, he must be selling, and when prices are going up he must be buying. Consequently, slippage has been defined as the absolute value of logarithmic returns. That is, $S_{t-n} = |\ln(P_{t-n}/P_{t-1}|$. Although pessimistic, this measure is still less conservative than existing measures of transaction costs. In fact, it is the absolute value of summed terms, not the sum of absolute values. Transactions price changes may be due to changes in the equilibrium price, rather than to movements between the bid and ask prices. By using the absolute value, we still consider that the average price is always more unfavourable than the first available price.

Slippage is by construction an increasing function of the number of contracts being traded. There are, however, sharp differences first between the times of the day at which the order is executed (Figure 3.4) and second between the varied subperiods (Figure 3.5). Transactions costs can even vary within a ratio 2 to 3. Unfortunately, there is no straightforward explanation to this phenomenon. For instance the increasing volume over the years might justify the lower slippage in 1997 but this does not tell us why slippage in 1994 was so much higher than in 1992. To get a proper understanding of these differences, a more detailed analysis of slippage has to be conducted. Studying variations of volume and volatility during the day and over the years might provide some valuable insights on slippage.

3.4   EMPIRICAL EVIDENCE AND ECONOMETRIC CHALLENGES

Statistics, volume, volatility and slippage data have been analysed over 70 quarterly periods from December 1991 to July 1997 at different times of the day: 08:00, 11:00, 14:30 and 16:00. Each observation represents average daily statistics over a quarter (more exactly 59 days). As an illustration, Figure 3.6 tells us that the average daily volume between 11:00 and 11:30 was 1051 lots for the first quarter starting in December 1991.

Rank correlation tests (Table 3.1) show that there is a significant positive relationship between market volatility and the total number of contracts traded,

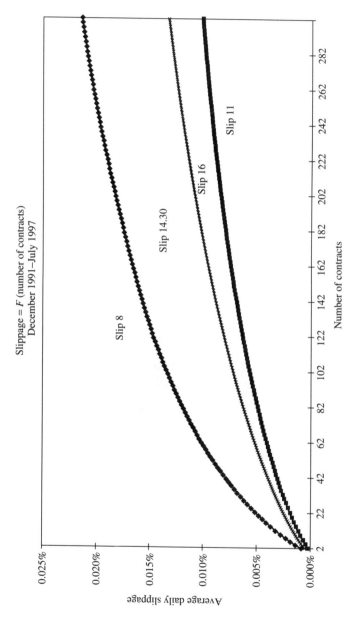

Figure 3.4 *Slippage at different times of the day*

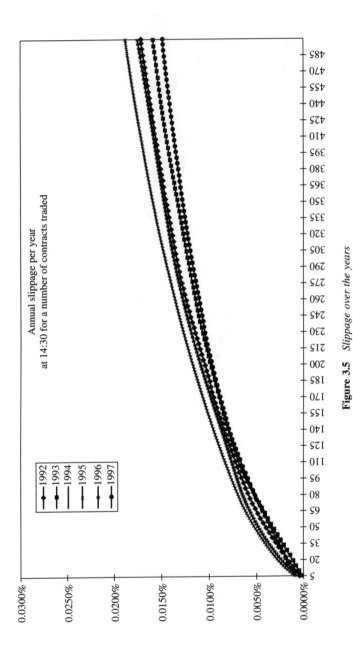

Figure 3.5   *Slippage over the years*

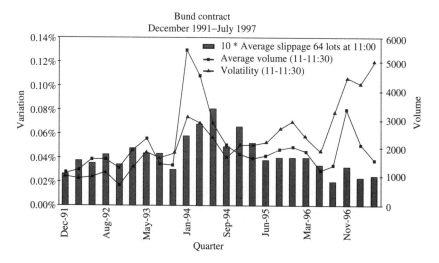

Figure 3.6 *Quarterly slippage, volume and volatility at 11:00*

Table 3.1 *Rank correlation between 30 minutes' volume and volatility*

Correlation/time	8:00	11:00	14:30	16:00
(Volume, volatility)	0.304*	0.528*	0.744*	0.719*

*Significantly positive at the critical levels of 5%.

confirming that periods of market stress are associated with high turnover. This is true at any time of the day.

Large positive volume shocks might increase volatility at a 30-minute frequency. However, at the tick frequency, prices in deep markets might move little in response to large volumes. Consequently, execution costs might increase far less than volatility and even decrease because of large volume. Therefore, to test each market's depth, slippage at different times of the day is regressed against volume and volatility measures. The problem with using raw statistics is that all of them, volume, volatility and slippage, exhibit massive asymmetry and positive serial dependencies.

Using logarithmic variations allows us to reduce persistent, time varying components in price variance, volume and slippage (Tables 3.2 to 3.4). Slippage on a small number of contracts (below 32) has not been considered in this section since this still exhibits too many zero values, even on a quarterly basis. Consequently, their log transformation might either be undefined or too asymmetric. For a larger number of contracts (above 32) this transformation stabilizes the variance of the error terms and allows the approximation of the error terms toward a symmetric distribution. Furthermore, resulting coefficients can be readily interpreted as the elasticities of quarterly slippage with respect

Table 3.2   *Quarterly logarithmic variations of 30 minutes' volume and volatility*

	Volume_8	Volume_11	Volume_14	Volume_16	Volatility_8	Volatility_11	Volatility_14	Volatility_16
Mean	1.6370%	2.8560%	3.2445%	3.4397%	-0.5827%	0.5707%	1.1545%	0.6573%
Min	39.7931%	28.2372%	26.3114%	27.7944%	37.9059%	41.6049%	42.7225%	37.5522%
Max	0.55	0.32	0.01	0.17	0.23	0.50	0.25	-0.09
Stdev	1.06	-0.26	2.49	0.39	-0.52	0.61	-0.24	-0.35
Skew	-0.17	-0.14	-0.20	-0.28	-0.25	-0.29	-0.36	-0.30
Kurt	-0.23	-0.31	-0.15	-0.01	-0.15	-0.20	-0.25	-0.15
r[1]	-0.28	-0.01	0.00	-0.12	-0.14	0.15	0.23	0.06
r[2]	0.29	0.15	0.02	0.06	0.18	0.01	-0.05	-0.07
r[3]	0.10	0.03	0.00	0.02	-0.19	0.00	-0.08	0.03
r[4]	-0.89	-0.63	-0.77	-0.61	-0.79	-0.76	-0.84	-0.79
r[5]	1.13	0.74	0.96	0.94	0.89	1.38	1.12	0.87

Table 3.3   *Quarterly logarithmic variations of slippage at 8:00 and 11:00*

	S8_32	S8_64	S8_128	S8_256	S11_32	S11_64	S11_128	S11_256
Mean	-5.5942%	-2.9933%	-2.0105%	-1.6055%	-0.1512%	-0.2665%	-0.1168%	-0.1895%
Min	77.8901%	52.4003%	45.1802%	36.8132%	78.5131%	44.9024%	33.1380%	28.8639%
Max	0.18	0.06	0.37	0.21	0.13	0.25	0.19	0.17
Stdev	-0.44	0.05	0.26	0.98	3.37	0.53	0.93	0.96
Skew	-0.56	-0.44	-0.50	-0.51	-0.40	-0.30	-0.36	-0.26
Kurt	0.01	-0.11	0.01	0.09	-0.18	-0.26	-0.13	-0.35
r[1]	0.15	0.09	-0.04	-0.08	0.06	0.04	0.03	0.24
r[2]	0.02	0.05	0.20	0.14	-0.10	-0.04	0.08	0.00
r[3]	-0.05	0.00	-0.15	-0.12	0.37	0.30	0.02	-0.09
r[4]	-1.84	-1.39	-0.97	-1.09	-2.83	-1.04	-0.88	-0.83
r[5]	1.73	1.27	1.19	1.09	2.76	1.30	0.99	0.78

Table 3.4 *Quarterly logarithmic variations of slippage at 8:00 and 11:00*

	S14_32	S14_64	S14_128	S14_256	S16_32	S16_64	S16_128	S16_256
Mean	−0.1492%	−0.6639%	−0.5217%	−0.5208%	−0.8383%	−1.1873%	−1.2724%	−0.7418%
Min	61.1220%	40.3733%	35.6176%	32.7661%	56.8530%	39.3584%	29.8675%	25.8982%
Max	−0.86	−0.13	0.09	−0.17	0.59	1.14	0.46	−0.07
Stdev	3.94	0.83	−0.08	0.03	2.28	3.23	0.87	−0.30
Skew	−0.33	−0.30	−0.41	−0.35	−0.45	−0.30	−0.15	−0.12
Kurt	−0.21	−0.16	0.06	0.01	−0.07	−0.18	−0.34	−0.30
r[1]	−0.07	−0.13	−0.19	−0.18	0.18	0.10	0.09	0.10
r[2]	0.25	0.13	0.07	0.06	−0.22	−0.06	−0.02	−0.20
r[3]	−0.01	0.14	0.02	−0.05	0.06	−0.05	−0.08	−0.06
r[4]	−2.56	−1.27	−0.84	−0.85	−1.45	−0.71	−0.68	−0.68
r[5]	1.47	0.92	0.88	0.76	2.05	1.61	0.85	0.48

to its explanatory variables, logarithmic variations in volume and volatility. We denote S_{i_j} the quarterly logarithmic variation of slippage at time i for j lots.

Slippage has been regressed against volume and volatility at the same time of the day. No dummy variables have been used given the small number of observations. Detailed results can be found in the Appendix. Overall R^2 are rather small and could be interpreted as disappointing. Nevertheless it seems that the cost of executing a large order is positively correlated with volatility and negatively correlated with volume.

Here it is interesting to note that statistical significance increases with the number of contracts and varies with the time of the day (Figure 3.7). In particular, the relationship between slippage and volatility is the strongest at 14:30 whereas the relationship between slippage and volume is the strongest at 8:00. The latter observation might be explained by the opening mechanism of the exchange. During the pre-opening period, traders influence the opening prices for option series or futures contracts through supply and demand, and the potential opening prices appear on the screens of all the traders. Orders and quotes can be entered that influence the formation of prices. During the netting phase, DTB nets all orders and quotes (netting) in order to determine the final opening prices for option series and futures contracts. Prices are determined on the basis of auctioning (the highest turnover principle). By nature, the opening volume is atypical and likely to be determinant in the evaluation of execution cost.

3.5   CONCLUSION

This chapter has highlighted some intraday statistics in the Bund futures market. Shapes of intraday volume, volatility have been established and a new measure of market liquidity has been defined as the cost of executing a given trading size. Slippage is an increasing function of the number of contracts. This is positively correlated with volatility and negatively correlated with volume. Our results confirm previous findings, namely that trading volume and transaction costs are jointly determined. Wang, Yau and Baptiste (1997) establish a positive relationship between trading volume and bid–ask spreads in many futures markets, after allowing for other factors. Our investigation shows, however, that the impact of volume and volatility on slippage differ greatly following the time of day. The variance of returns may not systematically translate into additional costs to liquidity traders.

Transaction costs could stay quite small despite a high variance of returns. Very large volumes might in fact 'absorb' any market shock. This phenomenon seems to occur in other markets. On the NYSE and AMEX, Brooks and Su (1997) report that the market-at-open order consistently produces better prices than market and limit orders executed during the trading day. In that market,

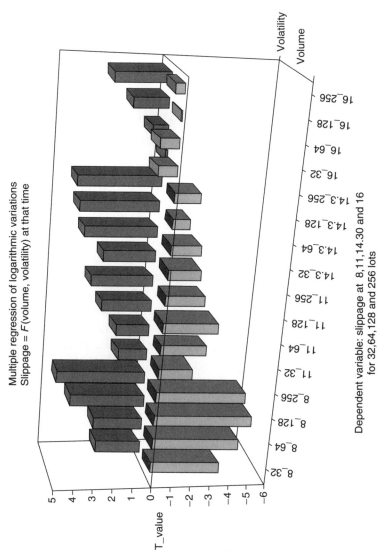

Figure 3.7 *Slippage regression: T_ values of volume and volatility coefficients*

a trader can reduce transaction costs by trading at the opening despite the fact that the variance in returns measured from opening prices is about 12% higher than that measured from closing prices.

Another issue of interest has been raised recently by many market participants and scholars. They have argued that open outcry markets should be substantially more liquid than computerized markets. However, Pirrong (1996) finds that the evidence from the DTB and LIFFE strongly suggests that an automated system can be more liquid and deeper than an open outcry market. It is hoped that volume statistics will be available in the LIFFE markets and that further research will say if the relationship between volume, volatility and slippage holds in the LIFFE market.

Finally, it must be recognized that liquidity is only one of the determinants of the cost of executing an order. Most importantly the cost of access may differ between LIFFE and DTB. For example, brokerage, exchange and clearing fees may differ between markets.

Further research is needed to refine the econometrics of this article and include an even larger data sample. In particular, dummy variables could be included in the regression. It might well be that volatility at different times of the day is a better explanatory variable of transaction costs. The purpose of this analysis has just been to introduce the concept of volume-weighted returns and their importance in assessing market liquidity. It has been argued here that intraday studies should not confine themselves to volume and volatility statistics but include some measurement of market deepness. Volume-weighted returns are just one measure of market liquidity. Price duration is another. Recent work has already started into time varying liquidity in the stock market (Engle and Lange, 1997). As the previous authors point out, market deepness is a simple concept but yet difficult to quantitatively measure.

3.6 APPENDIX   REGRESSION RESULTS

Table 3.5 R^2: *slippage at given times and number of lots against volume and volatility*

Time/No. of lots	32	64	128	256
8	0.174	0.239	0.313	0.319
11	0.050	0.080	0.126	0.134
14.3	0.097	0.178	0.232	0.234
16	0.017	0.045	0.060	0.155

Table 3.6 *Coefficients: slippage at given times and number of lots against volume and volatility*

Time	No. of lots	32		64		128		256	
		Coefficients	*t* Stat	Coefficients	*t* Stat	Coefficients	*t* Stat	Coefficients	*t* Stat
8	Intercept	−0.038	−0.443	−0.016	−0.289	−0.006	−0.141	−0.005	−0.142
	Volume	−0.864	−3.604*	−0.694	−4.484*	−0.649	−5.118*	−0.479	−4.659*
	Volatility	0.587	2.334*	0.414	2.549*	0.515	3.874*	0.503	4.659*
11	Intercept	0.015	0.158	0.010	0.197	0.010	0.259	0.004	0.128
	Volume	−0.655	−1.680*	−0.510	−2.325*	−0.441	−2.793*	−0.273	−1.993*
	Volatility	0.410	1.547	0.257	1.723*	0.275	2.569*	0.294	3.166*
14.30	Intercept	0.011	0.151	−0.002	−0.035	−0.005	−0.140	−0.003	−0.096
	Volume	−0.576	−1.699*	−0.328	−1.537	−0.155	−0.849	−0.210	−1.257
	Volatility	0.554	2.656*	0.485	3.684*	0.451	4.020*	0.433	4.203*
16	Intercept	−0.018	−0.257	−0.019	−0.405	−0.015	−0.407	−0.011	−0.373
	Volume	0.281	0.964	0.192	0.962	0.016	0.108	0.056	0.452
	Volatility	−0.029	−0.136	0.113	0.767	0.189	1.703*	0.248	2.719*

*Significantly different from zero at the 5% critical level.

REFERENCES

Amihud, Y. and Mendelson, H. (1987) Trading mechanisms and stock returns: an empirical investigation, *Journal of Finance*, **3**, 533–555.

Breedon, F. and Holland, A. (1997) *Bank of England*, Electronic versus open outcry markets: the case of the Bund futures contract, Working paper No. 76.

Brooks, R.M. and Su, T. (1997) A simple cost reduction strategy for small liquidity traders: Trade at the Opening, *Journal of Financial and Quantitative Analysis*, **32**(4), 525–539.

Buckle, M., Thomas, S.H. and Woodhams, M.S. (1995) Intraday empirical regularities in LIFFE data, working paper, European Business Management School, University of Wales.

Chang, E.C., Jain, P.C. and Locke, P.R. (1995) Standard & Poor's 500 index futures volatility and price changes around the New York Stock Exchange close, *Journal of Business*, **68**, 61–84.

Daigler, R.T. (1997), Intraday futures volatility and theories of market behaviour, *Journal of Futures Markets*, **17**, 45–74.

Engle, R.F. and Lange, J. (1997), Measuring, forecasting and explaining time varying liquidity in the stock market, University of California, San Diego, discussion paper 97–12R.

Engle, R.F. and Russell, J.R. (1998) Autoregressive conditional duration: a new model for irregularly spaced transaction data, (Forthcoming in *Econometrica*).

Hans Franses, P., van Ieperen, R., Kofman, P., Martens, M. and Menkveld, B. (1994) Volatility patterns and spillovers in Bund futures, Erasmus University Rotterdam, ECFR 94–02.

Harris, L.E. (1987) Transaction data tests of the mixture of distributions hypothesis, *Journal of Financial and Quantitative Analysis*, **22**, 127–142.

Karpoff, J.M. (1986) A theory of trading volume, *Journal of Finance*, **41**(5), 1069–1088.

Karpoff, J.M. (1987) The relationship between price changes and trading volume: a survey, *Journal of Financial and Quantitative Analysis*, **3**, 169–176.

Kleidon, A. and Werner, I. (1996) Round-the-clock trading: evidence from UK cross listed securities, *Review of Financial Studies*, **9**, 619–664.

Kofman, P. and Moser, J.T. (1995) Spreads, information flows and transparency across trading systems, Federal Reserve Bank of Chicago, WP 95–1.

Müller, U.A., Dacorogna, M.M., Olsen, R.B., Pictet, O.V., Schwarz, M. and Morgenegg, C. (1990) Statistical study of foreign exchange rates, empirical evidence of a price change scaling law and intra-day analysis, *Journal of Banking and Finance*, (14), 1189–1208.

Pirrong, C. (1996) Market liquidity and depth on computerised and open outcry trading systems: a comparison of DTB and LIFFE Bund contracts, *Journal of Futures Markets*, **16**, 519–543.

Stoll, H. and Whaley, R. (1990) Stock market structure and volatility, *Review of Financial Studies*, **3**, 37–71.

Thompson, S. and Waller, M. (1988) Determinants of liquidity costs in commodity futures markets, *Journal of Futures Markets*, **14**, 437–455.

Wang, G.H, Yau, J. and Baptiste, T. (1997) Trading volume and transaction costs in futures markets, *Journal of Futures Markets*, **17**, 757–780.

Wood, R.A., McInish, T.H. and Ord, J.K. (1985) An investigation of transactions data for NYSE stocks, *Journal of Finance*, **3**, 723–741.

NOTES

1. We would like to thank Eric Kuder for his computing assistance.
2. We are indebted to the DTB Business Development for their help in obtaining the data.

Chapter 4

Real trading volume and price action in the foreign exchange markets

PIERRE LEQUEUX*

SUMMARY

The information content of trading volume and its effect on the price structure of financial markets has always been an abundant topic in both the academic and market practitioner literature. Amongst market practitioners it is a generally accepted fact that the volume traded is closely tied to important turning points in market trends. This largely explains the numerous technical indicators that rely on both volume and price data. From the point of view of a market maker the distribution of volume through the day is a very important statistic not solely for the information contents it might carry but also because it might help him to execute orders at a better price by underlining recurrent intradaily pockets of liquidity. Due to the generalized lack of high-frequency data for both volume and price these relationships have not yet been fully investigated for the OTC currency markets. Indeed whereas transaction data is plentiful for exchange traded products most of the analysis for foreign exchange has to rely on samples made of indicative quotes contributed by market makers to data providers. Consequently the samples used in some research might not reflect what is the 'true price' action. Also, because there is no data on volume associated to these contributed prices, researchers generally have to resort to various schemes based on the frequency of information arrival to obtain estimates of the underlying volume without always being able to ascertain empirically the validity of their models. This chapter uses a two-week sample of *real traded price and associated volume* from US dollar

Continued on page 118

* Banque Nationale de Paris plc, UK.

___ *Continued from page 117* ___

versus Deutschemarks traded in the FX OTC market to investigate empirically some of the relationships that are thought to govern trading volume and price action in the OTC foreign exchange markets.

The information content of trading volume and its effect on the price structure of financial markets has always been an abundant topic in both the academic and market practitioner literature. Amongst market practitioners it is a generally accepted fact that the volume traded is closely tied to important turning points in market trends (Schwager, 1984; Kaufman, 1987). This largely explains the numerous technical indicators that rely on both volume and price data. From the point of view of a market maker the distribution of volume through the day is a very important statistic not solely for the directional information content it might carry but also because it might help him to execute orders at a better price by underlining recurrent intradaily pockets of liquidity. Due to the generalized lack of reliable high-frequency data for both volume and price these relationships have not yet been fully investigated in the OTC currency markets. Indeed whereas transaction data is plentiful for exchange traded products most of the analysis for foreign exchange generally rely on samples made of indicative quotes contributed by market makers to data providers. Consequently the samples used in past research might not reflect perfectly what is the 'true price' action. Because there is no data on volume associated to these prices contributed researchers had to resort to various schemes based on the frequency of information arrival to obtain estimates of the underlying volume without always being able to ascertain empirically the validity of their models other than by testing it on futures markets.

This chapter highlights some of the relationships that are thought to govern trading volume and price action by using a two-week sample of *real traded price and associated volume* from one of the most traded currency pairs in the FX OTC market. In a first part we give some general market statistics on the foreign exchange markets. We then give a description of EBS,[1] an electronic broking system which is used by a wide spectrum of foreign exchange market participants. Finally we look at some of the features of US dollar versus Deutschemark spot prices and traded volume by investigating a sample of transactions recorded over a period of two weeks.

4.1 THE CURRENCY MARKET

The foreign exchange market is without any doubt the largest financial market in the world. It has a turnover which exceeds by far other markets such as stocks

and bonds. In May 1996 the Bank for International Settlement reported an estimated daily turnover of $1260 bn in the FX currency market for the year 1995.
The figures computed in its previous surveys were respectively $880 bn in 1992
and $620 bn in 1989 (Table 4.1). Most of the foreign exchange trading volume
takes place within three main financial centres, the United Kingdom ($464 bn),
the United States ($244 bn) and Japan ($161 bn). These three centres accounted
for about 55% of the total turnover in FX markets according to the 1996 'BIS'
survey. The surplus of activity generated by these three centres can generally
be noticed through the statistical analysis of high-frequency returns and is often
quoted as a good explanation of the intradaily changing pattern of volatility.

Out of the total turnover declared, 60% is generated principally by the
trading of four currency pairs, namely, USD–DEM (22%), USD–JPY (21%),
GBP–USD (7%) and USD–CHF (5%). The estimated turnover for the major
currency pairs is shown in Table 4.2. An interesting feature is the market share
of each of these currencies which remained relatively stable through the years.

The foreign exchange market is characterized by the liquidity it offers on large
trades, the 24-hour access it provides to participants, the great number of traded
currencies and the absence of a pre-determined contract size. Leverage is readily
accessible for the investor/hedger with margin requirements that are usually
only 5%–10% of the face value of a contract. Contrary to stocks, transaction
costs are very small, they are estimated at 0.05% per trade in the inter-bank
foreign exchange at the most. Large operators are able to reduce brokerage fees
considerably and therefore incur mainly liquidity costs (bid–ask spread). Both
the low transaction costs feature and the high liquidity of Forex allows for high-
frequency trading which would not be possible for other markets (except some
future markets). Unlike most investments, trading on the currency markets can
produce profits not only when prices are rising but also when they are falling.
In spite of the widespread affirmation that in the long run, the return on passive
currency investment is nil, there is statistical evidence that active management
of currencies can significantly add value over time due to the low efficiency

Table 4.1 *Daily foreign exchange turnover ($bn)*

Type	1989	1992	1995
Spot	350	400	520
Forwards and swaps	240	420	670
Futures and options	30	60	70
Total	620	880	1,260

Source: Central bank survey of foreign exchange and
derivatives market activity conducted by the Monetary
and Economic Department of the Bank for International
Settlements, May 1996.

Table 4.2   *Daily turnover per currency pair in $bn*

	1992	% Total	1995	% Total	% Var
USD/DEM	192.2	24.50%	253.9	22.30%	−2.20%
USD/JPY	154.8	19.70%	242	21.30%	1.60%
GBP/USD	76.5	9.70%	77.6	6.80%	−2.90%
USD/CHF	48.8	6.20%	60.5	5.30%	−0.90%
USD/CAD	25.4	3.20%	51	4.50%	1.20%
GBP/DEM	23.3	3.00%	38.2	3.40%	0.40%
USD/FRF	18.6	2.40%	34.4	3.00%	0.70%
DEM/JPY	18.2	2.30%	28.7	2.50%	0.20%
AUD/USD	17.9	2.30%	24	2.10%	−0.20%
DEM/CHF	13.3	1.70%	21.3	1.90%	0.20%
Others	195.9	25.00%	305.3	26.90%	1.90%
Total	784.9		1136.90		

Source: Central bank survey of foreign exchange and derivatives market activity conducted by the Monetary and Economic Department of the Bank for International Settlements, May 1996.

of these markets (Arnott and Pham, 1993; Kritzman, 1989; Silber, 1994, to name only a few). These features have probably contributed tremendously to the increase in foreign exchange turnover (more than 100% from 1989 to 1995).

Whereas it was common practice to trade large transactions over telex only 10 years ago, the explosion in communication technology and demand for FX prices have radically changed the tools used in modern dealing rooms. Perhaps one of the most important features over the recent years as been the introduction of the electronic broking system that has succeeded in taking a large market share out of the voice brokers (which they probably will dwarf over the few years to come). Such systems were introduced in September 1992 in Japan and were reported, by the Bank of Japan, to account for 32% of the total brokered spot transactions in February 1996 (BIS, 1996). Similarly they have been introduced in other centres and are now an indispensable work tool for the spot trader. This new way of trading has undoubtedly brought some changes within the FX markets such as greater transparency of prices, better estimation of market liquidity, narrowing of bid–ask spread and reduction of execution costs. These systems are also a source of data for transaction records that are truly representative of what happens in FX markets contrary to the indicative quotes that banks contribute to data feeds.

When using indicative quotes contributed, for example, to a screen like Reuters FXFX (probably one of the most used sources of data source in academic and practitioner research), bid–ask spreads of 10 points in USD–DEM are commonly observed whereas the true spread quoted in the markets is usually around a couple of points. This probably raises some questions regarding results that have been conducted on the intraday behaviour of the Bid–Ask spread.

During periods of high activity there might be significant staleness of the indicative prices contributed due to the obvious priority for a spot dealer to trade instead of updating his indicative quotes. This will affect the results of some research conducted on price behaviour at the outset of economic figures. Some researchers have tried to eradicate the problem by using time and sales generated by spot trading desks of some banks. Though the approach is surely one step ahead of using indicative quotes there is still the impact of the credit rating of the bank which supplied the sample of data and the type of counterparts it works with. A bank with a high credit rating will obtain a better bid–ask spread than what a third name would get. Overall the quality of the data that is used by most of the analysts is not quite satisfactory. Saying that, quite a lot of features observed on indicative quotes remain satisfactory as long they do not address a too high-frequency time horizon. Interestingly, recently a few papers using samples of transactions obtained from electronic broking systems have been released (Evans, 1998; Goodhardt, Ito and Pague, 1996, for example). These papers emphasize the strong interest of researchers to use such data samples. Unfortunately due to the difficulty encountered in obtaining data samples with a statistically meaningful number of observations these papers remains sparse. The rarity of the data is principally linked to issues of confidentiality and transparency but we can probably expect to see the data providers yielding under the pressure of the demand to the benefit of risk management.

Electronic broking systems are multilateral trading platforms which market participants use to trade between themselves. These systems record all the transactions for a large panel of market participants. They are one of the most accurate sources of data for the transactions occurring in the FX markets. Contrary to samples of data obtained from bilateral dealing systems such as Reuters 2000-1 (Evans, 1998), they keep a timestamp for when the bargain occurred, whereas 2000-1 records the time at which the conversation started, hence the order of the event might vary depending on how much time the trader takes to quote its counterpart and on how many quotes it provided. Also one of the problems that might arise in using data coming from a bilateral system is that the trader quoting the price might well mark up or down his quote to show where his 'interest' is, consequently it might not reflect perfectly what the true 'market' was at this precise moment. Electronic broking systems as a data source by far outweigh other feeds in terms of quality, though they represent only part of the flow taking place in the market. In the following we review one such system.

4.2 DESCRIPTION OF THE EBS SYSTEM

In January 1990 12 of the world's leading foreign exchange market-making banks decided to finance the development of an electronic broking system for trading inter-bank spot foreign exchange. One of the main objectives was to provide effective competition to the system provided by Reuters (2002), then the main provider of transaction services to the foreign exchange community. Since then EBS has obtained a large share of the spot FX broking market. It is now considered the world's leading electronic foreign exchange broker with average traded volumes in excess of \$90 bn[2] a day. There are now around 800 banks using EBS to trade 19 currency pairs.[3] EBS is considered as one of the top five brokers in the London market with an estimated 45% of market share whilst it has 70% in Singapore and around 60% of all the dollar/Deutschemark and dollar/yen broking activity in Tokyo.

Figure 4.1 shows the typical screen-based system that a currency trader would use to trade spot foreign exchange transactions.

The EBS screen displays all the necessary trading information that a spot trader requires to trade efficiently in the currency markets. The screen is split in various sections:

- Rates section: Displays the best-quoted prices in real time and gives a continuous and comprehensive overview of the electronic broking market.
- Credit Information: Pre-trade credit screening and warning panels indicate that a counterparty is approaching its pre-determined credit limit (yellow) or has reached it (red), providing essential information critical to minimizing counterparty risk.
- Price section: The EBS multiple currency display allows for a dealer to trade up to three currency pairs simultaneously. All dealable prices displayed are prescreened for credit risk.
- Deals section: Where all relevant information of trades executed over EBS are listed by individual traders and on EBS as a whole.

The next section concentrates on the analysis of a sample of USD–DEM transactions executed through the EBS system.

4.3   EMPIRICAL STUDY OF RECORDED TRANSACTIONS

Our study concentrates on a sample of 170 369 transactions recorded from 1 October 1997 to 14 October 1997 for USD–DEM (Figure 4.2) which represented a total amount traded of US\$374 bn. We chose to use this parity because it is undoubtedly the most widely traded currency pair (Table 4.2). It also tends to be equally traded throughout the three main FX centres, London, New York and Tokyo, unlike the USD–JPY. For each record we were provided with a timestamp, a price and amount traded as well as the type of quote (given or paid).

4.4   NUMBER OF TRANSACTIONS, VOLUME AND VOLATILITY

Figure 4.3 shows how the trading volume and the associated number of transactions were distributed over an average day of 24 hours. During this

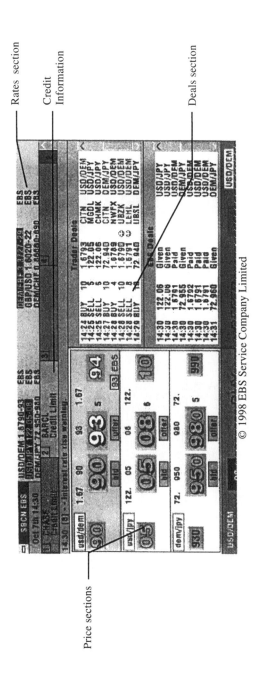

© 1998 EBS Service Company Limited

Figure 4.1 *EBS spot dealing system screen*

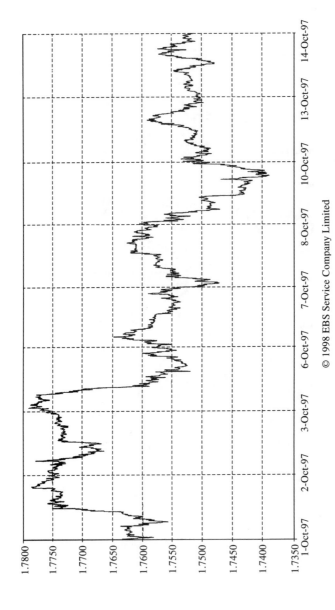

Figure 4.2 *Historical spot price of USD–DEM 1 October 1997 to 14 October 1997*

© 1998 EBS Service Company Limited

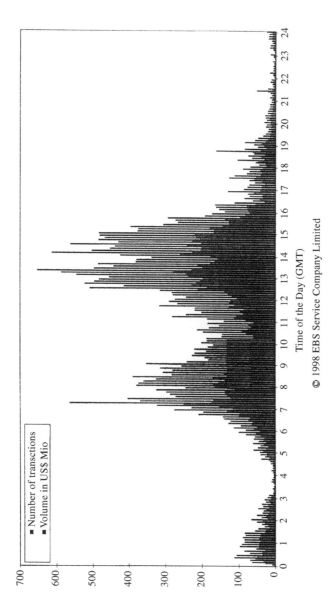

Figure 4.3 *Distribution of the volume traded and number of transaction throughout the day*

period of 24 hours the bulk of the trading is shared through three financial centres, Tokyo (23:00 to 07:00 GMT), London (7:00 to 16:00 GMT) and New York (13:00 to 21:00 GMT). We can observe that most of the activity seems to take place principally between 7:00 GMT and 15:00 GMT. This agrees with BIS research that designates London and New York as the two main centres for foreign exchange turnover; London covers most of the activity whilst New York enjoys only part of it. During this period the volume and number of transactions reach their highest peaks. The first peak occurs at 7:00 GMT and corresponds to the opening of Europe and close of Tokyo. Then the biggest surge in activity occurs between 13:00 and 16:00 GMT (respectively the estimated opening of New York and the close of London). It is made of two subpeaks a one corresponding to the opening of the US T-bond markets and the other one to the opening New York Stock Exchange respectively at 13:20 GMT and 14:30 GM. Such a pattern has been similarly observed by previous studies such as Bollerslev and Domovitz (1993) and Guillaume *et al.* (1995).

We can note a U-shape pattern occurring between 7:00 and 16:00 GMT for both volume and number of transactions. We can also notice an L-shape pattern from 16:00 to 24:00 and a smaller U-shape from 24:00 to 7:00. This clustering of volatility at the estimated open and close of trading sessions has been described extensively by the academic literature for a large number of markets (Sutcliffe, 1997). This pattern can be explained by the fact that the use of risk for a trader is not the same and depends an whether he is holding a position during or outside his trading session. If he keeps an overnight position he will have to use his overnight trading limits in conjunction with stops loss/take profit order; in fact most of the FX traders are intraday traders. Traders adjust their positions to reflect this utility for risk (and potential reward) at the open and close of their market session.

The intraday distribution of the volume displays the same type pattern seen for intraday volatility (Figures 4.3 and 4.4) due to the fact that volume is an estimator of volatility (Buckle, Thomas and Woodhams, 1995).

When investigating the data we note that there was slightly more paid transactions (52.75%) recorded than given ones (47.25%). The average size of each individual deal is quite small (around US\$ 2.5 Mio, Figure 4.5) when compared with the average transaction size usually undertaken over the phone or Reuters 2000-1 dealing system (US\$5 to 10 Mio). An interesting feature is the relative stability of the average trade put through EBS over a typical 24-hour trading day though ticket size slightly increases between 7:00 and 16:00.

Because electronic broking systems match one's order with counterparts for which there are trading limits available, it is highly likely that a market participant executing a large transaction will see his order matched by a series of smaller transactions adding up to his desired amount. For this reason our

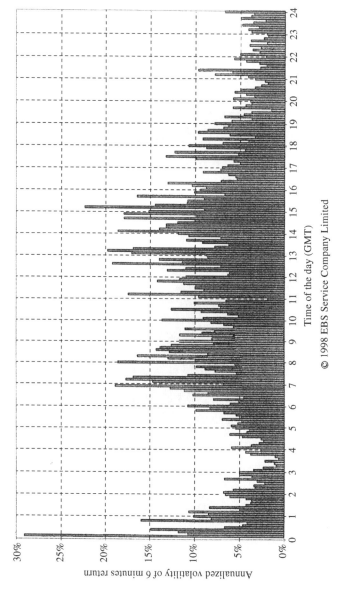

Figure 4.4 *Annualized intraday volatility returns*

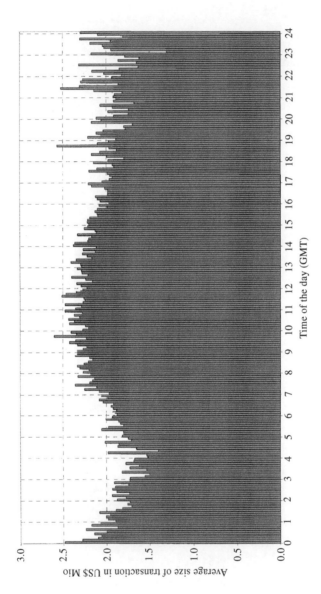

Figure 4.5   *Average ticket size throughout the trading day*

Table 4.3 *Summary statistics of the traded*

	Volume
Mean	6.51
Median	4.00
Min	1.00
Max	117.00
Std Dev.	7.29
Kurtosis	15.47
Skew	3.07
Sum	374147

following research is conducted on derived time series for which we aggregated all the transactions of the same type that follow each other. We created new time series for which we have the following information:

- Timestamp.
- Type of quote (given/paid).
- Price at the beginning of the (paid/given) segment.
- Weighted price over the (paid/given) segment.
- Number of transactions over the (paid/given) segment.
- Total volume transacted over the (paid/given) segment.

The average consecutive volume paid/given through EBS (Table 4.3) is US$6.51 Mio, which is more in line with the usual amount traded by market makers. We note a high kurtosis value indicating the presence of extreme values.

4.5 LIQUIDITY COST (PROFIT)

For a trader who handles customer flows the estimation of how 'deep' the market is, is crucial because his revenues will depend principally on the bid–ask spread he will earn on the transaction executed. Consequently it is paramount for a trader to be able to gauge market liquidity to anticipate what would be the effect of executing a large order and adjust the bid–ask spread accordingly to the level of risk taken. The liquidity cost, often referred to as slippage by the market practitioner, is calculated as being the variation between the average execution price and the initial execution price. This measure provides a good measure of liquidity contrary to other measures such as the number of transactions or the total amount traded which do not incorporate any notion of cost. To evaluate this cost we calculated for each of the string of given/paid transactions registered an estimated cost of liquidity as follows:

$$c = \left[\ln \left(\frac{Pw_t}{P_{t-1}} \right) - \ln \left(\frac{P_t}{P_{t-1}} \right) \right] \times Qt$$

where P_t = spot price, Pw_t = weighted spot price and Qt = quote type (paid $+1$, given -1).

The value c represents the cost/profit that a trader would have incurred whilst executing a transaction in the market. It is important to note that the slippage can be either a cost or a profit for the trader who executes an order. So in the following liquidity cost will have to be understood as the incertitude in the execution price. 'Reverse slippage' as best described in Taleb (1997) can occur when a trader 'quietly' establishes a long/short position in the market creating an imbalance in the market inventory and consequently using this imbalance to drive the market toward favourable price levels. In the following we look at the relationship between liquidy cost and the amount traded and also at how the 'liquidity cost' is distributed during the trading day.

4.6   LIQUIDITY COST AND VOLUME

The results obtained from our sample indicate that there is strong evidence of 'reverse slippage' but also that in general slippage tends to be a cost more than an 'unexpected' profit as indicated by the negative mean and skew of the series which shows an asymmetric distribution the tails of which extend more towards negative values (Table 4.4). The liquidity cost remains small overall and highly non-normal as shown by the high kurtosis value.

Maybe more interestingly we can clearly see that the bigger the amount traded the more likely the slippage will be a cost (Figures 4.6 and 4.7). The liquidity cost is a positive function of the size of the transaction. The higher the volume the higher the impact on the market (more noticeable by other market makers) and consequently the higher the cost of execution due to the price adjusting.

4.7   LIQUIDITY COST AND TIME OF THE DAY

Figure 4.8 indicates the bounds within which the liquidity cost varies during the trading day. Because of the changing intraday volatility (number of market participants active) we have the liquidity cost varying during the day. The liquidity cost tends to peak at the same time as the volatility and volume do.

Table 4.4 *Liquidity cost summary statisitics*

Average	−0.0002%
Max	0.0593%
Min	−0.0704%
Std Dev.	0.000037
Skew	−0.82
Kurtosis	26.29

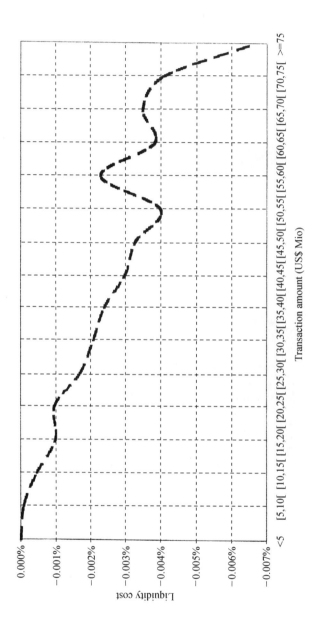

© 1998 EBS Service Company Limited

Figure 4.6 *Average liquidity cost as a function of the volume traded*

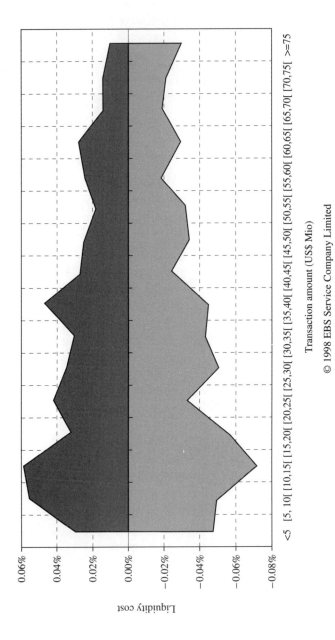

Figure 4.7 *Minimum and maximum liquidity cost as a function of the volume traded*

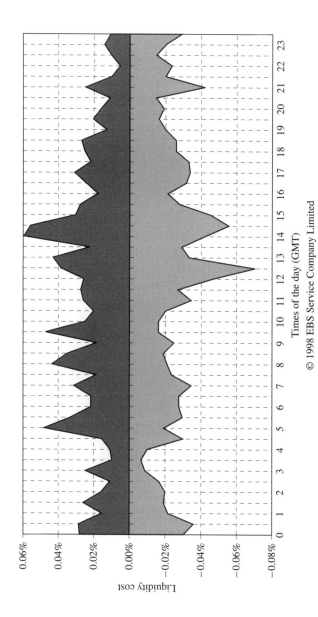

Figure 4.8 *Maximum/minimum liquidity cost observed as a function of the time of the day*

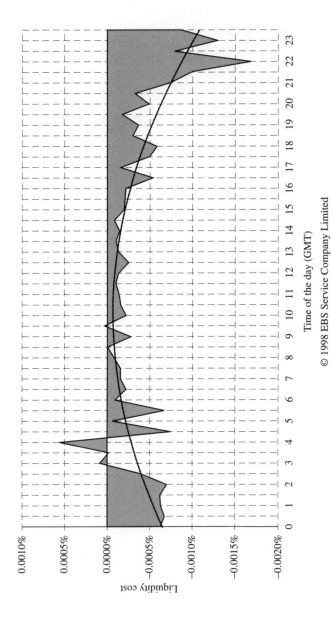

Figure 4.9   *Average liquidity cost as a function of the time of the day*

When we look at Figure 4.9 it is obvious that there is some period of the day were liquidity cost can be minimized. The best time for a large execution is probably between 6:00 and 15:00 and the worst time between 21:00 and 24:00 GMT. It would seem that the higher the volatility the smaller the liquidity cost and less likely it is to move the market by executing an order.

4.8   FINAL REMARKS

In this chapter we have highlighted some of the problems that may arise when using different sources of data to conduct empirical research in the foreign exchange market. We then reviewed some of the foreign exchange statistics and described an electronic broking system. Next we underlined how the volume was linked to number of transactions and volatility. We have also investigated the liquidity cost issue for the trader by estimating the cost of executing a transaction at various levels of size but also at various times of the day. We found that size and time matter when executing a transaction. There is some time of the day were slippage should be less. The transactions records provided by electronic broking systems can without doubt allow for a better understanding of how market participants interact. in the market place and how transactions can impact the price structure to an extent that was not possible when using indicative time price series.

REFERENCES

Arnott, R.D. and Pham, T.K. (1993) Tactical currency allocation, *Financial Analysts Journal*, 47–52.

Bank for International Settlements Monetary and Economic Department (1996) Central bank survey of foreign exchange and derivatives market activity 1995, Basle.

Bollerslev, T. and Domowitz, I. (1993) Trading patterns and prices in the interbank foreign exchange market, *Journal of Finance*, Vol. XLVIII, No. 4.

Buckle, S. Thomas, H. and Woodhams, M.S. (1995) Intraday empirical regularities in LIFFE data, Presentation at the International Conference Sponsored by Chemical Bank and Imperial College, March 1995, in London.

Evans, M. (1998) The microstructure of foreign exchange dynamics, HFDF 1998.

Guillaume, D., Dacorogna, M., Dave, R., Muller, U., Olsen, R. and Pictet, O. (1995) From the bird's eye to the microscope: a survey of new stylized facts of the intradaily foreign exchange markets, discussion paper by the O&A Research group.

Goodhart, C., Itô, T. and Payne, R. (1996) One day in June 1993: a study of the working of Reuters 2000-2 electronic foreign exchange trading system, in Frankel *et al.* (eds), *The Microstructure of Foreign Exchange Markets*, Chicago Press.

Kaufman, P.J. (1987) *The New Commodity Trading Systems and Methods*, John Wiley & Sons, New York.

Kritzman, M. (1989) Serial dependence in currency returns: investment implications, *Journal of Portfolio Management*, volume 16(1), 96–102.

Schwager, J. (1984) *A Complete Guide to the Futures Markets*, New York: John Wiley & Sons.

Silber, L.W. (1994) Technical trading: when it works and when it doesn't, *Journal of Derivatives*, Spring, 39–44.

Sutcliffe, C. (1997) *Stock Index Futures*, London: International Thompson Business Press.

Taleb, N. (1997) *Dynamic Hedging, Managing Vanilla and Exotic Options*, New York: John Wiley & Sons Inc.

NOTES

1. The author is thankful to EBS service company who provided the data sample used in this research and Tina Kane at EBS service company whose comments and remarks helped to further this chapter.
2. One side of the transaction only.
3. USD/DEM, DEM/FRF, USD/JPY, DEM/CHF, GBP/DEM, GBP/USD, DEM/JPY, USD/CHF, USD/FRF, USD/CAD, DEM/BEF, DEM/ITL, AUD/USD, XEU/DEM, DEM/ESP, DEM/SEK, DEM/DKK, DEM/FIM, DEM/NOK and USD/HKD.

Chapter 5

Implied risk-neutral probability density functions from option prices: a central bank perspective

BHUPINDER BAHRA*

5.1 INTRODUCTION

Apart from being a key component in financial option pricing models, estimates of future uncertainty have important implications in a wide range of decision-making processes, including portfolio selection, risk management, the evaluation of real investment options, the conduct of monetary and fiscal policy, and the management of financial guarantees by regulators.[1] The most widely used estimate of future uncertainty is the return variance that is implied by an option's price. This measure, known as the *implied volatility*, is the market's *ex-ante* estimate of the underlying asset's return volatility over the remaining life of the option. More interestingly, (European) option prices may be used to derive not only the implied variance of future asset values, but also their implied higher moments, for example skewness and kurtosis.[2] These can be extracted in the form of an *ex-ante* risk-neutral probability distribution of the underlying asset price at the maturity date (or terminal date) of the options.

The Black–Scholes (1973) option pricing formula assumes that the price of the underlying asset evolves according to a particular stochastic process known as *geometric Brownian motion* (GBM). Such a process is consistent with a lognormal probability distribution for the terminal value of the asset. However, the empirical observation that asset price (returns) distributions are fat tailed and

---

* Monetary Instruments and Markets Division, Bank of England, Threadneedle Street, London EC2R 8AH. E-mail: bhupi.bahra@bankofengland.co.uk

The views expressed in this chapter are those of the author and do not necessarily reflect those of the Bank of England. The author would like to thank Creon Butler (Bank of England), Neil S. Cooper (Bank of England), Simon Hayes (Bank of England), Stewart Hodges (University of Warwick, FORC), Cedric Kohler (Union Bank of Switzerland), Allan Malz (Federal Reserve Bank of New York), Jim Steeley (University of Cardiff), Charles Thomas (Federal Reserve Board), and Sanjay Yadav (Barclays Global Investors) for their comments and for many helpful discussions.

skewed relative to the lognormal (normal) distribution results in traders pricing options that are deeply away-from-the-money higher than is consistent with the Black–Scholes model. This chapter begins by showing how the prices of European options, on the same underlying asset and with the same time to maturity, observed across a range of different exercise prices, can be used to determine the market's implied risk-neutral density (RND) function for the price of the underlying asset on the maturity date of the options. We develop a technique for doing this and apply it to LIFFE short sterling futures options to estimate the market's implied RND for future levels of UK short-term interest rates.[3]

The implied RND, whilst encapsulating the information contained in implied volatilities, helps complete the market's profile of asset price uncertainty. This type of information is valuable to both monetary authorities and market participants. For monetary authorities, it provides a new way of gauging market sentiment. We illustrate how the information contained in implied RND functions can assist policy-makers in assessing monetary conditions, monetary credibility, the timing and effectiveness of monetary operations, and in identifying anomalous market prices. For market traders, it provides a quantitative probabilistic view, and hence an alternative way of examining the information embedded in option prices and comparing it across markets. The implied RND can help traders in pricing and hedging certain types of exotic options more efficiently, and in formulating optimal trading strategies.

That options are not priced strictly in accordance with the Black–Scholes model can be seen via the market's implied volatility *smile* curve, which usually shows implied volatility as a convex function of the exercise price of the option.[4] The existence of a convex smile curve poses a problem for volatility forecasters: which volatility estimate on the smile curve is the 'correct' market estimate of future volatility? A commonly used measure is the implied volatility backed out of the Black–Scholes price of the option that is trading *at-the-money* (ATM).[5] However, given that the smile curve is not flat, the ATM implied volatility is not necessarily the 'optimum' estimate of future volatility. So, a considerable amount of research has been carried out assessing the information content of Black–Scholes implied volatilities relative to that of alternative volatility forecasts.[6]

To overcome the 'smile effect', researchers sometimes take some sort of weighted average of the Black–Scholes implied volatilities observed across the smile curve as an alternative, and potentially more efficient, estimate of future volatility. In more recent studies analysing the information content of implied volatilities, the Black–Scholes model is dropped altogether and implied volatilities are instead backed out from option pricing models that better account for fat-tailed (non lognormal) empirical asset price distributions. These include time-varying volatility models allowing for systematic volatility risk.[7]

It is in the spirit of this latter strand of research that we conduct an analysis of the information content of different measures of future uncertainty in the UK short-term interest rate market. However, rather than assume a particular option pricing model to calculate implied volatilities, we illustrate how the implied RND function itself can be employed as a type of volatility forecasting tool by using it to calculate two alternative measures of uncertainty. This distributional approach is more general since it makes no assumptions about the underlying asset's stochastic price process. And, since the RND-based measures take into account the skewness and excess kurtosis components of the smile curve, they should, in principle, be informationally superior to Black–Scholes ATM implied volatilities.

Using a database of historical implied RND functions calculated using a two-lognormal mixture distribution approach, we are able to conduct an econometric analysis of the forecasting ability of the two implied RND-based uncertainty measures that we calculate. More specifically, we use non-overlapping options data on LIFFE short sterling futures going back to December 1987 to examine the out-of-sample performance (in terms of predictive power, unbiasedness and informational efficiency) of the two implied RND-based measures and compare it with that of traditional Black–Scholes ATM implied volatilities. We find consistent evidence for the predictive power of all three estimates of future uncertainty. We also find that over forecast horizons of 2 and 3 months the three measures are unbiased predictors of future volatility. However, we find no evidence that the RND-based measures are informationally superior to Black–Scholes ATM implied volatilities in the UK short-term interest rate market.

5.2 THE RELATIONSHIP BETWEEN OPTION PRICES AND RND FUNCTIONS

Consider that, under risk neutrality, the time-t price of a European call option with exercise price X and time-to-maturity $\tau = T - t$, denoted $c(X, \tau)$, can be written as the discounted sum of all expected future payoffs:[8]

$$c(X, \tau) = e^{-r\tau} \int_X^\infty q(S_T)(S_T - X)\, dS_T \tag{5.1}$$

where r is the (annualized) risk-free rate of interest over period τ, S_T is the terminal, or time-T, price of the underlying asset, and $q(S_T)$ is the RND function of S_T conditioned on the time-t price of the underlying asset, S.

The second partial derivative of the call pricing function, $c(X, \tau)$, with respect to the exercise price, gives the discounted RND function of S_T:[9]

$$\frac{\partial^2 c(X, \tau)}{\partial X^2} = e^{-r\tau} q(S_T | S_T = X) \tag{5.2}$$

This precise relationship – between the prices of European call options on the same underlying asset, and with the same time to maturity, T, but with a range of different exercise prices, X, and the weights attached by the representative risk-neutral agent to the possible outcomes for the price of the underlying asset on the maturity date of the options – was first noted by Breeden and Litzenberger (1978). The result can be interpreted more intuitively by noting that the difference in the price of two call options with adjacent exercise prices reflects the value attached to the ability to exercise the options when the price of the underlying asset lies between their exercise prices. This clearly depends on the probability of the underlying asset price lying in this interval.

5.3   THE BLACK–SCHOLES FORMULA AND ITS RND FUNCTION

We now review the assumptions of the classic Black–Scholes (1973) option pricing model and show how they relate to a lognormal implied terminal RND function. We will then show how the model is modified in practice, and how these modifications to the theoretical Black–Scholes prices result in non-lognormal implied terminal RND functions.

The call pricing function, given by equation (5.1), is somewhat general. To calculate an option's price, one has to make an assumption about how the price of the underlying asset evolves over the life of the option, and therefore what its RND function, conditioned on S, is at the maturity date of the option. The Black–Scholes (1973) model assumes that the price of the underlying asset evolves according to geometric Brownian motion with an instantaneous expected drift rate of μS and an instantaneous variance rate of $\sigma^2 S^2$:

$$dS = \mu S \, dt + \sigma S \, dw \tag{5.3}$$

where μ and σ are assumed to be constant and dw are increments from a *Wiener process*. Applying Ito's lemma to equation (5.3) yields the result:

$$\ln S_t \sim \phi \left[\ln S + \left(\mu - \tfrac{1}{2}\sigma^2 \right) \tau \right], \sigma\sqrt{\tau} \tag{5.4}$$

where $\phi(\alpha, \beta)$ denotes a normal distribution with mean α and standard deviation β. Therefore, the Black–Scholes GBM assumption implies that the RND function of S_T, $q(S_T)$ is lognormal with parameters α and β (or, alternatively, that the RND function of underlying *returns* is *normal* with parameters r and σ). The lognormal density function is given by:

$$q(S_T) = \frac{1}{S_T \beta \sqrt{2\pi}} e^{\{-(\ln S_T - \alpha)^2\}/2\beta^2} \tag{5.5}$$

Like Cox and Ross (1976), Black and Scholes (1973) show that options can be priced under the assumption that investors are risk neutral by setting the expected rate of return on the underlying asset, μ, equal to the risk-free interest rate, r. The formula that Black and Scholes (1973) derived for pricing European call options is as follows:

$$c(X, \tau) = SN(d_1) - e^{-r\tau} XN(d_2) \tag{5.6}$$

where

$$d_1 = \frac{\ln(S/X) + \left(r + \frac{1}{2}\sigma^2\right)\tau}{\sigma\sqrt{\tau}}$$

$$d_2 = \frac{\ln(S/X) + \left(r - \frac{1}{2}\sigma^2\right)\tau}{\sigma\sqrt{\tau}} = d_1 - \sigma\sqrt{\tau}$$

and $N(x)$ is the cumulative probability distribution function for a standardized normal variable, i.e. it is the probability that such a variable will be less than x.

Since the price of an option does not depend upon μ, the expected rate of return on the underlying asset, a distribution recovered from option prices will not be the true distribution unless universal risk neutrality holds, in which case $\mu = r$, the risk-free rate of interest.

5.4   THE IMPLIED VOLATILITY SMILE CURVE

Figure 5.1 shows an example of an implied volatility smile curve observed in the UK short-term interest rate market.

The existence of a convex implied volatility smile curve indicates that market participants make more complex assumptions than GBM about the future path of the underlying asset price: for example, the smile effect may arise if the underlying price follows a jump-diffusion process, or if volatility is stochastic.[10] And, as a result, they attach different probabilities to terminal values of the underlying asset price than those that are consistent with a lognormal distribution.[11] The extent of the convexity of the smile curve indicates the degree to which the market RND function differs from the Black–Scholes (lognormal) RND function. In particular, the more convex the smile curve, the greater the probability the market attaches to extreme outcomes for S_T. This causes the market RND function to have 'fatter tails' than are consistent with a lognormal density function. In addition, the direction in which the smile curve slopes reflects the skew of the market RND function: a positively (negatively) sloped implied volatility smile curve results in an RND function that is more (less) positively skewed than the lognormal RND function that would result from a flat smile curve.

Any variations in the shape of the smile curve are mirrored by corresponding changes in the slope and convexity of the call pricing function. The slope and convexity of the smile curve, or of the call pricing function, can be translated into probability space to reveal the market's (non-lognormal) implied RND

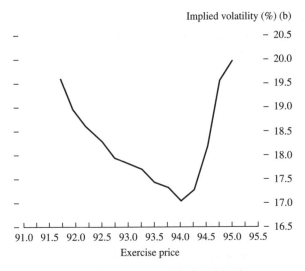

Implied volatility (%) (b)

(a) As at 16 April 1996. The price of the underlying future was
     93.49. The options expired on 18 December 1996.
(b) Implied volatility is an annualized estimate of the instantaneous
     standard deviation of the return on the underlying asset over the
     remaining life of the option.

Figure 5.1 *Implied volatility smile curve for LIFFE December 1996 option on the short sterling*
future[(a)]

function for S_T. In the next section we implement a technique for undertaking
this translation in the UK short-term interest rate market.

5.5 ESTIMATING IMPLIED TERMINAL RND FUNCTIONS

Implementation of the Breeden and Litzenberger (1978) result, which underlies
all of the techniques for empirically estimating implied terminal RND functions,
requires that a continuum of European options with the same time-to-maturity
exist on a single underlying asset spanning strike prices from zero to infinity.
Unfortunately, since option contracts are only traded at discretely spaced strike
price levels, and for a very limited range either side of the at-the-money (ATM)
strike, there are many RND functions that can fit their market prices. So,
any procedure for estimating RND functions essentially amounts to making an
assumption (either directly or indirectly) about the form of the call pricing function and interpolating between observed strike prices and extrapolating outside
of their range to model the tail probabilities.[12]

Rather than implement directly the Breeden and Litzenberger approach,
some researchers estimate the implied RND function by assuming a particular
stochastic process for the price of the underlying asset and using observed

option prices to recover the parameters of the assumed process. The estimated parameters can then be used to infer the RND function that is implied by the assumed stochastic process.[13] Alternatively, an assumption can be made about the functional form of the RND function itself and its parameters recovered by minimizing the distance between the observed option prices and those that are generated by the assumed parametric form.[14] Starting with an assumption about the terminal RND function, rather than the stochastic process by which the underlying price evolves, is a more general approach since any given stochastic process implies a unique terminal distribution, whereas any given RND function is consistent with many different stochastic price processes. This is the approach we adopt.

Consider equation (5.1) which expresses the time-t price of a European call option as the discounted sum of all expected future payoffs. In theory any sufficiently flexible functional form for the density function, $q(S_\tau)$, can be used in equation (5.1), and its parameters recovered by numerical optimization. Given that observed financial asset price distributions are in the neighbourhood of the lognormal distribution, it seems economically plausible to employ the same framework suggested by Ritchey (1990) and to assume that $q(S_\tau)$ is the weighted sum of k component lognormal density functions, that is:

$$q(S_\tau) = \sum_{i=1}^{k} [\theta_i L(\alpha_i, \beta_i; S_\tau)] \tag{5.7}$$

where $L(\alpha_i, \beta_i; S_\tau)$ is the i lognormal density function in the k-component mixture with parameters α_i and β_i;

$$\alpha_i = \ln S + \left(\mu_i - \tfrac{1}{2}\sigma_i^2\right)\tau \quad \text{and} \quad \beta_i = \sigma_i\sqrt{\tau} \quad \text{for each } i \tag{5.8}$$

(see equation (5.5) for the formula of the lognormal density function).

The weights, θ_i, satisfy the conditions:

$$\sum_{i=1}^{k} \theta_i = 1, \quad \theta_i > 0 \quad \text{for each } i \tag{5.9}$$

Moreover, the functional form assumed for the RND function should be flexible enough to be able to capture the main contributions to the smile curve, namely the skewness and the kurtosis of the underlying distribution. A weighted sum of independent lognormal density functions meets this requirement.[15] Each lognormal density function is completely defined by two parameters. The values of these parameters and the weights applied to each of the density functions together determine the overall shape of the mixture implied RND function, as given by equation (5.7).

Melick and Thomas (1994) apply this methodology to extract implied RND functions from the prices of American-style options on crude oil futures.[16] They assume that the terminal price distribution is a mixture of three independent lognormal distributions. However, given that, in the UK interest rate traded options market, contracts are only traded across a relatively small range of exercise prices, there are limits to the number of distributional parameters that can be estimated from the data. Therefore, on grounds of numerical tractability, we prefer to use a two-lognormal mixture, which has only five parameters: α_1, β_1, α_2, β_2 and θ. Under this assumption the value of a call option, given by equation (5.1), can be expressed as follows:

$$c(X, \tau) = e^{-r\tau} \int_X^{\infty} [\theta L(\alpha_1, \beta_1; S_\tau) + (1 - \theta) L(\alpha_2, \beta_2; S_\tau)](S_\tau - X) dS_\tau$$

$$(5.10)$$

For given values of X and τ, and for a set of values for the five distributional parameters and r, equation (5.10) can be used to provide a fitted value of $c(X, \tau)$. This calculation can be applied across all exercise prices to minimize the sum of squared errors, with respect to the five distributional parameters and r, between the option prices generated by the mixture distribution model and those actually observed in the market. In practice, since we can observe interest rates which closely approximate r, we use this information to fix r, and thereby reduce the dimensionality of the problem. Therefore, the minimization is carried out with respect to the five distributional parameters only.[17]

Since both calls and puts should be priced off the same underlying distribution, either set of prices could be included in the minimization problem. However, in practice, ITM options are often less actively traded than the OTM options, which causes traders of ITM options to demand an illiquidity premium. It may therefore be beneficial, before using a set of call prices in the minimization process, to remove this illiquidity effect by replacing the ITM calls with the call prices implied by put–call parity using the more liquid OTM puts. Also, in the absence of arbitrage opportunities, the mean of the implied RND function should equal the forward price of the underlying asset. In this sense we can treat the underlying asset as a zero-strike option and use the incremental information it provides by including its forward price as an additional observation in the minimization procedure. The minimization problem is:[18]

$$\underset{\alpha_1,\alpha_2,\beta_1,\beta_2,\theta}{\text{Min}} \sum_{i=1}^{n} [c(X_i, \tau) - \hat{c}_i]^2 + [\theta e^{\alpha_1+(1/2)\beta_1^2} + (1 - \theta)e^{\alpha_2+(1/2)\beta_2^2} - e^{r\tau}S]^{-2}$$

$$(5.11)$$

subject to $\beta_1, \beta_2 > 0$ and $0 \leq \theta \leq 1$, over the observed strike range $X_1, X_2, X_3, \ldots, X_n$. The first two exponential terms in the last bracket in equation (5.11) represent the means of the component lognormal RND functions. Their weighted sum therefore represents the mean of the mixture RND function. Figure 5.2 shows an example of an implied RND function derived using the two-lognormal mixture distribution approach. It also shows

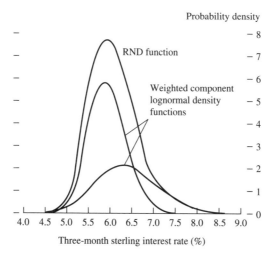

(a) Shown with its (weighted) component iognormal density
     functions. This RND function was derived using LIFFE
     December 1996 options on the short sterling future as at
     10 June 1996. These options expired on 18 December 1996.

Figure 5.2 *An implied RND function derived using the two-lognormal mixture distribution
approach[a]*

the (weighted) component lognormal density functions of the mixture RND
function.

We would expect the five distributional parameters to vary over time as news
changes and option prices adjust to incorporate changing beliefs about future
events. The two-lognormal mixture distribution can incorporate a wide variety
of possible functional forms which, in turn, are able to accommodate a wide
range of possible market scenarios, including a situation in which the market has
a bi-modal view about the terminal value of the underlying asset; for example,
if participants are placing a high weight on an extreme move in the underlying
price but are unsure of its direction.

It is important to remember that the implied density functions derived are risk
neutral, that is, they are equivalent to the true market density functions only
when investors are risk neutral. On the assumption that the market's aversion
to risk is relatively stable over time, changes in the RND function from one
day to the next should mainly reflect changes in investors' beliefs about future
outcomes for the price of the underlying asset.

5.6 APPLICATION OF THE TWO-LOGNORMAL MIXTURE APPROACH
TO OPTIONS ON SHORT-TERM INTEREST RATES

We now apply the two-lognormal mixture distribution approach outlined above
to LIFFE's short sterling futures options.[19] Although these options are American

style, due to LIFFE's unique option margining procedure, they are priced as European-style options.[20] They expire quarterly, in March, June, September and December. In order to avoid the problems associated with asynchronous intraday quotes we use exchange settlement prices, which are obtainable directly from LIFFE.[21]

When applied to LIFFE's short-rate futures options, equation (5.10), which gives the value of a call option under the assumption that the underlying asset is distributed as a mixture of two lognormal distributions, needs to be modified in two ways. The first modification takes into account the fact that the underlying instrument is the interest rate that is implied by the futures price, given by one hundred minus the futures price, $(100 - F)$, rather than the futures price itself. Therefore, a call (put) option on an interest rate futures price is equivalent to a put (call) option on the implied interest rate. And second, because the option buyer is not required to pay the premium up front, the options are priced at time T, that is, without the discount factor.

The objective function, given by equation (5.11), can be minimized using the modified version of equation (5.10) to obtain estimates for the five distributional parameters, α_1, β_1, α_2, β_2 and θ. Note that, in a risk-neutral world, the expected growth rate of a future is zero. So, the mean of the implied RND should equal the interest rate that is implied by the time-t futures price, which requires that $e^{rt}S$ in equation (5.11) be replaced by $(100 - F)$. The problem with using equation (5.10) in the optimization is that it requires numerical integration, which usually results in compounded numerical errors due to the upper limit of infinity. Because of this and for computational ease, we prefer to carry out the optimization using the following closed-form solution to equation (5.10):[22]

$$c(X, \tau) = \theta[-e^{\phi_1}N(-d_1) + (100 - X)N(-d_2)]$$
$$+ (1 - \theta)[-e^{\phi_2}N(-d_3) + (100 - X)N(-d_4)] \qquad (5.12)$$

where

$$\phi_1 = \alpha_1 + \tfrac{1}{2}\beta_1^2, \quad \phi_2 = \alpha_2 + \tfrac{1}{2}\beta_2^2$$

$$d_1 = \frac{-\ln(100 - X) + \alpha_1 + \beta_1^2}{\beta_1}, \quad d_2 = d_1 - \beta_1$$

$$d_3 = \frac{-\ln(100 - X) + \alpha_2 + \beta_2^2}{\beta_2}, \quad d_4 = d_3 - \beta_2$$

$$\alpha_i = \ln(100 - F) + \left(\mu_i - \tfrac{1}{2}\sigma_i^2\right)\tau \quad \text{and} \quad \beta_i = \sigma_i\sqrt{\tau} \quad \text{for } i = 1, 2 \ (5.13)$$

This two-lognormal mixture model is the weighted sum of two Black–Scholes solutions, where θ is the weight parameter, and α_1, β_1 and α_2, β_2 are the parameters of each of the component lognormal RND functions. The d terms are the same as those in the Black–Scholes model, but have been reformulated

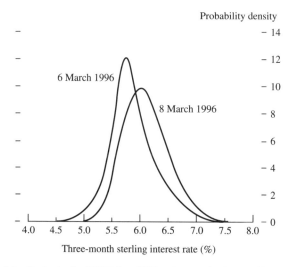

(a) Derived using LIFFE June 1996 options on the short sterling
future, as at 6 March and 8 March 1996. These options expired
on 19 June 1996.

Figure 5.3 *Implied RND functions for the three-month sterling interest rate in June 1996[a]*

here in terms of the relevant α and β parameters by applying the definitions given in equation (5.8).[23]

Figure 5.3 illustrates the use of the two-lognormal mixture distribution approach with LIFFE options on the short sterling future. It shows how the implied RND for the implied three-month interest rate on 19 June 1996 changed between 6 March and 8 March 1996.

5.7 MONETARY POLICY USES OF THE INFORMATION CONTAINED IN IMPLIED RND FUNCTIONS

5.7.1 Validating the two-lognormal mixture distribution approach

Much of the information contained in RND functions can be captured through a range of summary statistics, including the mean, mode, median, standard deviation, interquartile range (IQR), skewness and kurtosis. Such summary statistics provide a useful way of tracking the behaviour of RND functions over the life of a single contract and of making comparisons across contracts.

Table 5.1 shows the summary statistics of the RND functions, as at 4 June 1996, for the three-month sterling and Deutsche Mark interest rates in December 1996 and in March 1997.

The means of the distributions are equivalent to the interest rates implied by the current prices of the relevant futures contracts ($100 - F$) and are lower

Table 5.1   *Summary statistics for the three-month sterling and Deutsche Mark interest rates in December 1996 and March 1997[a]*

	December 1996	March 1997
Sterling		
Mean	6.33	6.66
Mode	6.18	6.43
Median	6.27	6.56
Standard deviation	0.66	1.01
Interquartile range	0.80	1.19
Skewness	0.83	0.76
Kurtosis[b]	4.96	4.67
Deutsche Mark		
Mean	3.45	3.73
Mode	3.29	3.47
Median	3.39	3.62
Standard deviation	0.55	0.84
Interquartile range	0.69	0.95
Skewness	0.75	1.16
Kurtosis[b]	4.27	6.06

[a]Derived using LIFFE December 1996 and March 1997 options on the short sterling and Euromark futures, as at 4 June 1996. The short sterling futures options expired on 18 December 1996 and 19 March 1997. The Euromark futures options expired on 16 December 1996 and 17 March 1997.
[b]Kurtosis is a measure of how peaked a distribution is and/or the likelihood of extreme outcomes: the greater this likelihood, the fatter the tails of the distribution. A normal distribution has a fixed kurtosis of three.

in Germany than in the United Kingdom. For both countries, the dispersion statistics (standard deviation and IQR) are higher for the March 1997 contract than for the December 1996 contract. One would expect this since, over longer time horizons, there is more uncertainty about the expected outcome. Figure 5.4 confirms this, showing the upper and lower quartiles with the mean and the mode for the three-month sterling interest rate on four different option maturity dates as at 15 May 1996. It can be seen that the IQR is higher for contracts with longer maturities. Also, the standard deviations of the two distributions for the sterling rate are higher than the corresponding standard deviations of those for the Deutsche Mark rate, suggesting greater uncertainty about the level of future short-term rates in the United Kingdom than in Germany. Another feature of all four distributions is that they are positively skewed, indicating that there is less probability to the right of each of the means than to their left. The fact that the mode is to the left of the mean is also indicative of a positive skew.

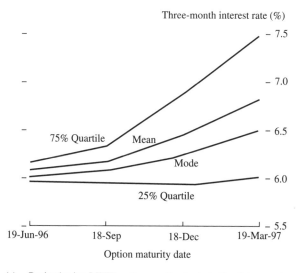

(a) Derived using LIFFE options on the short sterling future as at
      15 May 1996

Figure 5.4 *Implied RND summary statistics for the three-month sterling interest rate on four
different option maturity dates*[a]

   In deciding whether to place reliance on the information extracted using a
new technique, one not only needs to be confident in the theory, but must also
test whether in practice changes in the expectations depicted are believable
in light of the news reaching the market. In the case of short-term interest
rate expectations, we sought to do this by examining the way RND functions
for short-term sterling interest rates change over time, and by comparing the
RND functions for short-term sterling interest rates with those from Germany,
a country with different macroeconomic conditions and monetary history.
   Figures 5.5 and 5.6 show a convenient way of representing the evolution
of implied RND functions over the life of a single option contract. Figure 5.5
shows the market's views of the three-month sterling interest rate on 19 June
1996 (as implied by the prices of LIFFE June short sterling futures options)
between 22 June 1995 and 7 June 1996. Figure 5.6 shows the same type of
information for the three-month Deutsche Mark interest rate on 17 June 1996
(as implied by the prices of LIFFE June Euromark futures options) between
20 June 1995 and 7 June 1996. Both figures depict the mean, mode, and the
lower (25%) and upper (75%) quartiles of the distributions.
   These time series representations of implied RND functions convey how
market uncertainty about the expected outcome changed over time; an increase
in the distance between the lower and upper quartiles indicates that the market
became more uncertain about the expected outcome. Figures 5.5 and 5.6 also

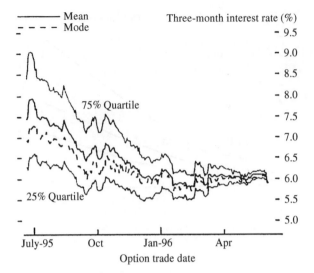

(a) Derived using LIFFE June 1996 options on the short
sterling future. These options expired on 19 June 1996.

Figure 5.5   *Implied RND summary statistics for the three-month sterling interest rate in June
1996[a]*

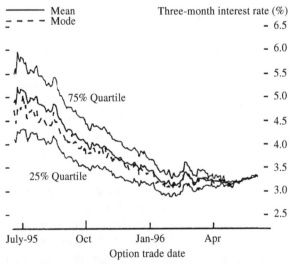

(a) Derived using LIFFE June 1996 options on the Euromark
future. These options expired on 17 June 1996.

Figure 5.6   *Implied RND summary statistics for the three-month Deutsche Mark interest rate in
June 1996[a]*

convey information about changes in the skewness of the implied distributions. For example, the location of the mean relative to the lower and upper quartiles is informative of the direction and extent of the skew. Movements in the mean relative to the mode are also indicative of changes in skewness.

Generally, both sets of implied RND functions depict falling forward rates over the period analysed, as evidenced by the downward trend in the mean and mode statistics. At the same time, the gaps between these measures narrowed, suggesting that the distribution of market participants' expectations was becoming more symmetrical as the time horizon shortened. Figures 5.5 and 5.6 also show that as the maturity date of a contract is approached, the distributions typically become less dispersed causing the quartiles to converge upon the mean. This is because as the time horizon becomes shorter, the market, all other things being equal, becomes more certain about the terminal outcome due to the smaller likelihood of extreme events occurring. Another feature of the distributions is that the mode is persistently below the mean in both countries, indicating a positive skew to expectations of future interest rates. In the United Kingdom this might be interpreted as reflecting political uncertainty ahead of the 1997 election, with the market attaching some probability to much higher short-term rates in the future. However, in Germany the macroeconomic and political conditions are different and yet the RND functions are also positively skewed.

One possible explanation is that the market perceives there to be a lower bound on nominal interest rates at zero. In this case, the range of possible outcomes below the current rate is restricted, whereas the range of possible outcomes above the current rate is, in principle, unlimited. If market participants are generally uncertain, that is, they attach positive probabilities to a wide range of possible outcomes, the lower bound may naturally result in the RND function having a positive skew. Moreover, the lower the current level of rates the more positive this skew may be for a given degree of uncertainty.

A further step towards validating the information contained in implied RND functions is to assess whether changes in their shapes are sensible around particular news events. For example, see Figure 5.7, which shows the change in the shape of the implied RND function for the three-month sterling interest rate in June 1996 around the publication of the May 1996 *Inflation Report* on 14 May. The *Inflation Report* concluded that it was marginally more likely than not that inflation would be above 2.5% in two years' time were official rates to remain unchanged throughout that period. This was followed by an upward revision of the market's expectation for short-term interest rates between 13 May and 15 May. However, it seems that this upward move was not driven so much by a parallel rightward *shift* in the distribution as by a change in the entire *shape* of the distribution; a reallocation of probability from outcomes between 5.6 and

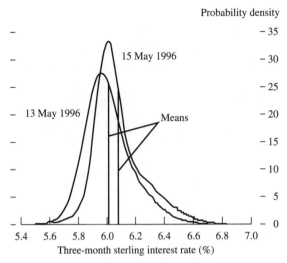

(a)   Derived using LIFFE June 1996 options of the short sterling
future, as at 13 May and 15 May 1996. These options expired on
19 June 1996.

Figure 5.7   *Change in the implied RND function for the three-month sterling interest rate in June 1996 around the publication of the May 1996* Inflation Report[a]

5.9% to outcomes between 5.9 and 6.6% resulted in a fatter right tail which was in part responsible for the upward movement in the mean.[24] This type of change in the shape of implied RND functions is illustrative of how they can add value to existing measures of market sentiment such as the mean.[25]

The above examples suggest that the two-lognormal mixture distribution approach is validated by recent market developments in the United Kingdom. Although the mean remains a key summary statistic, on the basis of these and other examples there is no reason to doubt that implied RND functions can add to our understanding of market views on short-term interest rates.

5.7.2   Assessing monetary conditions

Assuming that financial market expectations are indicative of those in the economy as a whole, RND functions have the potential to improve the authorities' ability to assess monetary conditions on a day-to-day basis. In principle, the whole probability distribution of future short-term interest rates is relevant to the determination of economic agents' behaviour. A lot of this information is captured in the mean of the distribution, which can already be observed directly from the yield curve or forward rates, but other summary statistics may add explanatory power. For example, suppose that agents tend to place less weight on extreme interest rate outcomes when taking investment or consumption decisions than is assumed in the mean of the interest rate probability distribution. In this case, a *trimmed mean* – in which the probabilities attached to extreme outcomes are ignored or given reduced weight – may reflect the information used by agents better than the standard mean, and so may provide a better indication of monetary conditions for the monetary authorities. Much of the time the standard mean and the trimmed mean may move together, but one could envisage circumstances in which the standard mean is influenced by an increase in the probabilities attached to very unlikely outcomes, while the trimmed mean is less affected.

Further empirical research is required to assess whether summary statistics such as an adjusted mean, the mode, median, interquartile range, skewness and kurtosis can add explanatory power to the standard mean interest rate in conventional economic models.[26] RND functions may also provide evidence of special situations influencing the formation of asset price expectations. For example, if two distinct economic or political scenarios meant that asset prices would take very different values according to which scenario occurred, then this might be revealed in bi-modal probability distributions for various asset prices.

Take the example of a foreign exchange rate that is managed within a target zone. Such bi-modal behaviour may conceivably be observed in the RND functions of the exchange rate if the credibility of the target zone is called into question – with one mode being observed within the boundaries of the target zone, and the other lying outside. So, for central banks attempting to maintain an exchange rate within a given target zone, either through formal arrangement or informal exchange rate management, the market implied RND function calculated from the prices of options on that exchange rate is a useful tool for gauging the credibility of the target zone as perceived by the market.[27]

5.7.3   Assessing monetary credibility

A monetary strategy to achieve a particular inflation target can be described as credible if the public believes that the government will carry out its plans. So, a relative measure of credibility is the difference between the market's perceived distribution of the future rate of inflation and that of the authorities.[28] Some information on this is already available in the United Kingdom in the form of implied forward inflation rates, calculated from the yields of index-linked and conventional gilts. However, this only gives us the mean of the market's probability distribution for future inflation. Even if this mean were the same as the authorities' target, this could mask a lack of credibility if the market placed higher weights on much lower and much higher inflation outcomes than the authorities.

Unfortunately for monetary authorities there are at present no exchange-traded options which enable the extraction of an implied RND function for inflation.[29]

However, implied probability distributions for long-term interest rates, revealed by options on long gilt futures, may be helpful in this respect, to the extent that most of the uncertainty over long-term interest rates – and hence news in the shape of a long gilt RND function – may plausibly be attributed to uncertainty over future inflation.

5.7.4   Assessing the timing and effectiveness of monetary operations

Implied RND functions from options on short-term interest rates indicate the probabilities the market attaches to various near-term monetary policy actions. These probabilities are in turn determined by market participants' expectations about news and their view of the authorities' reaction function.

In this context, implied RND summary statistics may help the authorities to assess the market's likely reaction to particular policy actions. For example, a decision to raise short-term interest rates may have a different impact on market perceptions of policy when the market appears to be very certain that rates will remain unchanged (as evidenced by a narrow and symmetric RND function for future interest rates) from when the mean of the probability distribution for future rates is the same, but the market already attaches non-trivial probabilities to sharply higher rates, albeit counterbalanced by higher probabilities attached to certain lower rates.

Equally, implied RND functions may help in the *ex-post* analysis of policy actions. For example, if the shape and location of the implied RND function for short-term interest rates three months ahead remains the same following a change in base rates, this suggests, all other things being equal, that the market fully expected the change in monetary stance. By contrast a constant mean is less informative because it could disguise significant changes in skewness and kurtosis.

Implied probability distributions may also be useful for analysing market reactions to money market operations which do not involve a change in official rates, or events such as government bond auctions. These can be assessed either directly by looking at probability distributions from the markets concerned, or indirectly by looking at related markets.

5.7.5   Identifying market anomalies

All of the above uses of RND data assume that markets are perfectly competitive and that market participants are rational. However, provided one has overall confidence in the technique used, RND functions may help to identify occasional situations where one or other of these assumptions does not hold, essentially because the story being told is not believable.[30]

For example, in the face of an 'abnormal' asset price movement – such as a stock market crash or a sharp jump in the nominal exchange rate, which is not easily explained by news – the information embedded in options prices for this and related assets may help the authorities to understand whether the movement in question is likely to be sustained with consequent macroeconomic effects, or whether it reflects a temporary phenomenon, possibly due to market failure. For example, if RND functions suggest that the market factored in the possibility of the very large asset price movement because it purchased insurance against the move in advance, then the amount of news required to trigger the change might reasonably be expected to be less than in the situation where there was no 'advance knowledge'. This in turn might make it more believable that the move reflected fundamentals and hence would be sustained.

5.8 USING THE IMPLIED RND FUNCTION AS A VOLATILITY FORECASTING TOOL

In the section above we showed how implied RND functions can be used by central banks in gauging current market sentiment. However, an interesting question, for both monetary authorities and market traders, is whether implied RND functions can also provide a better measure of future uncertainty than other available measures, such as implied volatilities. One possible criterion for assessing this is to see whether uncertainty measures derived from implied RND functions outperform implied volatilities as predictors of future volatility.

When calculating implied volatilities most researchers utilize specific option pricing models. In doing so they assume a particular stochastic process for the price of the underlying asset. We now illustrate how the market implied RND function itself, estimated via the two-lognormal mixture distribution approach, can be employed as a type of volatility forecasting tool. This distributional approach is more general since it makes no assumptions about the underlying asset's stochastic price process.

We calculate two alternative measures of future uncertainty from implied RND functions estimated using LIFFE short sterling futures options data since December 1987. We then use these time series of the RND-based uncertainty measures to conduct an econometric analysis of their forecasting ability. The literature has looked at three issues regarding the usefulness of any volatility estimate as a forecast of future uncertainty: (i) does the estimate have predictive power for subsequent realized volatility? (ii) is it an unbiased estimate of realized volatility? and (iii) is it informationally efficient, or do alternative estimates provide incremental predictive power? Whilst there is general agreement about the predictive power of option implied volatilities, disagreement remains about their bias and informational efficiency. The issue is further complicated by the possible existence of a time-varying volatility risk premium.[31]

We use non-overlapping data to examine the out-of-sample performance (in terms of predictive power, unbiasedness and informational efficiency) of the two implied RND-based uncertainty measures and compare it with that of traditional Black–Scholes ATM implied volatilities. Since, the RND-based measures take into account the skewness and excess kurtosis components of the smile curve they should, in principle, contain incremental information compared with that from Black–Scholes ATM implied volatilities. We assess if this has been the case in the UK short-term interest rate market.

5.8.1   Calculating RND-based uncertainty measures

The first RND-based estimate of future uncertainty that we look at is what Shimko (1993) calls an 'unambiguous instantaneous implied return volatility'. By this he means that, because it is calculated using the implied RND function, it obviates the need to calculate a weighted average of all the implied volatilities observed in the smile curve in order to arrive at a single working volatility figure. The measure, which we call σ^*, is given by:[32]

$$\sigma^* = \sqrt{\ln(q^2 + 1)/\tau} \tag{5.14}$$

where

$q = \frac{s}{m}$, the coefficient of variation for the implied RND
s = standard deviation of the implied RND
m = mean of the implied RND
τ = time remaining to option maturity

The second RND-based measure, which can be seen as a heuristic measure of risk, is calculated using the β parameter of each of the component lognormal distributions: $\beta_1 = \sigma_1\sqrt{\tau}$ and $\beta_2 = \sigma_2\sqrt{\tau}$, see equation (5.8). Given these parameter estimates and the time to option maturity, it is easy to compute σ_1 and σ_2. Each of these σ's can then be weighted by the estimated weight on the component distribution from which it is derived, θ or $(1 - \theta)$, to yield the following measure, which we call $\bar{\sigma}$:[33]

$$\bar{\sigma} = \theta\sigma_1 + (1 - \theta)\sigma_2 \tag{5.15}$$

The first option contract in the LIFFE data set expired in December 1987. Since then LIFFE short sterling futures option contracts have expired every March, June, September and December, which means that we can estimate implied RND functions for 41 quarterly option maturity dates over the life cycle of each contract. We calculate the alternative uncertainty measures, σ^* and $\bar{\sigma}$, from the implied RND functions derived at three fixed points in the life cycle of each option contract: one month, two months and three months before the maturity date.[34] The actual (realized) volatility is calculated over each of these forecast horizons across each of the option life cycles as the sample standard deviation of the daily changes in the log of the short-term interest rate that is implied by the price of the underlying futures contract, and the numbers are annualized. ATM implied standard deviations calculated from the option prices at one, two and three months before each maturity date provide volatility estimates which we can use as base cases.[35]

We start with individual univariate OLS regressions to assess the predictive power and unbiasedness of each of the uncertainty measures. The regressions, which are run separately for each forecast horizon, take the form:

$$\sigma_{t,T} = \alpha + \beta \sigma_{t,T}^F + \varepsilon_t \tag{5.16}$$

where T is the option maturity date, $\sigma_{t,T}$ is the realized volatility over a given forecast horizon and $\sigma_{t,T}^F$ is the uncertainty measure, either the Black–Scholes ATM implied volatility, σ^* or $\bar{\sigma}$, applying over the same forecast horizon. We also use Scott's (1992) specification which allows for a possible unit root in the volatility process:

$$(\sigma_{t,T} - \sigma_{h,t}) = \delta + \gamma(\sigma_{t,T}^F - \sigma_{h,t}) + \mu_t \tag{5.17}$$

where $\sigma_{h,t}$ is the historical standard deviation over the period just prior to the forecast window and of equivalent length. The interpretation of the R^2 of this regression would be the percentage of the variation in volatility changes that is predictable from the uncertainty measures. Note that by running these regressions separately for each forecast horizon we are employing a discrete sampling methodology, and so avoiding the econometric problems associated with overlapping observations.[36]

A significant slope coefficient indicates that the uncertainty estimate in question has some predictive power. If the *ex-ante* uncertainty estimate is an unbiased predictor of realized volatility, the intercept will be zero and the slope coefficient one. These hypotheses are tested jointly.

Next, we test the incremental information content of each of the RND-based measures over the Black–Scholes ATM implied volatilities. Given that the correlations between the Black–Scholes ATM implied volatilities and each of the RND-based measures are above 0.95 at all three forecast horizons, we choose not to implement the standard encompassing regression approach, as this would most likely result in large standard errors for the slope coefficients. Instead we assume that Black–Scholes ATM implied volatilities are unbiased predictors of future volatility, as indicated by the results of regression (5.16) reported in Table 5.2, and investigate whether each of the RND-based measures have any power in explaining the variation in the difference between realized and

Table 5.2 *Regression (5.16): OLS estimates from univariate regressions of realized volatility on a single uncertainty estimate*

Here we test for predictive power and unbiasedness.[a][b]

$$\sigma_{t,T} = \alpha + \beta \sigma_{t,T}^{F} + \varepsilon_t$$

where T is the option maturity date, $\sigma_{t,T}$ is the realized volatility over a given forecast horizon and $\sigma_{t,T}^{F}$ is the uncertainty measure, either the Black–Scholes ATM implied volatility, σ^* or $\bar{\sigma}$, applying over the same forecast horizon.

Forecast horizon	α	$\beta(\sigma^{IV})$	$\beta(\sigma^*)$	$\beta(\bar{\sigma})$	$\bar{R}^2$	F
$i = 1$ month	3.75 (0.70)[5.38]	0.77 (2.05)[0.37]			0.11	0.24
	3.24 (0.57)[5.70]		0.75 (2.01)[0.37]		0.11	0.23
	3.26 (0.64)[5.06]			0.88 (2.31)[0.38]*	0.14	0.39
$i = 2$ months	0.02 (0.00)[4.29]	1.02 (3.15)[0.32]*			0.20	0.02
	−0.06 (−0.01)[4.43]		0.97 (3.06)[0.32]*		0.19	0.05
	1.63 (0.40)[4.03]			0.94 (2.95)[0.32]*	0.18	0.28
$i = 3$ months	−3.04 (−0.55)[5.52]	1.20 (2.97)[0.40]*			0.42	0.41
	−3.72 (−0.65)[5.68]		1.21 (3.01)[0.40]*		0.43	0.58
	−3.90 (−0.82)[4.75]			1.34 (3.67)[0.36]*	0.49	1.47

[a]We examine the residuals for evidence of serial correlation and find that we can accept the null hypothesis of zero first-order autocorrelation in all regressions. We also conduct the same tests using regression (5.17), which allows for a possible unit root in the volatility process, and find the results to be the same.
[b]The t-statistics (shown in curved brackets) reflect standard errors (shown in square brackets) computed using the White (1980) correction for heteroscedasticity. The F-statistics are for a joint test of $H_0 \cdot \alpha = 0$ and $\beta = 1$. And * indicates significance at the 5% level. The number of observations are: 40 for the 3 month forecast horizon, 36 for the 2 month horizon, and 27 for the 1 month horizon.

Black–Scholes ATM implied volatilities. The regression takes the form:

$$\sigma_{t,T} - \sigma_{t,T}^{IV} = \alpha + \beta \sigma_{t,T}^{F} + \varepsilon_t \tag{5.18}$$

where, $\sigma_{t,T}^{IV}$ is the Black–Scholes ATM implied volatility (the base-case volatility estimate) and $\sigma_{t,T}^{F}$ is the RND-based uncertainty measure, either σ^* or $\bar{\sigma}$, being tested for incremental information content. If $\sigma_{t,T}^F$ has incremental predictive power its slope coefficient will be non-zero.

5.8.2 Results

Tables 5.2 and 5.3 report the OLS estimates, respectively, for regressions (5.16) and (5.18). Table 5.2 shows consistent evidence for the predictive power of the three uncertainty measures. The slope coefficients for all three are significantly different from zero for the two- and three-month forecast horizons. The highest set of $\overline{R}^2$ statistics are for the three-month horizon, and the highest one amongst these applies to the regression involving $\overline{\sigma}$. This estimate also has the greatest predictive power at the one-month horizon, and is the only one with a significant slope coefficient at that horizon. The slope coefficients for the other two estimates are only just insignificant at the 5% level. The lack of significance of these estimates at the one-month forecast horizon may be due to expiration month 'liquidity effects', caused by traders beginning to move out of expiring option positions and into the next contract.[37] Overall, the $\overline{R}^2$ statistics are higher than those reported by Day and Lewis (1992) and of the same order of magnitude as those reported by Strong and Xu (1997).

We now turn to the issue of unbiasedness. That the intercepts for the uncertainty measures are insignificant, and their slope coefficients within one standard error of 1 for all three forecast horizons indicates that they are unbiased predictors of future volatility. This is confirmed by insignificant F-statistics for the joint test of the null hypothesis that $\alpha = 0$ and $\beta = 1$. The smallest F-statistics pertain to the two-month forecast horizon indicating a greater degree of unbiasedness at that horizon. However, it is difficult to draw a sharp conclusion regarding the biasedness of σ^{IV} and σ^* at the one-month forecast horizon since their slope coefficients, although not significantly different from 1, are also not significantly different from zero. If the constraint $\alpha = 0$ is imposed in these two regressions, the slope coefficients become significant and still lie within one standard error of 1.

Table 5.3 reports the results of regression (5.18), which assesses the incremental information content of each of the RND-based measures at all three forecast horizons. The estimated slope coefficients reported in this table are all statistically insignificant which indicates that, at least in the UK short-term interest rate markets and for forecast horizons of up to three months, neither of the RND-based measures contain any incremental predictive information relative to that already contained in Black–Scholes ATM implied volatilities.

Since the RND-based uncertainty measures take into account the non-normality of the underlying return distribution, they are comparable to equivalent measures derived from option pricing models that allow for stochastic

Table 5.3   *Regression (5.18): OLS estimates from univariate regressions of the difference between realized and Black–Scholes ATM implied volatilities on RND-based uncertainty measures.*

Here we test for incremental information content of each of the RND-based measures.[a][b]

$$\sigma_{t,T} - \sigma_{t,T}^{IV} = \alpha + \beta \sigma_{t,T}^{F} + \varepsilon_t$$

where, $\sigma_{t,T}^{IV}$ is the Black–Scholes ATM implied volatility (the base-case volatility estimate) and $\sigma_{t,T}^{F}$ is the RND-based uncertainty measure, either σ^* or $\bar{\sigma}$, being tested for incremental information content.

Slope coefficient	1 month	2 months	3 months
$\beta(\sigma^*)$	−0.24 (−0.63) [0.37]	0.01 (0.03) [0.32]	0.21 (0.53) [0.40]
$\beta(\bar{\sigma})$	−0.15 (−0.37) [0.39]	0.00 (0.01) [0.32]	0.35 (0.91) [0.38]

[a] The intercept values for all the regressions are insignificantly different from zero. The $\bar{R}$-squared statistics are all close to zero. We examine the residuals for evidence of serial correlation and find that we can accept the null hypothesis of zero first-order autocorrelation in all regressions. We also conduct the same tests using Scott's (1992) specification, given by equation (5.17), and find the results to be the same.

[b] The t-statistics (shown in curved brackets) reflect standard errors (shown in square brackets) computed using the White (1980) correction for heteroscedasticity. The number of observations are: 40 for the 3-month forecast horizon, 36 for the 2-month horizon, and 27 for the 1-month horizon.

volatility. Such a comparison means that our finding is in line with that of Strong and Xu (1997), who look at the information content of implied volatilities from S&P 500 stock index options and find no evidence for the superiority of volatility estimates from a stochastic volatility model over those from the Black–Scholes model.

5.9   CONCLUSIONS

In this chapter we outline the theory that relates option prices to risk-neutral density (RND) functions for the terminal value of the underlying asset. We describe a technique for estimating such functions which assumes that the implied RND can be characterized by a weighted sum of two independent lognormal distributions. Although this mixture distribution methodology is similar in spirit to the approach taken by Bates (1991) and others in deriving the parameters of the underlying stochastic process, it is more general in that it focuses directly on possible future outcomes for the underlying price, thereby obviating the need to specify the price dynamics. We apply the technique to LIFFE data on UK short-term interest rate futures options.

We go on to show how the information contained in implied RND functions can add to the type of forward-looking information available to policy-makers, particularly in assessing monetary conditions, monetary credibility, the timing and effectiveness of monetary operations, and in identifying anomalous market prices. To the extent that the distribution around the mean is observed to change in shape over time, measures such as the standard deviation, mode, interquartile range, skewness and kurtosis are useful in quantifying these changes in market perceptions. However, a good deal of further research, including event studies and the use of RND summary statistics in addition to the mean in classic economic models, is required to extract the maximum benefit from such information.

As a first step, it is important to be able to identify when a particular change in an implied probability distribution is significant by historical standards. One way of doing this is to establish suitable benchmarks. This would enable a large change in the shape of an RND function to be compared with changes in market perceptions at the time of a significant economic event in the past. In addition, RND functions could be estimated over the life cycles of many historical contracts for the same underlying asset in order to calculate average values for their summary statistics at particular points in the life cycle. These average values would identify the characteristics of a typical implied RND function during its life cycle.

The fact that exchange-traded option contracts have a limited number of fixed maturity dates is problematic when deriving time series of distributions and when assessing changes in market perceptions of short-term rates in the very near future. For example, if there are three months remaining until the nearest option maturity date it is not possible, without making assumptions about the time dependency of the distributional parameters, to determine the market's perceptions of the short-term rate in one month's time. This is inconvenient for the policy-maker if he is interested in gauging market sentiment with regard to short-term interest rates at the next monetary meeting, or at a date between the fixed maturity dates of two option contracts. So, research into which model best characterises the time dependency of the distributional parameters may be a useful extension to this work.

In the latter part of this chapter, we examine the information content of Black–Scholes ATM implied volatilities and of two alternative measures of future uncertainty derived from the market's implied RND function. These RND-based uncertainty measures are comparable to equivalent measures derived from stochastic volatility option pricing models, and to those calculated by taking a weighted average of Black–Scholes implied volatilities observed across the smile curve. However, the advantage of using the RND-based measures is that there is no need to specify a particular stochastic volatility price process or to use a specific implied volatility weighting scheme, as the skewness and excess kurtosis features are already incorporated into the market's implied RND function.

We find consistent evidence for the predictive power of the three uncertainty measures. We also find that over two- and three-month forecast horizons all three measures are unbiased predictors of future volatility. These findings indicate that there may be a relatively straightforward risk adjustment between risk-neutral measures of future uncertainty and the realized return volatility over the forecast horizon. Finally, we find no evidence that the RND-based measures provide incremental predictive power over that of Black–Scholes ATM implied volatilities in the UK short-term interest rate markets. However, it may be the case that in equity markets, where the smile effect is more pronounced, Black–Scholes implied volatilities are not entirely informationally efficient and that alternative indicators of future uncertainty contain incremental information.[38]

REFERENCES

Aït-Sahalia, Y. and Lo, A. (1995) Nonparametric estimation of state-price densities implicit in financial asset prices, NBER, working paper No. 5351.

Bahra, B. (1997) Implied risk-neutral probability density functions from option prices: theory and application, Bank of England Working Paper No. 66, July.

Bakshi, G., Cao, C and Chen, Z. (1997) Empirical performance of alternative option pricing models (Forthcoming in *Journal of Finance*).

Bates, D.S. (1988) The crash premium: option pricing under asymmetric processes, with applications to options on Deutschemark Futures Rodney L. White Centre, University of Pennsylvania, working paper No. 36–88.

Bates, D.S. (1991) The crash of '87: was it expected? The evidence from options markets *Journal of Finance*, **46**(3), 1009–1044.

Bates, D.S. (1995) Post-'87 crash fears in S&P 500 futures options, working paper, The Wharton School.

Bates, D. (1996) Jumps and stochastic volatility: exchange rate processes implicit in Deutsche Mark options, *Review of Financial Studies*, **9** Winter, 69–107.

Bhundia, A. and Chadha, J. (1997) The information content of three-month sterling futures, mimeo, Bank of England.

Black, F. (1975) Fact and fantasy in the use of options, *Financial Analysts' Journal*, **31**, 36–41 and 61–72.

Black, F. (1976) The pricing of commodity contracts, *Journal of Financial Economics*, **3**, 167–179.

Black, F. and Scholes, M. (1973) The pricing of options and corporate liabilities, *Journal of Political Economy*, **81**, 637–659.

Bodie, Z. and Merton, R. (1995) The information role of asset prices: the case of implied volatility, in Crane, D., Froot, K., Mason, S., Perold, A., Merton, R., Bodie, Z., Sirri, E. and Tufano, P. (eds), *The Global Financial System: A Functional Perspective*, Boston, Massachusetts: Harvard Business School Press.

Breeden, D.T. and Litzenberger, R.H. (1978) Prices of state-contingent claims implicit in option prices, *Journal of Business*, vol. 51, no. 4, 621–651.

Campa, J. and Chang, K. (1996) Arbitrage-based tests of target-zone credibility: evidence from ERM cross-rate options, *American Economic Review*, **86**, 726–740.

Canina, L. and Figlewski, S. (1993) The information content of options prices and a test of market efficiency, *Review of Financial Studies*, **6**, 659–681.

Cox, J. and Ross, S. (1976) The valuation of options for alternative stochastic processes, *Journal of Financial Economics*, **3**, 145–166.

Day, T. and Lewis, C. (1992) Stock market volatility and the information content of stock index options, *Journal of Econometrics*, **52**, April/May, 289–311.

Day, T. and Lewis, C. (1997) Initial margin policy and stochastic volatility in the crude oil futures market, *Review of Financial Studies*, **10**, Summer, 303–332.

Fleming, J. (1996) The quality of market volatility forecasts implied by S&P 100 index options prices, working paper, Rice University, July.

Hull, J.C. (1993) *Options, Futures, and Other Derivative Securities*, 2nd ed., New Jersey: Prentice Hall International.

Jackwerth, J.C. and Rubinstein, M. (1995) Implied probability distributions: empirical analysis, Haas School of Business, University of California, working paper No. 250.

Jarrow, R. and Rudd, A. (1982) Approximate option valuation for arbitrary stochastic processes, *Journal of Financial Economics*, **10**, 347–369.

King, M. (1995) Credibility and monetary policy: theory and evidence, *Bank of England Quarterly Bulletin*, vol. 35, February, 84–91.

Lamoureux, C. and Lastrapes, W. (1993) Forecasting stock-return variance: toward an understanding of stochastic implied volatilities, *Review of Financial Studies*, **6**, 293–326.

Lieu, D. (1990) Option pricing with futures-style margining, *Journal of Futures Markets*, vol. 10, no. 4, 327–338.

Longstaff, F. (1992) An empirical examination of the risk-neutral valuation model, working paper, College of Business, Ohio State University, and the Anderson Graduate School of Management, UCLA.

Longstaff, F. (1995) Option pricing and the martingale restriction, *Review of Financial Studies*, vol. 8, no. 4, 1091–1124.

MacBeth, J. and Merville, L. (1980) Tests of the Black–Scholes and Cox call option valuation models, *Journal of Finance*, **35**, 285–303.

Malz, A. (1995a) Recovering the probability distribution of future exchange rates from option prices, mimeo, Federal Reserve Bank of New York.

Malz, A. (1995b) Using option prices to estimate realignment probabilities in the European Monetary System, *Federal Reserve Bank of New York Staff Reports*, No. 5.

Malz, A. (1997) Option-implied probability distributions and currency excess returns, *Federal Reserve Bank of New York Staff Reports*, No. 32.

Melick, W.R. and Thomas, C.P. (1994) Recovering an asset's implied PDF from option prices: an application to crude oil during the Gulf crisis, working paper, Federal Reserve Board, Washington.

Neuhaus, H. (1995) The information content of derivatives for monetary policy: implied volatilities and probabilities, Deutsche Bundesbank Economic Research Group, discussion paper No. 3/95.

Ritchey, R.J. (1990) Call option valuation for discrete normal mixtures, *Journal of Financial Research*, vol. XIII, no. 4, 285–296.

Rubinstein, M. (1985) Nonparametric tests of alternative option pricing models using all reported trades and quotes on the 30 most active CBOE option classes from August 23, 1976 through August 31, 1978, *Journal of Finance*, **40**, 445–480.

Rubinstein, M. (1994) Implied binomial trees, *Journal of Finance*, vol. 49, no. 3, 771–818.

Scott, L. (1992) The information content of prices in derivative security markets, *IMF Staff Papers*, **39**, no. 3, 596–625.

Shimko, D. (1993) Bounds of probability, *RISK*, vol. 6, no. 4.

Söderlind, P. and Svensson, L. (1997) New techniques to extract market expectations from financial instruments, NBER working paper No. 5877, January.

Strong, N. and Xu, X. (1997) The comparative performance of S&P 500 implied volatility forecasts, mimeo, University of Manchester, September.

Whaley, R. (1982) Valuation of American call options on dividend-paying stocks: empirical tests, *Journal of Financial Economics*, **10**, 29–58.

White, H. (1980) A heteroscedasticity-consistent covariance matrix estimator and a direct test for heteroscedasticity, *Econometrica*, **48**, 817–838.

Xu, X. and Taylor, S. (1995) Conditional volatility and the informational efficiency of the PHLX currency options market, *Journal of Banking and Finance*, **19**, 803–821.

NOTES

1. For applications of volatility estimates in these decision-making processes, see Bodie and Merton (1995).

2. A European call (put) option on a given underlying asset is a contract that gives the holder the right, but not the obligation, to buy (sell) that asset at a certain date in the future at a pre-determined price. The pre-determined price at which the underlying asset is bought or sold, which is stipulated in an option contract, is known as the *exercise price* or *strike price*. The date at which an option expires is known as the *maturity date* or *expiration date*. Options that can be exercised at any time up to and including the maturity date are known as *American* options.

3. For a more detailed analysis of how to estimate market implied RND functions, see Bahra (1997).

4. Under the Black–Scholes assumption that the price of the underlying asset evolves according to GBM, the implied volatility ought to be the same across all exercise prices of options on the same underlying asset and with the same maturity date.

5. An option is said to be trading *at-the-money* when its exercise price is equal to the current price of the underlying asset. Otherwise it is either *in-the-money* (ITM) or *out-of-the-money* (OTM).

6. For examples of studies looking at the information content of Black–Scholes implied volatilities, see Day and Lewis (1992), Canina and Figlewski (1993), Lamoureux and Lastrapes (1993), Xu and Taylor (1995), and Fleming (1996).

7. For examples of such studies see Bates (1996), Bakshi, Cao and Chen (1997), Day and Lewis (1997), and Strong and Xu (1997).

8. See Cox and Ross (1976) for the pricing of options under risk neutrality.

9. The call pricing function relates the call price to the exercise price for options on the same underlying instrument and with the same time-to-maturity. In the absence of arbitrage opportunities, $c(X, \tau)$ is convex and monotonic decreasing in exercise price. Such a call pricing function is consistent with a positive RND function.

10. Many markets exhibit a departure from normality in the form of leptokurtotic, skewed and time-varying asset returns. Jump-diffusion processes can account both for the skewness and the leptokurtosis in returns: for example, see Bates (1988) and Malz (1995b). Time-varying variance of returns can be represented by autoregressive conditional heteroscedasticity (ARCH) models, which can also account for leptokurtosis.

11. Early empirical studies that document the differences between theoretical Black–Scholes prices and observed market prices include Black (1975), MacBeth and Merville (1980), Rubinstein (1985), and Whaley (1982).

12. Note, to ensure that the estimated RND function is positive the interpolating and extrapolating procedure(s) employed must assume the absence of arbitrage opportunities. That is, the fitted call pricing function must be convex and monotonic decreasing in exercise price. See Bates (1991), Jarrow and Rudd (1982), and Longstaff (1992, 1995). Malz (1995a) and Shimko (1993) make an assumption about the functional form of the implied volatility smile curve and, from the fitted smile, derive the implied call pricing function. Aït-Sahalia and Lo (1995) take a non-parametric approach to fitting the call pricing function. Neuhaus (1995) avoids smoothing altogether and instead discretely differences the observed call prices to obtain the discretized implied *cumulative* distribution of the underlying price.

13. For applications of this approach, see Bates (1991, 1995), and Malz (1995b).

14. For example, see Bahra (1997), Jackwerth and Rubinstein (1995), Melick and Thomas (1994), Rubinstein (1994), and Söderlind and Svensson (1997).

15. Note that this functional form implicitly ensures that the fitted call pricing function is monotonic decreasing and convex in exercise price, and is therefore consistent with the absence of arbitrage.

16. To deal with the early exercise feature of the options that they examine, Melick and Thomas (1994) derive bounds on the option price in terms of the terminal RND function.

17. Alternatively, the value of r can be backed out of the put–call parity formula using the ATM call and put prices.

18. Note that the minimization problem, as depicted here, implies that all of the observations (i.e. the call prices and the forward price of the underlying asset) are given equal weight in the minimization process. However, this may not be the optimum weighting scheme, and further investigation of alternative weighting functions may be required.

19. For details on how to apply the approach to options on equity indices, long bond futures and foreign exchange rates, see Bahra (1997).
20. For an explanation of this point, see Lieu (1990).
21. Settlement prices are established at the end of each day and are used as the basis for overnight 'marking-to-market' of all open positions. So, they should give a fair reflection of the market at the close of business, at least for contracts on which there is open interest. However, note that options that are deeply ITM tend to be fairly illiquid so their settlement prices may have limited information content, or may simply not be available. This data limitation sometimes results in sudden changes in the degree of convexity of the option pricing function. The two-lognormal mixture distribution approach (and other techniques) may in turn be sensitive to this, which may consequently result in implausibly spiked RND functions. See Bahra (1997) for a further discussion of this point.
22. The relevant single lognormal model is Black (1976). For the complete derivation of equation (5.12), see Bahra (1997).
23. Notice that the closed-form solutions involve the cumulative normal distribution function rather that the lognormal density function. This obviates the need for numerical integration since the cumulative normal distribution can be calculated to six decimal place accuracy using a polynomial approximation: see Hull (1993), Chapter 10.
24. While the changes in the characteristics of the distributions are numerically distinct, they may not be statistically significantly different. Suitable tests could be designed to support the numerical results.
25. A similar type of analysis can be undertaken around the dates of key monetary meetings in order to infer to what extent a particular monetary policy decision was expected by the market.
26. For example, see Malz (1997) who tests the international capital asset pricing model using implied risk-neutral exchange rate moments as explanatory variables and finds them to have considerable explanatory value for excess returns.
27. See Malz (1995b) and Campa and Chang (1996) for applications to ERM currencies.
28. For further explanation, see King (1995).
29. To learn about the market's *ex-ante* inflation distribution, one would require a market in options on inflation, for example options on annual changes in the retail price index (RPI).
30. The R^2 values of fitted option prices computed from the estimated RND functions are generally high. However, problems are sometimes encountered when trying to fit a five-parameter functional form to option prices which are quoted across only a limited number of strike prices (as is usually the case during periods of low market volatility).
31. This implies a non-trivial risk adjustment between risk-neutral estimates of future volatility and the realized return volatility over the forecast horizon, and therefore affects the degree to which risk-neutral volatility measures are reliable forecasts of future uncertainty. Note that many of the tests used in determining the predictive power of implied volatilities follow those used to assess whether

forward prices are optimal predictors of spot prices: for example, see Bhundia and Chadha (1997).

32. Shimko (1993) proposes this measure as the variance of the risk-neutral distribution translated to return form – i.e. the annualized volatility of $\ln S_T$. No further explanation is provided for the formula.

33. Note that this proposed risk measure is not the same as the variance of the asset return process, as this would depend on both the means and the variances of the component distributions.

34. Due to problems with fitting a five-parameter distribution to LIFFE option prices during periods of low market volatility, we were only able to use 40 of the 41 contracts for the 3-month forecast horizon, 36 contracts for the 2-month horizon, and 27 contracts for the 1-month horizon.

35. We use the ATM implied volatilities calculated by LIFFE using the Black (1976) model for pricing futures options.

36. Due to the nature of the options expiration calendar a slight overlap occasionally arises at the 3-month forecast horizon. But, this is of the order of one or two days and should not have any significant bearing on the results.

37. These types of effects are also documented by Day and Lewis (1992).

38. For example, Bakshi, Cao and Chen (1997) find that incorporating stochastic volatility when pricing S&P 500 index options over the period 1988–1991 provides a significant improvement on the Black–Scholes model.

Chapter 6

Hashing GARCH: a reassessment of volatility forecasting performance

GEORGE A. CHRISTODOULAKIS* AND STEPHEN E. SATCHELL[†]

SUMMARY

A number of volatility forecasting studies have led to the perception that the ARCH-type models provide poor out-of-sample forecasts of volatility. This is primarily based on the use of traditional forecast evaluation criteria concerning the accuracy and the unbiasedness of forecasts.

In this chapter we provide an assessment of ARCH forecasting. We show how the inherent noise in the approximation of the actual and unobservable volatility by the squared return results in a misleading forecast evaluation. We characterize this noise and quantify its effects assuming normal errors. We extend our results using more general error structures such as the compound normal and the Gram–Charlier classes of distributions. We argue that evaluation problems are likely to be exacerbated by non-normality of the shocks and conclude that non-linear and utility-based criteria can be more suitable for the evaluation of volatility forecasts.

6.1 INTRODUCTION[1]

Following the seminal papers of Engle (1982) and Bollerslev (1986) the ARCH and GARCH models are now widely used in economics and finance. Although

* Department of Economics, Birkbeck College, University of London, 7–15 Gresse Street, London W1P 2LL, UK, e-mail gchristodoulakis@econ.bbk.ac.uk
† Faculty of Economics and Trinity College, University of Cambridge.

they appear to provide a very good in-sample fit, there are numerous studies (see, for example Tse, 1991; Lee, 1991; Figlewski, 1994; Xu and Taylor, 1995) criticizing their out-of-sample behaviour and questioning the usefulness of ARCH for volatility forecasting. There is a perception of poor out-of-sample performance on the basis of relatively high forecast error statistics as well as limited explanatory power of the ARCH forecasts for the 'true' volatility as quantified by the squared or absolute returns over the relevant forecast horizons. This view has not been seriously challenged in the literature, with the exception of a paper by Andersen and Bollerslev (1997) which we discuss in section 6.4.

In this chapter we investigate the noise inherent in such a forecast methodology. We measure its effects and show that it tends to significantly inflate the mean squared error statistic and remove the explanatory power of ARCH forecasts on realized volatility. The structure of the chapter is as follows. In section 6.2 we review the literature on ARCH forecasting theory. Section 6.3 reviews the literature on ARCH forecast evaluation. We conclude from this review that GARCH appears to forecast badly on the basis of conventional statistical tests but it does rather well when more advanced concepts such as utility- and profit-based criteria are used. In section 6.4 we reconcile the results and show why GARCH does forecast better than previously thought; we support our arguments with results from simulation experiments. In section 6.5 we prove results for more general error structures and show the robustness of our conclusions. Section 6.6 concludes.

6.2 ARCH FORECASTS AND PROPERTIES

One of the primary objectives in ARCH model building is to obtain out-of-sample forecasts of the conditional second moments of a process as well as to gain further insight on the uncertainty of forecasts of its conditional mean. In this section we will briefly assess what constitutes current practice in the ARCH forecasting literature.

To introduce a basic notation, let us assume a univariate discrete-time, real-valued stochastic process $\{y_t\}$ of asset returns be generated by the model

$$y_t = \sqrt{h_t} v_t \tag{6.1}$$

where $v_t \sim \text{iid}(0, 1)$ and h_t is any GARCH process. This is a basic data-generating structure on which several ARCH-type models have been built. The focus of our attention is on the implications of the presence of ARCH for the multistep prediction of the conditional first and second moments as well as the prediction error distribution.

Engle and Kraft (1983) examine the forecasting of ARMA processes with ARCH errors for which they derive the multistep prediction for the conditional mean and the associated prediction error variance. The presence of ARCH does not affect the expression for the minimum MSE predictor of y_{t+s} but only the associated forecast error uncertainty. Under homoscedastic ARMA, the latter is an increasing function of the prediction horizon independent of the origin of the forecast. However, in the presence of ARCH, the forecast error variance will depend non-trivially upon the current information set and its evaluation will require forecasts of h_{t+s}. As the forecast horizon increases, it will tend to converge to the unconditional variance of the process, assuming it exists. These results are extended to the GARCH case in Engle and Bollerslev (1986), who also consider the case of IGARCH for which the conditional forecast error variance will not only depend on the current information set but also grow linearly with the forecast horizon. A more unified treatment of the topic is given in Baillie and Bollerslev (1992) who consider a general ARMA(m,l)–GARCH(p,q) process and derive multistep prediction formulas for both the conditional mean and variance and the associated prediction error variances. Karanasos (1997) provides results for multistep prediction of the ARMA(m,l)–GARCH(p,q) model with mean effects.

The distribution of $(y_{t+s}/\sqrt{E_t(h_{t+s})})$ for $s > 1$ and h_t time varying will generally depend on the information set at time t and thus the question arises as how to approximate the prediction error distribution which is analytically intractable. Baillie and Bollerslev (1992) suggest the use of the Cornish–Fisher[2] asymptotic expansion which will require the evaluation of higher order conditional moments of y_{t+s}. Granger, White and Kamstra (1989) propose ARCH quantile regression techniques for combining forecasts as a method for the estimation of the time-varying prediction error intervals. Further, Geweke (1989) proposes a numerical methodology using Bayesian ideas for the evaluation of a multistep exact predictive density in a linear model with ARCH disturbances. The arguments of Nelson (1990, 1992) could also provide a basis to approximate the forecast error distribution. If a high-frequency ARCH can be seen as a good approximation of a continuous time diffusion process, then an approximation for the distribution of the long horizon ARCH forecasts could be taken from the unconditional distribution of the diffusion. A few studies provide analytical results, such as Cooley and Parke (1990) and Satchell and Yoon (1994). Cooley and Parke propose a general class of likelihood-based asymptotic prediction functions that approximate the entire distribution of future observations and illustrate their results in the context of the ARCH class. Satchell and Yoon present exact results for the distribution of the two- and three-step-ahead forecast error in the popular case of a variable with GARCH(1,1) volatility. Last, Christoffersen and Diebold (1994) study the general optimal prediction problem under asymmetric loss functions. They provide analytical solutions for the optimal predictor for the linex[3] and the linlin[4] functions and develop numerical procedures for more complicated cases. They illustrate their results with a GARCH (1,1) forecasting exercise under the linlin loss function.

6.3 FORECASTING PERFORMANCE EVALUATION

Conditional heteroscedasticity in financial data is encapsulated in the fact that y has thicker tails than v as defined in equation (6.1). The underlying philosophy in the ARCH class of models is that they reproduce (explain) the random variation in h and thus reverse this tail thickening. A fundamental question is what criteria should one use to judge the superiority of a volatility forecast.

From the traditional statistical point of view, we wish to pick up the forecast that incorporates the maximum possible information (or the minimum possible noise). By contrast, there is a growing literature examining the extent to which more natural criteria such as expected utility, profit or likelihood maximization can provide adequate forecast evaluation as opposed to the traditional statistical criteria. Fair and Shiller (1989, 1990) argue that the information content in alternative forecasting models differs and thus a particular forecast can contribute to the information set of a competing forecast with lower MSE, ideas that can be viewed in the light of the notion of 'full' and 'partial' optimality of forecasts of Brown and Maital (1981). The discussion has started outside the volatility literature, with a class of papers that could not reject the null of no value added by most sophisticated forecasts over simple ARMA or even random walk models. Among others, Cooper and Nelson (1975), Narashimhan (1975), Ahlers and Lakonishok (1983), Hsieh (1989), Diebold and Nason (1990) and Hsieh (1993) as well as Dimson and Marsh (1990) for volatility models, all report the poor out-of-sample performance of non-linear models. The common feature in these papers is that performance is assessed on the basis of traditional statistical criteria such as the MSE. For some models, this inherent weakness can be understood, e.g. Daccó and Satchell (1995) prove a proposition stating conditions under which forecasts based on the 'true', regime-based model, for example a two-state Markov-switching model for exchange rates, can be higher in MSE terms than those forecasts based on the (false) assumption of a random walk with or without drift.

Leitch and Tanner (1991) address the problem of the economic value of forecasts thus connecting forecast evaluation to the behaviour of the economic agent. Using profit measures, they show that a forecast can be of low value according to forecast error statistics but at the same time be very profitable. They also report a very weak relationship between the statistical forecast accuracy and the forecast's profits. Following this approach, Satchell and Timmermann (1995) prove a proposition which states the conditions under which standard forecasting criteria will not generally be suited for the assessment of the economic value of predictions from non-linear processes. Setting up a simple trading strategy they report results consistent with Leitch and Tanner.

Further, Diebold and Mariano (1991) propose that for the economic forecast evaluation one should go beyond the traditional statistical criteria and allow for a wider class of loss functions. Christoffersen and Diebold (1994) study optimal prediction under asymmetric loss while Granger and Pesaran (1996) adopt a decision-theoretic approach to forecast evaluation. Diebold and Lopez (1995) provide a very informative assessment of the existing technology on forecast evaluation and combination.

These findings are also reflected in the ARCH literature. In section 6.3.1 we discuss the ARCH forecasting papers that use statistical measures of forecast accuracy and unbiasedness. Sections 6.3.2 and 6.3.3 present more recent studies employing economic criteria as well, such as expected utility and profit maximization.

6.3.1   Statistics-based evaluation

We first review a class of ARCH forecasting exercises that utilizes exclusively forecast error statistics[5] focusing primarily on forecast accuracy. A second class of papers follows examining the issues of unbiasedness as well as the information content of volatility forecasts, employing regression-based tests.

Akgiray (1989) employs the classical forecast error measures to evaluate the performance of Historical, Exponentially Weighted Moving Average (EWMA), ARCH and GARCH models in monthly forecasts, using daily stock data over 1963–1986. Evidence suggests that GARCH forecasts are slightly less biased and more accurate but the significance of the difference between the error measures is not examined. Tse (1991) compares a range of models similar to Akgiray (1989) using daily stock market data over 1986–1989 to generate monthly volatility forecasts. The empirical findings show that EWMA outperforms GARCH for the particular period. Lee (1991) performs an evaluation exercise between GARCH and the Gaussian kernel models using five weekly exchange rate series over 1981–1989 to generate one-step-ahead volatility forecasts. In terms of accuracy the results show that GARCH performs well but cannot generally outperform the non-linear models in the RMSE criterion. In MAE criterion the Gaussian kernel is shown to be the most accurate. Further, Figlewski (1994) uses monthly returns on S&P 500 and 20-year Treasury Bond yields to perform long-term volatility forecasting (6, 12, 24 months' horizon), using historical volatility (over the previous five and 10 years) and the GARCH (1,1) models. The forecasting performance on the basis of RMSE for S&P is almost the same for both models at all three horizons, but for the Treasury Bond yield GARCH appears substantially less accurate than historical volatility, and gets worse the longer the forecast horizon. Xu and Taylor (1995) use PHLX daily currency option prices and exchange rates over 1985–1995 to evaluate the relative performance of implied volatility, historical and GARCH predictors. They find that implied volatility forecasts are best for both one- and four-week horizons. West and Cho (1995) perform a similar evaluation exercise for the predictive ability of alternative models of exchange rate volatility, and develop an asymptotic procedure to test for the equality of the forecast error statistics. Using weekly data they compare the performance of historical, autoregressive, GARCH and Gaussian kernel models in one-, 12- and 24-week-ahead forecasts. GARCH forecasts are found to be slightly more accurate for a one-week horizon while for longer horizons the results are ambiguous. Last, Brailsford and Faff (1996) evaluate the forecasting performance of eight alternative models: the random walk, historical mean, moving average, EWMA, exponential smoothing, regression, GARCH(1,1), and the GJR-GARCH of Glosten, Jaganathan and Runkle (1993). They use daily stock market data over 1974–1993 to perform one-step-ahead forecasts and find the various model rankings to be sensitive to the error statistic used.

The second class of measures concentrates on forecast unbiasedness by adapting the approach of Mincer and Zarnowitz (1969). If h_t and $\hat{h}_t$ represent the time t actual and predicted volatility respectively, then $\hat{h}_t$ will be an unbiased forecast of h_t if in the regression

$$h_{t+s} = \alpha + \beta \hat{h}_{t+s} + e_{t+s}$$

$\alpha = 0$, $\beta = 1$ and $E(e_{t+s}) = 0$. The error term should be white noise for one-step forecasts, but it will probably be autocorrelated for multistep forecasts. This approach to forecast evaluation is further studied by Hatanaka (1974). The information content of competing forecasts is examined in a similar approach introduced by Fair and Shiller (1989, 1990) in which the 'actual' series is regressed on two competing forecasts. If both models contain information not included in the other, then both regression coefficients will be non-zero. If the information in one model is completely contained in the other, the coefficient of the latter will be non-zero. This approach reflects the ideas of Brown and Maital (1981) on 'partial' and 'full' optimality of forecasts. In all the ARCH applications, h_t is approximated by the squared return, y_t^2.

Pagan and Schwert (1990) use this approach to test the in- and out-of-sample performance of GARCH, EGARCH, Markov-switching Gaussian kernel and Fourier models for conditional stock volatility. They run the above regression both in levels and logs, motivated by a symmetric and an asymmetric loss function respectively, test the regression coefficients and compare the R^2's. Their evidence suggests that EGARCH and GARCH models tend to be less biased in out-of-sample prediction. Cumby, Figlewski and Hasbrouck (1993) use weekly excess returns on five broad asset classes to assess the predictive performance of EGARCH, historical volatility and a forecast based on the last period's squared return. Their regression results suggest that all models perform badly, with EGARCH providing the less biased out-of-sample forecasts. West and Cho (1995) in addition to their standard analysis, perform this forecast bias-efficiency regression analysis. None of the competing models was shown to pass the efficiency test.

Day and Lewis (1992) compare the information content of implied volatilities from weekly prices of call options on the S&P 100 index to GARCH and EGARCH models. Their out-of-sample evidence suggests that implied volatility and the GARCH and EGARCH forecasts are on average unbiased but results regarding their relative information content are not as clear. Lamoureux and Lastrapes (1993) also perform an analysis similar to Day and Lewis with daily data on individual stock options. Their findings show that implied volatility tends to underpredict realized volatility while forecasts of variance from past returns contain relevant information not contained in the forecasts constructed from implied volatility. Jorion (1995) examines the information content and the predictive power of implied standard deviations versus moving average and GARCH models. The latter are found to be outperformed by implied standard deviations which is also a biased volatility forecast. Last, Canina and Figlewski (1993) find implied volatility to have virtually no correlation with future volatility, while it does not incorporate the information contained in recently observed volatility. We remind the reader that all the above statements should be interpreted in the following sense; observed volatility means squared returns.

Overall, forecast error statistics tend to show either poor or ambiguous out-of-sample performance for ARCH-type models, often even for short forecast horizons. On the basis of unbiasedness regressions, GARCH-type forecasts tend to be less biased than their competitors while they are shown to contain information not contained in other volatility forecasts. However, a common feature in all regression-based tests is that ARCH forecasts have low explanatory power with respect to squared returns. The extremely low R^2 coefficients reported along with the ambiguous forecast error statistics have been the basis for heavy criticism of ARCH forecasting. In section 6.4 we examine the extent to which such a criticism is justified.

6.3.2   Utility-based evaluation

Motivated by the assumption of utility-maximizing economic agents, it is natural to formulate utility-based metrics for model selection. McCulloch and Rossi (1990) provided the starting point of this approach by applying it to optimal portfolio choices.

West, Edison and Cho (1993) employ these ideas to evaluate the forecasting performance of alternative volatility models. Their approach is inspired by the asymmetry inherent in a utility-based criterion when forecasts of future variances are used for asset allocation decisions. For specific choices of utility functions, underpredictions of future variances will lead to more heavily penalized expected utility than equal overpredictions. Thus, for West, Edison and Cho 'a model of conditional variance is preferred if, on average, over many periods, it leads to higher expected utility'. The model is applied, under the alternative assumptions of jointly normal asset returns and exponential utility or finite means and variances of asset returns and quadratic utility, to evaluate the out-of-sample performance of homoscedastic, GARCH, autoregressive and Gaussian kernel models of conditional volatility. Using a data set of six weekly exchange rate returns, an investor is assumed to use forecasts from the alternative volatility models to produce a sequence of hypothetical asset allocations over a number of successive periods. The empirical evidence suggests that GARCH models tend on average to lead to higher expected utility.

Although this approach uses economic criteria to introduce asymmetries in the loss function, it still uses the squared error as a proxy to the unobserved volatility and thus introduces noise, while the use of specific utility functions is restrictive. In this framework the investor achieves higher expected utility using the true volatility rather than using a noisy forecast. Nelson (1996) shows that when choosing between two noisy forecasts, the investor will not necessarily prefer the less noisy forecast. Acting as if the volatility forecast were exactly correct permits him to increase expected utility by picking up a more noisy forecast. In addition, this exercise can be seen as a discrete-choice optimization problem as different models of uncertainty are being ranked by a measure of expected utility. It is by no means clear to the authors that this is actually consistent with expected utility maximization. Further, if it assumed that returns are unconditionally normal, as stated, then the investor knows that a GARCH model is not appropriate since GARCH implies non-normal unconditional returns. Such an investor would not be rational in the usual sense of the term. An alternative procedure, advocated by Klein and Bawa (1976) is to set up a class of models and optimize asset allocation using Bayesian arguments.

6.3.3 Profit-based/preference-free evaluation

This approach has recently been established with papers outside the volatility literature, such as Leitch and Tanner (1991) and Satchell and Timmermann (1995). The central idea is to construct a trading rule and examine which forecasting model produces the highest return on average, either on an unadjusted or on a risk adjusted basis. In both papers, empirical results show that a model with higher MSE may produce substantially higher return. This approach has also been applied in an S&P option market efficiency exercise using implied volatilities by Harvey and Whaley (1992), which find that the implied volatility predictors are unable to produce abnormal returns after taking into account transaction costs.

In the context of GARCH volatility forecasting Engle, Kane and Noh (1993a) use this approach to assess the performance of autoregressive models of implied volatility and the GARCH model. They assume two traders who trade straddles on the S&P 500 index option market, each forecasting volatility with one of the two alternative methods. In some cases both traders are found to generate abnormally high returns, but overall GARCH volatility predictions generate greater profits than implied volatility predictions. Engle *et al.* (1993) develop a framework where they assess the performance of several volatility models by comparing the cumulative profits from options trading in a simulated options market. The technique is demonstrated using the NYSE portfolio data over 1962–1989. They assume four traders, each one representing a competing volatility predictor over the exercise period, that price one-day options on $1 shares of the NYSE. Agents are also allowed to hedge their variance-forecast-driven transactions by taking positions in the NYSE stock. The relative performance of the four competing models (agents), that is moving average and ARMA(1,1) of squared errors, the variance from an OLS-AR(1) model and the GARCH(1,1), is assessed on the basis of the accumulated profits and losses over the exercise period, which support the superiority of the GARCH(1,1) specification. The analysis is extended to long-term options and long-term volatility forecasts in Engle, Kane and Noh (1993b). In this paper the authors use the NYSE index returns over 1968–1991 to examine (among other things) the relative performance of GARCH(1,1) and the simple moving average of squared returns. The simulation results show that the gains from using GARCH(1,1) instead of moving average apply to options of maturity of up to one month.

Both approaches of economics-oriented forecast evaluation discussed above have been successful in introducing asymmetries to the loss function and detecting possible limitations of the statistical approach to evaluate volatility forecasts appropriately. They show GARCH forecasts to be preferred to the usual alternatives. However, these conclusions are case specific, relying on assumptions that do not hold generally.

6.4   THE PATHOLOGY OF ARCH FORECAST EVALUATION

In the previous sections we have seen that simple measures of forecasting performance do not reward GARCH whilst more complex procedures seem to. In this section we offer an explanation of the poor performance of the statistical measures.

The statistical approach requires no economic assumptions and is thus more practical. When applied to evaluate ARCH forecasts it indicates a poor out-of-sample performance in terms of accuracy and explanatory power with respect to the true volatility. This result relies on the use of squared return[6] as a proxy to the true, unobservable, volatility. The analysis we present next is worked in natural logarithms rather than levels. This gives tractable results and since the approximation $\ln(x) = -(1 - x)$ is accurate for small x, differences in logs will be nearly equal to differences in levels for small positive numbers. Indeed, for stochastic volatility models the following calculation will be exact without any approximation. Squaring equation (6.1) and taking logs

$$\ln(y_{t+s}^2) = \ln(h_{t+s}) + \ln(v_{t+s}^2) \tag{6.2}$$

Clearly, the squared return approximates the true volatility h_t, augmented by a noise, v_{t+s}^2, which under a conditional normality assumption in (6.1) will be a $\chi^2(1)$ variable. Subtracting from both sides the volatility forecast generated by the model

$$\ln(y_{t+s}^2) - \ln(\hat{h}_{t+s}) = (\ln(h_{t+s}) - \ln(\hat{h}_{t+s})) + \ln(v_{t+s}^2) \tag{6.3}$$

where the LHS represents the approximated forecast error, the first term of the RHS the 'true' forecast error and the second term the forecast error noise. We explicitly calculate the mean and the variance of the forecast error noise in the appendix. We now see how the mean error (ME) and mean absolute error (MAE) are affected.

$$ME_{observed} = ME_{true} + E(\ln(v_{t+s}^2))$$

Under unbiased GARCH predictions ($ME_{true} = 0$) and squared returns as proxies of the true volatility, the observed ME will be equal to -1.27 (see appendix), suggesting a substantial underestimation of the true mean error. Also, by triangle inequality

$$MAE_{observed} \leq MAE_{true} + E\left|\ln(v_{t+s}^2)\right|$$

Squaring both sides of (6.3) and taking expectations we obtain

$$E((\ln(y_{t+s}^2) - \ln(\hat{h}_{t+s}))^2) = E((\ln(h_{t+s}) - \ln(\hat{h}_{t+s}))^2) + E((\ln(v_{t+s}^2))^2)$$

$$+ 2E((\ln(h_{t+s}) - \ln(\hat{h}_{t+s}))\ln(v_{t+s}^2)) \tag{6.4}$$

Under the assumptions of the GARCH model[7] the true forecast error and the noise will be uncorrelated and if $\hat{h}$ is an unbiased forecast of h, then the last term of the RHS will vanish. The estimated mean squared error will approximate the 'true' mean squared error increased by the amount of $E((\ln(v_{t+s}^2))^2)$. Since v_{t+s}^2 is a $\chi^2(1)$ random variable, this quantity is known and is equal to 6.5486, all relevant calculations are given in the appendix. Furthermore, the third term of (6.4) can be shown to be equal to

$$2E(\ln(h_{t+s}) - \ln(\hat{h}_{t+s}))E(\ln(v_{t+s}^2))$$

for which the second term is shown to be equal to -1.27. Thus we find the relationship

$$MSE_{\text{observed}} = MSE_{\text{true}} + 6.5486 - 2.54 * Bias_{\text{true}} \qquad (6.5)$$

Equivalently, in the forecast unbiasedness regression[8] framework

$$\ln(h_{t+s}) = \alpha + \beta \ln(\hat{h}_{t+s}) + e_{t+s} \qquad (6.6)$$

where $\hat{h}$ is an unbiased forecast of the true volatility h if $\alpha = 0$, $\beta = 1$ and $E(e) = 0$. Since h is unobservable, its approximation with $y^2 = hv^2$ leads to the following regression

$$\ln(y_{t+s}^2) = \alpha + \beta \ln(\hat{h}_{t+s}) + (e_{t+s} + \ln(v_{t+s}^2)) \qquad (6.7)$$

which implies that ME and MSE are inflated by the same factor as in (6.3) and (6.5). The applied literature has extensively used regression (6.7) to evaluate volatility forecasts. The estimated regression coefficient for the constant is now expected to be biased since the expected value of the noise term in (6.7) will be different than zero. Further, the signal-to-noise ratio decreases, which explains the extremely low R^2's reported in the literature, that have been a source of criticism on GARCH out-of-sample performance. To see this, we can simply write, dropping the subscripts,

$$R^2 = \frac{\text{Var}(\ln(\hat{h}))}{\text{Var}(\ln(y^2))} = 1 - \frac{\text{Var}(e)}{\text{Var}(\ln(y^2))} - \frac{\text{Var}(\ln(v^2))}{\text{Var}(\ln(y^2))}$$

$$= R_T^2 - \frac{\text{Var}(\ln(v^2))}{\text{Var}(\ln(y^2))} \qquad (6.8)$$

where R_T^2 is the coefficient of determination from regression (6.7) assuming that $\ln(v^2)$ is zero. The second term of the RHS in (6.8) is positive and explains the low R^2's found in empirical studies; the numerator is a known quantity equal to 4.9348 as shown in the appendix, while the denominator can easily be derived from the model assumed.

The above points have been referred to in the literature. For example, Nelson (1996) proves a general theorem in which the inclusion of a mean preserving spread (noise) to a volatility forecast error will thicken the tails of the distribution of its standardized residuals. An alternative interpretation to this standard practice in the applied literature, to approximate h with $y^2 = hv^2$, is that it tends to undo GARCH effects. While the 'true' model is described by (6.1) this practice implies that the econometrician believes a model of the form

$$y = (hv^2)^{1/2}v \quad \text{where} \quad v \sim N(0, 1)$$

for which the standardized residual $(y/h^{1/2}) = v^2$ will be a $\chi^2(1)$ variable.

6.4.1 A simulation experiment

We illustrate the relevance of our analysis with a simulation experiment. Let us assume the following data generating process

$$y_t = \sqrt{h_t}v_t \quad \text{where} \quad v_t \sim N(0, 1)$$
$$h_t = \alpha_0 + \alpha h_{t-1} + \beta y_{t-1}^2$$

Assuming some plausible values for the GARCH parameters, e.g. $\alpha_0 = 0.083$, $\alpha = 0.1$ and $\beta = 0.82$ taken from the applied literature and generating v_t as a standard normal variable, we can simulate[9] the 'true' volatility h_t and the return process y_t. We can now use y_t to estimate a GARCH(1,1), forecast h_t and record the 'true' forecast error $\ln(h) - \ln(\hat{h})$ as well as the approximated forecast error $\ln(y^2) - \ln(\hat{h})$. We repeat this simulation 10^4 times with a plausible sample size of 3000 'daily' observations and 10 forecasting steps and calculate all the relevant forecast error statistics for both the 'true' and the approximated forecast errors. We also run the forecast unbiasedness regressions for both the in-sample and the out-of-sample forecast errors. Our simulation results are presented in Tables 6.1 to 6.4.

Table 6.1 contains the 'true' and the approximate forecast error statistics for 10 forecasting steps. It is clear that in all cases the use of squared return results in inflated error statistics. In particular, the ME is decreased by a factor of -1.27, while the MSE is increased on average by a factor of 6.55 plus the bias λ^{10} which increases with the forecast horizon. Table 6.2 presents the in-sample Mincer–Zarnowitz regression results. GARCH forecasts are shown to be unbiased with high explanatory power with respect to the true volatility h. When squared return is used as a proxy to the true volatility this result is reversed; the estimated intercept term is biased, as shown in (6.7), while R^2's are strikingly low. In Tables 6.3 and 6.4 the out-of-sample regression results (for all forecasting steps) fully comply with the above conclusions.

Andersen and Bollerslev (1997) work on the same problem and report results complementary to those presented here. They use a continuous-time volatility framework, the Nelson (1990) continuous-time GARCH(1,1), to show that estimation of the actual volatility from higher frequency data substantially reduces

Table 6.1   *Forecast error statistics (logs)*

Step	ME(h)	ME(y)	MAE(h)	MAE(y)	MSE(h)	MSE(y)	MAPE(h)	MAPE(y)	λ
1	0.008	−1.266	0.035	1.760	0.002	6.635	0.229	7.991	−.002
2	−0.017	−1.284	0.146	1.765	0.035	6.628	1.074	13.09	.040
3	−0.035	−1.295	0.208	1.788	0.066	6.707	0.734	6.692	.078
4	−0.050	−1.314	0.255	1.800	0.098	6.927	0.836	5.759	.122
5	−0.063	−1.331	0.290	1.803	0.127	6.808	0.635	4.472	.141
6	−0.078	−1.348	0.318	1.839	0.153	7.166	0.570	3.755	.209
7	−0.089	−1.385	0.345	1.861	0.181	7.183	0.518	3.279	.267
8	−0.103	−1.381	0.371	1.857	0.209	6.974	0.521	2.691	.263
9	−0.116	−1.373	0.393	1.851	0.237	6.982	0.508	2.582	.285
10	−0.126	−1.410	0.414	1.88	0.261	7.219	0.496	2.350	.353

Definitions: $N = 10\,000$

$$ME(h) = \frac{1}{N}\sum_{i=1}^{N}(\ln(h) - \ln(\hat{h})), \quad ME(y) = \frac{1}{N}\sum_{i=1}^{N}(\ln(y^2) - \ln(\hat{h}))$$

$$MAE(h) = \frac{1}{N}\sum_{i=1}^{N}\left|\ln(h) - \ln(\hat{h})\right|, \quad MAE(y) = \frac{1}{N}\sum_{i=1}^{N}\left|\ln(y^2) - \ln(\hat{h})\right|$$

$$MSE(h) = \frac{1}{N}\sum_{i=1}^{N}(\ln(h) - \ln(\hat{h}))^2, \quad MSE(y) = \frac{1}{N}\sum_{i=1}^{N}(\ln(y^2) - \ln(\hat{h}))^2,$$

$$MAPE(h) = \frac{1}{N}\sum_{i=1}^{N}\left|\frac{\ln(h) - \ln(\hat{h})}{\ln(\hat{h})}\right|, \quad MAPE(y) = \frac{1}{N}\sum_{i=1}^{N}\left|\frac{\ln(y^2) - \ln(\hat{h})}{\ln(\hat{h})}\right|.$$

$\lambda = 2.54^{*}BIAS_{\text{true}}$ as shown in equations (6.4) and (6.5).

Table 6.2   *In-sample regression results*

Regression coefficient	Dependent variable: $\ln(h)$	Dependent variable: $\ln(y^2)$
α	−0.006	−1.263
β	1.008	0.990
R^2	0.998	0.103

Notes: $\ln(h)$: regression (6.6), $\ln(y^2)$: regression (6.7).

Table 6.3   *Out-of-sample regression results ($\ln(h)$)*

Coeff.	Step 1	Step 2	Step 3	Step 4	Step 5	Step 6	Step 7	Step 8	Step 9	Step 10
α	0.005	−0.009	−0.002	−0.037	−0.047	−0.056	−0.063	−0.07	−0.08	−0.076
β	0.995	0.991	0.987	0.987	0.984	0.978	0.975	0.971	0.966	0.955
R^2	0.998	0.977	0.957	0.937	0.920	0.904	0.888	0.872	0.856	0.843

Notes: $\ln(h)$: regression (6.6). For each forecasting step we run a cross-section regression over 10^4 data points, produced from an equal number of simulations. Step j means a j-period ahead forecast.

Table 6.4 *Out-of-sample regression results ($\ln(y^2)$)*

Coeff.	Step 1	Step 2	Step 3	Step 4	Step 5	Step 6	Step 7	Step 8	Step 9	Step 10
α	−1.237	−1.240	−1.318	−1.284	−1.319	−1.332	−1.380	−1.339	−1.32	−1.363
β	0.969	0.955	1.022	0.97	0.988	0.985	0.994	0.961	0.959	0.957
R^2	0.112	0.106	0.111	0.096	0.098	0.089	0.091	0.085	0.080	0.078

Notes: $\ln(y^2)$: regression (6.7). For each forecasting step we run a cross-section regression over 10^4 data points, produced from an equal number of simulations. Step j means a j-period ahead forecast.

the noise occurring when it is approximated by the squared return. This is equivalent to saying that as we increase the frequency of observation per day, the term $\ln(v_{t+s}^2)$ in (6.2) will converge in probability to zero and consequently $MSE_{\text{true}} = MSE_{\text{obs}}$. This is demonstrated empirically for tick-by-tick FX data based on quotes. Whilst this may be reasonable for such a data set, microstructure issues arise if we try and use equity tick-by-tick transactions data.[11] Their simulation results suggest that as the sampling frequency increases, the R^2 increases approaching a limit of 0.5. This result justifies the (perhaps intuitive) approach in many papers such as Akgiray (1989), Tse (1991), Figlewski (1994), West and Cho (1995), Brailsford and Faff (1996) as well as the RiskMetrics Technical Document (1995, 81–82) that use daily data to generate monthly forecasts for which the actual monthly volatility is estimated from the within-month daily observations. However, even in this case the forecast evaluation remains misleading as a significant component of noise is left out. Further, in many cases such as macro and monetary variables, interest rates or housing market series, higher frequency data are unavailable and the question of quantifying the effects of actual volatility approximation is still important.

6.5 SOME GENERAL RESULTS

In section 6.4 we concentrated our attention on the popular case of Gaussian standardized errors v. This can be restrictive since the conditional distribution of asset returns may be non-normal, in which case a Gaussian ARCH will fail to represent the data-generating process. There are many alternative distributions that have been proposed, such as the conditional t to accommodate for excess kurtosis (Bollerslev, 1987), a normal-poison mixture distribution (Jorion, 1988), the generalized exponential distribution (Nelson, 1991) and serially dependent mixture of normal variables (Cai, 1994).

We address the implications of non-normality to our previous results in section 6.4, under alternative assumptions for the standardized error v. In the following we present results for the compound normal class as well as the Gram–Charlier class of distributions.

6.5.1   The compound normal

We specify the error structure in equation (6.1) as follows

$$y_t = \sqrt{h_t}v_t' \quad \text{where} \quad v_t' = \sqrt{s_t}v_t \tag{6.9}$$

and

$$v_t \sim N(0,1), \quad \text{Prob}(s_t > 0) = 1, \quad s_t, v_t \text{ independent}$$

A popular choice is to make y_t t-distributed, see Hamilton (1995, 662) for details. This choice is equivalent to setting s_t equal to the reciprocal of a gamma variable. Other choices of s_t can be used, for example if s_t is Bernoulli we get a mixture of normals for y_t.

We now investigate the implications of (6.9), for which we see that $E(\sqrt{s_t}v_t) = 0$, $E(s_t v_t^2) = 1$ and thus $E(s_t) = 1$. Squaring (6.9) and taking logs

$$\ln(y_t^2) = \ln(h_t) + (\ln(s_t) + \ln(v_t^2))$$

where the second term of the RHS represents the noise occurring from the approximation of true volatility with squared returns. The mean of the noise term will simply be

$$E(\ln(y_{t+s}^2) - \ln(h_{t+s})) = E(\ln(s_{t+s})) + E(\ln(v_{t+s}^2)) < -1.27$$

since the second term of the RHS is a known quantity (see appendix) and the first term is negative by Jensen's inequality. Thus, under unbiased GARCH forecasts the estimated ME will be less than -1.27. Furthermore,

$$\text{Var}(\ln(y_{t+s}^2) - \ln(h_{t+s})) = \text{Var}(\ln(s_{t+s})) + \text{Var}(\ln(v_{t+s}^2)) > 4.9348$$

since the second term of the RHS is a known quantity (see appendix) and the first term is positive. In addition, from (6.9)

$$E(\ln(v_{t+s}'^2)^2) = E(\ln(s_{t+s})^2) + E(\ln(v_{t+s}^2)^2) + 2E(\ln(s_{t+s})\ln(v_{t+s}^2)) > 6.5486$$

given the previous results. Thus the estimated MSE for this error structure will now be greater than 6.5486.

6.5.2   The Gram–Charlier class

Similar arguments can be applied for more general distributions. We now consider v_t to have a Gram–Charlier[12] distribution. Namely, the probability density function (pdf) of v_t, $pdf_v(x)$, is given by the following equation

$$pdf_v(x) = \frac{1}{\sqrt{2\pi}} \exp\left(-\frac{1}{2}x^2\right)\left(1 + \frac{\lambda_3}{3!}H_3(x) + \frac{\lambda_4}{4!}H_4(x)\right) \tag{6.10}$$

where $H_j(x)$ is the Hermite polynomial of j; $H_3(x) = x^3 - 3x$, $H_4(x) = x^4 - 6x^2 + 3$. It is well known that $E(v_t) = 0$, $\text{Var}(v_t) = 1$, skewness of $v_t = \lambda_3$ and excess kurtosis of $v_t = \lambda_4$.

Let $Y = v_t^2$, then denoting the pdf of Y by $pdf_Y(y)$, $\text{Prob}(Y \le y) = \text{Prob}(v_t^2 \le y)$, and

$$pdf_Y(y) = \frac{d}{dy}(\text{Prob}(v_t \le y^{1/2}) - \text{Prob}(v_t \le -y^{1/2}))$$

$$= \frac{1}{2}y^{-1/2}pdf_v(y^{1/2}) + \frac{1}{2}y^{-1/2}pdf_v(-y^{1/2})$$

Now,

$$pdf_v(y^{1/2}) = \frac{1}{\sqrt{2\pi}} \exp\left(-\frac{y}{2}\right)\left(1 + \frac{\lambda_3}{6}(y^{3/2} - 3y^{1/2}) + \frac{\lambda_4}{24}(y^2 - 6y + 3)\right)$$

and

$$pdf_Y(y) = \frac{1}{\sqrt{2\pi}}y^{-1/2} \exp\left(-\frac{y}{2}\right)\left(1 + \frac{\lambda_4}{24}(y^2 - 6y + 3)\right) \qquad (6.11)$$

We recognize $pdf_Y(y)$ as a $\chi^2(1)$ pdf multiplied by a polynomial which *does not* depend on skewness but *does* depend on excess kurtosis.

We present our conclusions so far plus further results on the moment generating function (mgf) of Y in a proposition.

Proposition 1

If v_t has a Gram–Charlier distribution with pdf given by (6.10), then the pdf of $Y = v_t^2$ is given by equation (6.11). This is independent of λ_3 and has an mgf, $\Phi_Y(s)$, given by

$$\Phi_Y(s) = (1 - 2s)^{-\frac{1}{2}}\left(1 + \frac{\lambda_4}{8}((1 - 2s)^{-2} - 2(1 - 2s)^{-1} + 1)\right)$$

Proof   We have presented most of the proof earlier in the text. The mgf can be computed by noting that $(1 - 2s)^{-1/2} = E(\exp(sY'))$ for Y' a $\chi^2(1)$. Then, differentiating both sides by s, we see that

$$(1 - 2s)^{-3/2} = E(Y' \exp(sY'))$$
$$3(1 - 2s)^{-5/2} = E(Y'^2 \exp(sY'))$$

Thus,

$$\Phi_Y(s) = E_Y(\exp(sY)) = E_{Y'}\left(\left(1 + \frac{\lambda_4}{24}(Y'^2 - 6Y' + 3)\right)\exp(sY')\right)$$

$$= (1 - 2s)^{-1/2} + \frac{\lambda_4}{24}(3(1 - 2s)^{-5/2} - 6(1 - 2s)^{-3/2} + 3(1 - 2s)^{-1/2})$$

$$= (1 - 2s)^{-1/2}\left(1 + \frac{\lambda_4}{8}x((1 - 2s)^{-2} - 2(1 - 2s)^{-1} + 1)\right)$$

where $E_Y(\cdot)$ means expectation with respect to Y. $\qquad$ QED

Our main result is that equation (6.5) is robust for all λ_3 and depends only on λ_4. We have already noted that Y does not depend upon λ_3, we now show how the numbers -2.54 and 6.5486 in (6.5) are affected by the presence of excess kurtosis λ_4.

Proposition 2

If v_t has a Gram–Charlier distribution with pdf given by (6.10), then the weight on the bias in (6.5), -2.54, becomes $-(2.54 + (\lambda_4/3))$, whilst 6.5486 (the second central moment of a $\ln(\chi^2(1))$) becomes $6.5486 + (\lambda_4/3) - (\lambda_4^2/36)$.

Proof See appendix.

The observed mean error in (6.3) will now increase with λ_4 and thus the weight of the bias in (6.5) increases as well. Now, under unbiased GARCH volatility predictions the new form of (6.5) will lead to increasing observed mean square error with λ_4 which eventually, after $\lambda_4 = 6$ will be decreasing. In addition, R^2 in (6.8) initially increases with excess kurtosis, but eventually decreases allowing R^2 to approach unity. We note in passing, the study of Andersen and Bollerslev (1997) which specifies the intraday volatility structure and provides results for the limiting behaviour of R^2 as the dependent variable in (6.7) is estimated from higher frequency data; it is found to approach $\frac{1}{2}$ as the sampling frequency becomes infinite. Our analysis does not investigate intraday issues.

Remark Proposition 2 can be seen as a robustness result for equations (6.3) and (6.5) in which our results do not depend upon skewness. However, it is more a peculiarity due to the peculiar nature of Gram–Charlier pdf's. For zero excess kurtosis, Proposition 2 also includes our results under the normal distribution. It is also consistent with our results for compound normals in as much as they exhibit no skewness ($\lambda_3 = 0$) and positive excess kurtosis ($\lambda_4 > 0$).

Overall, our results on compound normals in section 6.5.1 suggest that for unbiased estimators, non-normality will increase the discrepancy between the observed and the true forecast error statistics. If the bias is negative the discrepancy will be even larger than in the normal case. If the bias is positive, the discrepancy will be partly offset. The results for normality presented in Table 6.1 suggest a small bias which increases with the forecast horizon. Our results on the Gram–Charlier class suggest no effects from the presence of skewness while for plausible values of excess kurtosis the discrepancy between the observed and the true forecast error statistics will increase.

6.6 CONCLUSIONS

We provide an assessment of the ARCH forecasting literature, with respect to theoretical as well as forecast evaluation aspects. Our motivation stems from the fact of poor out-of-sample ARCH forecasting performance when judged on the basis of traditional forecast accuracy criteria versus its good performance when more advanced procedures such as expected utility or profit maximization are employed.

The approximation of the true volatility by the squared return introduces a substantial noise, which effectively inflates the estimated forecast error statistics and removes any explanatory power of ARCH volatility forecasts with respect to the 'true' volatility. Under the GARCH model assumptions and normal errors we characterize this noise and quantify its effects. For an unbiased GARCH predictor, the true mean error (zero) for log volatility will be decreased by a factor of -1.27, while the true mean squared error for log volatility will be increased by a factor 6.5486 which is up to 3000 times greater than the true mean squared error (see Table 6.1). Further, its explanatory power with respect to the true volatility as measured by R^2 will be substantially reduced. We support our arguments with results from simulation experiments. These results are also extended theoretically in two directions; for compound normals as well as the Gram–Charlier class of distributions. We show that the misestimation of traditional forecast performance measures is likely to be worsened by non-normality known to be present in financial data.

Finally, we present our reconciliation of the fact that GARCH seems to do better when the performance measure is based on measures more complex than mean, absolute and squared errors between forecasts and squared returns. This follows simply from the fact, demonstrated in simulation, that GARCH forecasts well when the true model is GARCH and correct comparisons are made. Non-linear measures of forecast such as economic evaluation or expected utility of asset allocations based on GARCH forecasts will often reflect the impact of the forecast correctly without making any inappropriate comparisons. Inasmuch as a GARCH formulation is reasonably close to the true model generating the data, this chapter concludes that non-linear evaluation is likely to be more reliable than the traditional methods of forecast evaluation using squared returns as a proxy for unobserved volatility.

6.7 APPENDIX

6.7.1 Mean and variance of $\ln(v^2)$

For Gaussian standardized errors v^2 is a $\chi^2(1)$ variable. Then, the moment generating function will be (for notational simplicity let $v^2 = x$)

$$E\left(e^{s\ln(x)}\right) = \int_0^\infty \frac{x^s x^{(1/2)-1} e^{-x/2}}{\sqrt{2\pi}} dx$$

$$= \int_0^\infty \frac{x^{(s+(1/2))-1}e^{-x/2}}{\sqrt{2\pi}} dx$$

$$= \frac{\left(\frac{1}{2}\right)^{s+(1/2)}}{\sqrt{2\pi}\left(\frac{1}{2}\right)^{s+(1/2)}} \int_0^\infty x^{(s+(1/2))-1}e^{-x/2} dx$$

$$= \frac{2^s \Gamma\left(s + \frac{1}{2}\right)}{\sqrt{\pi}}$$

where $\Gamma(\cdot)$ is the gamma function. The cumulant generating function will now simply be

$$\kappa(s) = s\ln(2) + \ln\Gamma\left(s + \frac{1}{2}\right) - \ln(\sqrt{\pi})$$

from which

$$\kappa'(s) = \ln(2) + \frac{\Gamma'\left(s + \frac{1}{2}\right)}{\Gamma\left(s + \frac{1}{2}\right)} = \ln(2) + \Psi\left(s + \frac{1}{2}\right)$$

$$\kappa''(s) = \Psi'\left(s + \frac{1}{2}\right)$$

where $\Psi(\cdot)$ and $\Psi'(\cdot)$ are the digamma and trigamma functions respectively (see Abramowitz and Stegun, 1970, 6.3.3 and 6.4.4).

Thus,

$$E(\ln x) = \kappa'(0) = \ln(2) + \Psi\left(\frac{1}{2}\right) = -1.27037$$

$$\text{Var}(\ln x) = \kappa''(0) = \Psi'\left(\frac{1}{2}\right) = (2^2 - 1)\zeta(2) = 4.9348$$

where $\zeta(\cdot)$ is the Rieman z function (see Abramowitz and Stegun, 1970, 23.2.16). Now

$$E\left((\ln x)^2\right) = \text{Var}(\ln x) + (E(\ln x))^2 = 6.5486$$

6.7.2   Proof of proposition 2

Consider the moment generating function of $X = \ln(Y)$, for Y as defined in Proposition 1.

$$\Phi_X(\theta) = E(\exp(\theta\ln(Y))) = E_Y(Y^\theta)$$

From Proposition 1 and for $Y' \sim \chi^2(1)$,

$$E_Y(Y^\theta) = E_{Y'}\left(Y'^\theta\left(1 + \frac{\lambda_4}{24}(Y'^2 - 6Y' + 3)\right)\right)$$

$$= E_{Y'}(Y'^\theta) + \frac{\lambda_4}{24}E_{Y'}(Y'^{(\theta+2)}) - \frac{\lambda_4}{4}E_{Y'}(Y'^{(\theta+1)}) + \frac{\lambda_4}{8}E_{Y'}(Y'^\theta)$$

Since for $Y \sim \chi^2(n)$

$$E(Y^\theta) = \int_0^\infty \frac{\exp\left(-\dfrac{Y}{2}\right) Y^{(n/2)+\theta-1}}{\Gamma\left(\dfrac{n}{2}\right) 2^{n/2}} \, dY = \frac{\Gamma\left(\dfrac{n}{2}+\theta\right) 2^{(n/2)+\theta}}{\Gamma\left(\dfrac{n}{2}\right) 2^{n/2}}$$

$$= 2^\theta \frac{\Gamma\left(\dfrac{n}{2}+\theta\right)}{\Gamma\left(\dfrac{n}{2}\right)}$$

where $\Gamma(\cdot)$ is the gamma function, we have

$$\Phi_X(\theta) = \frac{2^\theta \Gamma\left(\theta+\frac{1}{2}\right)}{\sqrt{\pi}} \left(1+\frac{\lambda_4}{8}\right) + \frac{2^\theta \lambda_4}{6\sqrt{\pi}} \Gamma\left(\theta+\frac{5}{2}\right)$$

$$- \frac{2^\theta \lambda_4}{2\sqrt{\pi}} \Gamma\left(\theta+\frac{3}{2}\right)$$

Using $\Gamma(n) = (n-1)\Gamma(n-1)$ (see Abramowitz and Stegun, 1970, 6.1.15)

$$\Phi_X(\theta) = \frac{2^\theta \Gamma\left(\theta+\frac{1}{2}\right)}{\sqrt{\pi}} \left(1+\frac{\lambda_4}{6}(\theta^2-\theta)\right)$$

The cumulant generating function will be

$$\kappa_X(\theta) = \theta \ln(2) + \ln\left(\Gamma\left(\frac{1}{2}+\theta\right)\right) + \ln\left(1+\frac{\lambda_4}{6}(\theta^2-\theta)\right) - \ln(\sqrt{\pi})$$

and thus

$$\kappa'_X(\theta) = \ln(2) + \frac{\Gamma'\left(\frac{1}{2}+\theta\right)}{\Gamma\left(\frac{1}{2}+\theta\right)} + \frac{\left(\dfrac{\lambda_4}{6}\right)(2\theta-1)}{1+\left(\dfrac{\lambda_4}{6}\right)(\theta^2-\theta)}$$

$$\kappa''_X(\theta) = \Psi'\left(\theta+\frac{1}{2}\right)$$

$$+ \frac{\dfrac{\lambda_4}{3}\left(1+\dfrac{\lambda_4}{6}(\theta^2-\theta)\right) - \left(\dfrac{\lambda_4}{6}(2\theta-1)\right)^2}{\left(1+\dfrac{\lambda_4}{6}(\theta^2-\theta)\right)^2}$$

Now

$$E(X) = \kappa'_X(0) = \ln(2) + \Psi\left(\frac{1}{2}\right) - \frac{\lambda_4}{6} = -\left(1.27+\frac{\lambda_4}{6}\right)$$

$$\text{Var}(X) = \kappa''_X(0) = \Psi'\left(\frac{1}{2}\right) + \frac{\lambda_4}{3} - \left(\frac{\lambda_4}{6}\right)^2 = 4.9348 + \frac{\lambda_4}{3} - \frac{\lambda_4^2}{36}$$

where $\Psi(\cdot)$ and $\Psi'(\cdot)$ are the digamma and trigamma functions respectively. Therefore

$$E(X^2) = 6.5486 + \frac{\lambda_4}{3} - \frac{\lambda_4^2}{36}$$

QED

REFERENCES

Abramowitz, M. and Stegun, I.A. (1970) *Handbook of Mathematical Functions*, New York: Dover Publications Inc.

Ahlers, D. and Lakoni-shock, J. (1983) A study of economists' consensus forecasts, *Management Science*, October, **29**, 113–25.

Akgiray, V. (1989) Conditional heteroscedasticity in time series of stock returns: evidence and forecasts, *Journal of Business*, **62**(1), 55–80.

Andersen, T.G. and Bollerslev, T. (1997) Answering the critics: yes, ARCH models do provide good volatility forecasts, NBER working paper, No. 6023.

Baillie, R.T. and Bollerslev, T. (1992) Prediction in dynamic models with time-dependent conditional variances, *Journal of Econometrics*, **52**, 91–113.

Barndorff-Nielsen, O.E. and Cox, D.R. (1989) *Asymptotic Techniques for Use in Statistics*, New York, London: Chapman and Hall.

Barton, D.E. and Dennis, K.E. (1952) The conditions under which Gram–Charlier and Edgworth curves are positive definite and unimodal, *Biometrika*, **39**, 425.

Bollerslev, T. (1986) Generalised autoregressive conditional heteroscedasticity, *Journal of Econometrics*, **31**, 307–327.

Bollerslev, T, Engle, R.F. and Nelson, D.B. (1995) ARCH models, *Handbook of Econometrics*, vol. 4.

Brailsford, T.J. and Faff, R.W. (1996) An evaluation of volatility forecasting techniques, *Journal of Banking and Finance*, **20**, 419–438.

Brown, B.W. and Maital, S. (1981) What do economists know? an empirical study of experts expectations, *Econometrica*, **49**(2), 491–504.

Campbell, J., Lo, A.L. and MacKinlay, A.C. (1997) *The Econometrics of Financial Markets*, Princeton, New Jersey: Princeton University Press.

Canina, L. and Figlewski, S. (1993) The information content of implied volatility, *Review of Financial Studies*, **6**(3), 659–681.

Christoffersen, P.F. and Diebold, F.X. (1994) Optimal prediction under asymmetric loss, *NBER Technical Working Paper Series*, No. 167.

Cooley, T.F. and Parke, W.R. (1990) Asymptotic likelihood-based prediction functions, *Econometrica*, **58**(5), 1215–1234.

Cooper, J.P., and Nelson, C.R. (1975) The ex-ante prediction performance of the St Louis and FRB-MIT-PENN econometric models and some results on composite predictors, *Journal of Money, Credit and Banking*, February, **7**, 1–32.

Cumby, R., Figlewski, S. and Hasbrouck, J. (1993) Forecasting volatility and corre-lations with EGARCH models, *Journal of Derivatives*, Winter, 51–63

Daccó, R. and Satchell, S. (1995) Why do regime switching models forecast so badly? Discussion Paper in Financial Economics, FE-7/95, Birkbeck College, University of London.

Day, T.E. and Lewis, C.M. (1992) Stock market volatility and the information content of stock index options, *Journal of Econometrics*, **52**, 267–287.

Diebold, F.X. and Lopez, J.A. (1995) Forecast evaluation and combination, Federal Reserve Bank of New York, research paper No. 9525.

Diebold, F.X. and Mariano R. (1995) Comparing predictive accuracy, *Journal of Busi-ness and Economic Statistics*, **13**(3), 253–263.

Dimson, E and March, P. (1990) Volatility forecasting without data snooping, *Journal of Banking and Finance*, **14**, 399–421.

Engle, R.F. (1982) Autoregressive conditional heteroscedasticity with estimates of the Variance of UK inflation, *Econometrica*, **50**, 987–1008.

Engle, R.F. and Bollerslev, T. (1986) Modelling the persistence of conditional vari-ances, *Econometric Reviews*, **5**(1), 1–50.

Engle, R.F., Hong, C-H., Kane, A. and Noh, J. (1993) Arbitrage valuation of variance forecasts with simulated options, *Advances in Futures and Options Research*, **6**, 393–415.

Engle, R.F., Kane A. and Noh, J. (1993a) Index option pricing with stochastic volatility and the value of accurate variance forecasts, NBER Working Paper, No. 4519, and UCSD Discussion Paper, No. 93–43.

Engle, R.F., Kane, A. and Noh. J. (1993b) A test of the efficiency for the S&P 500 index option market using variance forecasts, NBER Working Paper, No. 4520, and UCSD Discussion Paper, No. 93–32.

Engle, R.F. and Kraft, D.F. (1983) Multiperiod forecast error variances of inflation estimated from ARCH models, in A. Zellner (ed.), *Proceedings of ASACensus-NBER Conference on Applied Time Series Analysis of Economic Data*, University of Chicago Press, Chicago.

Fair, R.C. and Shiller, R.J. (1989) The informational content of ex-ante forecasts, *Review of Economics and Statistics*, 325–331.

Fair, R.C. and Shiller, R.J. (1990) Comparing the information in forecasts from econo-metric models, *American Economic Review*, 375–389.

Figlewski, S. (1994) Forecasting volatility using historical data, New York University, Stern School of Business, discussion paper.

Geweke, J. (1989) Exact prediction densities for linear models with ARCH distur-bances, *Journal of Econometrics*, **40**, 63–86.

Granger, C.W.J. (1969) Prediction with generalized cost error function, *Operational Research Quarterly*, **20**, 199–207

Granger, C.W.J. (1992) Forecasting stock market: lessons for forecasters, *Interna-tional Journal of Forecasting*, **8**, 3–13.

Granger, C.W.J. (1996) Can we improve the perceived quality of economic forecasts?, *Journal of Applied Econometrics*, **11**, 455–473.

Granger, C.W.J. and Newbold, D. (1986) *Forecasting Economic Time Series*, 2nd ed., Academic Press, London.

Granger, C.W.J. and Pesaran, H. (1996) A decision theoretic approach to forecast evaluation, Cambridge University, DAE Working Paper.

Granger, C.W.J., White, H. and Kamstra, M. (1989) Interval forecasting: an analysis based upon ARCH-quantile estimators, *Journal of Econometrics*, **40**, 87–96.

Hamilton, J. (1995) *Time Series Analysis*, Princeton, New Jersey: Princeton University Press.

Harvey, C.R. and Whaley, R.E. (1992) Market volatility prediction and the efficiency of the S&P 100 index option market, *Journal of Financial Economics*, **31**, 43–73

Jorion, P. (1995) Predicting volatility in the foreign exchange market, *Journal of Finance*, **11**(2), 507–528.

Karanasos, M. (1997) Essays on financial time series models, PhD Thesis, Birkbeck College, University of London.

Kendall, M.G. and Stuart, A. (1969) *The Advanced Theory of Statistics*, vol. 1, Charles Griffin & Co., London.

Klein, R.W. and Bawa, V.S. (1976) The effect of estimation risk on optimal portfolio choice, *Journal of Financial Economics*, **3**, 215–231.

Lamoureux, C.G. and Lastrapes, W.D. (1993) Forecasting stock return variance: toward an understanding of stochastic implied volatilities, *Review of Financial Studies*, **6**(2), 293–326.

Lee, K.Y. (1991) Are the GARCH models best in out-of-sample performance?, *Economics Letters*, **37**, 305–308.

Leitch, G. and Tanner, J.E. (1991) Economic forecast evaluation: profits vs the conventional error measures, *American Economic Review*, **81**(3), 580–590.

McCulloch, R. and Rossi, P.E. (1990) Posterior, predictive and utility-based approaches to testing the arbitrage pricing theory, *Journal of Financial Economics*, **28**(1–2), 7–38.

Mincer, J. and Zarnowitz, V. (1969) The evaluation of economic forecasts, in J. Mincer (ed.), *Economic Forecasts and Expectations*, NBER, New York.

Narashimhan, G.V.L. (1975) A comparison of predictive performance of alternative forecasting techniques: time series versus econometric models, *Proceedings of the American Statistical Association, Business and Economic Statistics Section*, August, 459–64.

Nelson, D.B. (1990) ARCH models as diffusion approximations, *Journal of Econometrics*, **45**, 7–39.

Nelson, D.B. (1992) Filtering and forecasting with misspecified ARCH models I, *Journal of Econometrics*, **52**, 61–90.

Nelson, D.B. (1996) A note on the normalised error in ARCH and stochastic volatility models, *Econometric Theory*, **12**, 113–128.

Nelson, D. and Foster, D. (1994) A symptotic filtering theory of univariate ARCH models, *Econometrica*, **62**, 1–41.

Pagan, A.R. and Schwert, G.W. (1990) Alternative models for conditional stock volatility, *Journal of Econometrics*, **45**, 267–290.

RiskMetrics Technical Document (1995, 81–2), 4th edition, J.P. Morgan/Reuters, New York.

Satchell, S. and Timmermann, A. (1995) An assessment of the economic value of non-linear foreign exchange rate forecasts, *Journal of Forecasting*, **14**, 477–497.

Satchell, S and Yoon, Y. (1994) GARCH predictions and the prediction of option prices, mimeo, DAE, University of Cambridge.

Stuart, A and Ord, J.K. (1994) *Kendall's Advanced Theory of Statistics*, vol. 1, Edward Arnold.

Tse, Y.K. (1991) Stock returns volatility in the Tokyo Stock Exchange, *Japan and the World Economy*, **3**, 285–298.

Varian, H. (1974) A Bayesian approach to real estate investment, in S.E. Fienberg and A. Zellner (eds), *Studies in Bayesian Econometrics and Statistics in Honor of L.J. Savage*, 195–208, Amsterdam, North Holland.

West, K.D. and Cho, D. (1995) The predictive ability of several models of exchange rate volatility, *Journal of Econometrics*, **69**, 367–391.

West, K.D., Edison, H.J. and Cho, D. (1993) A utility-based comparison of some models of exchange rate volatility, *Journal of International Economics*, **35**, 23–45.

Xu, X. and Taylor, S.J. (1995) Conditional volatility and the informational efficiency of the PHLX currency options market, *Journal of Banking and Finance*, **19**, 803–821.

NOTES

1. We would like to thank John Knight for helpful comments, as well as participants of the Birkbeck Finance Seminar and the 1998 Royal Economic Society conference. The second author would like to acknowledge the financial assistance of INQUIRE (UK). All remaining errors are the responsibility of the authors.

2. See Barndorff-Nielsen and Cox (1989), 117–21, as well as Stuart and Ord (1994), vol. 1, 6.25–26, for more details.

3. Introduced by Varian (1974), its shape is almost linear on one side of the origin and almost exponential on the other.

4. Introduced by Granger (1969), increases linearly from both sides of the origin but with different slopes.

5. The typical statistics employed are the mean error (ME) = $E(\sigma_t^2 - \hat{\sigma}_t^2)$, mean absolute error (MAE) = $E|\sigma_t^2 - \hat{\sigma}_t^2|$, mean squared error (MSE) = $E(\sigma_t^2 - \hat{\sigma}_t^2)^2$, or root MSE, and mean absolute percentage error (MAPE) = $E|(\sigma_t^2 - \hat{\sigma}_t^2/\sigma_t^2)|$, where σ_t^2 and $\hat{\sigma}_t^2$ are the actual and the predicted volatility respectively.

6. Or squared error if the conditional mean is non-zero.

7. Note that this is a consequence of $h_t \in I_{t-1}$, where I represents the available information set. If we used stochastic volatility models where $h_t \in I_t$ such a step would not be appropriate.

8. MSE and the regression test (6.6) in 'levels' reflect a quadratic loss function that penalizes forecast errors symmetrically. Instead, following Pagan and Schwert

(1990) we use logs, reflecting a proportional loss function in which forecast errors of small variances are more heavily penalized.

9. For this simulation we use the RNDN procedure of GAUSS programing language to generate v_t. We also assume a starting value for the return series $y_0 = 0.05$ and volatility h_0 to be equal to the unconditional variance of the GARCH(1,1).

10. This is equal to $2.54 * \text{Bias}_{\text{true}}$ as shown in equations (6.4) and (6.5).

11. See Campbell, Lo and MacKinlay (1997), Chapter 3.

12. See Kendall and Stuart (1969) and Barton and Dennis (1952). Gram–Charlier distributions are general approximations to pdf's and are used because of their amenability to exact analysis. They have drawbacks in that the pdf's need not be positive everywhere.

Chapter 7

Implied volatility forecasting: a comparison of different procedures including fractionally integrated models with applications to UK equity options

SOOSUNG HWANG*‡ AND STEPHEN E. SATCHELL†‡

SUMMARY

The purpose of this chapter is to consider how to forecast implied volatility for a selection of UK companies with traded options on their stocks. We consider a range of GARCH and log-ARFIMA based models as well as some simple forecasting rules. Overall, we find that a log-ARFIMA model forecasts best over short and long horizons.

7.1 INTRODUCTION

The purpose of this chapter is to investigate various procedures for forecasting implied volatility. This topic should be of particular interest to option traders. There is a vast bibliography in finance on this topic and we refer readers to Day and Lewis (1992), Engle *et al.* (1993), Harvey and Whaley (1992), Lamoureux and Lastrapes (1993), Noh, Engle and Kane (1994), Hwang and Satchell (1997), and Figlewski (1997) for more details on volatility forecasting. In this study, we further the work of Hwang and Satchell (1997) (HS) on long memory volatility processes for the forecast of implied volatility.

* Department of Applied Economics, University of Cambridge.
† Faculty of Economics and Politics and Trinity College, University of Cambridge.
‡ The authors are grateful to Mr. Carl Moss of Dresdner Kleinwort Benson and Professor Bill Ziemba for some valuable insights. The first author would like to thank the Newton Trust and Kleinwort Benson for financial support and the second author would like to thank Inquire for financial support.

Fractionally integrated processes which are a subclass of long memory processes have recently attracted considerable attention in volatility studies. Following the introduction of the Autoregressive Conditional Heteroscedasticity (ARCH) model (Engle, 1982) and the popular Generalized ARCH (GARCH) model (Bollerslev, 1986), many empirical studies on volatility in finance have reported the extreme degree of persistence of shocks to the conditional variance process. The Integrated GARCH (IGARCH) of Engle and Bollerslev (1986) was formulated to capture this effect. However, in the IGARCH model, the unconditional variance does not exist and a shock remains important for the forecasts of the variance for all future horizons. Ding, Granger and Engle (1992), using the S&P 500 stock market daily closing price index, show that the autocorrelations of the power transformation of the absolute return are quite high for long lags. The autocorrelations may not be explained properly by either an I(0) or an I(1) process. Motivated by these and other findings, Baillie, Bollerslev and Mikkelsen (1996) proposed the Fractionally Integrated GARCH (FIGARCH) model by applying the concept of fractional integration to the GARCH model. In the FIGARCH process, the conditional variance decays at a slow hyperbolic rate for the lagged squared innovations.

Recently, HS investigated model specification and forecasting performance of FIGARCH, log-FIGARCH, Autoregressive Fractionally Integrated Moving Average (ARFIMA), log-ARFIMA models for both return volatility and implied volatility. They suggested log-ARFIMA models for implied volatility processes. Log-ARFIMA models are well specified and do not need the non-negativity constraints on their parameters. In addition, using out-of-sample forecast tests, HS showed that for the forecast of implied volatility, log-ARFIMA models using implied volatility are preferred to conventional GARCH models using return volatility.

Leading on from this work, we further investigate log-ARFIMA models for the prediction of implied volatility. For a practical usage of long memory processes in volatility, two modified versions of long memory processes are also suggested: scaled truncated log-ARFIMA and detrended log-ARFIMA models. For comparative purposes, we use the GARCH(1,1) model and moving average models. In the next section, we describe the data used here and section 7.3 explains the models used in this study. In section 7.4, our results follow, and in section 7.5 we present conclusions.

7.2   DATA

We use two daily variance series; implied variance (IV) and historical return variance (RV). The IV is provided by the London Financial Options and Futures Exchange (LIFFE) and is calculated from the Black and Scholes (1973) option pricing formula. At-the-money call option IVs are used and to minimize term structure effects in volatility, options with the shortest maturity but with at least 15 trading days to maturity are used as in Harvey and Whaley (1991, 1992). In this chapter IV is used for the log-ARFIMA(0,d,1) model. The quantity, x_t, represents the implied standard deviation and x_t^2 the IV at time t.

The return series of the underlying asset is provided by Datastream. The RV is calculated from the log-return of the underlying asset less the mean log-return. The RV at time t is y_t^2. More formally, y_t^2 is obtained from log-return series, r_t, as follows:

$$y_t^2 = 250 \left[r_t - \frac{1}{T} \sum_{t=1}^{T} r_t \right]^2$$

where the number 250 is used to annualize the squared return series. This study uses a GARCH(1,1) process to model RV.

The following nine UK equities and their call options data are used: Barclays, British Petroleum, British Steel, British Telecommunication, BTR, General Electric Co., Glaxo Wellcome, Marks and Spencer, Unilever. In addition, American and European call options on FTSE100 are also used. However, the results of British Steel and Glaxo Wellcome are the only ones reported in this chapter.[1]

7.3 MODELS FOR VOLATILITY

In this section, we give details of the models used in this study. In addition, estimation methods and other topics related with forecasting will be explained. Two modified log-ARFIMA models are suggested for the forecast of volatility.

7.3.1 GARCH models

A GARCH(p,q) model introduced by Bollerslev (1986) for the residual process, y_t, can be expressed as

$$y_t = \xi_t \sqrt{ht} \quad \xi_t \sim N(0, 1)$$
$$h_t = \omega + B(L)h_t + A(L)y_t^2 \tag{7.1}$$

where $B(L) = \beta_1 L + \beta_2 L^2 +, \cdots, +\beta_p L^p, A(L) = \alpha_1 L + \alpha_2 L^2 +, \cdots, +\alpha_q L^q, L$ is a lag operator, and $h_t = E_{t-1}(y_t^2)$.

For the GARCH(1,1) model, the conditional variance is

$$h_t = \omega + \beta h_{t-1} + \alpha y_{t-1}^2 \tag{7.2}$$

The log likelihood function of the GARCH(1,1) model is

$$L(\Xi : y_1, y_2, \ldots, y_T) = -0.5T \ln(2\pi) - 0.5 \sum_{t=1}^{T} \left[\ln(h_t) + \frac{y_t^2}{h_t} \right] \tag{7.3}$$

where h_t is given by equation (7.2) and $\Xi' = (\omega, \alpha, \beta)$. The likelihood function is maximized using the Berndt *et al.* (1974) algorithm. Weiss (1986) and Bollerslev and Wooldridge (1992) show that even if the assumption that ξ_t is iid $N(0, 1)$ is not valid, the quasi maximum likelihood (QML) estimates obtained by maximizing (7.3) are both consistent and asymptotically normally distributed.

The h-step-ahead forecast of implied variance from the GARCH(1,1) model is

$$E_t(y_{t+h}^2) = \omega \sum_{i=0}^{h-1} (\alpha + \beta)^i + (\alpha + \beta)^{h-1} \beta h_t + (\alpha + \beta)^{h-1} \alpha y_t^2 \quad h > 1$$

$$= \omega \sum_{i=0}^{h-2} (\alpha + \beta)^i + (\alpha + \beta)^{h-1} h_{t+1} \quad h > 2 \qquad (7.4)$$

Therefore, when $\alpha + \beta < 1$, for large h, the conditional expectation of variance can be represented as

$$E_t(y_{t+h}^2) = \omega \sum_{i=0}^{h-2} (\alpha + \beta)^i + (\alpha + \beta)^{h-1} h_{t+1}$$

$$\approx \omega \sum_{i=0}^{\infty} (\alpha + \beta)^i \quad \text{as } h \to \infty$$

$$= \frac{\omega}{1 - \alpha - \beta} \qquad (7.5)$$

Note that $1/(1 - \alpha - \beta)$ is always positive for $0 < \alpha + \beta < 1$. For large forecasting horizons, the forecasts converge to $\omega/(1 - \alpha - \beta)$ at an exponential rate. When the unconditional variance is larger than the first-step-ahead forecast, the forecasts will show a concave form as the forecast horizon increases. On the other hand, when the unconditional variance is smaller than the first-step-ahead forecast, the forecasts will show a convex form.

7.3.2   Log-ARFIMA models

7.3.2.1   *Properties of fractionally integrated processes*

There are two major models for the long memory process: continuous time models such as the Fractional Gaussian Noise (FGN) model introduced by Mandelbrot and Van Ness (1968), and discrete time models such as the Autoregressive Fractionally Integrated Moving Average (ARFIMA) model introduced by Granger and Joyeux (1980) and Hosking (1981).[2] In this study, discrete time long memory processes are used.

Let us describe the discrete time long memory process. A simple model, the ARIMA(0,1,0), is defined as

$$(1 - L)x_t = \varepsilon_t \tag{7.6}$$

where ε_t is an independent identically distributed random variable. The equation (7.6) means that the first difference of x_t is a discrete time white noise process. The idea of fractional integration permits the degree of difference to take any real value rather than integral values. More formally, a fractionally integrated process is defined to be a discrete time stochastic process which is represented as

$$\nabla^d x_t = (1 - L)^d x_t = \varepsilon_t \tag{7.7}$$

The fractional difference operator ∇^d is defined by the binomial series expansion:

$$
\begin{aligned}
\nabla^d &= (1 - L)^d \\
&= \sum_{j=0}^{\infty} \frac{\Gamma(j - d)}{\Gamma(j + 1)\Gamma(-d)} L^j
\end{aligned}
\tag{7.8}
$$

where $\Gamma(\cdot)$ is the gamma function. Let $\gamma_j = (\Gamma(j - d))/(\Gamma(j + 1)\Gamma(-d))$. Then, via Stirling's approximation, it can be shown that $\gamma_j \approx (j^{-d-1})/(\Gamma(-d))$ as $j \to \infty$.

Certain restrictions on the long memory parameter d are necessary for the process x_t to be stationary and invertible. The covariance stationarity condition needs the squared coefficients of the infinite order moving average representation to be summable. The moving average representation of equation (7.7) is

$$
\begin{aligned}
x_t &= (1 - L)^{-d} \varepsilon_t \\
&= \sum_{j=0}^{\infty} \frac{\Gamma(j + d)}{\Gamma(j + 1)\Gamma(d)} \varepsilon_{t-j}
\end{aligned}
\tag{7.9}
$$

The variance of x_t can be represented as

$$
\begin{aligned}
\mathrm{Var}(x_t) &= \sigma_\varepsilon^2 \left[1 + \sum_{j=1}^{\infty} \left(\frac{\Gamma(j + d)}{\Gamma(j + 1)\Gamma(d)} \right)^2 \right] \\
&\approx \sigma_\varepsilon^2 \left[1 + \Gamma(d)^{-2} \sum_{j=1}^{\infty} j^{2d-2} \right]
\end{aligned}
\tag{7.10}
$$

where σ_ε^2 is the variance of ε_t. Therefore, for the variance of x_t to exist, we need $2d - 2 < -1$ from the theory of infinite series. The long memory parameter which satisfies this condition is $d < 0.5$. Thus, when $d < 0.5$, x_t is a (weakly) stationary process. On the other hand, to obtain a convergent autoregressive representation of equation (7.7), we can replace d in equation (7.10) with $-d$. In this case, the invertibility condition is $-0.5 < d$ for x_t. The following table summarizes the properties of the long memory process for various d in the frequency domain context. Values of d outside the range $-0.5 < d < 0.5$ can be understood by differencing the series and examining the properties of the differenced process.

Properties of the discrete time long memory process in the frequency domain

d	S	I	Properties
$d = -0.5$	Yes	No	$s(\omega) \sim 0$ as $\omega \to 0$
$-0.5 < d < 0$	Yes	Yes	short memory with negative correlation and high spectral density at high frequencies. $s(\omega) \sim 0$ as $\omega \to 0$
$d = 0$	Yes	Yes	white noise with zero correlation and constant spectral density. $s(\omega) = \sigma^2/2\pi$
$0 < d < 0.5$	Yes	Yes	long memory with positive correlation and high spectral density at low frequencies. $s(\omega) \sim \infty$ as $\omega \to 0$
$d = 0.5$	No	Yes	$s(\omega) \sim \infty$ as $\omega \to 0$

Note: S and I represent stationarity and invertibility, respectively. $s(\omega)$ represents the spectral density function of the discrete time long memory process.

Table 7.1 reports some examples of long memory coefficients at various lags. The key property of a long memory process is that its coefficients decay at a hyperbolical rate rather than the exponential rate of a short memory process such as ARMA models. Therefore, the long memory process is a sensible process to describe high persistence in time series such as volatility.

7.3.2.2 Log-ARFIMA models

Many empirical applications of GARCH models find an apparent persistence of volatility shocks in high-frequency financial time series. In order to explain the persistence, Engle and Bollerslev (1986) introduce an Integrated GARCH (IGARCH) model. However, it is difficult to ascertain whether or not the apparent persistence indicates integration (see Diebold and Lopez, 1994). HS show that low but persistent positive autocorrelations frequently found in volatility processes may be more appropriately described by the long memory process rather than conventional ARCH-based short memory processes.

Table 7.1 *Comparison of coefficients on moving average representation between long and short memory processes*

	ARFIMA(0,d,0) process				AR(1) process			
Lags	$d = 0.2$	$d = 0.4$	$d = 0.6^*$	$d = 0.8^*$	$\phi = 0.2$	$\phi = 0.4$	$\phi = 0.6$	$\phi = 0.8$
1	0.2000	0.4000	0.6000	0.8000	0.2000	0.4000	0.6000	0.8000
2	0.1200	0.2800	0.4800	0.7200	0.0400	0.1600	0.3600	0.6400
3	0.0880	0.2240	0.4160	0.6720	0.0080	0.0640	0.2160	0.5120
4	0.0704	0.1904	0.3744	0.6384	0.0016	0.0256	0.1296	0.4096
5	0.0591	0.1676	0.3444	0.6129	0.0003	0.0102	0.0778	0.3277
6	0.0513	0.1508	0.3215	0.5924	0.0001	0.0041	0.0467	0.2621
7	0.0454	0.1379	0.3031	0.5755	0.0000	0.0016	0.0280	0.2097
8	0.0409	0.1275	0.2880	0.5611	0.0000	0.0007	0.0168	0.1678
9	0.0372	0.1190	0.2752	0.5487	0.0000	0.0003	0.0101	0.1342
10	0.0342	0.1119	0.2642	0.5377	0.0000	0.0001	0.0060	0.1074
15	0.0248	0.0881	0.2255	0.4971	0.0000	0.0000	0.0005	0.0352
20	0.0197	0.0743	0.2014	0.4699	0.0000	0.0000	0.0000	0.0115
25	0.0165	0.0650	0.1844	0.4498	0.0000	0.0000	0.0000	0.0038
30	0.0143	0.0583	0.1716	0.4339	0.0000	0.0000	0.0000	0.0012
35	0.0126	0.0532	0.1614	0.4209	0.0000	0.0000	0.0000	0.0004
40	0.0114	0.0491	0.1531	0.4099	0.0000	0.0000	0.0000	0.0001
45	0.0103	0.0458	0.1461	0.4005	0.0000	0.0000	0.0000	0.0000
50	0.0095	0.0430	0.1401	0.3922	0.0000	0.0000	0.0000	0.0000
60	0.0082	0.0386	0.1303	0.3782	0.0000	0.0000	0.0000	0.0000
70	0.0073	0.0352	0.1225	0.3668	0.0000	0.0000	0.0000	0.0000
80	0.0065	0.0325	0.1162	0.3572	0.0000	0.0000	0.0000	0.0000
90	0.0059	0.0303	0.1109	0.3489	0.0000	0.0000	0.0000	0.0000
100	0.0055	0.0284	0.1063	0.3417	0.0000	0.0000	0.0000	0.0000
110	0.0051	0.0268	0.1023	0.3352	0.0000	0.0000	0.0000	0.0000
120	0.0047	0.0255	0.0988	0.3295	0.0000	0.0000	0.0000	0.0000
130	0.0044	0.0243	0.0957	0.3243	0.0000	0.0000	0.0000	0.0000
140	0.0042	0.0232	0.0929	0.3195	0.0000	0.0000	0.0000	0.0000
150	0.0040	0.0223	0.0904	0.3151	0.0000	0.0000	0.0000	0.0000
160	0.0038	0.0214	0.0881	0.3111	0.0000	0.0000	0.0000	0.0000
170	0.0036	0.0207	0.0860	0.3074	0.0000	0.0000	0.0000	0.0000
180	0.0034	0.0200	0.0841	0.3039	0.0000	0.0000	0.0000	0.0000
190	0.0033	0.0193	0.0823	0.3006	0.0000	0.0000	0.0000	0.0000
200	0.0031	0.0188	0.0806	0.2976	0.0000	0.0000	0.0000	0.0000
250	0.0026	0.0164	0.0737	0.2846	0.0000	0.0000	0.0000	0.0000
300	0.0023	0.0147	0.0686	0.2744	0.0000	0.0000	0.0000	0.0000
350	0.0020	0.0134	0.0645	0.2661	0.0000	0.0000	0.0000	0.0000
400	0.0018	0.0124	0.0611	0.2591	0.0000	0.0000	0.0000	0.0000
450	0.0016	0.0115	0.0583	0.2531	0.0000	0.0000	0.0000	0.0000
499	0.0015	0.0108	0.0559	0.2479	0.0000	0.0000	0.0000	0.0000

Notes: *means that the process is not stationary. The coefficients on the moving average representation of discrete time long memory processes are calculated using the following equation:

$$x_t = (1 - L)^{-d}\varepsilon_t = \sum \gamma_j \varepsilon_{t-j}$$

where $\gamma_j = \Gamma(j + d)/(\Gamma(j + 1)\Gamma(d))$ and $\Gamma(\cdot)$ is the gamma function. The coefficients on the moving average representation of AR processes are calculated using the following equation:

$$x_t = (1 - \phi L)^{-1}\varepsilon_t = \sum \phi^j \varepsilon_{t-j}$$

Baillie, Bollerslev and Mikkelsen (1996) suggest the FIGARCH model to capture the long memory present in volatility. They introduce the concept of the fractional integration to GARCH models to make the following FIGARCH(p,d,q) model:

$$(1 - \Phi(L))(1 - L)^d y_t^2 = w + (1 - \Theta(L))v_t \tag{7.11}$$

where $0 \le d \le 1$, $v_t = y_t^2 - h_t$, $\Phi(L) = \phi_1 L +, \cdots, +\phi_q L^q$ and $\Theta(L) = \theta_1 L +, \cdots, +\theta_p Lp$. The conditional variance of the above FIGARCH model is expressed as

$$h_t = w + \Theta(L)h_t + [1 - \Theta(L) - (1 - \Phi(L))(1 - L)^d]y_t^2 \tag{7.12}$$

In the FIGARCH model, the long memory parameter, d, is defined to have a value, $0 \le d \le 1$, while in the ordinary long memory return process, d is defined as $-0.5 < d < 0.5$ to be covariance stationary and invertible. In the FIGARCH model, d must not be less than zero because of the non-negativity conditions imposed on the conditional variance equation.

There is a difference between the definition of the stationarity in the long memory return process and the long memory volatility process. In the long memory return process of section 7.3.2.1, the covariance stationary condition needs the summability of the squared moving average coefficients. However, in the FIGARCH model, the stationary condition depends on the summability of the moving average coefficients.[3] That is, stationarity in the FIGARCH model is defined as having an infinite moving average representation in L^1 space rather than L^2 space. The stationary condition in L^1 space is satisfied only when $d < 0$. Therefore, when $0 \le d \le 1$, FIGARCH models are not covariance stationary.

Baillie, Bollerslev and Mikkelsen (1996) suggest that FIGARCH models with $0 \le d \le 1$ are strictly stationary and ergodic by applying Bougerol and Picard (1992): IGARCH models are strictly stationary and ergodic. As explained in Baillie, Bollerslev and Mikkelsen (1996), equation (7.12) is equivalent to $h_t = (1 - \Theta(1))^{-1}w + y_t^2$ at $L = 1$. Therefore, $w > 0$ in FIGARCH models can be interpreted in the same way as in IGARCH models, and the unconditional distribution of y_t^2 has infinite mean. This is a property of the long memory volatility process: every fractionally integrated volatility process with a drift does not have an unconditional distribution with finite mean.[4] This seems to be a major drawback as it says that, unconditionally, the expected value of implied volatility is infinite.

In this study, we use log-ARFIMA models instead of FIGARCH models to model IV, since log-ARFIMA models do not need the non-negativity conditions and their out-of-sample forecasts are not inferior to those of FIGARCH models, see HS. When equation (7.7) is combined together with conventional ARMA models, we can obtain ARFIMA(k,d,l) models. The model used in this study is a log-ARFIMA model which is represented as

$$(1 - \Phi(L))(1 - L)^d \ln(x_t^2) = \mu + (1 - \Theta(L))\psi_t \quad 0 \le d \le 1 \qquad (7.13)$$

where $\Phi(L) = \phi_1 L + \phi_2 L^2 +, \cdots, + \phi_k L^k$, and $\Theta(L) = \theta_1 L + \theta_2 L^2 +, \cdots, + \theta_l L^l$, and ψ_t is a white noise zero mean process ($\psi_t = \ln(x_t^2) - E_{t-1}(\ln(x_t^2))$). The conditional log-variance of the log-ARFIMA model which follows from (7.13) is

$$H_t = \mu + \Theta(L)\psi_t + (1 - (1 - \Phi(L))(1 - L)^d)\ln(x_t^2)$$
$$= \mu - \Theta(L)H_t + (1 - \Theta(L) - (1 - \Phi(L))(1 - L)^d)\ln(x_t^2) \qquad (7.14)$$

where $H_t = E_{t-1}(\ln(x_t^2))$. The log-ARFIMA model is defined as an ARFIMA model for log-variance and does not need non-negativity constraints. The above relationship expresses the conditional log-variance (H_t) in terms of lagged values of $\ln(x_t^2)$ and H_t.

Equation (7.14) is equivalent to $H_t = (1 + \Theta(1))^{-1}\mu + \ln(x_t^2)$ at $L = 1$. In log-ARFIMA models, therefore, $\mu \ne 0$ has the same interpretation as in FIGARCH models. That is, the unconditional distribution of $\ln(x_t^2)$ has infinite mean.

The model we use for the forecast of implied volatility is the log-ARFIMA(0,d,1) model. The conditional log-variance function for the log-ARFIMA(0,d,1) model is

$$H_t = \mu + \theta\psi_{t-1} + (1 - (1 - L)^d)\ln(x_t^2))$$
$$= \mu + \theta\psi_{t-1} - \sum_{j=1}^{\infty} \frac{\Gamma(j - d)}{\Gamma(j + 1)\Gamma(-d)} \ln(x_{t-j}^2) \qquad (7.15)$$

For the log-ARFIMA(0,d,1) model, the quasi maximum likelihood function is

$$L(\Xi : x_1, x_2, \ldots, x_T) = -0.5T \ln(2\pi) - 0.5 \sum_{t=1}^{T} \left(\ln(\sigma_\psi^2) + \frac{(\ln(x_t^2) - H_t)^2}{\sigma_\psi^2} \right) \qquad (7.16)$$

where H_t is given by equation (7.15) and $\Xi' = (\mu, d, \theta, \sigma_\psi)$. In log-ARFIMA models, we may not assume that innovations are iid normally distributed, and thus QML estimation is used. The Broyden, Fletcher, Goldfard and Shanno (BFGS) algorithm is used for the maximization of the likelihood function. The h-step-ahead conditional log-variance from the log-ARFIMA(0,d,1) model at time t is given by

$$E_t(\ln(x_{t+h}^2)) = \mu - \sum_{j=1}^{h-1} \frac{\Gamma(j - d)}{\Gamma(j + 1)\Gamma(-d)} H_{t+h-j}$$
$$- \sum_{j=h}^{\infty} \frac{\Gamma(j - d)}{\Gamma(j + 1)\Gamma(-d)} \ln(x_{t+h-j}^2), \quad h \ge 2 \qquad (7.17)$$

When fractionally integrated models are estimated, we need pre-sample values and a truncation lag (m) of the infinite lag polynomial in log-conditional variances of (7.14). In this study, the unconditional sample log-variance is used for all the pre-sample values as in Baillie, Bollerslev and Mikkelsen (1996). On the other hand, the truncation lag (m) is set to 100 as in HS, while previous studies such as Baillie, Bollerslev and Mikkelsen (1996) and Psaradakis and Sola (1995) set the truncation lag at 1000 for all estimates.[5]

In log-ARFIMA models, the h-step-ahead conditional variance cannot be represented as an exponential form of the h-step-ahead conditional log-variance. By Jensen's inequality, the forecast $h^*_{t+h} = \exp(H_{t+h})$ obtained from equation (7.17) is less than the appropriate forecast h_{t+h}, namely

$$h_{t+h} = E_t(\exp(\ln y^2_{t+h})) > \exp(E(\ln y^2_{t+h})) = \exp(H_{t+h}) = h^*_{t+h} \qquad (7.18)$$

If ψ_t is normal and ζ_i is the i-th coefficient of the moving average representation of the log-ARFIMA model, the appropriate forecast for the log-ARFIMA model is

$$h_{t+h} = E_t(\exp(\ln y^2_{t+h}))$$

$$= E_t\left(\exp(H_{t+h} + \sum_{i=0}^{h-1} \zeta_i \psi_{t+h-i}\right) \qquad (\zeta_0 = 1)$$

$$= \exp(H_{t+h})\exp\left(\frac{1}{2}\sum_{i=0}^{h-1} \zeta_i^2 \sigma_\psi^2\right) \qquad (7.19)$$

since for a normally distributed variable a, $E(\exp(a)) = \exp\left(m + \frac{1}{2}\sigma^2\right)$ where m and σ^2 are the mean and variance of a. The correction factor, $\exp\left(\frac{1}{2}\sum_{i=0}^{h-1} \zeta_i^2 \sigma_\psi^2\right)$, is always larger than 1. Therefore, $\exp(H_{t+h})$ gives downward biased forecasts, and the bias is an increasing function of the forecasting horizon, σ_ψ^2, and ζ_i.

We address systematic forecast bias in log-ARFIMA models.[6] As explained above, the long memory volatility process with a drift has infinite unconditional variance. In practice, we have only finite observations, and a truncation lag, m, should be chosen for long memory processes. In this case, the long memory volatility process has an unconditional variance. Consider the following simple log-ARFIMA(0,d,0) model with a drift, $(1 - L)^d \ln(x_t^2) = \mu + \psi_t$. The process can be represented as

$$\ln(x_t^2) = \mu - \sum_{j=1}^{\infty} \gamma_j \ln(x_{t-j}^2) + \psi_t \qquad (7.20)$$

where $\gamma_j = (\Gamma(j - d))/(\Gamma(j + 1)\Gamma(-d))$. With infinite observations, $-\sum_{j=1}^{\infty} \gamma_j = 1$ and unconditional variance does not exist. When we use a truncation lag, the process is

$$\ln(x_t^2) = \tilde{\mu} - \sum_{j=1}^{m} \gamma_j \ln(x_{t-j}^2) + \psi_t \qquad (7.21)$$

where $\tilde{\mu} = \mu - \sum_{j=m+1}^{\infty} \gamma_j \ln(x_{t-j}^2)$. The drift, $\tilde{\mu}$, varies with m, d, and the magnitude of the log-variances beyond the truncation lag. Treating $\tilde{\mu}$ as a constant yields the following unconditional log-variance:

$$E(\ln(x_t^2)) = \frac{\tilde{\mu}}{\sum_{j=0}^{m} \gamma_j} \qquad (7.22)$$

where $0 < \sum_{j=0}^{m} \gamma_j$. Therefore, when we use a truncation lag, an unconditional log-variance exists. The unconditional log-variance is achieved with a hyperbolic rate rather than an exponential rate as in GARCH and ARMA processes. Let A_h be a parameter on the drift term ($\tilde{\mu}$) in the h-step-ahead conditional log-variance of the log-ARFIMA(0,d,0) model. Then, A_h evolves hyperbolically as h increases as follows:

$$A_1 = 1 \quad \text{and} \quad A_h = 1 - \sum_{j=1}^{h-1} \gamma_j A_{h-j}, \quad h \geq 2 \qquad (7.23)$$

Therefore, the forecasts from the log-ARFIMA(0,d,1) model approach to an unconditional variance with a slow decay rate.

7.3.2.3 Scaled truncated fractionally integrated process and log-ARFIMA models

In theory, we define long memory volatility models such as FIGARCH or log-ARFIMA models under the assumption that the sample size is infinite. However, in practice, we only have finite samples. As we have seen in the previous section, there is a gap between theory and actual application, and this issue is focused on whether an unconditional variance exists. The same problem arises in conventional ARMA or GARCH models. However, they are short memory processes and their actual application and results will be consistent with their theory, since the impact of the initial observation becomes negligible even for a small sample size.

In long memory processes, we need to consider an infinite number of observations which are not available in practice. Thus, there is a need to consider a truncated long memory process where $-\sum_{j=1}^{m} \gamma_j < 1$. Consider the sum of the AR coefficients, $-\sum_{j=1}^{m} \gamma_j$. It is far from 1 when d is small and m is moderate. Table 7.2 reports the sum of the AR coefficients over various values of d when a truncation is used. When d is close to 1, the sum of the AR coefficients

Table 7.2 *Sum of AR coefficients of fractionally integrated processes*

Truncation lag \d	0.1	0.2	0.3	0.4	0.5	0.6	0.7	0.8	0.9	0.99
50	0.3678	0.6078	0.7623	0.8599	0.9204	0.9570	0.9784	0.9905	.9969	0.9998
100	0.4098	0.6583	0.8067	0.8937	0.9437	0.9716	0.9867	0.9945	.9983	0.9999
300	0.4711	0.7256	0.8609	0.9314	0.9674	0.9853	0.9938	0.9977	.9994	1.0000
500	0.4974	0.7522	0.8806	0.9441	0.9748	0.9892	0.9957	0.9985	.9996	1.0000
800	0.5204	0.7744	0.8963	0.9537	0.9801	0.9918	0.9969	0.9990	.9997	1.0000
1 000	0.5310	0.7843	0.9030	0.9576	0.9822	0.9929	0.9973	0.9991	.9998	1.0000
1 500	0.5496	0.8011	0.9141	0.9640	0.9854	0.9944	0.9980	0.9994	.9999	1.0000
2 000	0.5624	0.8122	0.9212	0.9679	0.9874	0.9953	0.9984	0.9995	.9999	1.0000
2 500	0.5721	0.8204	0.9263	0.9706	0.9887	0.9959	0.9986	0.9996	.9999	1.0000
3 000	0.5798	0.8268	0.9302	0.9727	0.9897	0.9963	0.9988	0.9996	.9999	1.0000
5 000	0.6007	0.8436	0.9402	0.9777	0.9920	0.9973	0.9991	0.9998	1.0000	1.0000
7 000	0.6139	0.8538	0.9459	0.9805	0.9933	0.9978	0.9993	0.9998	1.0000	1.0000
10 000	0.6275	0.8639	0.9514	0.9831	0.9944	0.9982	0.9995	0.9999	1.0000	1.0000

Notes: A fractionally integrated process can be transformed into the following AR process:

$$x_t = -\sum \delta_j x_{t-j} + \varepsilon_t$$

where $\delta_j = \Gamma(j-d)/(\Gamma(j+1)\Gamma(-d))$ and $\Gamma(\cdot)$ is the gamma function. The numbers in the above table are sums of the AR coefficients for given lag and d.

becomes one for a relatively small truncation lag. However, when d is close to zero (e.g. $d = 0.1$), the sum of the AR coefficients is far less than 1 even with the truncation lag of 10 000 and we may obtain a large significant $\tilde{\mu}$, where $\tilde{\mu}$ is defined in equation (7.21). In this case, applying such long memory processes with finite valued interpretations needs to be done in such a way as to preserve as many of the salient features of the theoretical process as possible.

Facing these problems in long memory models, we suggest the following scaled truncated long memory model for a variable z:

$$(1 - L)^{d_{ST}} z_t = \varepsilon_t. \tag{7.24}$$

The properties of the scaled truncated long memory process are expressed in the AR representation

$$z_t = \sum_{j=1}^{m} \gamma_j^* z_{t-j} + \varepsilon_t \tag{7.25}$$

where $\gamma_j^* = ((\Gamma(j-d))/(\Gamma(j+1)\Gamma(-d)))/((\sum_{j=1}^{m}(\Gamma(j-d)))/(\Gamma(j+1)\Gamma(-d)))$ and d is the original long memory parameter. The sum of the scaled AR coefficients is always 1, $\sum_{j=1}^{m} \gamma_j^* = 1$, while $0 < -\sum_{j=1}^{m} \gamma_j < 1$ in equation (7.21).

We shall now discuss the properties of the scaled truncated long memory process. The scaled truncated long memory process can be regarded as an AR(m) model with the sum of the AR coefficients constrained to be 1. However, in the scaled truncated long memory model, only one parameter, d_{ST}, is used for the long range dependence instead of m parameters as in the case of the AR(m) model. Furthermore, the decay rate retains the hyperbolic character associated with a long memory process. The invertibility conditions are the same as those of the ordinary fractionally integrated process in equation (7.7), since the AR coefficients in the scaled truncated long memory process are increased by a multiplication factor of $1/\sum_{j=1}^{m}((\Gamma(j-d))/(\Gamma(j)\Gamma(-d)))$. Stationarity conditions will require checking if the roots of the appropriate polynomial lie outside the unit circle. There seem to be no results available on this question.

The scaled truncated fractionally integrated process does not result in the same degree of divergence between theory and practice as other forms of truncation imply for estimated models. In addition, it is worth noting that the long memory parameter of the scaled truncated fractionally integrated process is always less than the original long memory parameter for $0 < d < 1$. The gap between the two long memory parameters is smaller as d goes to 1 and vice versa. As the truncation lag increases, the long memory parameter of the scaled truncated fractionally integrated process will approach that of the ordinary fractionally integrated process. Therefore, with infinite samples and an infinite truncation lag, the scaled truncated fractionally integrated process is equivalent to the ordinary fractionally integrated process.

Using the scaled truncated fractionally integrated process, we suggest the scaled truncated log-ARFIMA(k,d,l) model:

$$(1 - \Phi(L))(1 - L)^{d_{ST}}(\ln(y_t^2) - \delta) = (1 + \Theta(L))\psi_t \qquad (7.26)$$

In this model, the zero mean process is used instead of a drift term, since the assumption of a trend in a volatility process can lead to the non-existence of expected volatility. For forecasting purposes, the standard deviation of the forecasts is expected to be smaller than that of the random walk model, since the forecasts of the scaled truncated log-ARFIMA(0,d,1) model are obtained by the weighted average of past variances.

The conditional log-variance of the log-ARFIMA model which follows from (7.26) is

$$H_t + \delta + \Theta(L)\psi_t + (1 - (1 - \Phi(L))(1 - L)^{d_{ST}})(\ln(x_t^2) - \delta) \qquad (7.27)$$

where $H_t = E_{t-1}(\ln(x_t^2))$. Therefore, the scaled truncated log-ARFIMA(0,d,1)-IV model is

$$(1 - L)^{d_{ST}}(\ln(x_t^2) - \delta) = (1 + \theta L)\psi_t \qquad (7.28)$$

and using the same method as in equation (7.17), the h-step-ahead conditional log-variance from the scaled truncated log-ARFIMA(0,d,1)-IV model is

$$H_{t+h}^{ST} = \delta - \sum_{j=1}^{h-1} \gamma_j^*(H_{t+h-j}^{ST} - \delta) - \sum_{j=h}^{m} \gamma_j^*(\ln(x_{t+h-j}^2) - \delta) \quad h \geq 2 \qquad (7.29)$$

where γ_j^* is defined in equation (7.25) and with m is a truncation lag.

7.3.2.4 Detrended log-ARFIMA models

An alternative and simple method to reduce the systematic forecast bias in log-ARFIMA models is to detrend the forecasts. The detrended h-step-ahead conditional log-variance of the log-ARFIMA(0,d,1) model is

$$H_{t+h}^D = H_{t+h} - \frac{(H_{t+h^*} - H_{t+1})}{h^*}h \qquad (7.30)$$

where h^* is the longest forecast horizon, that is, $h^* = 120$ in this study.

This method is based on the stationarity of volatility process. If there is a downward or upward trend in volatility for a short time period, the detrended method may not be used. If the forecast biases were a linear function of forecast horizons, then detrended log-ARFIMA models would work. However, as we have already noticed in the previous subsection, the systematic forecast bias changes at a hyperbolic rate over forecasting horizons. Therefore, even if we use this method, there still exists some bias especially in relatively short horizons.

Despite all these difficulties, this method has the merit that it is straightforward to use.

7.3.3 Moving average methods

Another frequently used method for the forecast of future implied volatility is the moving average method. We include this procedure as a benchmark. Any sensible forecasting procedure should do just as well as a moving average method. This method is used widely in practice, since traders tend to add a value to the past return volatility to cover their trading costs and other expenses. In this sense, the difference between the implied volatility and return volatility may be called 'traders' premium'.

Using the n most recent observations, we can use the following formulae as the forecasts of future volatility.

$$FIV_t^{n,RV} = \sqrt{\frac{1}{n} \sum_{j=0}^{n-1} y_{t-j}^2}$$

$$FIV_t^{n,IV} = \sqrt{\frac{1}{n} \sum_{j=0}^{n-1} x_{t-j}^2} \tag{7.31}$$

Since the forecasts are not changed for the forecasting horizons in this moving average method, the statistical properties of the forecasts are the same across all horizons.

Table 7.3 *Mean and standard deviation of moving average forecasts of RV and IV*

A. British Steel

Moving average lag (n)		1	5	10	15	20	60
Return volatility	Mean	0.1767	0.1759	0.1753	0.1742	0.1734	0.1711
	STD	0.1443	0.0755	0.0546	0.0479	0.0433	0.0282
Implied volatility	Mean	0.2428	0.2426	0.2424	0.2422	0.2420	0.2401
	STD	0.0245	0.0198	0.0171	0.0153	0.0140	0.0106

B. Glaxo Wellcome

Moving average lag (n)		1	5	10	15	20	60
Return volatility	Mean	0.1473	0.1469	0.1464	0.1452	0.1438	0.1415
	STD	0.1346	0.0651	0.0476	0.0397	0.0325	0.0154
Implied volatility	Mean	0.1938	0.1938	0.1938	0.1937	0.1936	0.1958
	STD	0.0129	0.0118	0.0112	0.0104	0.0095	0.0110

Note: Return and implied volatilities from 23 March 1992 to 7 October 1996 for a total of 1148 observations are used.

Table 7.3 reports mean and standard deviation of the forecasts. As expected, the mean of return volatility is smaller than that of implied volatility, while standard deviation of return volatility is larger than that of implied volatility.

7.4   OUT-OF-SAMPLE FORECASTING PERFORMANCE TESTS

7.4.1   Forecasting procedure

Noh, Engle and Kane (1994) investigate the forecasting performance of the implied and actual return volatilities in the simulated options. Here, we directly compare the forecasting performance of the alternative models using mean absolute forecast error (MAFE) and mean squared forecast error (MSFE), which are represented as follows:

$$MAFE_h = \frac{1}{240} \sum_{t=1}^{240} |FIV_{h,t} - x_{t+h}|$$

$$MSFE_h = \frac{1}{240} \sum_{t=1}^{240} (FIV_{h,t} - x_{t+h})^2 \tag{7.32}$$

where $MAFE_h$ and $MSFE_h$ represent the MAFE and MSFE at horizon h, respectively, x_{t+h} is the realized implied standard deviation at time $t + h$, and $FIV_{h,t}$ is the forecasted implied standard deviation for horizon h at time t. Note that the $FIV_{h,t}$ for the models used in this study is calculated by equation (7.4) for the GARCH(1,1)-RV model, equation (7.17) for the log-ARFIMA(0,d,1)-IV model, equation (7.29) for the scaled truncated log-ARFIMA(0,d,1)-IV model, equation (7.30) for the detrended log-ARFIMA(0,d,1)-IV model, and equation (7.31) for the moving average methods, respectively. In addition, we investigate the forecasting performance of the models over various horizons rather than just one-step-ahead.

We use a rolling sample of the past volatilities. On day t, the conditional volatility of one period ahead, $t + 1$, is constructed by using the estimates which are obtained from only the past observations (i.e. 778 observations in this study). By recursive substitution of the conditional volatility, forecasts for up to 120 horizons are constructed. On the next day $(t + 1)$, using 778 recent observations (i.e. 778 observations from the second observation to the 779 observation), we estimate the parameters again and get another forecast for up to 120 horizons. The estimation and forecasting procedures are performed 240 times using rolling windows of 778 observations. Each forecast is expressed as a standard deviation to be compared with the realized implied standard deviation, and MAFE and MSFE statistics are calculated as in (7.32) above.

7.4.2 Results

Table 7.4 reports the QML estimates of the GARCH(1,1) model using return volatility (GARCH(1,1)-RV), the log-ARFIMA(0,d,1) model using implied volatility (log-ARFIMA(0,d,1)-IV), and the scaled truncated log-ARFIMA(0,d,1)-IV for British Steel and Glaxo Wellcome. As frequently found in empirical finance, $\alpha + \beta$ in the GARCH(1,1)-RV model is close to 1 and highly persistent. In this case, long memory processes may be more appropriate for return volatility than the GARCH(1,1) model.

The middle part of each panel reports the estimates of the log-ARFIMA(0,d,1)-IV model. As expected, the drift is not equivalent to zero and for the truncation lag used in this study there exists an unconditional log-variance. The lowest parts of panels A and B show the estimates of the scaled truncated log-ARFIMA(0,d,1)-IV model. As explained in the previous subsection, the long memory parameter of the scaled truncated log-ARFIMA(0,d,1) model is smaller than that of the log-ARFIMA(0,d,1) model. However, for both models, the estimates of the long memory parameter are significantly different from 0 and 1.

Table 7.5 reports the results of an out-of-sample forecasting performance test for British Steel and Glaxo. The first two columns in panels A and B of

Table 7.4 *Maximum likelihood estimates of GARCH(1,1)-RV, log-ARFIMA(0,d,1)-IV, and truncated log-ARFIMA(0,d,1)-IV models*

A. British Steel

Models		$\omega(\mu, \delta)$	$\alpha(\theta)$	$\beta(d, d_{ST})$
GARCH(1,1)	Estimates	0.0004	0.0091	0.9559
	Robust standard deviation	(0.0002)	(0.0079)	(0.0091)
Log-ARFIMA(0,d,1)-IV	Estimates	−0.0509	−0.1309	0.6425
	Robust standard deviation	(0.0135)	(0.0491)	(0.0348)
Scaled truncated	Estimates	−2.2998	−0.0259	0.5104
log-ARFIMA(0,d,1)-IV	Robust standard deviation	(0.0295)	(0.0551)	(0.0527)

B. Glaxo Wellcome

Models		$\omega(\mu, \delta)$	$\alpha(\theta)$	$\beta(d, d_{ST})$
GARCH(1,1)	Estimates	0.0019	0.0518	0.9170
	Robust standard deviation	(0.0008)	(0.0128)	(0.0235)
Log-ARFIMA(0,d,1)-IV	Estimates	−0.0221	−0.1792	0.7674
	Robust standard deviation	(0.0072)	(0.0477)	(0.0362)
Scaled truncated	Estimates	−2.7311	−0.1285	0.7062
log-ARFIMA(0,d,1)-IV	Robust standard deviation	(0.0295)	(0.0546)	(0.0493)

Note: Return and implied volatilities from 23 March 1992 to 7 October 1996 for a total of 1148 observations are used.

Table 7.5 *Comparison of forecasting performance of GARCH(1,1)-RV, log-ARFIMA(0,d,1)-IV, and moving average method*

A. British Steel

Forecasting horizons	GARCH(1,1)-RV		Log-ARFIMA (0,d,1)-IV		Detrended log-ARFIMA (0,d,1)-IV		Scaled truncated log-ARFIMA (0,d,1)-IV		Return volatility (n = 60) increased by 0.0661		Implied volatility (n = 20)	
	MAFE	MSFE	MAFE	MSFE	MAFE	MSFE	MAFE	MSFE	MAFE	MSFE	MAFE	MSFE
1	0.0308	0.0016	0.0117	0.0003	0.0117	0.0003	**0.0116**	**0.0003**	0.0207	0.0008	0.0142	0.0005
5	0.0288	0.0015	0.0165	0.0006	0.0162	0.0006	0.0156	0.0006	0.0205	0.0008	**0.0153**	**0.0006**
10	0.0270	0.0014	0.0186	0.0007	0.0182	0.0007	0.0174	0.0007	0.0208	0.0008	**0.0165**	**0.0006**
20	0.0255	0.0013	0.0195	0.0007	0.0191	0.0007	**0.0178**	**0.0006**	0.0221	0.0009	0.0181	0.0006
30	0.0259	0.0013	0.0200	0.0008	0.0189	0.0007	**0.0175**	**0.0006**	0.0240	0.0010	0.0188	0.0007
40	0.0274	0.0014	0.0219	0.0008	0.0202	0.0007	0.0190	0.0007	0.0247	0.0010	**0.0176**	**0.0006**
50	0.0256	0.0012	0.0208	0.0007	0.0186	0.0006	**0.0173**	**0.0006**	0.0247	0.0009	0.0182	0.0006
60	0.0250	0.0011	0.0217	0.0007	0.0181	0.0006	**0.0168**	**0.0005**	0.0271	0.0011	0.0200	0.0007
70	0.0265	0.0012	0.0239	0.0009	0.0208	0.0007	**0.0193**	**0.0007**	0.0293	0.0013	0.0205	0.0007
80	0.0262	0.0011	0.0257	0.0010	0.0216	0.0008	**0.0203**	**0.0007**	0.0301	0.0013	0.0210	0.0008
90	0.0254	0.0010	0.0259	0.0010	0.0215	0.0008	**0.0206**	**0.0007**	0.0314	0.0013	0.0228	0.0008
100	0.0255	0.0011	0.0281	0.0012	0.0230	0.0008	0.0229	0.0008	0.0307	0.0013	**0.0227**	**0.0008**
120	0.0260	0.0011	0.0293	0.0012	0.0241	0.0009	**0.0226**	**0.0008**	0.0308	0.0014	0.0230	0.0008

B. Glaxo Wellcome

Forecasting horizons	GARCH(1,1)-RV		Log-ARFIMA (0,d,1)-IV		Detrended log-ARFIMA (0,d,1)-IV		Scaled truncated log-ARFIMA (0,d,1)-IV		Return volatility (n = 6) increased by 0.0465		Implied volatility (n = 20)	
	MAFE	MSFE	MAFE	MSFE	MAFE	MSFE	MAFE	MSFE	MAFE	MSFE	MAFE	MSFE
1	0.0281	0.0013	**0.0048**	**0.0000**	0.0048	0.0001	**0.0048**	**0.0000**	0.0130	0.0002	0.0075	0.0001
5	0.0351	0.0016	0.0076	0.0001	0.0074	0.0001	**0.0073**	**0.0001**	0.0137	0.0003	0.0089	0.0002
10	0.0416	0.0020	0.0103	0.0002	0.0100	0.0002	**0.0098**	**0.0002**	0.0140	0.0003	0.0101	0.0002
20	0.0457	0.0024	0.0120	0.0003	0.0114	0.0002	**0.0111**	**0.0002**	0.0149	0.0003	0.0114	0.0003
30	0.0490	0.0027	0.0128	0.0003	0.0120	0.0003	**0.0117**	**0.0002**	0.0159	0.0003	0.0120	0.0003
40	0.0538	0.0032	0.0145	0.0003	0.0132	0.0003	0.0129	0.0003	0.0155	0.0003	**0.0123**	**0.0003**
50	0.0564	0.0036	0.0150	0.0004	0.0131	0.0003	0.0128	0.0003	0.0141	0.0003	**0.0119**	**0.0002**
60	0.0574	0.0037	0.0144	0.0003	0.0128	0.0003	0.0125	0.0003	0.0145	0.0003	**0.0121**	**0.0002**
70	0.0585	0.0038	0.0146	0.0004	0.0130	0.0003	0.0127	0.0003	0.0133	0.0003	**0.0118**	**0.0002**
80	0.0587	0.0038	0.0147	0.0004	0.0127	0.0003	**0.0125**	**0.0003**	0.0136	0.0003	0.0125	0.0003
90	0.0583	0.0038	0.0147	0.0004	**0.0121**	**0.0003**	**0.0121**	**0.0003**	0.0142	0.0003	0.0132	0.0003
100	0.0575	0.0037	0.0163	0.0005	0.0140	0.0003	**0.0137**	**0.0003**	0.0162	0.0004	0.0140	0.0003
120	0.0574	0.0036	0.0167	0.0005	0.0152	0.0004	**0.0146**	**0.0004**	0.0170	0.0005	0.0149	0.0004

Notes: GARCH(1,1)-RV forecasts for implied standard deviation (ISD) are obtained using return volatility, while log-ARFIMA(0,d,1)-IV forecasts for ISD are calculated using implied volatility. Return and implied volatilities from 23 March 1992 to 7 October 1996 for a total of 1148 observations are used. The most recent 778 observations are used for estimating models and predicting future ISDs over 120 horizons. The results are based on 240 out-of-sample forecasts. Bold numbers represent the smallest MAFE and the smallest MSFE for given forecasting horizons. In the case of a tie or a non-ranking, both are recorded in bold.

Table 7.2 report the results of an out-of-sample forecasting performance test for British Steel and Glaxo based on the MAFE and the MSFE of the forecasts of implied volatility over the horizons from 1 to 120. Columns 3 and 4 are the results of calculations based on the detrended log-ARFIMA(0,d,1) model of subsection 7.3.2.4 and the scaled truncated log-ARFIMA(0,d,1) model of section 7.3.2.3, respectively. The final two columns are obtained from Table 7.7. They describe forecasts based on simple moving averages of RV plus a constant and implied volatility, respectively. The moving average methods were explained in section 7.3.3 and a more detailed explanation on the empirical results are reported in section 7.4.2.2. We also report in the table the 'efficient set' of methods based on smallest MAFE and smallest MSFE. If, for example, $\text{MAFE}_{\text{method 1}} < \text{MAFE}_{\text{method 2}}$ and $\text{MSFE}_{\text{method 1}} > \text{MSFE}_{\text{method 2}}$, then both methods 1 and 2 are in the efficient set and are reported in bold.

7.4.2.1   Log-ARFIMA(0,d,1)-IV and GARCH(1,1)-RV models

This subsection compares the forecasts from the long memory volatility model (i.e. the log-ARFIMA(0,d,1)-IV model) with those from the conventional short memory volatility model (i.e. the GARCH(1,1)-RV model) in detail.

The first two columns of Table 7.5 show that the MAFE and MSFE of the log-ARFIMA(0,d,1)-IV model are smaller than those of the GARCH(1,1)-RV model over all horizons. In particular, in short horizons, the forecasting performance of the log-ARFIMA(0,d,1)-IV model is much better than that of the GARCH(1,1)-RV model. Therefore, for the prediction of implied volatility, the log-ARFIMA(0,d,1)-IV model outperforms the GARCH(1,1)-RV model at least in this context.

The MAFE and MSFE used here show only the magnitude of the forecast error and do not show systematic forecast bias (FB) and forecast standard deviation (FSTD).[7] Figures 7.1 and 7.3 plot the average forecast errors over forecasting horizons for British Steel and Glaxo. During the forecasting period, the realized IV of Glaxo is relatively less volatile than that of British Steel. The magnitude of the average forecast errors tends to increase as forecasting horizons increase for both models. In short horizons, the log-ARFIMA(0,d,1)-IV average forecast errors are very small. Over long horizons, the log-ARFIMA(0,d,1)-IV forecasts are less biased than the GARCH(1,1)-RV forecasts for Glaxo, while the log-ARFIMA(0,d,1)-IV forecasts are more biased than the GARCH(1,1)-RV forecasts for British Steel. This shows that, as explained in subsection 7.3.2.2, a drift term together with the truncation lag may result in a large forecast bias in the log-ARFIMA model.

Figures 7.2 and 7.4 plot the FSTDs of the forecasts for the two companies. The log-ARFIMA(0,d,1)-IV model has lower FSTD than the GARCH(1,1)-RV model in short forecasting horizons. However, in long horizons, the

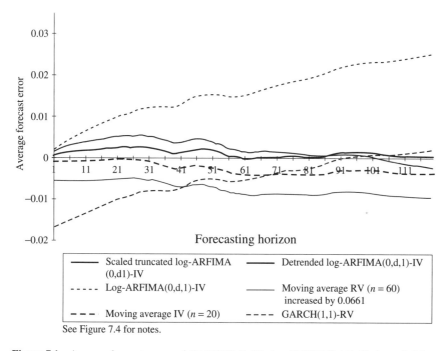

Figure 7.1 *Average forecast error of GARCH(1,1)-RV, log-ARFIMA(0,d,1)-IV detrended log-ARFIMA(0,d,1)-IV scaled truncated log-ARFIMA(0,d,1)-IV, averaged RV, and averaged IV British Steel Plc*

FSTD of the GARCH(1,1)-RV model is little different from that of the log-ARFIMA(0,d,1)-IV model for Glaxo. Although it is not reported in this chapter, British Petroleum and Barclays also show that the FSTD of the log-ARFIMA(0,d,1)-IV model is lower than that of the GARCH(1,1)-RV model. Our conclusion is that the log-ARFIMA(0,d,1)-IV model has less FSTD than the GARCH(1,1)-RV model.

We need to address the issue of when to re-estimate the models. In practice, daily estimation of a model may be time consuming work. If there is little difference in forecasting performance between daily estimation and longer estimation intervals, e.g. weekly, monthly, and quarterly, we need not estimate the models daily. Table 7.6 reports the results. For British Steel, the forecasting performance gets better as the estimation interval increases for the GARCH(1,1)-RV model, while it becomes slightly worse for the larger estimation intervals for the log-ARFIMA(0,d,1)-IV model. On the other hand, for Glaxo, the forecasting performance gets worse as the estimation interval increases for both log-ARFIMA(0,d,1)-IV and GARCH(1,1)-RV models. However, we find that the GARCH(1,1)-RV model still does not outperform the log-ARFIMA(0,d,1)-IV model, and the difference between the forecasting performances from the

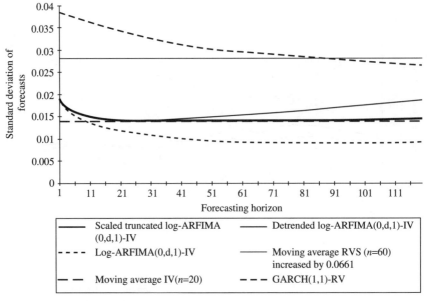

See Figure 7.4 for notes.

Figure 7.2   *Standard deviation of forecasts of GARCH(1,1)-RV, log-ARFIMA(0,d,1)-IV, detrended log-ARFIMA(0,d,1)-IV, scaled truncated log-ARFIMA(0,d,1), average RV, and average IV British Steel Plc*

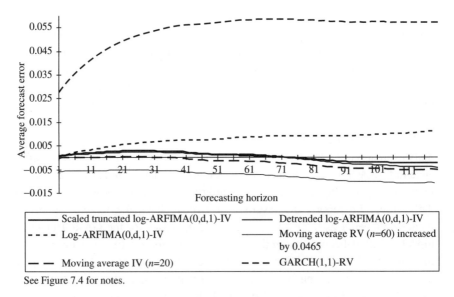

See Figure 7.4 for notes.

Figure 7.3   *Average forecast error of GARCH(1,1)-RV, log-ARFIMA(0,d,1)-IV detrended log-ARFIMA(0,d,1)-IV scaled truncated log-ARFIMA(0,d,1)-IV, averaged RV, and averaged IV Glaxo Wellcome Plc*

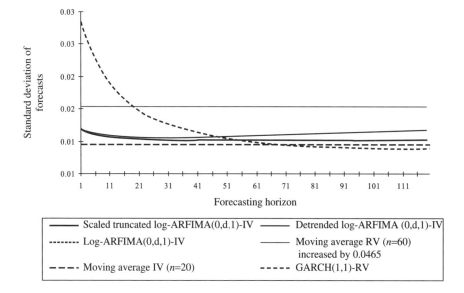

Notes: Figures 7.1 and 7.3 plot average forecast errors over forecasting horizons for British Steel and Glaxo Wellcome and Figures 7.2 and 7.4 plot forecast standard deviations over forecasting horizons for the two companies. The GARCH(1,1)-RV log-ARFIMA(0,d,1)-IV, scaled truncated log-ARFIMA(0,d,1)-IV, and detrended log-ARFIMA(0,d,1)-IV models are explained in sections 7.3.1, 7.3.2.2, 7.3.2.3 and 7.3.2.4, respectively. The moving average IV ($n = 20$) represents forecasts based on averaged value of last 20 IVs. The moving average RV ($n = 60$) increased by a number (0.0661 for British Steel and 0.0465 for Glaxo Wellcome) represents forecasts based on averaged value of last 60 RVs plus the optimal increase. The moving average methods were explained in section 7.3.3 and a more detailed explanation on the empirical results is reported in section 7.4.2. The MAFE and MSFE of the forecasts are summarized in Table 7.5.

Figure 7.4 *Standard deviation of forecasts of GARCH(1,1)-RV, log-ARFIMA(0,d,1)-IV, detrended log-ARFIMA(0,d,1)-IV, scaled truncated log-ARFIMA(0,d,1)-IV, averaged RV, and averaged IV Glaxo Wellcome Plc*

different estimation intervals is marginal for the log-ARFIMA-IV model. Therefore, on the ground of the results in Table 7.6, we can conclude that the log-ARFIMA(0,d,1)-IV model need not be estimated daily and can be estimated monthly without particularly increasing the forecasting error.

7.4.2.2 Forecasting performance of the moving average methods

We need to investigate the forecasting performance of the practically widely used moving average methods in detail. The moving average forecasts for implied volatility using IV and RV with the n most recent observations at time t, $FIV_t^{n,IV}$ and $FIV_t^{n,RV}$, are discussed in section 7.3.3. The forecasting performances of $FIV_t^{n,IV}$ and $FIV_t^{n,RV}$ are reported in Table 7.7. Table 7.7 also

Table 7.6 *Forecasting performance of the GARCH(1,1)-RV and log-ARFIMA(0,d,1)-IV models considering estimation intervals*

A. British Steel

Estimation interval		1 (daily)		5 (weekly)		10 (fortnightly)		20 (monthly)		60 (quarterly)	
		MAFE	MSFE	MAFE	MSFE	MAFE	MSFE	MAFE	MSFE	MAFE	MSFE
Forecasting performance of RV-GARCH(1,1) model	1	0.0308	0.0016	0.0304	0.0015	0.0303	0.0015	0.0294	0.0014	0.0273	0.0013
	5	0.0288	0.0015	0.0285	0.0015	0.0282	0.0015	0.0279	0.0014	0.0261	0.0013
	10	0.0270	0.0014	0.0267	0.0014	0.0266	0.0014	0.0266	0.0014	0.0248	0.0012
	15	0.0255	0.0013	0.0254	0.0013	0.0254	0.0013	0.0250	0.0013	0.0240	0.0011
	20	0.0259	0.0013	0.0257	0.0013	0.0256	0.0012	0.0249	0.0012	0.0240	0.0011
	30	0.0274	0.0014	0.0269	0.0013	0.0265	0.0013	0.0262	0.0012	0.0256	0.0012
	40	0.0256	0.0012	0.0253	0.0012	0.0252	0.0012	0.0252	0.0012	0.0243	0.0011
	50	0.0250	0.0011	0.0248	0.0010	0.0250	0.0010	0.0247	0.0010	0.0234	0.0009
	60	0.0265	0.0012	0.0265	0.0012	0.0266	0.0011	0.0261	0.0011	0.0237	0.0009
	70	0.0262	0.0011	0.0263	0.0011	0.0262	0.0010	0.0256	0.0010	0.0241	0.0009
	80	0.0254	0.0010	0.0250	0.0010	0.0250	0.0009	0.0248	0.0009	0.0236	0.0008
	100	0.0255	0.0011	0.0254	0.0010	0.0250	0.0010	0.0245	0.0010	0.0226	0.0008
	120	0.0260	0.0011	0.0258	0.0010	0.0253	0.0010	0.0247	0.0010	0.0242	0.0009
Forecasting performance of IV - log-ARFIMA(0,d,1) model	1	0.0117	0.0003	0.0117	0.0003	0.0118	0.0003	0.0117	0.0003	0.0117	0.0003
	5	0.0165	0.0006	0.0165	0.0006	0.0165	0.0006	0.0164	0.0006	0.0165	0.0006
	10	0.0186	0.0007	0.0186	0.0007	0.0186	0.0007	0.0184	0.0007	0.0186	0.0007
	15	0.0195	0.0007	0.0195	0.0007	0.0195	0.0007	0.0195	0.0007	0.0197	0.0007
	20	0.0200	0.0008	0.0200	0.0008	0.0200	0.0008	0.0201	0.0008	0.0204	0.0008
	30	0.0219	0.0008	0.0219	0.0008	0.0219	0.0008	0.0219	0.0008	0.0222	0.0008
	40	0.0208	0.0007	0.0208	0.0007	0.0209	0.0007	0.0211	0.0007	0.0216	0.0008

	1 (daily)		5 (weekly)		10 (fortnightly)		20 (monthly)		60 (quarterly)	
	MAFE	MSFE	MAFE	MSFE	MAFE	MSFE	MAFE	MSFE	MAFE	MSFE
Forecasting performance of IV - log-ARFIMA(0,d,1) model										
50	0.0217	0.0007	0.0218	0.0008	0.0220	0.0008	0.0221	0.0008	0.0229	0.0008
60	0.0239	0.0009	0.0242	0.0009	0.0243	0.0009	0.0243	0.0009	0.0247	0.0009
70	0.0257	0.0010	0.0259	0.0010	0.0262	0.0010	0.0263	0.0010	0.0266	0.0010
80	0.0259	0.0010	0.0261	0.0010	0.0264	0.0010	0.0267	0.0010	0.0273	0.0011
100	0.0281	0.0012	0.0283	0.0012	0.0286	0.0012	0.0293	0.0012	0.0310	0.0013
120	0.0293	0.0012	0.0295	0.0012	0.0299	0.0012	0.0306	0.0012	0.0320	0.0013

B. Glaxo Wellcome

Estimation interval	1 (daily)		5 (weekly)		10 (fortnightly)		20 (monthly)		60 (quarterly)	
	MAFE	MSFE	MAFE	MSFE	MAFE	MSFE	MAFE	MSFE	MAFE	MSFE
1	0.0281	0.0013	0.0281	0.0013	0.0286	0.0013	0.0300	0.0014	0.0319	0.0015
5	0.0351	0.0016	0.0353	0.0016	0.0360	0.0016	0.0376	0.0018	0.0405	0.0020
10	0.0416	0.0020	0.0420	0.0020	0.0427	0.0021	0.0443	0.0022	0.0478	0.0026
15	0.0457	0.0024	0.0462	0.0024	0.0469	0.0025	0.0484	0.0027	0.0521	0.0031
Forecasting performance of RV-GARCH(1,1) model										
20	0.0490	0.0027	0.0495	0.0028	0.0501	0.0028	0.0516	0.0030	0.0551	0.0034
30	0.0538	0.0032	0.0543	0.0033	0.0550	0.0034	0.0561	0.0035	0.0593	0.0039
40	0.0564	0.0036	0.0569	0.0036	0.0574	0.0037	0.0584	0.0038	0.0613	0.0042
50	0.0574	0.0037	0.0578	0.0037	0.0583	0.0038	0.0591	0.0039	0.0618	0.0042
60	0.0585	0.0038	0.0588	0.0038	0.0593	0.0039	0.0600	0.0040	0.0625	0.0043
70	0.0587	0.0038	0.0589	0.0038	0.0594	0.0039	0.0601	0.0040	0.0624	0.0043
80	0.0583	0.0038	0.0586	0.0038	0.0591	0.0039	0.0596	0.0039	0.0618	0.0042
100	0.0575	0.0037	0.0578	0.0037	0.0582	0.0037	0.0587	0.0038	0.0608	0.0041
120	0.0574	0.0036	0.0577	0.0036	0.0581	0.0037	0.0585	0.0037	0.0605	0.0040

(continued)

Table 7.6 *(continued)*

B. Glaxo Wellcome

Estimation interval	1 (daily)		5 (weekly)		10 (fortnightly)		20 (monthly)		60 (quarterly)	
	MAFE	MSFE	MAFE	MSFE	MAFE	MSFE	MAFE	MSFE	MAFE	MSFE
1	0.0048	0.0000	0.0048	0.0000	0.0049	0.0000	0.0049	0.0000	0.0049	0.0000
5	0.0076	0.0001	0.0076	0.0001	0.0076	0.0001	0.0077	0.0001	0.0077	0.0001
10	0.0103	0.0002	0.0104	0.0002	0.0104	0.0002	0.0104	0.0002	0.0105	0.0002
15	0.0120	0.0002	0.0120	0.0002	0.0120	0.0002	0.0120	0.0002	0.0122	0.0002
20	0.0128	0.0003	0.0128	0.0003	0.0128	0.0003	0.0128	0.0003	0.0132	0.0003
30	0.0145	0.0003	0.0145	0.0003	0.0145	0.0003	0.0146	0.0003	0.0152	0.0004
40	0.0150	0.0004	0.0150	0.0004	0.0150	0.0004	0.0151	0.0004	0.0160	0.0004
50	0.0144	0.0003	0.0145	0.0003	0.0144	0.0003	0.0146	0.0003	0.0155	0.0004
60	0.0146	0.0004	0.0147	0.0004	0.0146	0.0004	0.0149	0.0004	0.0158	0.0004
70	0.0147	0.0004	0.0148	0.0004	0.0148	0.0004	0.0150	0.0004	0.0163	0.0005
80	0.0147	0.0004	0.0148	0.0004	0.0147	0.0004	0.0149	0.0004	0.0164	0.0005
100	0.0163	0.0005	0.0164	0.0005	0.0164	0.0005	0.0167	0.0005	0.0185	0.0006
120	0.0167	0.0005	0.0168	0.0005	0.0167	0.0005	0.0171	0.0005	0.0190	0.0006

Forecasting performance of IV - log-ARFIMA(0,d,1) model

Notes: GARCH(1,1)-RV forecasts for implied standard deviation (ISD) are obtained using return volatility, while log-ARFIMA(0,d,1)-IV forecasts for ISD are calculated using implied volatility. Return and implied volatilities from 23 March 1992 to 7 October 1996 for a total of 1148 observations are used. The most recent 778 observations are used for estimating models and predicting future ISDs over 120 horizons. The results are based on 240 out-of-sample forecasts. For the case of daily estimation, each model is estimated and the forecasts are obtained on the daily basis, whilst for the quarterly estimation, the models are estimated once every 60 days and the estimates are used for the forecasts. Therefore, the number of estimations is 240 for the daily estimation while it is only four for the quarterly estimation. Note that forecasting is always performed on a daily basis.

Table 7.7 *Forecasting performance of averaged RV and IV*

A. British Steel

		1		10		20		60	
Average Lag (*n*)		MAFE	MSFE	MAFE	MSFE	MAFE	MSFE	MAFE	MSFE
	1	0.13383	0.02506	0.07286	0.00752	0.07210	0.00669	0.07170	0.00590
	5	0.13343	0.02518	0.07359	0.00760	0.07178	0.00665	0.07163	0.00588
	10	0.13371	0.02540	0.07401	0.00758	0.07096	0.00662	0.07175	0.00588
Return	20	0.13206	0.02494	0.07268	0.00730	0.06970	0.00652	0.07123	0.00592
volatility	40	0.13470	0.02551	0.07304	0.00782	0.07127	0.00695	0.07337	0.00626
	60	0.13511	0.02549	0.07481	0.00793	0.07405	0.00723	0.07527	0.00668
	80	0.13497	0.02557	0.07532	0.00833	0.07464	0.00749	0.07585	0.00685
	100	0.13542	0.02551	0.07665	0.00844	0.07615	0.00768	0.07463	0.00679
	120	0.13821	0.02627	0.07863	0.00854	0.07676	0.00778	0.07568	0.00702
	1	0.12479	0.02282	0.05982	0.00523	0.05513	0.00431	0.05184	0.00343
	5	0.12407	0.02294	0.06051	0.00530	0.05507	0.00427	0.05187	0.00341
Return	10	0.12415	0.02316	0.06041	0.00528	0.05443	0.00424	0.05195	0.00342
volatility	20	0.12294	0.02271	0.05914	0.00502	0.05249	0.00417	0.05159	0.00347
increased	40	0.12509	0.02321	0.05973	0.00546	0.05383	0.00452	0.05367	0.00374
by 0.02	60	0.12522	0.02312	0.06145	0.00550	0.05671	0.00473	0.05631	0.00409
	80	0.12503	0.02320	0.06243	0.00590	0.05789	0.00498	0.05858	0.00425
	100	0.12571	0.02316	0.06410	0.00604	0.06102	0.00520	0.05665	0.00422
	120	0.12830	0.02387	0.06547	0.00608	0.06113	0.00525	0.05725	0.00440
	1	0.11736	0.02137	0.05084	0.00373	0.04275	0.00274	0.03373	0.00176
	5	0.11637	0.02150	0.05125	0.00380	0.04199	0.00270	0.03347	0.00175
Return	10	0.11651	0.02172	0.05069	0.00378	0.04130	0.00266	0.03337	0.00175
volatility	20	0.11613	0.02129	0.04923	0.00354	0.04093	0.00261	0.03388	0.00182
increased	40	0.11732	0.02171	0.05039	0.00391	0.04125	0.00288	0.03618	0.00201
by 0.04	60	0.11738	0.02155	0.05215	0.00387	0.04401	0.00302	0.04091	0.00229
	80	0.11723	0.02162	0.05304	0.00427	0.04587	0.00327	0.04370	0.00246
	100	0.11793	0.02162	0.05549	0.00444	0.04982	0.00353	0.04309	0.00245
	120	0.12037	0.02227	0.05566	0.00443	0.04876	0.00352	0.04197	0.00258
	1	0.11116	0.02069	0.046156	0.002974	0.03479	0.00188	0.02072	0.00079
	5	0.11036	0.02082	0.045719	0.003055	0.03402	0.00185	0.02046	0.00078
Return	10	0.11033	0.02103	0.045123	0.003029	0.03434	0.00181	0.02077	0.00078
volatility	20	0.11005	0.02063	0.043493	0.002814	0.03523	0.00178	0.02211	0.00087
increased	40	0.11019	0.02095	0.045859	0.003084	0.03607	0.00195	0.02471	0.00096
by 0.0661*	60	0.11071	0.02069	0.046274	0.002945	0.03485	0.00199	0.02713	0.00114
	80	0.11062	0.02077	0.048408	0.003345	0.03945	0.00225	0.03014	0.00131
	100	0.11118	0.02080	0.050181	0.003556	0.04242	0.00254	0.03071	0.00135
	120	0.11362	0.02139	0.049591	0.00348	0.04034	0.00247	0.03075	0.00140
	1	**0.01238**	**0.00038**	0.01411	0.00050	0.01417	0.00052	0.01449	0.00050
	5	0.01826	0.00084	0.01686	0.00069	**0.01527**	**0.00060**	0.01534	0.00054
	10	0.02128	0.00104	0.01908	0.00074	0.01646	0.00061	**0.01622**	**0.00056**
Implied	20	0.02310	0.00100	0.01929	0.00069	0.01813	0.00063	**0.01743**	**0.00061**
volatility	40	0.02252	0.00098	0.01923	0.00064	**0.01756**	**0.00057**	0.01776	0.00060
	60	0.02402	0.00106	0.02192	0.00081	0.01997	0.00070	**0.01883**	**0.00063**
	80	0.02562	0.00108	0.02323	0.00087	0.02099	0.00076	**0.01973**	**0.00066**
	100	0.02585	0.00106	0.02444	0.00088	0.02272	0.00080	**0.02105**	**0.00075**
	120	0.02679	0.00119	0.02381	0.00083	0.02302	0.00081	**0.02137**	**0.00076**

(continued)

Table 7.7 *(continued)*

B. Glaxo Wellcome

		1		10		20		60	
Average lag (n)		MAFE	MSFE	MAFE	MSFE	MAFE	MSFE	MAFE	MSFE
	1	0.11477	0.01977	0.05636	0.00416	0.05254	0.00337	0.05219	0.00294
	5	0.11403	0.01963	0.05765	0.00430	0.05315	0.00343	0.05203	0.00296
	10	0.11496	0.02000	0.05802	0.00437	0.05343	0.00339	0.05201	0.00299
Return	20	0.11428	0.01992	0.05767	0.00423	0.05312	0.00336	0.05176	0.00299
volatility	40	0.11584	0.02030	0.05925	0.00455	0.05431	0.00365	0.05230	0.00303
	60	0.11577	0.02034	0.06075	0.00470	0.05569	0.00373	0.05349	0.00310
	80	0.11616	0.02023	0.05895	0.00439	0.05530	0.00356	0.05517	0.00325
	100	0.11726	0.02022	0.06153	0.00476	0.05790	0.00392	0.05667	0.00351
	120	0.11764	0.02078	0.06361	0.00518	0.05987	0.00421	0.05725	0.00365
	1	0.10658	0.01832	0.04379	0.00267	0.03663	0.00178	0.03221	0.00125
	5	0.10586	0.01818	0.04408	0.00281	0.03728	0.00184	0.03211	0.00128
Return	10	0.10659	0.01855	0.04491	0.00288	0.03741	0.00181	0.03204	0.00130
volatility	20	0.10572	0.01848	0.04455	0.00275	0.03734	0.00179	0.03207	0.00132
Increased	40	0.10702	0.01884	0.04682	0.00305	0.03979	0.00205	0.03270	0.00134
by 0.02	60	0.10700	0.01884	0.04825	0.00316	0.04062	0.00208	0.03355	0.00136
	80	0.10719	0.01866	0.04484	0.00278	0.03809	0.00185	0.03532	0.00144
	100	0.10833	0.01859	0.04753	0.00308	0.04169	0.00215	0.03679	0.00164
	120	0.10857	0.01912	0.04994	0.00349	0.04356	0.00242	0.03802	0.00176
	1	0.09891	0.01762	0.03321	0.00192	0.02431	0.00090	0.01301	0.00024
	5	0.09836	0.01750	0.03337	0.00208	0.02415	0.00097	0.01374	0.00028
Return	10	0.09888	0.01786	0.03334	0.00215	0.02350	0.00094	0.01402	0.00031
volatility	20	0.09823	0.01781	0.03342	0.00203	0.02372	0.00093	0.01494	0.00034
Increased	40	0.09853	0.01815	0.03648	0.00230	0.02685	0.00117	0.01554	0.00034
by 0.0465	60	0.09917	0.01808	0.03706	0.00234	0.02648	0.00113	0.01453	0.00029
	80	0.09861	0.01780	0.03247	0.00187	0.02238	0.00081	0.01359	0.00028
	100	0.09962	0.01766	0.03495	0.00210	0.02546	0.00103	0.01620	0.00040
	120	0.09962	0.01816	0.03707	0.00248	0.02749	0.00127	0.01704	0.00050
	1	0.09641	0.01781	0.03276	0.00208	0.02303	0.00099	0.01326	0.00027
	5	0.09607	0.01769	0.03365	0.00224	0.02330	0.00106	0.01394	0.00032
Return	10	0.09670	0.01805	0.03346	0.00231	0.02296	0.00104	0.01428	0.00034
volatility	20	0.09632	0.01801	0.03295	0.00220	0.02270	0.00103	0.01525	0.00038
increased	40	0.09661	0.01833	0.03590	0.00246	0.02610	0.00126	0.01451	0.00036
by 0.06	60	0.09694	0.01823	0.03566	0.00247	0.02506	0.00119	0.01302	0.00029
	80	0.09590	0.01791	0.03132	0.00195	0.02114	0.00083	**0.01183**	**0.00023**
	100	0.09706	0.01773	0.03273	0.00214	0.02264	0.00100	**0.01423**	**0.00031**
	120	0.09673	0.01821	0.03454	0.00250	0.02476	0.00123	**0.01400**	**0.00039**
	1	**0.00509**	**0.00005**	0.00650	0.00008	0.00749	0.00011	0.01027	0.00020
	5	**0.00764**	**0.00012**	0.00844	0.00014	0.00889	0.00015	0.01091	0.00023
	10	**0.01007**	**0.00020**	0.01024	0.00019	**0.01010**	**0.00019**	0.01175	0.00025
Implied	20	0.01240	0.00028	0.01176	0.00026	**0.01145**	**0.00025**	0.01280	0.00030
volatility	40	0.01332	0.00033	0.01243	0.00029	**0.01231**	**0.00027**	0.01348	0.00033
	60	0.01358	0.00030	0.01272	0.00026	**0.01211**	**0.00024**	0.01413	0.00034
	80	0.01271	0.00027	0.01209	0.00024	0.01249	0.00026	0.01524	0.00040
	100	0.01466	0.00037	0.01413	0.00035	**0.01401**	**0.00034**	0.01518	0.00041
	120	0.01573	0.00041	0.01526	0.00040	**0.01493**	**0.00036**	0.01565	0.00039

Notes: The results are based on 240 out-of-sample moving average forecasts, see section 7.3.3 for the moving average forecasts for implied volatility using IV and RV with the n most recent observations. The forecasting procedure is described in section 7.4.1. Bold numbers represent the smallest MAFE and the smallest MSFE for given forecasting horizons. In the case of a tie or a non-ranking, both are recorded in bold.

reports the forecast performance of $FIV_t^{n,RV}$ increased by some numbers from the original $FIV_t^{n,RV}$. This is because RV is generally less than IV and the original $FIV_t^{n,RV}$ may result in downward FB if unadjusted. The optimal increase (i.e. 0.0661* for British Steel and 0.0465* for Glaxo) is chosen to match with $FIV_t^{1,RV}$ with $FIV_t^{1,IV}$. $FIV_t^{n,RV*}$ is used for $FIV_t^{n,RV}$ with the optimal increase. Therefore, $FIV_t^{n,RV*}$ is the sum of the moving average forecasts at time t and the optimal increase which is obtained using all *ex-post* moving average forecasts. In this sense, $FIV_t^{n,RV*}$ is not an out-of-sample forecast, but we use it for purposes of comparison.

Note that the MSFE of $FIV_t^{n,RV*}$ with $n > 1$ are smaller than those of the original $FIV_t^{1,RV}$. Since MSFE can be decomposed into the sum of squared forecast bias and forecast variance, this can be explained by follows; as the moving average lag (n) increases, the FSTD of $FIV_t^{n,RV}$ reduces and as the mean of $FIV_t^{n,RV}$ goes to $FIV_t^{n,RV*}$, FB decreases. Therefore, the table shows that, when we use moving averaged RV as a forecast of future volatility, large n and an appropriate increase should be considered.

Note that $FIV_t^{n,RV*}$ may have less MAFE and MSFE than the GARCH(1,1)-RV method. However, we calculated the optimal increase by 'data snooping', and since we do not know how much we increase $FIV_t^{n,RV}$, the simple moving average method may not be preferred to the GARCH(1,1)-RV method. Moreover, even though we choose the optimal increase and a large lag, the forecasting performance of the $FIV_t^{n,RV*}$ does not outperform $FIV_t^{n,IV}$; see the last lows of panels A and B of Table 7.7. Therefore, we can conclude that for the forecast of IV, IV should be used rather than RV.

In addition, we investigate the selection of n for $FIV_t^{n,IV}$. Table 7.7 shows that for the forecast of short horizons, $FIV_t^{1,IV}$ outperforms $FIV_t^{n,IV}$ with $n > 1$. However, for long forecasting horizons, $n = 20$ seems to be appropriate.[8] The last rows of panels A and B in Table 7.7 show that MAFE and MSFE tend to decrease as n becomes larger. For large n, there is little difference in MSFE and MAFE and in particular, for Glaxo, some MSFEs and MAFEs of $FIV_t^{60,IV}$ are larger than those of $FIV_t^{n,IV}$ with the smaller n.

7.4.2.3 Comparison of forecasting performance of the models

In this subsection, the results of the forecasting performance for all methods described in section 7.3 are compared: GARCH(1,1)-RV, log-ARFIMA(0,d,1)-IV, detrended log-ARFIMA(0,d,1)-IV, scaled truncated log-ARFIMA(0,d,1)-IV, and the moving average method for the RV and IV. Table 7.5 shows the MAFE and MSFE of six methods. As shown in subsections 7.4.2.1 and 7.4.2.2, the GARCH(1,1)-RV model and $FIV_t^{60,RV*}$ are not preferred to the other methods. Thus, from now on, the following four models are considered: log-ARFIMA(0,d,1)-IV in section 7.3.2.2, scaled truncated log-ARFIMA(0,d,1)-IV in section 7.3.2.3, detrended log-ARFIMA(0,d,1)-IV in section 7.3.2.4, and the moving average method for the IV in section 7.3.3.

For short horizons, the long memory volatility models are preferred to $FIV_t^{20,IV}$. In this case, $FIV_t^{1,IV}$ will give smaller forecast errors than $FIV_t^{20,IV}$ (see Table 7.7). The forecasting performances of $FIV_t^{1,IV}$ and the long memory volatility models are indistinguishable in short horizons. For long horizons, we may not differentiate the forecasting power of $FIV_t^{20,IV}$ from that of the detrended and scaled truncated log-ARFIMA(0,d,1)-IV models. Therefore, $FIV_t^{1,IV}$ and $FIV_t^{20,IV}$ can be used for short and long horizons, respectively.

The forecasting performance of the detrended log-ARFIMA(0,d,1) model is reported in Table 7.5. The detrended forecasts have less MAFE and MSFE than those of the log-ARFIMA(0,d,1)-IV model. Figures 7.1 to 7.4 suggest that the systematic forecast bias in the log-ARFIMA(0,d,1)-IV model can be reduced by this simple detrend method. Despite the increase in FSTD in long forecasting horizons, Table 7.5 and Figures 7.1 to 7.4 suggest that the detrended method is not worse than the log-ARFIMA(0,d,1)-IV model, and performs well in long horizons.

The forecasting performance of the scaled truncated log-ARFIMA(0,d,1)-IV model is reported in Table 7.5. The scaled truncated log-ARFIMA(0,d,1)-IV model performs well over all forecasting horizons. Figures 7.1 and 7.3 show that the scaled truncated log-ARFIMA(0,d,1) model reduces the systematic forecast bias found in the log-ARFIMA(0,d,1) model to a trivial level. In addition, the scaled truncated log-ARFIMA(0,d,1) model reduces FSTD in long horizons; see Figures 7.2 and 7.4. Therefore, by reducing systematic forecast bias and standard deviation, the scaled truncated log-ARFIMA(0,d,1)-IV model outperforms the log-ARFIMA(0,d,1)-IV in long forecasting horizons, while it holds the same forecasting power in short horizons as the log-ARFIMA(0,d,1)-IV. We suggest that the scaled truncated log-ARFIMA(0,d,1) model is preferred to the log-ARFIMA(0,d,1)-IV.

To make sure that our results are not dependent on the stock chosen or the time period, we selected seven other stocks and FTSE100 index and three separate time periods. Although we only report two stocks for the period, the other results, available on request from the authors, are broadly similar and do not change our qualitative evaluations. However, we find that for some companies such as BTR, British Telecommunication, General Electric and FTSE100 European call options, the log-ARFIMA(0,d,1)-IV model outperforms the scaled truncated log-ARFIMA(0,d,1)-IV for the forecast of implied volatility. These implied volatilities have a common character that they have increasing trends during the forecasting period. In this case, the systematic forecasting bias in the log-ARFIMA(0,d,1)-IV model gives better forecasts. However, when an increasing trend in implied volatility is not anticipated, the scaled truncated log-ARFIMA(0,d,1)-IV performs well.

7.5 CONCLUSION

We can summarize our conclusions as follows. First, for the forecast of implied volatility, IV rather than RV should be used. Second, log-ARFIMA(0,d,1)-IV is preferred to GARCH(1,1)-RV. Besides the forecasting performance results reported above, the log-ARFIMA(0,d,1) model does not need non-negativity constraints and estimates are easily obtained. Third, the moving average method outperforms the more sophisticated methods such as GARCH and log-ARFIMA models for the forecast of long horizons. In addition, the estimate of d which is greater than 0.5 for our long memory models means that our models are actually random walks with some short memory correlation. Such a structure will favour short-term forecasts, not long-term forecasts. Finally, we also address the important issue of scaled truncation in ARFIMA(k,d,l) models and suggest a procedure that eliminates bias-induced trending in the forecasts whilst preserving the essential pattern of hyperbolic decay if it is present in the process. Our final recommendation for the forecast of implied volatility is scaled truncated ARFIMA(k,d,l) models for both short and long horizons.

Our evidence shows that the long memory in volatility may be eliminated by differencing, that is, $\ln(x_t^2 - \ln(x_{t-1}^2)$, the growth rate in implied variance is covariance stationary with autocorrelation that decays exponentially. This means that whilst there is evidence of integration in IV models, there is no compelling evidence of long memory effects.

REFERENCES

Baillie, R.T., Bollerslev, T. and Mikkelsen, H.O. (1996) Fractionally integrated generalized autoregressive conditional heteroscedasticity, *Journal of Econometrics*, **75**(1), 3–30.

Berndt, E.K., Hall, B.H., Hall, R.E. and Hausman, J.A. (1974) Estimation and inference in nonlinear structure models, *Annals of Economic and Social Measurement*, **3/4**, 653–665.

Black, F. and Scholes, M. (1973) The pricing of options and corporate liabilities, *Journal of Political Economy*, **81**, 637–659.

Bollerslev, T. (1986) Generalized autoregressive conditional heteroscedasticity, *Journal of Econometrics*, **31**, 307–327.

Bollerslev, T., Chou, R.Y. and Kroner, K. (1992) ARCH modeling in finance, *Journal of Econometrics*, **52**, 5–59.

Bollerslev, T. and Wooldridge, J.M. (1992) Quasi-maximum likelihood estimation and inference in dynamic models with time-varying covariances, *Econometric Reviews*, **11**(2), 143–172.

Bougerol, P. and Picard, N. (1992) Stationarity of GARCH processes and of some nonnegative time series, *Journal of Econometrics*, **52**, 115–128.

Day, E.T. and Lewis, C.M. (1992) Stock market volatility and the information content of stock index options, *Journal of Econometrics*, **52**, 267–287.

Diebold, F.X. and Lopez, J.A. (1994) ARCH models, mimeo, Department of Economics, University of Pennsylvania.

Ding, Z., Granger, C. and Engle, R.F. (1992) A long memory property of stock market returns and a new model, discussion paper 92–21, Department of Economics, University of California, San Diego.

Engle, R.F. (1982) Autoregressive conditional heteroscedasticity with estimates of the variance of the United Kingdom inflation, *Econometrica*, **50**(4), 987–1007.

Engle, R.F. and Bollerslev, T. (1986) Modeling the persistence of conditional variances, *Econometric Reviews*, **5**, 1–50.

Engle, R.F., Hong, C., Kane, A. and Noh, J. (1993) Arbitrage valuation of variance forecasts with simulated options, *Advances in Futures and Options Research*, **6**, 393–415.

Figlewski, S. (1997) Forecasting volatility, *Financial Markets, Institutions and Instruments*, **6**(1), 1–88.

Granger, C., and Joyeux, R. (1980) An introduction to long memory time series models and fractional differencing, *Journal of Time Series Analysis*, **1**(1), 15–29.

Harvey, C.R. and Whaley, R.E. (1991) S&P 100 index option volatility, *Journal of Finance*, **46**(4), 1551–1561.

Harvey, C.R. and Whaley, R.E. (1992) Market volatility prediction and the efficiency of the S&P 100 index option market, *Journal of Financial Economics* **31**, 43–73.

Hosking, J.R.M. (1981), Fractional differencing, *Biometrika*, **68**, 165–176.

Hwang, S. and Satchell, S. (1997) Alternative models for implied and return volatilities, outliers, and further investigation of the integration of volatility, unpublished manuscript, Department of Applied Economics, University of Cambridge.

Lamoureux, C.G. and Lastrapes, W.D. (1993) Forecasting stock-return variance: toward an understanding of stochastic implied volatilities, *Review of Financial Studies*, **6**(2), 293–326.

Mandelbrot, B. and Van Ness, J. (1968) Fractional Brownian motions, fractional noises and applications, *SIAM Review*, **10**, 422–437

Noh, J.R., Engle, F. and Kane, A. (1994) Forecasting volatility and option prices of the S&P 500 Index, *Journal of Derivatives*, 17–30.

Psaradakis, Z. and Sola, M. (1995) Modelling long memory in stock market volatility: A fractionally integrated generalised ARCH approach, Discussion Paper in Financial Economics FE-2/95, Birkbeck College, University of London.

Weiss, A.A. (1986) Asymptotic theory for ARCH models: estimation and testing, *Econometric Theory*, **2**, 107–131.

NOTES

1. The results for the other companies can be obtained from authors on request.
2. The ARFIMA model is generally preferred to the FGN model. The main reason is that the former can describe economic and financial time series better than the latter. Moreover, by capturing both long and short memory, the ARFIMA model is a generalization of the more familiar ARIMA model, and it is easier to use than the FGN model. Furthermore, it need not assume Gaussianity for the innovations.

3. See Baillie, Bollerslev and Mikkelsen (1996) for further discussion.
4. The following log-ARFIMA model has the same property.
5. See the explanation of HS. To reduce the calculation time, they used the log-ARFIMA(1,d,1) model and searched for the best or at least equivalent truncation lag compared with the 1000 truncation lag. Lags of length, 100, 300, 500, 700 and 1000, were investigated, and the truncation lag which has the maximum log-likelihood value was chosen. The differences in the maximum values between the truncation lags were marginal but the log-ARFIMA(1,d,1) model achieved maximum values when the truncation lags were set at 100.
6. The following explanation applies to all discrete time long memory processes.
7. Note that MSFE may be decomposed into the sum of squared forecast bias and forecast variance. For the models such as log-ARFIMA(0,d,1)-IV model which have systematic forecast bias, the FB includes both the systematic forecast bias and the differences between forecasts and realized IVs for given forecasting horizons. On the other hand, for models such as the GARCH(1,1)-RV model which do not have systematic forecast bias, the FB simply represents the sum of the differences between forecasts and realized IVs for a given forecasting horizon.
8. Although it is not reported in this chapter, British Petroleum and Barclays also show that $n = 20$ is an appropriate value.

Chapter 8

GARCH predictions and the predictions of option prices*

JOHN KNIGHT[†] AND STEPHEN E. SATCHELL[‡]

In a rout of the civilized world unequalled since the onslaught of the Golden Horde, GARCH has overwhelmed the financial profession, sweeping aside all existing models of asset return volatility. One of the reasons for its success is the property of GARCH models that volatility can be forecast; indeed, it assumes that it is known one-period-ahead. This should have important implications for forecasting asset prices and instruments contingent upon asset prices, such as options and futures.

Baillie and Bollerslev (1992), henceforth B and B, have written a rather general paper, examining the predictions implied by GARCH models. Their paper provides more generality than is required for many practical problems, especially when one is modelling option prices. Several papers have emerged that price options on GARCH processes, see Duan (1993), Engle and Mustafa (1992), and Satchell and Timmermann (1993).

Financial practitioners, inasmuch as they announce what they do, seem to use GARCH to predict volatility but use the traditional Black and Scholes (BS) coupled with GARCH to price the option. This hybrid procedure, whilst lacking theoretical rigor, can be partially justified by the arguments of Amin and Jarrow (1991) and by the empirical results of the previously mentioned papers and others which demonstrate a remarkable robustness for BS values of options, even when they may not be theoretically appropriate.

The purpose of this chapter is to discuss in detail the properties of predictions based on a GARCH(1,1) model since this is a popular choice for applied economists. We find exact results for the forecast error two-steps-ahead for a variable whose volatility process is GARCH(1,1). Contrary to expectation,

* Financial support from the Newton Trust, ESRC, and INQUIRE(UK) is gratefully acknowledged by the authors. The research assistance of Y. Yoon is acknowledged.
† Department of Economics, University of Western Ontario.
‡ Trinity College, University of Cambridge.

there seems to be little gain in using GARCH models for prediction for feasible parameter values found in daily data for UK stocks. We also discuss the properties of predictions of BS options with GARCH volatility. In section 8.1, we present the prediction results for the GARCH model. Numerical results of forecasting errors are presented in section 8.2. In section 8.3, we discuss the properties of BS predictions and present forecasting results.

8.1 PREDICTION OF GARCH MODELS

Let the model generating y_t be given by

$$y_t = \mu + \sigma_t e_t \tag{8.1}$$

where e_t is iid$(0, 1)$ and $\sigma_t^2 = \omega + \alpha\sigma_{t-1}^2 e_{t-1}^2 + \beta\sigma_{t-1}^2$. The variable y_t is typically an asset return with constant mean and variance modelled by a GARCH(1,1) process. We proceed with the prediction of $y_{t+s}|I_t$ where I_t is the information set at time t. Then

$$E(y_{t+s}|I_t) = \mu$$

so the prediction error is

$$y_{t+s} - E(y_{t+s}|I_t) = (\sigma_{t+s}|I_t)e_{t+s}$$

Now

$$(\sigma_{t+s}^2|I_t) = \omega + (\sigma_{t+s-1}^2|I_t)(\alpha e_{t+s-1}^2 + \beta) \tag{8.2}$$

Let $X_s = \sigma_{t+s}^2|I_t$, $a_s = \alpha e_{t+s}^2 + \beta$ then (8.2) becomes

$$X_s = \omega + X_{s-1}a_{s-1}$$

which can be solved recursively to yield

$$X_s = \omega\left(\gamma + \sum_{j=1}^{s-2}\left(\prod_{k=1}^{j}a_{s-k}\right)\right) + \left(\prod_{k=1}^{s-1}a_{s-k}\right)X_1 \quad \text{for } s > 2 \tag{8.3}$$

$$X_2 = \omega + X_1 a_1 (s = 2)$$

This seems different from B and B (Baillie and Bollersler (1992), p. 98, after equation (28)). We define $\phi_s(\theta) = E(\exp(iX_s\theta))$ and E is conditional on I_t. It follows upon differentiating j times that

$$\phi_s^j(\theta) = E\left((iX_s)^j \exp(iX_s\theta)\right)$$

$$\therefore (-i)^j\phi_s^j = E((X_s^j \exp(iX_s\theta)) \tag{8.4}$$

Now returning to (8.2)

$$E(\exp(iX_s\theta)) = E(\exp(iw\theta + i\theta X_{s-1}a_{s-1}))$$

$$\phi_s(\theta) = \exp(iw\theta)E(\exp(i\theta X_{s-1}a_{s-1}))$$

Using iterated expectation, and the extra assumption of normality[1]

$$\phi_s(\theta) = \exp(iw\theta) \times E\left(\exp(i\theta X_{s-1}\beta)(1 - 2i\theta\alpha X_{s-1})^{-1/2}\right)$$

$$= \exp(iw\theta)E\left[(\exp(i\theta\beta X_{s-1}) \cdot \sum_{j=0}^{\infty} \frac{(2i\theta\alpha X_{s-1})^j \left(\frac{1}{2}\right) j}{j!}\right]$$

Assuming uniform convergence and noting that $(a)_j = a(a+1)\ldots(a+j-1)$, we see that

$$\phi_s(\theta) = \exp(iw\theta)\left[\sum_{j=0}^{\infty} \frac{(2\theta\alpha)^j i^j \left(\frac{1}{2}\right)_j}{j!} E\left[\exp(i\theta\beta X_s - 1)X_{s-1}^j\right]\right], \quad (8.5)$$

$$\therefore \phi_s(\theta) = \exp(iw\theta)\left[\sum_{j=0}^{\infty} \left(\frac{1}{2}\right)_j \frac{(2\theta\alpha)^j}{j!} \phi_{s-1}^j(\theta\beta)\right]$$

We present our results in Proposition 1.

Proposition 1

For the model given by equation (8.1) where e_t is assumed iid $N(0, 1)$, the characteristic function of the s-step-ahead forecast error of $\sigma_{t+s}^2 \phi_s(\theta)$ satisfies a (non-linear) recursion given by equation (8.5) for $s \geq 2$.

Corollary

If $s = 2$, then

$$\phi_2(\theta) = \exp(iw\theta)\sum_{j=0}^{\infty} \frac{(2\theta\alpha)^j}{j!}(1/2)_j i^j(\sigma_{t+1}^{2j}\exp(i\theta B\sigma_{t+1}^2)$$

Proof   We use equation (8.5) to derive $\phi_2(\theta)$, a direct proof is very easy. From (8.5)

$$\phi_2(\theta) = \exp(iw\theta)\sum_{j=0}^{\infty} \frac{(2\theta\alpha)^j}{j!}\left(\frac{1}{2}\right)_j i^j(\sigma_{t+1}^{2j})\exp(i\theta B\sigma t + 1^2)$$

$$= \exp\left(i\theta(w + B\sigma_{t+1}^2)\right)\sum_{j=0}^{\infty} \frac{(2\theta\alpha i\sigma_{t+1}^2)^j \left(\frac{1}{2}\right)_j}{j!} \qquad (8.6)$$

$$\therefore \phi_2(\theta) = \exp\left(i\theta(w + B\sigma_{t+1}^2)\right)(1 - 2i\theta\alpha\sigma_{t+1}^2)^{-1/2}$$

Note that

$$\phi_1(\theta) = E_t \left(\exp(i\theta \sigma_{t+1}^2 / I_t) \right)$$
$$= \exp(i\theta \sigma_{t+1}^2)$$

and $\phi_1^j(\theta) = i^j \sigma_{t+1}^{2j} \exp(i\theta \sigma_{t+1}^2)$.

$\phi_3(\theta)$ will depend upon the jth derivatives of $\phi_2(\theta)$. Now $\phi_2(\theta)$ can be inverted quite easily. Before we do this, we shall derive results for z_s, the prediction error, conditional on I_t. Now

$$z_s = (y_{t+s} - E(y_{t+s}|I_t))$$
$$= (\sigma_{t+s}|I_t)e_{t+s} = \sqrt{X_s}e_{t+s}$$

and $\Phi_s(\theta)$ is defined by

$$\Phi_s(\theta) = E_t \left(\exp(i\sqrt{X_s}e_{t+s}\theta) \right)$$
$$= E_t \left(\exp\left(-\frac{1}{2}X_s\theta^2 \right) \right) \tag{8.7}$$
$$\therefore \; \Phi_s(\theta) = \phi_s \left(\frac{i\theta^2}{2} \right)$$

so that $\Phi_s(\theta)$ could, in principle, be calculated via Proposition 1. We recollect the results about $\Phi_s(\theta)$ in Proposition 2.

Proposition 2
For the model described in Proposition 1, the characteristic function of forecast error $\Phi_s(\theta)$ satisfies a recursion

$$\Phi_2(\theta) = \exp\left(-\frac{\omega\theta^2}{2} \right) \left[\sum_{j=0}^{\infty} \left(\frac{1}{2} \right)_j \frac{(i\theta^2\alpha)^j}{j!} \phi_{s-1}^j \left(\frac{i\theta^2\beta}{2} \right) \right]$$

Hence, for $s = 2$, we see, using (8.6) and (8.7) that

$$\Phi_2(\theta) = \exp\left(\frac{-\theta^2}{2}(\omega + \beta\sigma_{t+1}^2) \right)(1 + \alpha\theta^2\sigma_{t+1}^2)^{-1/2} \tag{8.8}$$

For this case it is possible to invert (8.7), term by term, to get a series expansion for the pdf of z_2. Let $H_j(x)$ be the Hermite polynomial of degree j.

Proposition 3

The pdf of z_2 can be represented in a formal series expansion as

$$\text{pdf}(z_2) = \left(\sum_{j=0}^{\infty} \frac{\left(\frac{1}{2}\right)_j (\alpha \sigma_{t+1}^2)^j}{j!} \frac{1}{(\omega + \beta \sigma_{t+1}^2)^j} H_{2j} \left(\frac{z_2}{\sqrt{\omega + \beta \sigma_{t+1}}} \right) \right)$$

$$\times \exp \frac{\left(-\dfrac{z_2^2}{2(\omega + \beta \sigma_{t+1}^2)} \right)}{\sqrt{2\pi(\omega + \beta \sigma_{t+1}^2)}}$$

where z_2 is the two-step-ahead prediction error for a GARCH(1,1) model with constant mean. Of course, the expansion in Proposition 3 is purely formal, there is no guarantee that such a series converges, an issue we do not address. For the purpose of calculation, the characteristic function given by (8.8) will be more tractable. We note that inspection of (8.8) gives us a further characterization of the pdf of z_2:

$$\Phi(z_2) = \exp\left(-\frac{\theta^2}{2}(\omega + \beta \sigma_{t+1}^2) \right) (1 + i\sqrt{\alpha\theta\sigma_{t+1}})^{-1/2} (1 - i\sqrt{\alpha\theta\sigma_{t+1}})^{-1/2}$$

(8.9)

so that we can interpret z_2 as being generated by three independent random variables X_1, X_2, X_3 where $X_1 \sim N(0, \omega + \beta\sigma_{t+1}^2)$, X_2 is $\sqrt{\alpha\sigma_{t+1}}/2$ times a chi-squared one and X_3 has the same distribution as X_2, then $z_2 \overset{d}{=} X_1 + X_2 - X_3$ where $\overset{d}{=}$ means equal in distribution.

8.2   NUMERICAL RESULTS

We now consider the numerical calculation of the pdf of z_2. The importance of this investigation will become clear later when we need to construct confidence intervals. For one period prediction, the forecasting error z_1 can be shown to follow a normal distribution with mean zero and variance σ_{t+1}^2. Therefore, our interest focuses on the forecasting errors of longer than one period. For two-period prediction, Proposition 3 tells us the pdf of z_2 and, in principle, we can derive the distribution function from it. However, since issues of convergence arise, we use the characteristic function of z_2 in equation (8.8). By using the inversion theorem in Kendall and Stuart (1977) and the symmetry of the distribution, the distribution function of z_2 is derived as

$$F(x) = \frac{1}{2} + \int_{-\infty}^{\infty} \frac{1 - e^{-ix\theta}}{2\pi i\theta} \phi(\theta)\, d\theta$$

$$= \frac{1}{2} + \int_{-\infty}^{\infty} \frac{1 - \cos(x\theta)}{2\pi i\theta} \phi(\theta)\, d\theta + \int_{-\infty}^{\infty} \frac{i\sin(x\theta)}{2\pi i\theta} \phi(\theta)\, d\theta \qquad (8.10)$$

$$= \frac{1}{2} + \frac{1}{\pi} \int_{0}^{\infty} \frac{\sin(x\theta)}{\theta} \phi(\theta)\, d\theta$$

We remark that it is obvious that the two-period forecasting error is not normally distributed. This is easy to prove from the definition of z_2:

$$z_2 = (\sigma_{t+2}|I_t)\varepsilon_{t+2} = \sqrt{\omega + \alpha\sigma_{t+1}^2 + \beta\sigma_{t+1}^2} \cdot \varepsilon_{t+2} \tag{8.11}$$

In order to compare equation (8.10) with the standard normal distribution, we standardize (8.8) by the standard deviation of $\sigma_{t+2}\varepsilon_{t+2}$, $\sqrt{\omega + (\alpha + \beta)\sigma_{t+1}^2}$, and the standardized characteristic function is

$$\Phi_2\left(\frac{\theta}{\sqrt{\omega + (\alpha + \beta)\sigma_{t+1}^2}}\right) = \exp\left(\frac{\theta^2(\omega + \beta\sigma_{t+1}^2)}{2(\omega + (\alpha + \beta)\sigma_{t+1}^2)}\right)$$

$$\times \left(1 + \frac{\theta^2\alpha\sigma_{t_1}^2}{\omega + (\alpha + \beta)\sigma_{t+1}^2}\right)^{-1/2}$$

We present the result for the distribution function in Table 8.1 for particular sets of three parameters (ω, α, β). A historical value,[2] 0.2E-4 is used for ω. Also, different values of σ_{t+1}^2 are selected in proportion to the steady state variance, $\omega/(1 - \alpha - \beta)$. Table 8.1 clearly shows that as α increases relative to β, the distribution of the two-period forecasting error becomes fat tailed. This can be explained by the kurtosis of z_2

$$\kappa_4 = \frac{6\alpha^2\sigma_{t+1}^4}{(\omega + (\alpha + \beta)\sigma_{t+1}^2)^2} \tag{8.12}$$

Inspection of equation (8.12) reveals that the conditional kurtosis of equation (8.7) depends upon α, that is, higher α implies higher conditional kurtosis. Moreover, this kurtosis is affected by the estimate of σ_{t+1}^2: a higher value relative to the steady state variance implies fatter tails.

For longer period prediction, in principle, it is possible to apply Proposition 1. However, it is difficult to use a characteristic function, for example $\phi_3(\theta)$ depends upon the jth derivatives of $\phi_2(\theta)$. Simulation is easier for $s \geq 3$ and we can simulate forecasting errors by using three independent random variables, that is, for z_3

$$z_3 = \sigma_{t+3}\varepsilon_{t+3} = \sqrt{\omega + \alpha\sigma_{t+2}^2\varepsilon_{t+2}^2 + \beta\sigma_{t+2}^2} \cdot \varepsilon_{t+3}$$

$$= \sqrt{\omega + (\alpha\varepsilon_{t+2}^2 + \beta)(\omega + \alpha\sigma_{t+1}^2\varepsilon_{t+1}^2 + \beta\sigma_{t+1}^2)} \cdot \varepsilon_{t+3} \tag{8.13}$$

We now describe our simulation experiment. We generate 10 000 observations of equation (8.13) with different values of three parameters (ω, α, β). We have chosen the sum of α and β equal to 0.9 since this is the amount we usually find in the empirical data. The configurations (0.1, 0.8), (0.45, 0.45) and (0.8, 0.1)

Table 8.1   *Probability function of two-period forecasting errors*

					Pr[$|x| \leq$ value]					
		GARCH with $\sigma^2_{t+1} = 0.5\omega/(1-\alpha-\beta)$			GARCH with $\sigma^2_{t+1} = \omega/(1-\alpha-\beta)$			GARCH with $\sigma^2_{t+1} = 2\omega/(1-\alpha-\beta)$		
Value	$N(0,1)$	$\alpha=0.1$ $\beta=0.8$	$\alpha=0.45$ $\beta=0.45$	$\alpha=0.8$ $\beta=0.1$	$\alpha=0.1$ $\beta=0.8$	$\alpha=0.45$ $\beta=0.45$	$\alpha=0.8$ $\beta=0.1$	$\alpha=0.1$ $\beta=0.8$	$\alpha=0.45$ $\beta=0.45$	$\alpha=0.8$ $\beta=0.1$
2.576	0.010	0.008	0.014	0.024	0.011	0.017	0.027	0.008	0.017	0.027
2.326	0.020	0.019	0.026	0.036	0.021	0.027	0.037	0.019	0.028	0.039
2.170	0.030	0.028	0.033	0.044	0.031	0.036	0.045	0.028	0.035	0.049
2.054	0.040	0.037	0.043	0.053	0.040	0.044	0.052	0.038	0.044	0.057
1.690	0.050	0.048	0.051	0.060	0.050	0.052	0.059	0.047	0.052	0.064
1.881	0.060	0.058	0.061	0.067	0.060	0.061	0.066	0.059	0.063	0.070
1.812	0.070	0.068	0.069	0.073	0.070	0.069	0.072	0.068	0.069	0.075
1.751	0.080	0.080	0.076	0.079	0.080	0.077	0.078	0.079	0.076	0.081
1.695	0.090	0.091	0.086	0.084	0.090	0.085	0.085	0.091	0.085	0.088
1.645	0.100	0.098	0.096	0.093	0.100	0.093	0.091	0.098	0.095	0.094
1.598	0.110	0.109	0.105	0.100	0.110	0.102	0.097	0.109	0.102	0.100
1.555	0.120	0.119	0.113	0.106	0.119	0.110	0.103	0.118	0.111	0.116
1.514	0.130	0.128	0.121	0.112	0.129	0.118	0.109	0.127	0.118	0.111
1.476	0.140	0.139	0.130	0.116	0.139	0.127	0.115	0.138	0.127	0.117
1.444	0.150	0.151	0.138	0.125	0.149	0.135	0.121	0.151	0.137	0.124
Kurtosis	0.0	0.050	1.004	3.174	0.060	1.215	3.840	0.066	1.346	4.255

are actually used to examine the effect of the magnitude of α. The value of ω is set to its historical value, 0.2E-4. We also change the value of σ_{t+1}^2 from half of the steady state variance, $\omega/(1 - \alpha - \beta)$, to double it. It is interesting to investigate how this influences the distribution because practitioners tend to use this value relative to the implied volatility of the BS option to impute future patterns of risk. A check on the accuracies of our simulation experiment is provided by a comparison of the results from (8.11) with the theoretical version (8.10). The results of three-period forecasting error are reported in Table 8.2. As before, kurtosis is increasing with the magnitude of α and of σ_{t+1}^2. This implies that constructing confidence intervals for forecasting errors based on the normal table underestimates the length of the confidence interval. In particular, a process whose volatility is substantially determined by random effects[3] such as exchange rates will amplify this bias. Similar results can be found for four-period forecasting error in Table 8.3. These results confirm the findings of B and B, the dependence in the higher order moments for the GARCH model substantially complicates conventional multi-step prediction exercises. However, we should note that empirically common values found in UK data tend to be approximately $\alpha = 0.1$ and $\beta = 0.8$. For these values the tail probabilities for all choices of initial variances (see the columns read by $\alpha = 0.1$ and $\beta = 0.8$ in Tables 8.2 and 8.3) are very close to the normal. This does suggest that empirically, if you wish to use GARCH(1,1) for prediction just adjust your variance and assume normality.

We have considered the case of the normal distribution, but this is not necessary to characterize a GARCH model. A similar experiment can be applied to a t-distribution. Two t-distributions with degree of freedoms 10 and 5 are chosen and the results are presented in Tables 8.4 and 8.5. In both cases, kurtosis is very clear and the same conclusion can be drawn as the normal case. For small degrees of freedom (5), kurtosis is more apparent. Indeed, examination of Table 8.5 reveals that the tail probabilities of the standardized predictions are longer than that of the t-distribution with 5 degrees of freedom, thus for this case the GARCH predictions have the effects of amplifying the probability of outliers.

8.3   APPLICATION TO OPTION PRICING MODELS

In this section we shall use our theoretical model in order to predict option prices. It is interesting to investigate the effect of the GARCH process on option pricing models since option prices are substantially influenced by the volatility of underlying asset prices as well as the price itself. Furthermore, the small differences between GARCH and normal predictions seen in the previous section will be multiplied up by the censored aspect of option leading possibly to larger errors; it is this issue we wish to investigate. Assuming the stock price follows a diffusion process with constant variance, Black and Scholes (1973)

Table 8.2 Simulated probability function of three-period forecasting errors

		GARCH with $\sigma^2_{t+1} = 0.5\omega/(1-\alpha-\beta)$			GARCH with $\sigma^2_{t+1} = \omega/(1-\alpha-\beta)$			GARCH with $\sigma^2_{t+1} = 2\omega/(1-\alpha-\beta)$		
	$N(0,1)$	$\alpha=0.1$ $\beta=0.8$	$\alpha=0.45$ $\beta=0.45$	$\alpha=0.8$ $\beta=0.1$	$\alpha=0.1$ $\beta=0.8$	$\alpha=0.45$ $\beta=0.45$	$\alpha=0.8$ $\beta=0.1$	$\alpha=0.1$ $\beta=0.8$	$\alpha=0.45$ $\beta=0.45$	$\alpha=0.8$ $\beta=0.1$
Value										
2.576	0.010	0.010	0.019	0.028	0.010	0.022	0.030	0.010	0.022	0.031
2.326	0.020	0.018	0.030	0.035	0.018	0.031	0.037	0.018	0.032	0.038
2.170	0.030	0.020	0.039	0.042	0.029	0.041	0.042	0.029	0.041	0.043
2.054	0.040	0.040	0.047	0.047	0.039	0.048	0.047	0.039	0.049	0.048
1.690	0.050	0.048	0.053	0.051	0.048	0.054	0.054	0.048	0.056	0.053
1.881	0.060	0.057	0.063	0.057	0.057	0.062	0.058	0.058	0.063	0.059
1.812	0.070	0.068	0.070	0.063	0.067	0.070	0.063	0.067	0.068	0.062
1.751	0.080	0.077	0.075	0.068	0.077	0.077	0.067	0.075	0.077	0.067
1.695	0.090	0.086	0.083	0.072	0.086	0.083	0.074	0.087	0.084	0.072
1.645	0.100	0.098	0.094	0.078	0.098	0.091	0.077	0.098	0.090	0.078
1.598	0.110	0.108	0.104	0.083	0.107	0.100	0.082	0.107	0.098	0.083
1.555	0.120	0.119	0.110	0.089	0.119	0.109	0.088	0.118	0.107	0.087
1.514	0.130	0.129	0.118	0.094	0.128	0.114	0.092	0.129	0.114	0.091
1.476	0.140	0.139	0.126	0.101	0.139	0.123	0.097	0.140	0.122	0.096
1.444	0.150	0.148	0.133	0.107	0.147	0.131	0.101	0.149	0.128	0.100
Kurtosis	0.0	0.086	1.733	5.478	0.109	2.199	3.840	0.125	2.540	8.029

Table 8.3 *Simulated probability function of four-period forecasting errors*

		Pr[$|x| \leq$ value]								
Value	$N(0,1)$	GARCH with $\sigma_{t+1}^2 = 0.5\omega/(1-\alpha-\beta)$			GARCH with $\sigma_{t+1}^2 = \omega/(1-\alpha-\beta)$			GARCH with $\sigma_{t+1}^2 = 2\omega/(1-\alpha-\beta)$		
		$\alpha=0.1$ $\beta=0.8$	$\alpha=0.45$ $\beta=0.45$	$\alpha=0.8$ $\beta=0.1$	$\alpha=0.1$ $\beta=0.8$	$\alpha=0.45$ $\beta=0.45$	$\alpha=0.8$ $\beta=0.1$	$\alpha=0.1$ $\beta=0.8$	$\alpha=0.45$ $\beta=0.45$	$\alpha=0.8$ $\beta=0.1$
2.576	0.010	0.008	0.019	0.022	0.009	0.022	0.024	0.009	0.023	0.025
2.326	0.020	0.018	0.029	0.029	0.019	0.031	0.029	0.019	0.032	0.030
2.170	0.030	0.028	0.038	0.035	0.028	0.039	0.035	0.029	0.040	0.034
2.054	0.040	0.038	0.047	0.041	0.038	0.047	0.038	0.039	0.048	0.038
1.690	0.050	0.047	0.053	0.047	0.048	0.053	0.045	0.049	0.053	0.044
1.881	0.060	0.056	0.061	0.051	0.055	0.059	0.049	0.055	0.060	0.048
1.812	0.070	0.067	0.066	0.057	0.066	0.067	0.054	0.067	0.066	0.052
1.751	0.080	0.075	0.073	0.062	0.076	0.072	0.058	0.076	0.072	0.056
1.695	0.090	0.086	0.079	0.066	0.087	0.078	0.062	0.086	0.078	0.059
1.645	0.100	0.099	0.085	0.071	0.097	0.085	0.067	0.096	0.084	0.064
1.598	0.110	0.107	0.095	0.074	0.106	0.091	0.071	0.106	0.090	0.068
1.555	0.120	0.116	0.102	0.079	0.116	0.096	0.075	0.115	0.095	0.071
1.514	0.130	0.124	0.109	0.084	0.123	0.104	0.078	0.123	0.101	0.074
1.476	0.140	0.133	0.117	0.088	0.131	0.113	0.083	0.131	0.108	0.078
1.444	0.150	0.142	0.127	0.092	0.140	0.121	0.088	0.141	0.117	0.082
Kurtosis	0.0	0.115	3.159	18.544	0.151	4.391	27.705	0.181	5.453	35.735

Table 8.4   *Simulated probability function of forecasting errors from t-distribution with degree of freedom 10*

		Pr[|x| ≤ value]										
		Two period $\sigma_{t+2}\varepsilon_{t+2}$			Three period $\sigma_{t+3}\varepsilon_{t+3}$				Four period $\sigma_{t+4}\varepsilon_{t+4}$			
	t-dist(10)	$\alpha = 0.1$ $\beta = 0.8$	$\alpha = 0.45$ $\beta = 0.45$	$\alpha = 0.8$ $\beta = 0.1$	$\alpha = 0.1$ $\beta = 0.8$	$\alpha = 0.45$ $\beta = 0.45$	$\alpha = 0.8$ $\beta = 0.1$	$\alpha = 0.1$ $\beta = 0.8$	$\alpha = 0.45$ $\beta = 0.45$	$\alpha = 0.8$ $\beta = 0.1$
Value											
3.169	0.010	0.007	0.020	0.032	0.013	0.020	0.031	0.012	0.026	0.030
2.764	0.020	0.017	0.033	0.045	0.023	0.033	0.041	0.021	0.038	0.039
2.527	0.030	0.028	0.041	0.055	0.034	0.044	0.052	0.031	0.048	0.046
2.054	0.040	0.039	0.051	0.065	0.046	0.054	0.060	0.040	0.058	0.050
1.690	0.050	0.048	0.060	0.072	0.056	0.063	0.067	0.049	0.069	0.056
1.881	0.060	0.057	0.069	0.081	0.068	0.070	0.075	0.060	0.078	0.061
1.812	0.070	0.066	0.077	0.087	0.081	0.080	0.082	0.072	0.088	0.065
1.751	0.080	0.078	0.087	0.092	0.091	0.086	0.086	0.084	0.097	0.071
1.695	0.090	0.087	0.097	0.101	0.100	0.095	0.091	0.092	0.104	0.076
1.645	0.100	0.096	0.105	0.107	0.111	0.103	0.097	0.103	0.111	0.082
1.598	0.110	0.107	0.114	0.114	0.123	0.110	0.102	0.110	0.119	0.086
1.555	0.120	0.116	0.125	0.120	0.133	0.118	0.106	0.120	0.127	0.090
1.514	0.130	0.129	0.131	0.126	0.145	0.128	0.111	0.132	0.135	0.095
1.476	0.140	0.138	0.140	0.133	0.153	0.136	0.117	0.143	0.141	0.100
1.444	0.150	0.150	0.148	0.139	0.163	0.144	0.122	0.153	0.149	0.104
Kurtosis	1.069	0.866	3.951	6.611	1.129	12.896	17.058	1.819	25.937	49.319

Table 8.5 *Simulated probability function of forecasting errors from t-distribution with degree of freedom 5*

| | | | Pr[\|x\| ≤ value] | | | | | | | |
| | | Two period $\sigma_{t+2}\varepsilon_{t+2}$ | | | Three period $\sigma_{t+3}\varepsilon_{t+3}$ | | | Four period $\sigma_{t+4}\varepsilon_{t+4}$ | | |
Value	t-dist(5)	$\alpha=0.1$ $\beta=0.8$	$\alpha=0.45$ $\beta=0.45$	$\alpha=0.8$ $\beta=0.1$	$\alpha=0.1$ $\beta=0.8$	$\alpha=0.45$ $\beta=0.45$	$\alpha=0.8$ $\beta=0.1$	$\alpha=0.1$ $\beta=0.8$	$\alpha=0.45$ $\beta=0.45$	$\alpha=0.8$ $\beta=0.1$
4.032	0.010	0.011	0.022	0.026	0.016	0.029	0.035	0.016	0.035	0.044
3.365	0.020	0.022	0.034	0.037	0.025	0.047	0.052	0.028	0.049	0.057
3.003	0.030	0.034	0.043	0.049	0.035	0.060	0.063	0.039	0.063	0.067
2.756	0.040	0.043	0.054	0.061	0.047	0.068	0.072	0.048	0.077	0.076
2.571	0.050	0.052	0.065	0.070	0.058	0.079	0.083	0.061	0.087	0.082
2.422	0.060	0.065	0.075	0.080	0.071	0.088	0.091	0.073	0.095	0.089
2.297	0.070	0.075	0.084	0.086	0.082	0.098	0.098	0.084	0.104	0.097
2.191	0.080	0.085	0.095	0.094	0.093	0.108	0.106	0.095	0.116	0.104
2.098	0.090	0.096	0.106	0.100	0.104	0.118	0.114	0.103	0.125	0.113
2.015	0.100	0.106	0.117	0.109	0.118	0.124	0.121	0.115	0.134	0.117
1.940	0.110	0.115	0.124	0.117	0.129	0.134	0.129	0.126	0.144	0.121
1.873	0.120	0.125	0.136	0.126	0.138	0.140	0.135	0.133	0.152	0.127
1.810	0.130	0.135	0.145	0.132	0.148	0.149	0.141	0.144	0.162	0.133
1.753	0.140	0.147	0.153	0.138	0.160	0.158	0.148	0.157	0.170	0.140
1.699	0.150	0.158	0.160	0.145	0.171	0.169	0.153	0.169	0.179	0.146
Kurtosis	1.069	3.428	37.325	24.963	3.851	608.772	122.867	4.814	308.112	231.202

developed a closed form of the option pricing model and it has been commonly used by academics and practitioners. However, it has been widely recognized that asset returns exhibit both fat-tailed marginal distributions and volatility clustering. These factors are now interpreted as evidence that the volatility of financial asset prices is stochastic and that the volatility process has innovations with a slow rate of decay as defined by GARCH-type processes.

The pricing of contingent claims on assets with stochastic volatility has been studied by many researchers such as, for example, Hull and White (1987), Johnson and Shanno (1987), Scott (1987), Wiggins (1987), and Melino and Turnbull (1990). In general, there is not a closed-form solution for option prices and, even more seriously, there is not a preference-free valuation function. Duan (1993), Amin and Ng (1993), and Satchell and Timmermann (1994) derived solutions under special assumptions about the agents' utility function. Instead, we shall focus on forecasting future option prices and construct their confidence interval when the underlying asset price follows a GARCH(1,1) process and the option price is treated as a known non-linear transformation of the data.

Our data are option prices on the FTSE100 share index from 1 May to 30 May 1992. Our choice of this period is due to relatively stable movements of the index. The closing bid and ask prices of all options on this index over the period were supplied by the LIFFE. One hundred and sixteen contracts were quoted which were half calls and half puts. In each case, there are 15 contracts for May closing, 13 for June, six for July, eight for September, eight for December 1992, and eight for March 1993. Strike prices from 2125 to 2825 were taken although not all of the contracts were actively traded over the sample period. Our data represent a variety of options out-of-, at-, and in-the-money with maturities varying from less than 1 month to 11 months. Those contracts which were not traded have quoted prices calculated by the Exchange, a so-called automatic quotation system.[4] The contracts are written as European options and cannot be exercised until maturity.

To obtain estimates of the GARCH(1,1) process of the underlying asset price in equation (8.1), we collected daily observations on the FTSE100 share index from 1 January 1988 up to the day when we forecast future option prices, i.e. 30 April 1992 for one-day-ahead predictions and 29 April 1992 for two-day-ahead predictions to forecast the option price on 1 May 1992. This period excludes the October 1987 stock market crash which substantially increases the volatility estimates of the daily stock prices when included in the sample. We also tried different sample sizes and found that, as the length of the sample period was shortened, the significance of the parameter representing persistency was noticeably reduced. Although a short period can reflect temporary phenomena, the GARCH model is much less evident. The estimates of the GARCH(1,1) model over our sample period are presented in Table 8.6. During

Table 8.6 *Estimates of the GARCH(1,1) process**

	μ	ω	α	β
1 May	.00039	.00007	.0723	.7794
	(1.52)	(15.01)	(2.68)	(8.48)
5 May	.00036	.00007	.0760	.7509
	(1.44)	(15.74)	(2.72)	(7.26)
6 May	.00037	.00007	.0772	.7475
	(1.44)	(15.71)	(2.76)	(7.40)
7 May	.00038	.00007	.0754	.7590
	(1.50)	(15.52)	(2.77)	(7.67)
8 May	.00039	.00007	.0758	.7568
	(1.53)	(15.51)	(2.75)	(7.76)
11 May	.0004	.00007	.0759	.7572
	(1.59)	(15.49)	(2.79)	(7.82)
12 May	.00042	.00007	.0751	.7557
	(1.64)	(15.60)	(2.74)	(7.70)
13 May	.00041	.00007	.0770	.7528
	(1.62)	(15.48)	(2.80)	(7.78)
14 May	.00041	.00007	.0793	.7478
	(1.61)	(15.36)	(2.83)	(7.89)
15 May	.00037	.00007	.0782	.7478
	(1.47)	(15.64)	(2.90)	(7.89)
18 May	.00036	.00007	.0789	.7469
	(1.44)	(15.57)	(2.89)	(7.87)
19 May	.00038	.00007	.0787	.7469
	(1.52)	(15.60)	(2.86)	(7.86)
20 May	.00039	.00007	.0787	.7476
	(1.55)	(15.61)	(2.92)	(8.03)
21 May	.0004	.00007	.0792	.7475
	(1.57)	(15.53)	(2.90)	(8.00)
22 May	.00038	.00007	.0801	.7450
	(1.51)	(15.58)	(2.97)	(8.07)
26 May	.00039	.00007	.0801	.7469
	(1.54)	(15.49)	(2.94)	(8.13)
27 May	.00038	.00007	.0802	.7496
	(1.52)	(15.38)	(2.95)	(8.32)
28 May	.00038	.00007	.0806	.7522
	(1.50)	(15.24)	(2.97)	(8.53)
29 May	.00037	.00007	.0812	.7516
	(1.46)	(15.21)	(3.02)	(8.60)

*These coefficients of the GARCH model are re-estimated with an updated sample for each extra date from 4 January 1988. Numbers in parentheses are *t*-statistics.

May 1992, the coefficients of volatility are significant and the volatility is determined mainly by the previous volatility given our sample size. We also observe the stability of those estimates over the sample period. These parameter values will be used when we proceed to compute option prices later in this section.[5]

In principle, we cannot use the BS option pricing model since the underlying asset price no longer follows the diffusion process. However, previous experience, see Satchell and Timmermann (1994), suggests that a volatility adjusted BS option should be a good predictor of the actual price. Indeed, it is what is widely used by practitioners. Our strategy is simply to replace the underlying stock price and its volatility modelled by a GARCH(1,1) process. Then intervals with 95% confidence can be constructed for future option prices. To measure the efficiency of the model's predictability, a similar prediction is carried out using the Black and Scholes formula with the original assumption that the underlying stock price follows a diffusion process. This corresponds for discrete observations on the continuous process to the case where the unconditional volatility is equal to the historical variance. It implies that $\omega = \sigma^2$, $\alpha = \beta = 0$ in our model. Our result will be exact in the following sense. Since our confidence interval is exact and we apply a monotonic transformation, the resulting Black and Scholes function will have an exact confidence interval.

From equation (8.1), we can express future spot prices at time t. For example, one- and two-day-ahead prices are

$$S(t+1) = S(t)\exp[\mu + \sigma_{t+1}\varepsilon_{t+1}]$$

$$S(t+2) = S(t)\exp\left[2\mu + \sigma_{t+1}\varepsilon_{t+1} + \sqrt{\omega + \alpha\sigma_{t+1}^2\varepsilon_{t+1}^2 + \beta\sigma_{t+1}^2}\cdot\varepsilon_{t+2}\right]$$

$$(8.14)$$

Similarly, expected future prices based on the diffusion process are

$$S(t+1) = S(t)\exp[\mu + \sigma\varepsilon_{t+1}]$$

$$S(t+2) = S(t)\exp[2\mu + \sigma(\varepsilon_{t+1} + \varepsilon_{t+2})]$$

$$(8.15)$$

First, using the estimates from our data set, we compare the prediction of the two models for the index itself. In the case of $S(t+2)$ in equation (8.14), Monte Carlo simulations are used to draw 10 000 sequences of normally distributed innovations in ε_t. We find that actual index levels are within 95% confidence intervals in both cases for one- and two-day-ahead predictions. However, the diffusion process has narrower intervals than the GARCH(1,1) model. In other words, the diffusion process can describe the index more precisely given our sample period, not surprisingly since the unconditional volatility of GARCH will be larger.

The same practice is carried out for future option prices. In the case of a one-day forecast, the confidence interval for option prices becomes

$$\text{Prob}[-1.96 < \varepsilon_{t+1} < 1.96] = 0.95$$

$$\text{Prob}[S(t)\exp(\mu - 1.96\sigma_{t+1}) < S(t+1)$$

$$< S(t)\exp(\mu + 1.96\sigma t + 1)] = 0.95$$

$$\text{Prob}[BS(-1.96) < BS(S(t+1)) < BS(1.96)] = 0.95 \tag{8.16}$$

since the Black and Scholes formula is monotonically increasing with the underlying stock price. Note that σ_{t+1}^2 is estimated by the steady state volatility in the GARCH(1,1) model, and $BS(S)$ means the value of BS evaluated at S. However, the confidence interval for two-day-ahead prediction has to be simulated from the predicted option price:

$$BS(\varepsilon_{t+1}, \varepsilon_{t+2}) = S(t)\exp\left[2\mu + \sigma_{t+1}\varepsilon_{t+1} + \sqrt{\omega + \alpha\sigma_{t+1}^2\varepsilon_{t+1}^2 + \beta\sigma_{t+1}^2}\,\varepsilon_{t+2}\right]$$

$$\times N(d_1) - e^{rT}XN(d_2) \tag{8.17}$$

where

$$d_1 = \frac{\left(\ln(S(t)/X) + \left(2\mu + \sigma t + 1\varepsilon_{t+1} + \sqrt{\omega + \alpha\sigma_{t+1}^2\varepsilon_{t+1}^2 + \beta\sigma_{t+1}^2}\,\varepsilon_{t+2}\right)\right.}{\left. + \left(r + \frac{\omega + \alpha\sigma_{t+1}^2\varepsilon_{t+1}^2 + \beta\sigma_{t+1}^2}{2}\right)T\right)}{\sqrt{\omega + \alpha\sigma_{t+1}^2\varepsilon_{t+1}^2\beta\sigma_{t+1}^2}\sqrt{T}}$$

$$d_2 = d_1 - \sqrt{\omega + \alpha\sigma_{t+1}^2\varepsilon_{t+1}^2 + \beta\sigma_{t+1}^2}\sqrt{T}$$

We apply a similar exercise to the diffusion process, which gives us the original Black and Scholes option prices. For the interest rate, it seems appropriate to use a Treasury Bill whose maturity matches the maturity of the option contract; therefore, the interest rate that we used is a linear interpolation using one- and three-month Treasury Bill rates, one could achieve greater accuracy if necessary.

We present the results of forecasting option prices. The total number of option prices which falls within the 95% confidence interval is calculated in Table 8.7. For the May contracts, the two models perform similarly. The difference becomes apparent when the maturity is more than a month. The GARCH(1,1) process predicts much better for June, July and September contracts whilst December and March contracts are better predicted by the original Black and Scholes formula. This is almost certainly due to the fact that long maturity options are traded in very small quantities if at all. Consequently, the prices calculated will be by the autoquote program which assumes *BS*. We find that in-the-money options with maturity less than five months are better predicted by the GARCH process. In the out-of-the-money case, the diffusion process

Table 8.7 *Forecasting* of different call option prices during May 1992*

Expiry		2125	2175	2225	2275	2325	2375	2425	2475	2525	2575	2625	2675	2725	2775	2825
May	G†	19	19	19	19	19	19	19	19	19	17	15	8	0	0	0
	BS	19	18	18	19	19	19	19	19	19	19	19	17	15	6	4
Jun.	G	19		19		19	19	19	19	19	19	19	15	7	0	0
	BS	18		14		6	5	5	5	5	6	8	10	15	17	8
Jul.	G					15		8		4		1		1		1
	BS					0		0		0		0		0		0
Sep.	G	17		18		18		19		19		19		19		19
	BS	8		16		17		8		1		0		0		0
Dec.	G	0		0		0		0		0		0		0		0
	BS	0		4		14		19		15		8		2		1
Mar. 1993	G	0		0		0		0		0		0		0		0
	BS	0		0		2		10		17		18		18		15

*Numbers indicate the frequency of actual option prices falling in the 95% confidence interval; in columns where there are numbers 19 option prices are quoted due to the 19 trading days in May 1992. Blank columns imply no contracts available.
† G denotes the process generated by the GARCH model.

seems preferable to explain the behaviour of option prices except for July and September contracts. In particular, neither models predict July contracts. This may be due to the infrequent tradings of July contracts. In conclusion, this chapter suggests that the simple adjustment used by practitioners for pricing options with GARCH coupled with our forecasted confidence intervals captures the actual outcomes better than *BS* at least for the short time period examined. We note that *BS* does outperform for out-of-the-money options.

REFERENCES

Amin, K.I. and Jarrow, R. (1991) Pricing foreign currency options under stochastic interest rates, *Journal of International Money and Finance*, **10**, 310–329.

Amin, K.I. and Ng, V.N. (1993) Option valuation with systematic stochastic volatility, *Journal of Finance*, **48**, 881–910.

Baillie, R. and Bollerslev, T. (1992) Prediction in dynamic models with time-dependent conditional variances, *Journal of Econometrics*, **52**, 91–113.

Black, F. and Scholes, M. (1973) The pricing of options and corporate liabilities, *Journal of Political Economy*, 637–659.

Bollerslev, T. (1986) Generalized autoregressive heteroscedasticity, *Journal of Econometrics*, **31**, 307–327.

Duan, J.C. (1993) The GARCH option pricing model, mimeo, faculty of management, McGill University.

Engle, R. and Mustafa, C. (1992) Implied ARCH models from options prices, *Journal of Econometrics*, **52**, 289–311.

Hull, J. and White, A. (1987) The pricing of options on assets with stochastic volatilities, *Journal of Finance*, **42**, 281–300.

Johnson, H. and Shanno, D. (1987) Option pricing when the variance is changing, *Journal of Financial and Quantitative Analysis*, **22**, 143–151.

Kendall, M. and Stuart, A. (1977) *The Advanced Theory of Statistics*, Charles Griffin & Company, London.

Melino, A. and Turnbull, S.M. (1990) Pricing foreign currency options with stochastic volatility, *Journal of Econometrics*, **45**, 239–265.

Satchell, S. and Timmermann, A. (1994) Option pricing with GARCH and systematic consumption risk, Financial Economic Discussion Paper (FE/10), Birkbeck College, University of London.

Scott, L. (1987) Option pricing when the variance changes randomly: theory, estimation, and an application, *Journal of Financial and Quantitative Analysis*, **22**, 419–438.

Wiggins, J.B. (1987) Option values under stochastic volatility: theory and empirical estimates, *Journal of Financial Economics*, **19**, 351–372.

NOTES

1. If e_t is iid $N(0, 1)$, then the characteristic function of e_t^2 is $(1 - 2it)^{-1/2}$.
2. This is a typical variance for daily rates of return on UK stocks.

3. This would mean for equation (8.1) that α is larger relative to β.
4. These are based on a binomial pricing model used by LIFFE, hence these observations will always bias us towards Black–Scholes results.
5. The library size is kept fixed and updated as we carry out our prediction.

Chapter 9

Volatility forecasting in a tick data model[*]

L.C.G. ROGERS[†]

SUMMARY

In the Black–Scholes paradigm, the variance of the change in log price during a time interval is proportional to the length t of the time interval, but this appears not to hold in practice, as is evidenced by implied volatility smile effects. In this chapter, we find how the variance depends on t in a tick data model first proposed in Rogers and Zane (1998).

9.1 INTRODUCTION

The simple model of an asset price process which is the key to the success of the Black–Scholes approach assumes that the price S_t at time t can be expressed as $\exp(X_t)$, where X is a Brownian motion with constant drift and constant volatility. A consequence of this is that if we consider the sequence $X_{n\delta} - X_{(n-1)\delta}$, $n = 1, \ldots, N$ of log price changes over intervals of fixed length $\delta > 0$, then we see a sequence of independent Gaussian random variables with common mean and common variance, and we can estimate the common variance $\sigma^2\delta$ by the sample variance in the usual way. Dividing by δ therefore gives us an estimate of σ^2, which (taking account of sample fluctuations) should not depend on the choice of δ–but in practice it does. As the value of δ increases, we see that the estimates tend to settle down, but for small δ (of the order of a day or less) the estimates seem to be badly out of line. Given these empirical observations, we may not feel too confident about estimating σ^2, or about forecasting volatility of log price changes over coming time periods. Of course, if we are interested in a particular time interval (say, the time to expiry of an option), we can estimate

---

[*] Research supported in part by EPSRC grant GR/J97281.
[†] University of Bath, email lcgr@maths.bath.ac.uk

using this time interval as the value of δ, but this is only a response to the problem, not a solution to it.

The viewpoint taken here is that this problem is due to a failure of the underlying asset model, and various adjustments of the model will never address the basic issue. The basic issue is that the price data simply do not look like a diffusion, at least on a small timescale; trades happen one at a time, and even 'the price' at some time between trades is a concept that needs careful definition. Aggregating over a longer timescale, the diffusion approximation looks much more appropriate, but on shorter timescales we have to deal with quite different models, which acknowledge the discrete nature of the price data.

In this chapter, we will consider a class of tick data models introduced in Rogers and Zane (1998), and will derive an expression for

$$v(t) \equiv \text{Var}(\log(S_t/S_0)) \tag{9.1}$$

in this context. Under certain natural assumptions, we find that there exist positive constants σ and b such that for times which are reasonably large compared to the inter-event times of the tick data

$$v(t) \sim \sigma^2 t + b \tag{9.2}$$

Section 9.2 reviews the modelling framework of Rogers and Zane (1998) in the special case of a single asset, and section 9.3 derives the functional form of v. Section 9.4 concludes.

9.2　THE MODELLING FRAMEWORK

The approach of Rogers and Zane (1998) is to model the tick data itself. An event in the tick record of the trading of some asset consists of three numbers: the time at which the event happened, the price at which the asset traded, and an amount of the asset which changed hands. The assumptions of Rogers and Zane (1998) are that the amounts traded at different events are IID (independent, identically distributed), and that there is some underlying 'notional' price process z with stationary increments such that the log price y_i at which the asset traded at event time τ_i is expressed as

$$y_i = z(\tau_i) + \varepsilon_i \tag{9.3}$$

Here, the noise terms ε_i are independent conditional on $\{\tau_i, a_i; i \in \mathbb{Z}\}$, where a_i denotes the amount traded at the ith event, and the distribution of ε_i depends only on a_i. The rationale for this assumption is that an agent may be prepared to trade at an anomalous price as a way of gaining information about market sentiment, or as a way of generating interest; but he is unlikely to be willing to trade a *large* amount at an anomalous price. In short, large trades are likely to be more keenly priced than small ones. This modelling structure permits such an effect. Of course, we could for simplicity assume that the ε_i were independent with a common distribution.

It remains to understand how the process of times τ_i of events is generated. The model is based on a Markov process X which is stationary and ergodic with invariant distribution π. Independent of X we take a standard Poisson counting process $\tilde{N}$, and consider the counting process

$$N_t \equiv \tilde{N}\left(\int_0^t f(X_s)\,ds\right)$$

where f is a positive function on the statespace of X. As is explained in Rogers and Zane (1998), it is possible to build in a deterministic dependence on time to model the observed pattern of intraday activity, but for simplicity we shall assume that all such effects have been corrected for. Even when this is done, though, there are still irregularities in the trading of different shares, with periods of heightened activity interspersed with quieter periods, and these do not happen in any predictable pattern. So some sort of stochastic intensity for the event process seems unavoidable; moreover, when we realize that a deterministic intensity would imply that changes in log-prices of *different* assets would be uncorrelated, a stochastic intensity model is more or less forced on us.

Rogers and Zane (1998) present a few very simple examples, and discuss estimation procedures for them, so we will say no more about that here. Instead we turn to the functional form of v implied by this modelling framework.

9.3   THE FUNCTIONAL FORM OF v

The first step in finding the form of v is to determine the meaning of S_t in the expression (9.1). Since the price jumps discretely, we propose to take as the price at time t the price at the last time prior to t that the asset was traded; if

$$T_t \equiv \sup\{\tau_n : \tau_n \leq t\} \equiv \tau_{v(t)}$$

then we define $\log S_t \equiv y_{v(t)}$. It is of course perfectly possible that for $t > 0$ we may have $T_t = T_0$; this is equivalent to the statement that there is no event in the interval $(0, t]$. We have to bear this possibility in mind. It follows from (9.3) that

$$\log\left(\frac{S_t}{S_0}\right) = z(T_t) - z(T_0) + \varepsilon_{v(t)} - \varepsilon_{v(0)} \tag{9.4}$$

so that

$$E\left[\log\left(\frac{S_t}{S_0}\right)\right] = E[z(T_t) - z(T_0)] \tag{9.5}$$

$$= \mu E[T_t - T_0] \tag{9.6}$$

Here, we have used the assumption that z has stationary increments, which implies in particular that for some μ

$$E[z(t) - z(s)] = \mu(t - s)$$

for all s, t. Rather remarkably, the expression (9.6) simplifies. Indeed, because the underlying Markov process X is assumed to be stationary, T_t is the same in distribution as $T_0 + t$, so we have more simply that

$$E\left[\log\left(\frac{S_t}{S_0}\right)\right] = \mu t \tag{9.7}$$

We may similarly analyse the second moment of the change in log price over the interval $(0, t]$:

$$E\left[\left\{\log\left(\frac{S_t}{S_0}\right)\right\}^2\right] = E[(z(T_t) - z(T_0))^2] + E[(\varepsilon_{v(t)} - \varepsilon_{v(0)})^2]$$
$$= E[\text{Var}(z(T_t) - z(T_0))] + \mu^2 E[(T_t - T_0)^2]$$
$$+ 2\,\text{Var}(\varepsilon)P[T_t > T_0] \tag{9.8}$$

which we understand by noting that if $T_t = T_0$ then $\varepsilon_{v(t)} - \varepsilon_{v(0)} = 0$, whereas if $T_t > T_0$ then the difference of the ε terms in (9.4) is the difference of two (conditionally) independent variables both with the same marginal distribution. In general, no simplification of (9.8) is possible without further explicit information concerning the underlying probabilistic structure. In particular, the term $E[(T_t - T_0)^2]$ does not reduce simply, and the term

$$P[T_t > T_0] = 1 - E\exp\left(-\int_0^t f(X_s)\,ds\right) \tag{9.9}$$

cannot be simplified further without knowledge of the process X (and perhaps not even then!). Nevertheless, if we were to assume that *the increments of the notional price process z are uncorrelated* (which would be the case if we took z to be a Brownian motion with constant volatility and drift), then we can simplify

$$E[\text{Var}(z(T_t) - z(T_0))] = \sigma^2 E[T_t - T_0]$$
$$= \sigma^2 t \tag{9.10}$$

Under these assumptions, we may combine and find

$$\text{Var}\left(\log\left(\frac{S_t}{S_0}\right)\right) = \sigma^2 t + \mu^2\,\text{Var}(T_t - T_0) + 2\,\text{Var}(\varepsilon)P[T_t > T_0] \tag{9.11}$$

While the exact form of the different terms in (9.11) may not be explicitly calculable except in a few special cases, the asymptotics of (9.11) are not hard to understand. The term $\mathrm{Var}(T_t - T_0)$ is bounded above by $4ET_0^2$, and tends to zero as $t \downarrow 0$. Assuming that the Markov process X satisfies some mixing condition, we will have for large enough t that

$$\mathrm{Var}(T_t - T_0) \doteq 2\,\mathrm{Var}\,T_0$$

The term $P[T_t > T_0]$ is increasing in t, bounded by 1, and behaves as $Ef(X_0)$ as $t \downarrow 0$. For times which are large compared to the mean time between trades, this probability will be essentially 1. So except for thinly traded shares viewed over quite short time intervals, we may safely take the probability to be 1, which justifies the form (9.2) asserted earlier for the variance of the log-price.

9.4 DISCUSSION AND CONCLUSIONS

We have shown how a natural model for tick data leads us to the functional form

$$\sigma(t) \sim \sqrt{\sigma^2 + b/t}$$

for the 'volatility' $\sigma(t)$ over a time period of length t. This appears to be consistent with observed non-Black–Scholes behaviour of share prices in various ways. First, implied volatility typically decreases with time to expiry, and the 'volatility' in this model displays this feature. Second, log returns look more nearly Gaussian over longer time periods, and we may see this reflected here in that if we assume the notional price is a Brownian motion with constant volatility and drift, then the log return is a sum of a Gaussian part (the increment of z) and two noise terms with common variance. For small times, the noise terms dominate, but as the time interval increases, the variance of $z(t)$ increases while the variance of the two noise terms remains constant; it follows that the distribution will look more nearly Gaussian for longer time periods, but could be very different for short time periods. Third, there is the empirical result of Roll (1984) who studies the direction of successive price jumps in tick data, and finds that the next price change is much more likely to be in the opposite direction from the one just seen; this is easily explained by a model in which there is some notional underlying price, and observed prices are noisy observations of it.

Given tick data on some asset, the ideal would be to fit the entire Markovian intensity structure of section 9.2, though this may not always be easy. However, in terms of forecasting volatility, if we accept the modelling assumptions which led to (9.2), this level of fitting is not needed. We could form estimates $\hat{\sigma}(\delta_i)$ of the variance of $\log(S(\delta_i)/S(0))$ for a range of time intervals δ_i (for example, hourly, daily, weekly and monthly) and then fit the functional form (9.2) to the estimates, a linear regression problem. Of course, we would want to be confident that all of the time intervals δ_i chosen were long enough for negligible probability of no event in such an interval; but if that is not satisfied, how are we going to be able to form the estimator $\hat{\sigma}(\delta_i)$?! In this way, we are able to extract *more* information from the record of tick-by-tick data than would have been possible had we imposed the log-Brownian model on that data. It seems likely that tick data *should* tell us much more than just a record of end-of-day prices, but until we have suitable models of tick data, we cannot hope to extract this additional information.

REFERENCES

Rogers, L.C.G. and Zane, O. (1998) Designing and estimating models of high-frequency data, University of Bath preprint.

Roll, R. (1984) A simple implicit measure of the effective bid–ask spread in an efficient market, *Journal of Finance*, **39**, 1127–1139.

Chapter 10

An econometric model of downside risk*

SHAUN BOND[†]

SUMMARY

The use of semivariance as a measure of risk in financial markets is intuitively appealing. However, despite this appeal, little attention has been devoted to modelling this risk measure in a time series framework. This chapter explores one avenue for developing a dynamic model of semivariance by modifying existing members of the ARCH class of models. The resulting models are found to capture the unusual features of conditional semivariance. Furthermore, the flexibility provided by the ARCH framework enables a family of semivariance models to be developed to capture different features of the data. By developing a methodology to model and forecast semivariance the benefits of using downside risk measures in financial activities (such as portfolio management) can be more readily assessed.

10.1 INTRODUCTION

The use of econometric techniques to model volatility in financial markets, has grown rapidly following the seminal work of Engle (1982). Well-defined techniques, discussed elsewhere in this book, are available for modelling the conditional variance of a series and such techniques readily gained acceptance

* The financial support of the Cambridge Commonwealth Trust and the Overseas Research Students Award Scheme is gratefully acknowledged. The author would also like to thank Dr Steve Satchell for enthusiastically supervising this research, and participants in the finance seminar group at Cambridge University for their comments. Remaining errors are, of course, the responsibility of the author.
† Hughes Hall, Cambridge CB1 2EW.

in areas where forecasts of the conditional variance were required, such as portfolio management and derivative pricing. However, variance (or the standard deviation) is just one, albeit a well-used, measure of risk in financial markets. A range of alternative risk measures exist which may perform as well as, or better than, variance in some circumstance. One alternative risk measure that has a long association with investment management is the semivariance.

The importance of semivariance as a measure of downside volatility was first highlighted by Markowitz (1959, 1991) and since then numerous other authors have extended the concept in the finance literature (see for instance Mao, 1970a; Hogan and Warren, 1972, 1974; Bawa and Lindenberg, 1977; Fishburn, 1977; Satchell, 1996). The measure is intuitively appealing as it is consistent with the generally held notion that risk is related to failure to achieve a target or a below target outcome. For example, such issues are commonly discussed in investment decision making, where they are clearly important in fields such as investment strategies for a defined benefits pension scheme, or performance of a fund against a given benchmark. Despite the seemingly useful nature of semivariance it is not a widely used risk measure in practice. There are several reasons for this, and some of the limitations of semivariance are discussed more fully in the section below. However, one reason for the underutilization of semivariance is that its wider application has been hindered by the absence of a suitable dynamic modelling framework. There are no comparable econometric techniques to the widely used ones for modelling variance, which can be used to model or forecast alternative measures of risk such as semivariance. This chapter goes some way towards correcting that by modifying existing members of the ARCH class of models, to develop a dynamic model of semivariance.

In the process of developing a class of dynamic models of semivariance it will be shown how some asymmetric members of the ARCH class of models can be reinterpreted in a semivariance framework. That is, with some ARCH models the potential to model semivariance already existed and this interpretation has not been fully considered. Indeed, many readers will detect the similarities which exist between some members of the asymmetric class of ARCH models and members of the dynamic semivariance class of models. In light of this overlap it is important to realize that the contribution of this chapter lies more in the development of a conceptual framework for modelling semivariance and drawing out the semivariance interpretation from existing ARCH models, rather than so much in the development of the specification of the models themselves.

The outline of the material in this chapter is as follows. Semivariance as a measure of downside volatility is introduced in section 10.2, with attention paid to developing a broad understanding of the advantages and disadvantages of this measure of risk. In section 10.3, the history of dynamic volatility models is briefly reviewed. Most emphasis is placed on reviewing the ARCH class of models, although some mention is also paid to stochastic volatility models. The development of dynamic models of semivariance is presented in section 10.4, and the relationship between semivariance models and asymmetric ARCH models is also discussed in this section. The new models are applied to UK stock price data in section 10.5 and section 10.6 concludes the chapter.

10.2   OVERVIEW OF SEMIVARIANCE

10.2.1   Introduction to semivariance

Semivariance as a measure of downside volatility was introduced by Markowitz (1959), in his seminal book on portfolio analysis. For the most part, Markowitz used standard deviation or variance as a measure of asset risk. However, an entire chapter of his book was devoted to a discussion of the advantages and disadvantages of semivariance (and semi-standard deviation) as a risk measure. Markowitz defined semivariance as:

$$sv = \frac{\sum_{i=1}^{n} \text{Min}^2[0, x_i - \tau]}{n}$$

where x_i is (in this case) an asset return and τ is a target return. Returns which fall below this target rate are considered undesirable. This notion of risk is consistent with the research of Mao (1970b), who found that business decision makers defined risk in terms of the failure to achieve a given target. This contrasts with a risk measure based on variance, in which both extreme gains and extreme losses are considered undesirable. To illustrate the calculation of semivariance consider the asset returns in Table 10.1.

Table 10.1   *Calculation of semivariance FTSE100 monthly share returns January to June 1996**

Month	Monthly return x_i	Target rate (0.1) $\text{Min}(0, x_i - 0.1)$	Semivariance calculation $\text{Min}^2(0, x_i - 0.1)$
Jan.	1.78	0.00	0.00
Feb.	0.60	0.00	0.00
Mar.	−1.09	−1.19	1.42
Apr.	2.53	0.00	0.00
May.	−0.90	−1.00	1.00
Jun.	−0.65	−0.75	0.56
Total			2.98
Semivariance			0.50

*No importance should be attached to the dates chosen. The data were selected merely to illustrate the calculation of the semivariance.

The semivariance for returns over the period January to June was 0.50 (given a target rate of 0.1%). In comparison, the corresponding value for the variance of returns was 1.92.[1]

The calculation of semivariance (or more correctly the lower partial moment in this case) shown above is a sample measure. Sortino and Forsey (1996) suggest that the population measure be estimated by integrating over a fitted empirical distribution with the limits of integration given by $-\infty$ and τ (the target rate), that is:

$$sv = \int_{-\infty}^{\tau} (x - \tau)^2 f(x)\, dx \qquad (10.1)$$

In the empirical example given by Sortino and Forsey, a three-parameter lognormal distribution is fitted to Japanese stock market data and it is found that the sample method understates the level of downside risk. They conclude that 'fitting a continuous probability distribution is superior to discrete sample calculations' (Sortino and Forsey, 1996, p. 41).

10.2.2   Limitations of variance as a risk measure

A major limitation in the use of variance as a measure of risk is that extreme gains as well as extreme losses are treated as equally undesirable. Hence, a procedure such as portfolio optimization will penalize assets which have extreme returns, regardless of whether these returns are positive or negative. This is clearly an undesirable result.

Markowitz was aware of this anomaly in his early work of portfolio analysis. Indeed, he even states that 'analyses based on S [semivariance] tend to produce better portfolios than those based on V [variance]' (Markowitz, 1959, p. 194). However, he continued to emphasize the role of variance as a measure of risk because of the cost, convenience and familiarity of using it. To emphasize this point consider Table 10.2. This table lists a series of fictitious returns and the associated semivariance and variance measures.

In Table 10.2, two 'risk' measures are calculated for each series (semivariance and variance). The first series consists of a period of six consecutive losses. Overall the cumulative *loss* on this hypothetical investment amounts to 20.3%. However, there is a noticeable difference in the magnitude of the two risk measures. Semivariance is considerably larger than variance. The high risk of capital loss is clearly evident from the semivariance measure.[2]

In contrast to the first series, the second series in Table 10.2, consists of six consecutive gains of the same absolute magnitude as the first series. The cumulative *gain* resulting from the compounding of these returns totals 24.0%. The magnitude of variance is unchanged from the first series. Risk as measured by variance is identical for both series. In contrast, the semivariance measure is

Table 10.2 *Extreme returns and risk measurement: a hypothetical example*

Observation	Series 1	Series 2
1	−3.5	3.5
2	−5.7	5.7
3	−0.5	0.5
4	−8.3	8.3
5	−2.4	2.4
6	−1.7	1.7
Cumulative loss/gain (%)	−20.3	24.0
Semivariance*	20.4	0.0
Variance	6.9	6.9

*Semivariance is calculated with a target rate of 0.

zero, indicating no risk of capital loss. Clearly, the use of semivariance in this instance provides a better measure of risk (if risk is defined in terms of a loss of funds).

10.2.3 Limitations of semivariance

One factor that has limited the use of semivariance in investment analysis has been the absence of a suitable method for modelling the conditional semivariance through time. This compares to the extensive knowledge of the modelling of the conditional variance in the econometrics literature (see for instance the survey by Bollerslev, Chou and Kroner, 1992). This situation appears to have occurred as a result of the time series properties of the semivariance series. To see this, consider the following approximation to the conditional semivariance of a series of returns:

$$sv_t = \text{Min}^2[0, x_t - \tau] \tag{10.2}$$

where x_t and τ are the return at time t and the target rate, respectively, and $E(x_t) = 0$. Now consider the situation where the unconditional distribution of x_t is symmetrically distributed around zero,[3] and the target rate is set at zero. Then, on average, half the sample of observations would fall below the target rate. This implies that a semivariance time series, based on equation (10.2) above, would consist of a large number of zero observations. Should the distribution of returns be positively skewed, the proportion of zero observations would be even larger. Indeed, when the semivariance is calculated for a series of monthly returns on the FT30 share index (over the period February 1963 to June 1997) almost 41% of the 413 observations are zero observations when a target rate of zero is used. This high proportion of zero observations distinguishes a semivariance time series from most other financial time series used in econometrics.

It also suggests that the traditional linear analysis techniques commonly used in financial econometrics are unlikely to be the most appropriate methods to capture this unusual feature of the data.

10.2.4　Asymmetry of returns and semivariance

Another possible limitation on the use of semivariance in financial applications concerns the situation when the distribution of returns is symmetric. As Markowitz (1991) and many other authors have since explained (see for instance Bawa and Lindenberg, 1977; Nantell and Price, 1979; Homaifar and Graddy, 1991; Bond and Satchell, 1998), for symmetric distributions, semivariance is equal to half of the variance:

$$\text{Var}(x) = 2sv(x) \tag{10.3}$$

when measured around the expected value of the distribution. It follows that semivariance measured below target rates, other than the expected value, will also exhibit a similar proportionality when the distribution of returns is symmetric. Because of this proportionality, efficient portfolios constructed on the basis of semivariance will contain the same set of securities as a portfolio derived by using variance. This finding will also hold if the distribution of returns for all securities in a portfolio has the same degree of skewness (Markowitz, 1991; Bawa and Lindenberg, 1977).

10.3　RISK MODELLING TECHNIQUES

Interest in the dynamic modelling of risk (or conditional variance/volatility) has expanded rapidly since the early 1980s. The seminal paper which sparked significant interest in conditional volatility was by Engle (1982). The class of AutoRegressive Conditional Heteroscedasticity (ARCH) models introduced by Engle has dominated the risk modelling literature. Engle's framework provided a simple yet highly intuitive base upon which more complex models could be developed. This section follows the development of the ARCH class of models from the simple ARCH(1) model to more complex asymmetric specifications. In particular, much attention is focused on reviewing asymmetric ARCH specifications, and also regime-based models of volatility, because such models have important linkages with dynamic semivariance models (this is discussed more fully in section 10.4.7). To complete the review, stochastic volatility models are also briefly discussed. However, extensions of the semivariance modelling methodology to the stochastic volatility class of models are not considered in this chapter.

10.3.1 The ARCH class of models

Engle (1982) proposed a model which allowed the conditional variance to depend on lagged values of a squared innovations series. To explain Engle's model, consider an autoregressive representation of the series of interest:

$$x_t = g(\Omega_{t-1}, \beta) + \varepsilon_t \tag{10.4}$$

where Ω_{t-1} is the information set at time $t-1$ (usually consisting of, though not restricted to, a matrix of lagged dependent variables), and β a vector of parameters. The ARCH(q) model is then expressed in terms of the innovations ε_t conditioned on elements of the information set Ω_{t-1}, that is:

$$\varepsilon_t = z_t \sigma_t$$

$$\sigma_t^2 = \alpha_0 + \alpha_1 \varepsilon_{t-1}^2 + \alpha_2 \varepsilon_{t-2}^2 + \cdots + \alpha_q \varepsilon_{t-q}^2 \tag{10.5}$$

where $z_t \sim \text{iid}(0, 1)$, $\alpha_0 > 0$ and $\alpha_i \geq 0$, $i = 1, \ldots, q$. To assist in estimation, it is typically assumed that:

$$\varepsilon_t | \Omega_{t-1} \sim N(0, \sigma_t^2) \tag{10.6}$$

The simple linear lag structure of the ARCH model allows reasonably easy estimation of the model. However, it was frequently found in practice that when the model was estimated in an unrestricted format, the non-negativity restrictions were violated. As a means of overcoming this problem a declining linear restriction was placed on the model parameters. While implementation of this lag structure aided estimation, there were concerns about the arbitrariness of the linear lag structure. As a means of alleviating these concerns Bollerslev (1986) proposed the Generalized ARCH (GARCH) model.

The GARCH(p,q) model generalizes the specification of the conditional variance equation of the ARCH model by adding an autoregressive conditional variance term, that is:

$$\sigma_t^2 = \alpha_0 + \alpha_1 \varepsilon_{t-1}^2 + \alpha_2 \varepsilon_{t-2}^2 + \cdots + \alpha_q \varepsilon_{t-q}^2 + \beta_1 \sigma_{t-1}^2 + \cdots + \beta_p \sigma_{t-p}^2 \tag{10.7}$$

with inequality restrictions:[4]

$$\alpha_0 > 0$$

$$\alpha_i \geq 0 \quad \text{for } i = 1, \ldots, q$$

$$\beta_j \geq 0 \quad \text{for } j = 1, \ldots, p \tag{10.8}$$

A related issue is that of the stationarity of σ_t^2. Bollerslev (1986) has shown that the stationarity condition will be satisfied if $\alpha(1) + \beta(1) < 1$. However, in many applications there is evidence of strong persistence in the conditional variance, and this has led to another extension of the GARCH model, referred to as the Integrated GARCH (IGARCH) model (Bollerslev and Engle, 1986). The IGARCH model is estimated with the stationarity condition imposed on the parameters.

Nelson's (1991) EGARCH model grew out of dissatisfaction with the limitations of the GARCH model. In particular Nelson points out that the GARCH model: rules out asymmetries in volatility; imposes restrictions on the parameters of the model which may not be consistent with the data; and there are difficulties in determining the persistence of shocks. Nelson's model is:

$$\ln(\sigma_t^2) = \alpha_0 + \sum_{i=1}^{q} \beta_i h(z_{t-i}) + \sum_{i}^{p} \alpha_i \ln(\sigma_{t-i}^2) \tag{10.9}$$

where $h(\cdot)$ is some suitable function of the lagged z terms. The model expresses the relationship in terms of the natural logarithm which ensures the non-negativity of the conditional variance. One possible choice for $h(\cdot)$ which allows for asymmetry in the response of σ_t^2 to shocks is:

$$h(z_t) = \theta z_t + \gamma[|z_t| - E|z_t|] \tag{10.10}$$

Note that the term z_t can be viewed as a standardized innovation ($z_t = \varepsilon_t/\sigma_t$).

Threshold ARCH and GARCH models were introduced by Zakoian (1991), Rabemananjara and Zakoian (1993) and Glosten, Jagannathan and Runkle (1993). As the models are essentially similar this chapter focuses on the latter paper. The starting point for this model is the GARCH framework, where the conditional volatility is modelled as a linear function of the lagged conditional variance and lagged squared residuals. To allow for possible asymmetric behaviour in volatility, an indicator function is incorporated into the conditional volatility specification by Glosten, Jagannath and Runkle (1993, hereafter GJR). This model permits volatility to react differently depending on the sign of past innovations, that is:

$$\sigma_t^2 = \alpha_0 + \sum_{i=1}^{p} \alpha_i^1 \varepsilon_{t-i}^2 + \sum_{i=1}^{p} \alpha_i^2 \varepsilon_{t-i}^2 I_{t-i} + \sum_{i=1}^{q} \beta_i \sigma_{t-i}^2 \tag{10.11}$$

where $I_t = 0$ when $\varepsilon_t \leq 0$ and $I_t = 1$ when $\varepsilon_t > 0$. By including the indicator function in the conditional variance specification, the impact of the lagged innovation terms will differ depending on the sign of ε_{t-i}. For example, when $\varepsilon_{t-i} > 0$, the coefficient will be $\alpha_i^1 + \alpha_i^2$. For $\varepsilon_{t-i} \leq 0$, the coefficient will be given by α_i^1.

Further developing the ideas from this model is the work of Li and Li (1996). These authors propose a Double-Threshold ARCH (DTARCH) model, in which both the conditional mean and conditional volatility of a series are modelled in a piecewise framework. Their model builds on the work of Tong (1990), who proposed a SETAR–ARCH model.

A series $\{x_t\}$ is assumed to follow a DTARCH process if:

$$x_t = \Phi_0^{(j)} + \sum_{i=1}^{p_j} \Phi_i^{(j)} x_{t-i} + \varepsilon \quad \text{for } r_{j-1} < X_{t-d} < r_j \tag{10.12}$$

$$\sigma_t^2 = \alpha_0^{(j)} + \sum_{r=1}^{q_j} \alpha_r^{(j)} \varepsilon_{t-r}^2 \tag{10.13}$$

where $j = 1, 2, \ldots, m$ and d is the delay parameter. The threshold parameter is denoted by $-\infty = r_0 < r_1 < r_2 < \cdots < r_m = \infty$. The model above is denoted as a DTARCH($p_1, p_2, \ldots, p_m; q_1, q_2, \ldots, q_m$), with the p values indicating the order of the AR process, and the q variables indicating the order of the ARCH process.

Another approach to the modelling of a changing conditional variance structure is provided by Hamilton and Susmel (1994). Their approach allows for changes in the parameter values of the ARCH conditional variance equation in a similar way to the Markov switching model of Hamilton (1989). Part of the reason for allowing for changing parameter values in the conditional variance is the tendency of the GARCH model to overpredict the persistence of volatility. This has been noted by Engle and Mustafa (1992) and Lamoureux and Lastrapes (1993). Hamilton and Susmel present evidence from the literature to suggest that the persistence of a series may be lowered by allowing for regime changes.

An alternative approach to modelling volatility which moves away from the ARCH class of models is the stochastic volatility class of models. In a similar way to the EGARCH model, stochastic volatility models consider the natural logarithm of σ_t^2 (denoted h_t), and in common with ARCH models this process is assumed to have an autoregressive form. However, an important distinction with such models is that the stochastic process h_t is not directly observable. To see this consider the model

$$x_t = \sigma_t \varepsilon_t \tag{10.14}$$

where $t = 1, \ldots, T$, and $\varepsilon_t \sim N(0, 1)$.

Let $h_t \equiv \sigma_t^2$, and assume the process follows an autoregressive form, such that

$$h_t = \gamma + \varphi h_{t-1} + \eta \tag{10.15}$$

where $\eta_t \sim N(0, 1)$. The returns equation can then be re-expressed to reflect this specification

$$\ln x_t^2 = h_t + \ln \varepsilon_t^2 \tag{10.16}$$

A quasi-maximum likelihood estimator based on the Kalman filter is proposed by Harvey, Ruiz and Shephard (1993) to estimate the model, although other approaches have been suggested which use the method of moments (see for instance Chesney and Scott, 1989, or Melino and Turnbull, 1990).

While stochastic volatility models are useful tools in modelling conditional volatility, the rest of this chapter focuses on the ARCH class of models and develops models of dynamic semivariance from this class. The review of stochastic volatility models is included for completeness although it should be noted that it may indeed be possible to build a semivariance model by applying the approach used in the rest of this chapter to the stochastic volatility framework. The next section considers the construction of a dynamic model of semivariance.

10.4   DYNAMIC MODELS OF SEMIVARIANCE

Section 10.3 provided an overview of the major strands of the risk modelling literature. This section extends the previous work on risk modelling by using the ARCH framework to model downside risk. The need for such a model was outlined in section 10.2, as the lack of a suitable modelling strategy has been one factor which has limited the adoption of downside risk measures. To begin with the dynamic semivariance model is explained in terms of a simple first-order model; however, extension of the model to higher orders is discussed later, as are other extensions to the model.

10.4.1   ARCH-semivariance (ARCH-SV)

To develop the dynamic semivariance model consider the standard ARCH(1) decomposition of returns (or returns less the conditional mean) as presented in Engle (1982):

$$x_t = a + \sum_{i=1}^{p} b_i x_{t-i} + \varepsilon_t \qquad (10.17)$$

$$\varepsilon_t = \sigma_t z_t \qquad (10.18)$$

where x_t is the return at time t, $z_t \sim \text{iid}(0, 1)$ and σ_t^2 is the conditional variance modelled as a function of past returns (or return shocks). That is:

$$\sigma_t^2 = \alpha_0 + \alpha_1 \varepsilon_{t-1}^2 \qquad (10.19)$$

In developing a dynamic model of semivariance one possible starting point is to consider the specification of the conditional variance when the return is below target (that is, when $x_t < \tau$). This point is of interest because when the return is below target the variance and semivariance are equivalent (where $\tau = E(x_t) = 0$). That is:

$$sv_t = \sigma_t^2 = E(x_t^2 | x_t < \tau) \tag{10.20}$$

To show this, recall that:

$$\sigma_t^2 = E(x_t^2) \tag{10.21}$$

so when $x_t < \tau$, then:

$$\sigma_t^2 = E(x_t^2) = E(x_t^2 | x_t < \tau) = sv_t \tag{10.22}$$

A simple semivariance model could then be developed by modifying the conditional variance equation in the ARCH(1) model above. This gives the following semivariance model:

$$\varepsilon_t = \sigma_t z_t$$

$$sv_t = \sigma_t^2 = \alpha_0 + \alpha_1 \varepsilon_{t-1}^2 \quad \text{for } x_t < \tau \tag{10.23}$$

However, there is clearly an inconsistency with this approach. Equation (10.19) expresses σ_t^2 as belonging to the information set Ω_{t-1} whereas sv_t belongs to the information set Ω_t (because of the x_t term in equation (10.23)). To maintain the consistency of the model with respect to the information set, and to introduce a dynamic element into the model, it is necessary to make the semivariance a function of the Ω_{t-1} information set.

In order to meet the criteria suggested in the above paragraph of making the semivariance a function of the Ω_{t-1} information set, the concept of dynamic semivariance is proposed. The dynamic semivariance (or dynamic downside risk) is defined as:

$$dsv_t^- = E(x_t^2 | x_{t-d} < \tau) \tag{10.24}$$

where $d = 1, \ldots, T - 1$, and the $(-)$ superscript of dsv_t signifies that the variable is downside risk. Of interest in some situations would be the complementary concept of upside volatility or:

$$dsv_t^+ = E(x_t^2 | x_{t-d} \geq \tau) \tag{10.25}$$

The two partial elements of risk introduced above are related to conditional variance in the following manner:

$$\sigma_t^2 = dsv_t^- \Pr(x_{t-d} < \tau) + dsv_t^+ \Pr(x_{t-d} \geq \tau) \tag{10.26}$$

or for the sample analogue the conditional variance is expressed as:

$$\sigma_t^2 = I_t dsv_t^- + (1 - I_t) dsv_t^+ \tag{10.27}$$

where I_t is an indicator function, such that:

$$I_t = 1 \quad \text{if } x_{t-d} < \tau$$
$$= 0 \quad \text{otherwise} \tag{10.28}$$

It is clear that this is the case, as when $x_{t-d} < \tau$, then:

$$I_t = 1 \tag{10.29}$$

and

$$\sigma_t^2 = dsv_t^- \tag{10.30}$$

which is consistent with equation (10.22).

Having introduced the concept of dynamic semivariance it is now possible to propose a dynamic model of semivariance using the ARCH framework. In particular, it is postulated that the dynamic semivariance is a function of past returns (or return shocks depending on whether the conditional mean was removed from the returns series), in a manner similar to the specification of conditional variance in an ARCH model. For the first-order dynamic semivariance model (ARCH-SV(1)), the conditional semivariance is given as:

$$dsv_t^- = \alpha_0^- + \alpha_1^- \varepsilon_{t-1}^2 \quad \text{for } x_{t-d} < \tau$$
$$dsv_t^+ = \alpha_0^+ + \alpha_1^+ \varepsilon_{t-1}^2 \quad \text{for } x_{t-d} \geq \tau \tag{10.31}$$

where the variable definitions are as before.

10.4.2   Extension of model and other issues

The above exposition of the ARCH-SV model was limited to a simple first-order model for ease of presentation. It is of course readily extended to higher order models. Indeed, given the evidence of long lag lengths commonly found in ARCH models (for example, Bollerslev, 1986), it would be highly unusual to only use a first-order model. The extended model takes the form of:

$$x_t = a + \sum_{i=1}^{p} b_i x_{t-i} + \varepsilon_t \tag{10.32}$$

and

$$dsv_t^- = \alpha_0^- + \sum_{i=1}^{p} \alpha_i^- \varepsilon_{t-i}^2 \quad \text{for } x_{t-d} < \tau$$

$$dsv_t^+ = \alpha_0^+ + \sum_{i=1}^{p} \alpha_i^+ \varepsilon_{t-i}^2 \quad \text{for } x_{t-d} \geq \tau \tag{10.33}$$

Given the evidence for long lag lengths in ARCH models, estimation efficiency may be increased by imposing restrictions on the model parameters. The most obvious restriction is the non-negativity requirement, though this is imposed to ensure economic validity rather than to increase efficiency. Engle (1982, 1983) was aware of the benefits of imposing restrictions, and recommends applying a linear declining weight structure of the form (see also the discussion in Bera and Higgins, 1993)

$$w_i = \frac{(p+1) - i}{\frac{1}{2}p(p+1)} \tag{10.34}$$

where p is the order of the autoregressive terms, and

$$\sum_{i=1}^{p} w_i = 1$$

The conditional semivariance equations of the ARCH-SV model would then be estimated as:

$$dsv_t^- = \alpha_0^- + \alpha^- \sum_{i=1}^{p} w_i \varepsilon_{t-i}^2 \quad \text{for } x_{t-d} < \tau$$

$$dsv_t^+ = \alpha_0^+ + \alpha^+ \sum_{i=1}^{p} w_i \varepsilon_{t-i}^2 \quad \text{for } x_{t-d} \geq \tau \tag{10.35}$$

10.4.3   A generalized ARCH-SV model

An important development in the field of volatility models occurred when Bollerslev (1986) generalized the ARCH model of Engle (1982) to capture persistence effects in volatility. As discussed in the review above, this extension of the ARCH model has now become the standard model for studies on volatility modelling. To allow for the persistence of volatility to be incorporated in the ARCH-SV model, it is possible to generalize the semivariance model in a similar manner.

By generalizing the ARCH-SV model in this way, one limitation of semivariance measures is overcome. This is, that semivariance is a less efficient risk measure because not all of the observations are used in performing the calculations, because by generalizing the model, the impact of past conditional variance (whether upper or lower semivariance) is included. Thus, the effect of all observations (either implicitly or explicitly) is included in modelling semivariance.

The starting point for this extension is the relationship between conditional volatility and the upper and lower dynamic semivariance variance, contained in equation (10.27) and reproduced below:

$$\sigma_t^2 = I_t dsv_t^- + (1 - I_t)dsv_t^+ \tag{10.36}$$

where I_t is an indicator function, such that:

$$I_t = 1 \quad \text{if } x_{t-d} < \tau$$
$$ = 0 \quad \text{otherwise} \tag{10.37}$$

This information can be used in the conditional semivariance equation in the same way that the lagged conditional variance is used in the GARCH equations. However, it is not possible to include the lagged conditional variance in the standard way that the GARCH model does. Instead the persistence in conditional variance must be captured by including the two asymmetric components of volatility, detailed in equation (10.36). Thus the conditional semivariance equations for a GARCH-SV model become:

$$dsv_t^- = \alpha_0^- + \sum_{i=1}^p \alpha_i^- \varepsilon_{t-i}^2 + \sum_{i=1}^q \beta_i^- [I_{t-i} dsv_{t-i}^- + [1 - I_{t-i}]dsv_{t-i}^+]$$
$$\text{for } x_{t-d} < \tau \tag{10.38}$$

$$dsv_t^+ = \alpha_0^+ + \sum_{i=1}^p \alpha_i^+ \varepsilon_{t-i}^2 + \sum_{i=1}^q \beta_i^+ [I_{t-i} dsv_{t-i}^- + [1 - I_{t-i}]dsv_{t-i}^+]$$
$$\text{for } x_{t-d} \geq \tau \tag{10.39}$$

If $\sum_{i=1}^q \beta_i^+ = 0$ and $\sum_{i=1}^q \beta_i^- = 0$ the model reduces to the ARCH-SV model discussed in the section above.

The GARCH-SV model is expected to hold the same advantages for estimation of a dynamic semivariance model as the GARCH model has for the ARCH model. In particular, initial attempts to estimate the ARCH-SV model have found long lag lengths to be needed to properly specify the model. Estimation of the GARCH-SV model is expected to occur with shorter lag lengths because of the property of the model to replicate an infinite length ARCH-SV model.

The model also has advantages over the traditional GARCH model, allowing for possible asymmetric behaviour of variance to be readily handled. GARCH-SV also has advantages over many (though not necessarily all) asymmetric GARCH models, such as EGARCH, by explicitly including a pre-specified target rate. The model also extends closely related models such as the DTARCH model by incorporating lagged conditional semivariance, to capture the persistence in variance noted by Bollerslev (1986). The next section discusses the estimation of the GARCH-SV model.

10.4.4 Estimation of the model

To this point nothing has been said about the estimation of the model, the choice of lag in the threshold variable x_{t-d}, or regarding whether the target rate (τ) is known or unknown. The latter two issues will be discussed first and then the issue of model estimation can be discussed.

10.4.4.1 Selection of τ and d

The choice of lag length for the threshold variable is very similar to the choice of delay parameter in a TAR or SETAR modelling framework (see Tong, 1980, or Tsay, 1989). Recall that a SETAR model has the following form:

$$Y_t = \Phi_0^{(j)} + \sum_{i=1}^{p} \Phi_i^{(j)} Y_{t-i} + a_t^{(j)}, \quad \text{for } r_{j-1} \leq Y_{t-d} < r_j \tag{10.40}$$

where $j = 1, \ldots, k$ and d is a positive integer (Tsay, 1989, p. 231). One difference between this model and the ARCH-SV model is that the threshold variable in the SETAR model is the same as the dependent variable in the autoregressive equation. However, this is not the case in the ARCH-SV model, where the threshold variable x_{t-i} differs from the dependent variable dsv_t^- or dsv_t^+. This is only a minor matter as the non-linearity F-test proposed by Tsay (Tsay, 1989) could be easily calculated from arranged autoregression ordered on the threshold variable x_{t-d}. However, in practice is it highly likely that a threshold variable of x_{t-1} will prove to be the most suitable choice. This matter is discussed further in section 10.5.2.

The selection of the level of the target rate τ in the ARCH-SV model is different in principle from the choice of threshold parameter in a SETAR model. In the ARCH-SV model it is expected that the level of the target rate will be set exogenously. In practice there are a number of candidate values which are commonly used in semivariance calculations – the most intuitive being zero, as this is the point of distinction between capital gains and losses. Other rates which may be relevant are a prespecified 'hurdle' rate of investment consistent with a user cost of capital or a threshold rate consistent with a long-term investment objective (which may be used in the case of defined benefit pension schemes, see comments in Balzer, 1994). Ultimately this choice will depend upon the investment objectives of the investor.

10.4.4.2 Estimation of GARCH-SV

Quasi-maximum likelihood estimation of the GARCH-SV (or ARCH-SV) model can be considered in a similar way to the estimation of the GARCH model of Bollerslev (1986). To develop the numerical maximum likelihood estimation of the model, it is necessary to assume a form for the conditional distribution of the innovation term. In keeping with Bollerslev (1986), we let:

$$\varepsilon_t | \Omega_{t-1} \sim N(0, (I_t dsv_t^- + [1 - I_t] dsv_t^+)) \tag{10.41}$$

This allows simpler estimation of the model by making use of well-known likelihood techniques. However, this assumption does have implications for the semivariance measures derived from the model. Recall from section 10.2.4 that many authors have shown that when the unconditional distribution of the model is symmetric, the semivariance will reduce to a known proportion of variance. This means that portfolios constructed on the basis of either semivariance or variance will contain the same set of securities, diluting the arguments in favour of replacing variance with a semivariance measure. The same arguments are expected to hold for the conditional variance and conditional semivariance based on a symmetric conditional distribution. However, this does not mean that estimating a dynamic semivariance model using a symmetric conditional distribution is of no use. First, it illustrates the techniques involve, and highlights that dynamic models of semivariance can be constructed. Second, it provides a general model that can be enhanced after further research to allow for an asymmetric conditional distribution to be used in the maximum likelihood estimation of the model. At present the use of asymmetric conditional distributions in GARCH is a developing field. There are strong *prima facie* reasons for expecting that the conditional distribution of some series, such as interest rates (which are bounded from below, see Lee and Tse, 1991), or the equity returns on small capitalization companies (see discussion in Bollerslev, Chou and Kroner, 1992), are conditionally skewed. Research is continuing on estimating the ARCH-SV class of models with a non-normal conditional distribution.

The log-likelihood function can be written as:

$$L = \sum_{t=1}^{n} \left\{ -\frac{1}{2} \ln 2\pi - \frac{1}{2} \ln \sigma_t^2 - \frac{1}{2} \frac{\varepsilon_t^2}{\sigma_t^2} \right\} \tag{10.42}$$

Extending the model to incorporate the component elements of variance gives:

$$L = \sum_{t=1}^{n} \left\{ -\frac{1}{2} \ln 2\pi - \frac{1}{2} \ln(I_t dsv_t^- + (1 - I_t) dsv_t^+) \right.$$

$$\left. -\frac{1}{2} \frac{\varepsilon_t^2}{I_t dsv_t^- + (1 - I_t) dsv_t^+} \right\} \tag{10.43}$$

where ε_t and I_t are defined above, and

$$dsv_t^- = \alpha_0^- + \sum_{i=1}^{p} \alpha_i^- \varepsilon_{t-i}^2 + \sum_{i=1}^{q} \beta_i^- [I_{t-i} dsv_{t-i}^- + [1 - I_{t-i}] dsv_{t-i}^+]$$

$$\text{for } x_{t-d} < \tau \tag{10.44}$$

$$dsv_t^+ = \alpha_0^+ + \sum_{i=1}^{p} \alpha_i^+ \varepsilon_{t-i}^2 + \sum_{i=1}^{q} \beta_i^+ [I_{t-i} dsv_{t-i}^- + [1 - I_{t-i}] dsv_{t-i}^+]$$

$$\text{for } x_{t-d} \geq \tau \tag{10.45}$$

This likelihood function for the ARCH-SV would be essentially identical with the exception of the recursive components. Numerical techniques can be used to obtain estimates of the model parameters.

10.4.5 Extensions of the GARCH-SV model (GARCH-SV(M))

A common extension of ARCH models is to allow the conditional variance of an asset to influence returns. Such an extension allows one of the basic tenets of finance theory, that return is proportional to risk, to be empirically measured. Engle, Lilien and Robins (1987) and French, Schwert and Stambaugh (1987) were among the first researchers to quantify this relationship. Of particular importance was the work by Engle, Lilien and Robins which lead to the development of the ARCH in mean (ARCH-M) model. French, Schwert and Stambaugh extended this approach to the GARCH model. The GARCH-SV model provides an ideal framework for assessing the impact of risk on asset returns. In particular, it has an important advantage over the ARCH-M and GARCH-M models of allowing for the impact of semivariance on returns to be measured; thereby permitting the value of asymmetric risk measures to be assessed.

An asymmetric component of risk can be incorporated into the GARCH-SV model in the following way:

$$x_t = a + \sum_{i=1}^{p} b_i x_{t-i} + \delta^- dsv_t^- + \varepsilon_t \tag{10.46}$$

$$dsv_t^- = \alpha_0^- + \sum_{i=1}^{p} \alpha_i^- \varepsilon_{t-i}^2 + \sum_{i=1}^{q} \beta_i^- [I_{t-i} dsv_{t-i}^- + [1 - I_{t-i}] dsv_{t-i}^+]$$

$$\text{for } x_{t-d} < \tau \tag{10.47}$$

$$dsv_t^+ = \alpha_0^+ + \sum_{i=1}^{p} \alpha_i^+ \varepsilon_{t-i}^2 + \sum_{i=1}^{q} \beta_i^+ [I_{t-i} dsv_{t-i}^- + [1 - I_{t-i}] dsv_{t-i}^+]$$

$$\text{for } x_{t-d} \geq \tau \tag{10.48}$$

Estimation of the model parameters can be conducted through numerical optimization of the likelihood function as explained above for the GARCH-SV model.

10.4.6 The differential impact of lagged volatility

The specification of the conditional semivariance variance equations above constrains the impact of lagged conditional semivariance to be equal for both upper and lower semivariance. However, this presumption may not necessarily be valid. That is the persistence of the lower semivariance may differ from that of the upper semivariance. To allow for the testing of this hypothesis a differential impact GARCH-SV model (GARCH-SV(D)) can be estimated. To estimate the unrestricted model, the conditional semivariance variance equations can be written as:

$$dsv_t^- = \alpha_0^- + \sum_{i=1}^p \alpha_i^- \varepsilon_{t-i}^2 + \sum_{i=1}^q \beta_i^- dsv_{t-i}^- + \sum_{i=1}^q \phi_i^- dsv_{t-i}^+$$

$$\text{for } x_{t-d} < \tau \qquad (10.49)$$

$$dsv_t^+ = \alpha_0^+ + \sum_{i=1}^p \alpha_i^+ \varepsilon_{t-i}^2 + \sum_{i=1}^q \beta_i^+ dsv_{t-i}^- + \sum_{i=1}^q \phi_i^+ dsv_{t-i}^+$$

$$\text{for } x_{t-d} \geq \tau \qquad (10.50)$$

Estimation can then be carried out using the quasi-maximum likelihood approach of the GARCH-SV model.

An interesting question with the GARCH-SV(D) model is what form the stationarity conditions take. In the GARCH-SV model, similar stationarity conditions to the GARCH model exist, that is for, say dsv_t^-, $\sum_{i=1}^p \alpha_i^- + \sum_{i=1}^q \beta_i^- < 1$. In the first order GARCH-SV(D) model, when similar reasoning is used, the stationarity restriction are

$$\alpha_1^- + \beta_1^- < 1 \qquad (10.51)$$

when $x_t < \tau$, and

$$\alpha_1^+ + \phi_1^+ < 1 \qquad (10.52)$$

when $x_t \geq \tau$ (a proof is available on request).

However, Tong (1990) finds the conditions for stationarity are more complicated for threshold models than for linear models. A simple empirical method of determining the model's stability is to use an empirical simulation, based on the estimated parameters, to check the overall properties of the model. This procedure was adopted for the estimated GARCH-SV(D) model in section 10.5.

10.4.7   Semivariance and asymmetric ARCH models

The issue of modelling conditional semivariance is very closely related to the asymmetric modelling of the conditional variance. In many cases the similarities between the models reviewed in section 10.3 and the ARCH-SV and GARCH-SV models are surprisingly clear. However, an important contribution of this chapter and the goal of the present section is to draw out the implicit semivariance models already embedded in many of the asymmetric ARCH models. Indeed, it appears that the relationship between the asymmetric ARCH models and dynamic semivariance models has often been overlooked, despite the closeness of the two concepts. The reasons for this oversight are probably many, although one of the most obvious being that the authors' developing asymmetric ARCH models were more concerned with empirical issues in modelling volatility, reflecting the widespread dominance of mean-variance portfolio analysis in finance.

A related issue is the broader importance of the threshold parameter in semivariance modelling than in the asymmetric ARCH specifications. With the exception of the AGARCH model of Hentschel (1994), the asymmetric ARCH models generally only consider asymmetry around zero. In the dynamic semivariance models, the threshold parameter is given a more central role as it represents a prespecified target rate, below which investors are concerned about downside loss. While it may often be the case that zero is the chosen target rate, the semivariance models do allow for the possibility that target rates other than zero could be used. The rationale behind the selection of the target rate is discussed elsewhere in this chapter.

This section begins by examining perhaps one of the most clearly related asymmetric models to the dynamic semivariance model, the Double Threshold ARCH model of Li and Li (1996). The relationship between the other models discussed in section 10.3 and the dynamic semivariance models follows.

10.4.7.1   *DTARCH model and semivariance*

It is interesting to note the similarities between a DTARCH model and the issue of estimating semivariance. In both cases a target rate of return is an important input into the model (in the DTARCH model the target rate operates as the threshold parameter). The structure of the conditional variance also depends on what 'state' the model is in. To see this more clearly consider the model used by Li and Li in a simulation exercise:

$$X_t = \begin{cases} -0.3X_{t-1} + a_t, & X_t \le 0 \\ 0.35X_{t-1} + a_t, & X_t > 0 \end{cases} \tag{10.53}$$

$$\sigma_t^2 = \begin{cases} 0.002 + 0.42a_{t-1}^2, & X_t \le 0 \\ 0.004 + 0.24a_{t-1}^2, & X_t > 0 \end{cases}$$

Ignoring the threshold component for the conditional mean, the threshold model for the conditional variance seems to be modelling the semivariance (for $X_t \leq 0$), and also the upper semivariance component (for $X_t > 0$). A problem with this specification is that the threshold variable is contemporaneously related to return. However, in applied work Li and Li allow the threshold variable to take the values X_{t-d} for $d = 1, \ldots, N$. When this modification is incorporated the ARCH-SV model can be seen to be essentially identical to the DTARCH model. However, Li and Li do not consider extensions to generalize the model to a GARCH-type framework.

While the models appear numerically identical, it is important to distinguish the different underpinnings of the model. In particular, the target rate and delay parameter in the DTARCH model are determined from the data set. Whereas, in the ARCH-SV model, the target rate is set exogenously, depending on the needs of the analyst.

10.4.7.2 Asymmetric GARCH models and semivariance

Just as the DTARCH model was shown to have a semivariance interpretation, other members of the ARCH class of models can also be shown to implicitly model semivariance. A simple example of this is the EGARCH model of Nelson (1991). Recall that Nelson's model is given by:

$$\ln(\sigma_t^2) = \alpha_0 + \sum_{i=1}^{q} \beta_i h(z_{t-i}) + \sum_{i}^{p} \alpha_i \ln(\sigma_{t-i}^2) \tag{10.54}$$

and

$$h(z_t) = \theta z_t + \gamma[|z_t| - E |z_t|] \tag{10.55}$$

where $z_t = \varepsilon_t / \sigma_t$.

To show that one measure of semivariance is implicitly embedded within the model, let the standardized innovation z_t be redefined as a standardized return:

$$\left(z_t = \frac{x_t}{\sigma_t} \right) \tag{10.56}$$

When returns fall below a target rate of zero (that is $x_{t-1} < 0$), the lower semivariance can be expressed as (and ignoring the lagged conditional variance term for simplicity):

$$\ln dsv_t^+ = \alpha_0^- + \beta_1^- h(z_{t-1}) \tag{10.57}$$

with

$$h(z_{t-1}) = (\theta - \gamma)z_{t-1} - \gamma E |z_{t-1}| \tag{10.58}$$

When returns are above the target rate, the upper conditional semivariance equation is:

$$\ln dsv_t^+ = \alpha_0^+ + \beta_1^+ h(z_{t-1}) \tag{10.59}$$

and

$$h(z_{t-1}) = (\theta + \gamma)z_{t-1} - \gamma E |z_{t-1}| \tag{10.60}$$

for $x_{t-1} \geq 0$.

Hence, a simple dynamic semivariance model can be shown to exist within an EGARCH framework. Indeed, many members of the ARCH class of models can be re-expressed in this way. However, this presentation of the model raises an important issue. The semivariance models presented in the previous section, while using the squared innovations (ε_{t-i}^2) to model dynamic semivariance, base the regime of the model on the sign of the x_{t-d} variable and not on the sign of the innovation (ε_{t-i}). This is in contrast to most of the asymmetric ARCH models which consider asymmetry in the innovations (see paper by Engle and Ng, 1993).

The simple dynamic semivariance variance models based on the EGARCH model, above, overcome this problem by replacing the innovations with the elements of the returns series (as in equation (10.56)). However, semivariance models based directly on the return series do not first remove the predictable component from returns and this may overstate the size of the semivariance. In keeping with recent presentations of ARCH models (see Bollerslev, Chou and Kroner, 1992), a semivariance model based on EGARCH could be written in terms of a regime-based model (such as GARCH-SV). This also allows the information from the innovations to be incorporated into the conditional semi-variance equation. In addition, it allows the regime to be determined by x_t rather than ε_t, which is more consistent with the nature of a semivariance measure (and is also more consistent with the leverage principle of Black (1976) and Christie (1982) than other asymmetric ARCH models). The EGARCH model could be incorporated into a semivariance framework by rewriting the model in the following way:

$$x_t = a + \sum_{i=1}^{p} b_i x_{t-i} + \varepsilon_t \tag{10.61}$$

$$\ln dsv_t^- = \alpha_0^- + \alpha_1^- h^-(z_{t-1}) + \beta_1^- \ln[I_{t-1}dsv_{t-1}^- + [1 - I_{t-1}]dsv_{t-1}^+]$$
$$h^-(z_{t-1}) = \theta^- z_{t-1} + \gamma^- [|z_{t-1}| - E |z_{t-1}|] \quad \text{for } x_{t-d} < \tau \tag{10.62}$$

$$\ln dsv_t^+ = \alpha_0^+ + \alpha_1^+ h^+(z_{t-1}) + \beta_1^+ \ln[I_{t-1}dsv_{t-1}^- + [1 - I_{t-1}]dsv_{t-1}^+]$$
$$h^+(z_{t-1}) = \theta^+ z_{t-1} + \gamma^+ [|z_{t-1}| - E |z_{t-1}|] \quad \text{for } x_{t-d} \geq \tau \tag{10.63}$$

where

$$z_{t-1} = \frac{\varepsilon_{t-1}}{\sqrt{\exp[\ln(I_{t-1}dsv_{t-1}^- + [1 - I_{t-1}]dsv_{t-1}^+)]}} \qquad (10.64)$$

This then allows for any asymmetry in ε_t to be captured along with any asymmetry around past returns. It also confers other advantages possessed by the EGARCH model, such as the use of logs to avoid non-negativity restrictions.

Another interesting asymmetric ARCH model with implications for modelling semivariance is the model by Glosten, Jagannathan and Runkle (1993), which is referred to as the GJR model. As discussed in section 10.3.1, the conditional variance equation for the GJR GARCH(1,1) model can be expressed as:

$$\sigma_t^2 = \alpha_0 + \alpha_1 \varepsilon_{t-1}^2 + \alpha_2 \varepsilon_{t-1}^2 I_{t-1} + \beta \sigma_{t-1}^2 \qquad (10.65)$$

where $I_t = 1$ if $\varepsilon_t > 0$. Therefore when $\varepsilon_t > 0$

$$\sigma_t^2 = \alpha_0 + (\alpha_1 + \alpha_2)\varepsilon_{t-1}^2 + \beta \sigma_{t-1}^2 \qquad (10.66)$$

and for $\varepsilon_t \leq 0$,

$$\sigma_t^2 = \alpha_0 + \alpha_1 \varepsilon_{t-1}^2 + \beta \sigma_{t-1}^2 \qquad (10.67)$$

The similarity between this model and the GARCH-SV is clear. However, the GARCH-SV model uses a different indicator function, with I_t taking its value from x_{t-d} rather than ε_t, as in the GJR model. Another important difference is that GARCH-SV separates the lagged conditional variance into the lower and upper semivariance terms in the conditional semivariance equations. While this separation does not numerically distinguish the model, it does make explicit the relationship between semivariance and variance, and allows for the development of alternative models, such as the GARCH-SV(M) and GARCH-SV(D) models.

The regime switching ARCH model of Hamilton and Susmel (1994) is another model that displays a similarity to semivariance ARCH models. In particular, conditional variance is modelled over a number of regimes, with movements between regimes determined by an unobserved indicator variable. The ARCH-SV class of models mirrors this regime-based approach, although a major difference is the number of regimes and the indicator variable used to move between states. In the ARCH-SV model, only two states are considered, an upper and lower semivariance state, whereas in the regime switching model, the number of states is determined by the data.[5] Movement between states in the regime switching model is determined by an unobserved Markov variable, whereas in the ARCH-SV models, movements between the states are determined by the value of past returns in relation to the target rate.

This section has shown that a number of asymmetric ARCH models implicitly contain a version of a semivariance model embedded within them. In particular, the DTARCH model was shown to be equivalent to the ARCH-SV model. Other GARCH models were shown to be similar to the semivariance GARCH models, however, differences in the incorporation of asymmetry remain. The next section applies the ARCH-SV class of models to daily financial data on UK shares.

10.5 APPLICATION OF THE DYNAMIC SEMIVARIANCE MODELS

10.5.1 Data

To illustrate the application of the dynamic semivariance models, a series of daily returns on the FTSE100 index was chosen. The series extends from 2 January 1984 to 30 June 1997 providing 3412 observations (after excluding the nil returns recorded on public holidays). Note that in common with many similar studies of equity returns, all the analysis is in terms of the log return of the index.[6] Dividend returns are excluded from the analysis as total return data were only available for a shorter period of time. In any case, it is typically found that almost all of the volatility in total returns is attributed to price movements rather than dividend changes (see for instance Poon and Taylor, 1992). A table displaying a statistical summary of the data is shown in Table 10.A1 contained in the appendix.

The choice of the series was influenced by a number of factors. An important consideration was that the FTSE100 is a well-known series and has been used in a number of other studies. This allows for the results of the present analysis to be compared with other studies. However, initially the preferred choice of data was return data relating to utility stocks. Return data on utility companies were preferred because the performance of semivariance risk measures has been extensively discussed in relation to this class of securities. This is typically because the return distribution is usually found to be (negatively) skewed as a result of the regulatory framework in which these companies operate (see discussion in Homaifar and Graddy, 1991). As discussed in section 10.2.4, the use of semivariance as a risk measure is more limited when applied to a symmetric series. Unfortunately, equities for utility companies (both in the UK and the United States markets) tend to be less actively traded and this results in a high number of zero returns. There was some concern that the high number of zero observations may have an adverse impact on the model results, hence a more actively traded series (the FTSE100) was chosen. It is noted, however, from Table 10.A1 in the appendix, that the FTSE100 returns used to estimate the models do display skewness (even after allowing for the effects of the stock market crash). The comments of section 10.4.4.2 should be borne in mind when considering the implications of skewness for the conditional semivariance.

In keeping with other studies of volatility, no adjustment is made to the data for the October 1987 stock market crash (see for instance Nelson, 1991).

However, because of the uncommonly large magnitude of the returns recorded in that month, the model was also estimated over a shorter time period from 1 January 1988. It was found that for some of the regime GARCH models convergence problems were encountered. Possible reasons for this convergence problem are discussed in the appropriate sections.

The target rate chosen for the present analysis was zero. This choice has a number of advantages, it is intuitively appealing because it distinguishes between capital gains and losses. Another reason for favouring this target rate is that many previous studies have found variance to be asymmetric around this point, and it is consistent with the leverage effect of Black (1976) and Christie (1982). An alternative choice was to use a variable target rate, such as a risk-free interest rate. This would be equivalent to modelling excess returns around zero. Such an approach was considered for this chapter; however, it proved difficult to obtain daily interest rate data over the sample period used in this study. Future research will consider the application of the ARCH-SV class of models to excess returns.

Apart from choosing the target rate, it was also necessary to select the delay parameter (d). As discussed in section 10.3.3.2, the delay parameter could be chosen by performing a sequential search over a range of d values and selecting the value which maximized a criteria function. In this study, the search procedure was not followed. Rather the delay parameter was set to 1. This omission of the search procedure was mainly due to time constraints; however, the choice of one is intuitively appealing and consistent with similar studies (for example, Li and Li, 1996).

10.5.2   Dynamic models of semivariance

In this section the application of the ARCH-SV and GARCH-SV models to daily returns on the FTSE100 index is discussed. The extensions of the basic model (GARCH-SV(M) and GARCH-SV(D)) are discussed in the next section. Unless otherwise stated the models were estimated using the Maxlik routines in GAUSS (Aptech Systems, 1993). The numerical algorithm used was the BHHH algorithm (Berndt *et al.*, 1974) and this is consistent with the choice of Bollerslev (1986) in estimating the GARCH model.

10.5.2.1   *ARCH-SV*
The starting point for modelling the conditional volatility of the data is the ARCH model of Engle (1982). Before commencing model estimation, the data is first checked to ensure that ARCH effects are present. If such effects are shown not to be present, it is of little use modelling the conditional second moment. In his paper, Engle proposes a simple Lagrange multiplier test for detecting the presence of autoregressive conditional heteroscedasticity. The test

is based on a regression of a squared residual term (from an OLS regression) on a constant and squared lagged residuals. The test results provide strong evidence of ARCH effects.

To provide a benchmark model, the ARCH model of Engle (1982) is first estimated and then two versions of the ARCH-SV model are estimated, and the results compared. The lag length chosen for the ARCH and ARCH-SV models is seven, and this was selected from a search of autoregressions of the squared OLS of residuals (using the AIC criterion). The lag order of the returns equation was also chosen on the basis of the minimum AIC value over a range of lag lengths.

To assist in the estimation of the model, the linear declining lag structure discussed in section 10.4.2 was imposed on the model. The estimation results for the ARCH(7) model are as follows.

Table 10.3 *ARCH model parameters*

Coefficient	Est. parameter	Std err.
a	0.0586	0.0159
b	0.0701	0.0190
α_0	0.3784	0.0298
α_1	0.5344	0.0884

Log-likelihood: -4238.55.

where

$$w_i = \frac{(p+1)-i}{\frac{1}{2}p(p+1)} \qquad (10.69)$$

and the standard errors are shown in parentheses. All estimated parameters are highly significant. The coefficients for the lag parameters can be calculated from the above formula. The parameters estimates are:

Table 10.4 *ARCH model parameters (lag coefficients)*

Lag number	Weight	DSV$^-$
1	0.2500	0.1336
2	0.2413	0.1145
3	0.1786	0.0954
4	0.1429	0.0763
5	0.1071	0.0573
6	0.0714	0.0382
7	0.0357	0.0191

The results for the ARCH-SV model are presented below:

Table 10.5 *ARCH model parameters*

Coefficient	Est. parameter	Std err.
a	0.0633	0.0197
b	0.0694	0.0190
α_0^-	0.3944	0.0405
α_1^-	0.4492	0.0780
α_0^+	0.3576	0.0445
α_1^+	0.6241	0.1758

Log-likelihood: -4235.99

Overall the results are generally similar to the alternative model version discussed above. As before, individual parameter estimates can be calculated from the estimated parameters, and these are shown in the table below:

Table 10.6 *ARCH-SV model parameters (lag coefficients)*

Lag number	Weight	DSV$^-$	DSV$^+$
1	0.2500	0.1047	0.1560
2	0.2413	0.0898	0.1337
3	0.1786	0.0748	0.1114
4	0.1429	0.0598	0.0892
5	0.1071	0.0449	0.0669
6	0.0714	0.0299	0.0446
7	0.0357	0.0150	0.0223

Using a likelihood ratio test, the equality restrictions implicitly imposed by the ARCH model on the model coefficients (that $\alpha_0^- = \alpha_0^+$ and $\alpha^- = \alpha^+$) can be tested:

$$LR = 2\{\ln L(\text{unrestricted}) - \ln L(\text{restricted})\} \sim \chi^2(2)$$

$$= 2\{-4235.99 + 4238.55\}$$

$$= 5.12[0.077]$$

where the *p*-value of the distribution is shown in brackets after the test statistic.

The equality restrictions imposed by the ARCH model are rejected by the data at a 10% level of significance, which lends moderate support to the hypothesis that it is important to model the individual components of variance (that is the upper and lower semivariance) separately.

10.5.2.2 GARCH-SV

The previous section found ARCH models could be adapted to model conditional semivariance (both upper and lower semivariance), and that such models were preferred to the traditional ARCH model for modelling conditional variance. This section of the chapter applies the generalized ARCH-SV model to FTSE100 data to assess the performance of the model. To provide a comparative model, the GARCH(1,1) model of Bollerslev was used. The estimation results for this model were:

Table 10.7   *GARCH model parameters*

Coefficient	Est. parameter	Std err.
a	0.0579	0.0152
b	0.0658	0.0186
α_0	0.0396	0.0132
α_1	0.0907	0.0225
β	0.8608	0.0300

Log-likelihood: -4234.63

All parameter estimates are statistically significant at traditional significance levels. In addition, all parameters are correctly signed and of expected magnitude. The sum of α_1 and β is 0.9542, which is close to one. To check whether an IGARCH model may represent the data more accurately, a likelihood ratio test of the integration constraint $(\alpha_1 + \beta = 1)$ was conducted. It was found that the integration constraint was rejected by the data.[7]

In contrast to the GARCH(1,1) model, the results for the GARCH-SV(1,1) are shown below:

Table 10.8   *GARCH-SV model parameters*

Coefficient	Est. parameter	Std err.
a	0.0478	0.0134
b	0.0672	0.0183
α_0^-	0.0459	0.0331
α_1^-	0.1265	0.0455
β^-	0.8412	0.0608
α_0^+	0.0331	0.0239
α_1^+	0.0417	0.0170
β^+	0.8870	0.0453

Log-likelihood: -4218.40

The estimated model results are correctly signed and significant at the 10% level. It is interesting to note the different magnitudes of the lagged innovation coefficients (that is α_1^- and α_1^+). As the innovation terms can be interpreted as *news*, the results imply that news has more impact on the lower semivariance variance (that is volatility when the market is falling), than on the upper semivariance (interpreted as volatility when the market is rising). This finding is similar to the result discussed by Engle and Ng (1993), who found that 'negative shocks induce more volatility than positive shocks'. However, the results in this chapter are more general because the GARCH-SV model examines the impact of all news innovations on conditional semivariance, implying that both positive and negative news induces greater (lower) volatility when the market is falling (rising).

In testing whether the GARCH-SV model differs significantly from the standard GARCH model, the likelihood ratio test can once again be used. The equality restrictions ($\alpha_0^- = \alpha_0^+$, $\alpha_1^- = \alpha_1^+$ and $\beta_1^- = \beta_1^+$) are implicitly imposed by the GARCH model, and the validity of this can be assessed. The likelihood ratio results are:

$$LR = 2\{\ln L(\text{unrestricted}) - \ln L(\text{restricted})\} \sim \chi^2(3)$$

$$= 2\{-4218.40 + 4234.63\}$$

$$= 32.45[0.00]$$

which strongly rejects the constraints. The lagged conditional semivariance coefficient is also highly significant, which emphasizes the importance of capturing the persistence in volatility.

The sum of the α_1^- and β_1^- parameters in the dsv_t^- equation is very close to one (0.9677). A likelihood ratio test was once again used to examine whether the integration constraint should be imposed on the data. The resulting model was:

Table 10.9   *IGARCH-SV model parameters*

Coefficient	Est. parameter	Std err.
a	0.0473	0.0134
b	0.0673	0.0183
α_0^-	0.0277	0.0208
α_1^-	0.1289	0.0474
β^-	0.8711	–
α_0^+	0.0469	0.0159
α_1^+	0.0412	0.0165
β^+	0.8633	0.0327

Log-likelihood: -4218.67

and the hypothesis that $\alpha_1^- + \beta_1^- = 1$ cannot be rejected ($LR = 0.5454[0.460]$).

This model provides a very interesting insight into the dynamic nature of variance. In the original GARCH model, the sum of the parameters was very close to, but not equal to, one. On the basis of the evidence from the simple GARCH model, variance could be characterized as a highly persistent but stationary process. However, on more careful examination with the GARCH-SV model, a clearer insight into the nature of the variance could be obtained. The lower semivariance component was indeed found to be non-stationary (which implies downside shocks persist), whereas shocks to the upper semivariance are found to be much less persistent than implied by the GARCH model. Hence, not only does the GARCH-SV model provide a framework in which downside semivariance may be modelled, it also provides interesting insights into the nature of the dynamic structure of variance.

A chart of the conditional semivariance derived from the IGARCH-SV model is shown in Figure 10.1 and the appendix.

10.5.3   Model extensions

10.5.3.1   GARCH-SV(M)

As explained in section 10.4.5, above, the GARCH-SV in mean model provides a way of testing whether the downside component of conditional volatility (the lower semivariance) has a different impact on mean returns from the conditional variance. A GARCH-M model was first estimated to provide a comparison model. The resulting parameter estimates are presented below:

Table 10.10   *GARCH-M model parameters*

Coefficient	Est. parameter	Std err.
a	0.0607	0.0284
b	0.0657	0.0185
δ	−0.0043	0.0354
α_0	0.0396	0.0132
α_1	0.0906	0.0224
β	0.8609	0.0299

Log-Likelihood = −4229.99

From the estimated results, it is evident that the risk term in the mean return equation is not of the correct sign, although as the coefficient is not significantly different from zero, no implication can be drawn from this. The downside risk parameter estimate for the GARCH-SV(M) model (shown below) also displays an unexpected negative relationship between volatility and returns. However, once again neither of these terms are significant. The lack of significance of these terms also indicates that, at least in this case, separating the components of volatility does not add any insight into the relationship between risk and return.

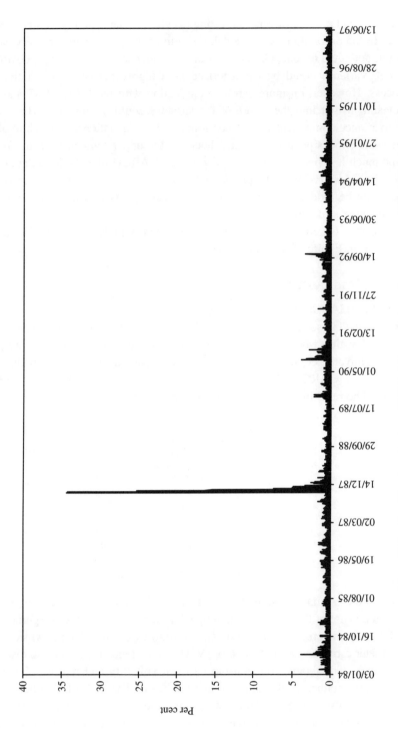

Figure 10.1   *Conditional semivariance FT100–daily semivariance 3 January 1984–30 June 1997*

Table 10.11   *GARCH-SV(M) model parameters*

Coefficient	Est. parameter	Std err.
a	0.0519	0.0185
b	0.0619	0.0244
δ^-	−0.0123	0.0403
α_0^-	0.0444	0.0339
α_1^-	0.1265	0.0455
β^-	0.8438	0.0616
α_0^+	0.0337	0.0241
α_1^+	0.0416	0.0169
β^+	0.8859	0.0455

Log-likelihood: −4218.33

10.5.3.2 GARCH-SV(D)

A further extension to the basic GARCH-SV model was outlined in section 10.4.6. This extension considered the question of whether there was a differential impact on current period conditional volatility from the lagged elements of conditional volatility (that is the lower and upper semivariance). Initially the model was estimated with no integration constraint, and this resulted in the following parameter estimates:

Table 10.12   *GARCH-SV(D) model parameters*

Coefficient	Est. parameter	Std err.
a	0.0488	0.0135
b	0.0630	0.0189
α_0^-	0.0414	0.0336
α_1^-	0.1244	0.0395
β^-	0.8365	0.0667
ϕ^-	0.7482	0.1303
α_0^+	0.0519	0.0355
α_1^+	0.0507	0.0179
β^+	1.0131	0.1313
ϕ^+	0.8199	0.0930

Log-likelihood: −4213.05

The most obvious feature of the estimated results is that the coefficient of the dsv_{t-1}^- term in the second conditional semivariance equation is greater than one, suggesting that there is strong persistence between these two terms. Despite the high value of this parameter, the dsv_t^+ equation meets the stationarity conditions presented earlier (that is $\alpha_1^+ + \phi_1^+ < 1$). On the other hand, the sum of the estimated parameters of the dsv_t^- equation is close to the value implied by the stationarity conditions ($\alpha_1^- + \beta_1^- < 1$) and requires further investigation for possible IGARCH effects.

A likelihood ratio test can be used to test whether the sum of the parameters equals one. Lumsdaine (1995, 1996) shows that unlike the analogous unit root test for the mean, the estimated parameters in an IGARCH model are asymptotically normal and consistent estimates of the covariance matrix are available. Hence using a standard likelihood ratio test, it is found that the null hypothesis (that the parameters sum to unity) cannot be rejected (test statistic is 0.880 with p value 0.348). Note that the joint hypothesis that $\alpha_0^- = 0$ and $\alpha_1^- + \beta_1^- = 1$ was rejected by the data. The model is re-estimated with the integration condition imposed. The new results are:

Table 10.13   *IGARCH-SV(D) model parameters*

Coefficient	Est. parameter	Std err.
a	0.0480	0.0135
b	0.0638	0.0187
α_0^-	0.0221	0.0195
α_1^-	0.1256	0.0414
β^-	0.8744	–
ϕ^-	0.7767	0.1256
α_0^+	0.0675	0.0325
α_1^+	0.0497	0.0175
β^+	0.9824	0.1215
ϕ^+	0.7966	0.0894

Log-likelihood: −4213.49

Another feature to note is that the coefficients of the dsv_t^- terms are always larger than the coefficients of the dsv_{t-i}^+ term. However, whether the two coefficients are statistically significant for each other requires a formal hypothesis test. Using a likelihood ratio test, this hypothesis can be evaluated. Comparing the likelihood value in this unrestricted model to the likelihood value of the GARCH-SV model (which implicitly imposes the restrictions that $\beta_1^- = \phi_1^-$ and that $\beta_1^+ = \phi_1^+$) gives the following test statistic:

$$LR = 2\{\ln L(\text{unrestricted}) - \ln L(\text{restricted})\} \sim \chi^2(2)$$

$$= 2\{-4213.9 + 4218.7\}$$

$$= 9.6[0.01]$$

It is found that the restrictions are rejected by the data set. This highlights the importance of not only modelling the individual components of volatility, but also allowing such components to have different persistence effects.

10.6   CONCLUSION

Semivariance has been discussed in the finance literature as an alternative volatility measure to variance. Algorithms have been developed which allow for mean-semivariance portfolios to be constructed, and research exists on calculating semivariance 'betas'. Despite the attention that semivariance measures have received, there have, to date, been no attempts to model the series over time. In contrast, modelling the conditional second moment of a series is a very well-established field in econometrics. This chapter has proposed extensions to the existing ARCH class of models which allow conditional semivariance to be modelled. The resulting GARCH-SV models, while similar to some existing GARCH models, provide for the explicit identification of conditional semivariance.

The GARCH-SV models were applied to a historical series of daily FTSE100 returns. The data rejected the traditional GARCH models in favour of the GARCH-SV approach. One version of the GARCH-SV model (GARCH-SV(D)) was also found to provide valuable information about the differential persistence of the components of volatility.

Further research is continuing on the evaluation of the models developed in this chapter. In particular, attention is being devoted to considering the forecasting performance of the ARCH-SV class of models relative to simple threshold autoregressive models (such as the SETAR model of Tsay, 1989) of downside risk. More work is also being done on assessing the value of forecasts of conditional semivariance in portfolio management.

An additional contribution of this chapter is to show that while attempts have not been previously made to explicitly model semivariance, a number of existing asymmetric ARCH models do implicitly model a form of downside volatility.

10.7   STATISTICAL APPENDIX

Table 10.A1   *Summary statistics for FTSE100 daily returns*
2 January 1984 to 30 June 1997

	No adjustment	Four std devs*
Mean	0.0451	0.0507
Variance	0.8518	0.7258
Standard deviation	0.9229	0.8519
Semivariance	0.4537	0.3490
Skewness	-1.5072	-0.1838
(p-value)	0.0000	0.0368
Excess kurtosis	22.3766	1.7440
(p-value)	0.0000	0.0000
Maximum	7.5970	3.7367
Minimum	-13.0286	-3.6465

*Observations greater than four standard deviations from the mean are set equal to the four standard deviation limit.

REFERENCES

Aptech Systems, Inc. (1993) *The Gauss System Version 3.1*, Aptech Systems, Inc., Maple Valley, WA, USA.

Balzer, L.A. (1994) Measuring investment risk: a review, *Journal of Investing*, Fall, 47–58.

Bawa, V.S. and Lindenberg, E.B. (1977) Capital market equilibrium in a mean-lower partial moment framework, *Journal of Financial Economics*, **5**, 189–200.

Bera, A.K. and Higgins, M.L. (1993) ARCH models: properties, estimation and testing, *Journal of Economic Surveys*, **7**, 305–366.

Berndt, E.K., Hall, B.H., Hall, R.E. and Hausman, J. (1974) Estimation and inference in non-linear structural models, *Annals of Economic and Social Measurement*, **4**, 653–665.

Black, F. (1976) Studies in stock volatility changes, *Proceedings of the 1976 Meeting of the Business and Economics Statistics Section, American Statistical Association*, 177–181.

Bollerslev, T. (1986) Generalized autoregressive conditional heteroscedasticity, *Journal of Econometrics*, **31**, 307–327.

Bollerslev, T., Chou, R.Y. and Kroner, K.F. (1992) ARCH modelling in finance: a review of the theory and empirical evidence, *Journal of Econometrics*, **52**, 5–59.

Bollerslev, T. and Engle, R.F. (1986) Modelling the persistence of conditional variances, *Econometric Reviews*, **5**(1), 1–50.

Bond, S.A. and Satchell, S.E. (1998) Statistical properties of the sample semi-variance, with applications to emerging markets data, mimeo, Faculty of Economics and Politics, University of Cambridge.

Chesney, M. and Scott, L. (1989) Pricing European currency options: a comparison of the modified Black–Scholes model and a random variance model, *Journal of Financial and Quantitative Analysis*, **24**, 267–284.

Christie, A.A. (1982) The stochastic behavior of common stock variances: value, leverage and interest rate effects, *Journal of Financial Economics*, **10**, 407–432.

Engle, R.F. (1982) Autoregressive conditional heteroscedasticity with estimates of the variance of United Kingdom inflation, *Econometrica*, **50**, 987–1007.

Engle, R.F. (1983) Estimates of the variance of US inflation based on the ARCH model, *Journal of Money Credit and Banking*, **15**, 286–301.

Engle, R.F., Lilien, D.M. and Robins, R.P. (1987) Estimating time-varying risk premia in the term structure: the ARCH-M model, *Econometrica*, **55**, 392–407.

Engle, R.F. and Mustafa, C. (1992) Implied ARCH models from option prices, *Journal of Econometrics*, **52**, 289–311.

Engle, R.F. and Ng, V.K. (1993) Measuring and testing the impact of news on volatility, *Journal of Finance*, **48**, 1749–1778.

Fishburn, P.C. (1977) Mean-risk analysis with risk associated with below-target returns, *American Economic Review*, **67**, 116–126.

French, K.R., Schwert, G.W. and Stambaugh, R.F. (1987) Expected stock returns and volatility, *Journal of Financial Economics*, **19**, 3–29.

Glosten, L.R., Jagannathan, R. and Runkle, D.E. (1993) On the relation between the expected value and the volatility of the nominal excess return on stocks, *Journal of Finance*, **48**, 1779–1801.

Hamilton, J.D. (1989) A new approach to the economic analysis of non-stationary time series and the business cycle, *Econometrica*, **37**, 357–384.

Hamilton, J.D. and Susmel, R. (1994) Autoregressive conditional heterskedasticity and changes in regime, *Journal of Econometrics*, **64**, 307–333.

Hentschel, L. (1995) All in the family: nesting symmetric and asymmetric GARCH models, *Journal of Financial Economics*, **39**, 71–104.

Hogan, W.W. and Warren, J.M. (1972) Computation of the efficient boundary in the E-S portfolio selection model, *Journal of Financial and Quantitative Analysis*, **7**, 1881–1896.

Hogan, W.W. and Warren, J.M. (1974) Toward the development of an equilibrium capital-market model based on semivariance, *Journal of Financial and Quantitative Analysis*, **9**(1), 1–11.

Homaifar, G. and Graddy, D.B. (1991) Variance and lower partial moment betas as bases for costing equity capital among regulated utilities, *Applied Economics*, **23**, 1771–1777.

Lamoureux, C.G. and Lastrapes, W.D. (1993) Forecasting stock return variance: towards an understanding of stochastic implied volatilities, *Review of Financial Studies*, **6**, 293–326.

Lee, Y.K. and Tse, T.K.Y. (1991) Term structure of interest rates in the Singapore Asian dollar market, *Journal of Applied Econometrics*, **6**, 143–152.

Li, C.W. and Li, W.K. (1996) On a double threshold autoregressive heteroscedastic time series model, *Journal of Applied Econometrics*, **11**, 253–274.

Lumsdaine, R.L. (1995) Finite-sample properties of the maximum likelihood estimator in GARCH(1,1) and IGARCH(1,1) models: a Monte Carlo investigation, *Journal of Business and Economic Statistics*, **13**, 1–10.

Lumsdaine, R.L. (1996) Consistency and asymptotic normality of the quasi-maximum likelihood estimator in IGARCH(1,1) and covariance stationary GARCH(1,1) models, *Econometrica*, **64**, 575–596.

Mao, J.C.T. (1970a) Models of capital budgeting E-V vs E-S, *Journal of Financial and Quantitative Analysis*, **4**(5), 657–675.

Mao, J.C.T. (1970b) Survey of capital budgeting: theory and practice, *Journal of Finance*, **25**, 349–360.

Markowitz, H.M. (1959) *Portfolio Selection: Efficient Diversification of Investments*, John Wiley and Sons, New York.

Markowitz, H.M. (1991) *Portfolio Selection: Efficient Diversification of Investments*, 2nd ed. Basil Blackwell, Oxford, UK.

Melino, A. and Turnbull, S.M. (1990) Pricing foreign currency options with stochastic volatility, *Journal of Econometrics*, **45**, 239–265.

Nantell, T.J. and Price, B. (1979) An analytical comparison of variance and semivariance capital market theories, *Journal of Financial and Quantitative Analysis*, **14**, 221–242.

Nelson, D.B. (1991) Conditional heteroscedasticity in asset returns: a new approach, *Econometrica*, **59**, 347–370.

Nelson, D.B. and Cao, C.O. (1992) Inequality constraints in the univariate GARCH model, *Journal of Business and Economic Statistics*, **10**, 229–235.

Poon, S-H. and Taylor, S.J. (1992) Stock returns and volatility: an empirical study of the UK stock market, *Journal of Banking and Finance*, **16**, 37–59.

Rabemananjara, R. and Zakoian, J.M. (1993) Threshold ARCH models and asymmetries in volatility, *Journal of Applied Econometrics*, **8**, 31–49.

Satchell, S.E. (1996) Lower partial moment capital asset pricing models: a re-examination, IFR Birkbeck College Discussion Paper, No. 20.

Sortino, F.A. and Forsey, H.J. (1996) On the use and misuse of downside risk, *Journal of Portfolio Management*, Winter, 35–42.

Tong, H. (1990) *Nonlinear Time Series: A Dynamical System Approach*, Oxford University Press, London.

Tsay, R.S. (1989) Testing and modelling threshold autoregressive processes, *Journal of the American Statistical Association*, **84**(405), 231–240.

Zakoian, J.M. (1991) Threshold heteroscedastic models, Discussion Paper, INSEE.

NOTES

1. The semi-standard deviation and standard deviation are 0.70 and 1.38, respectively.
2. Although it is noted that the means of the two series are very different, and such information would also be considered by investors.
3. Admittedly, this may be an unrealistic assumption, it is only used to illustrate the example.
4. For an extensive discussion of the imposition of inequality restrictions see Nelson and Cao (1992).
5. In their paper, Hamilton and Susmel find that the number of states ranges from 2 to 4.
6. That is:

$$x_t = \ln\left(\frac{p_t}{p_{t-1}}\right) \times 100 \tag{10.68}$$

7. $LR = 21.14$ [0.000].

Chapter 11

Variations in the mean and volatility of stock returns around turning points of the business cycle*

GABRIEL PEREZ-QUIROS[†] AND ALLAN TIMMERMANN[‡]

SUMMARY

This chapter studies the patterns and magnitude of variations in the mean and volatility of US stock returns around turning points of the business cycle. During the brief spell from the peak to the trough of the post-war business cycle, mean excess returns increased by approximately 40% in annualized terms. Volatility of stock returns peaked for the period leading official recessions by a single month and was 50% higher in recessions than in expansions. We also report the presence around turning points of the business cycle of an important asymmetry in the conditional distribution of stock returns given standard forecasting instruments and analyse the economic and statistical importance of accounting for this asymmetry.

11.1 INTRODUCTION

Predictability of the mean and volatility of stock returns over the course of the business cycle have generated considerable interest in the financial community.

* For comments on the chapter and discussions we would like to thank John Campbell, Wouter den Haan, Rob Engle, Gloria Gonzalez-Rivera, Jim Hamilton, Bruce Lehmann, Hashem Pesaran, Josh Rosenberg, and seminar participants at UC Riverside, UC San Diego, University of Southern California, London School of Economics, the NBER/NSF conference on Forecasting and Empirical Methods in Macro, Simposia de Analisis Economico, Barcelona, Bank of Spain, University of Murcia, Federal Reserve Bank of New York, and Eastern Economic Association Meetings. The views expressed are those of the authors and do not necessarily reflect those of the Federal Reserve Bank of New York or the Federal Reserve System.
† Federal Reserve Bank of New York.
‡ University of California, San Diego.

This interest is easy to understand from the perspective of managing risk: economic theory suggests that we should expect to see non-trivial variations in the investment opportunity set and the expected risk-return ratio around turning points in the economic cycle, at which point changes in investors' intertemporal marginal rates of substitution between current and future consumption are largest. Hence investment strategies based on market timing can potentially benefit considerably from an improved understanding of variations in the expected return and the volatility of stocks during such periods.

This chapter provides such an analysis of the variation in the mean and volatility of US stock returns around turning points of the business cycle. In view of the few official recessions after the Second World War US stock returns display surprisingly systematic and significant patterns related to the official dating of the business cycle. For the period 1954–1994 the annualized mean excess returns around peaks and troughs were −22 and 21%, respectively. Hence, during the few months from the peak of the business cycle to the trough, mean excess returns increase by approximately 40%. A pattern related to the state of the business cycle is also observed in the volatility of stock returns; volatility peaks for the period preceding official recessions by a month or so. At 6% per month during post-war recessions, volatility was approximately 50% higher than its level during expansions.

Based on conditioning information such as lagged interest rates and dividend yields, the existing literature on predictability of the mean and volatility of stock returns provides indirect evidence on the existence of a business cycle component in expected stock returns.[1] We take the more direct approach of relating variations in stock returns to the NBER recession indicator. Some studies have alluded to a relationship between the NBER indicator and stock returns (e.g. Fama and French, 1989; Whitelaw, 1994), but have stopped short of a formal analysis of this relationship. Other studies (e.g. Ferson and Merrick, 1987; Schwert, 1989) undertake regressions of either the mean or the volatility of returns on the contemporaneous value of the NBER indicator. However, since prices in financial markets incorporate the expectations of forward looking agents, additional information on the business cycle variation in stock returns can be gained by considering the relationship between stock returns and leads and lags of the NBER indicator.

Using the NBER indicator as conditioning information in an analysis of stock returns raises a host of statistical and economical issues. Caution should be excercised when interpreting the results since there were only 13 recessions in the full sample (1926–1994), while the post-war sample contains seven recessions. Second, the NBER recession indicator, which takes on a value of one if the economy was judged by the NBER to have been in a recession in a given month and is otherwise zero, is only reported with a considerable time lag and hence represents *ex-post* information. This makes it critical to use instrumental variables estimation based on *ex-ante* information in the statistical analysis. Despite these problems we find that the variation in stock returns around turning points of the business cycle is so economically and statistically significant that it allows us to gain new insights into a variety of findings in the literature. For example, we find that an analysis based on the relationship between mean stock returns and the contemporaneous value of the NBER indicator understates the variation in mean stock returns around turning points of the business cycle. We also find a strong business cycle asymmetry in the conditional mean of stock returns suggesting that models which assume a time-invariant linear relation between stock returns and standard regressors may be misspecified.

The plan of this chapter is as follows. Variations in the mean and volatility of stock returns over different stages of the business cycle are analysed in section 11.2. Section 11.3 looks into how the distribution of stock returns conditional on standard regressors depends on the state of the business cycle. Section 11.4 concludes.

11.2 VARIATIONS IN STOCK RETURNS AROUND TURNING POINTS OF THE BUSINESS CYCLE

Our measure of the state of the business cycle is based on the binary recession indicator published by the NBER. There are several reasons for this choice. First, it provides a comprehensive summary measure of the state of the economy. The NBER examines a variety of data on economic activity before deciding on the state of the economy. By contrast, variables such as growth in industrial production only account for a particular aspect of economic activity and generate their own problems concerning how to extract a cyclical component from the series. Second, although the NBER indicator does not reflect the severity of a recession, its format facilitates computation of simple summary statistics on the variation in the distribution of stock returns as a function of 'business cycle time'. Thus our analysis allows us to measure the month-by-month variation in the moments of stock returns as the cycle progresses. Finally, turning points in the economic cycle are easily defined by reference to the NBER indicator, while they may not be so clearly defined by reference to alternative series.

11.2.1 Business cycle variation in expected excess returns

To measure the variation in the mean and volatility of excess returns (ρ_t) around turning points of the business cycle, we simply compare mean excess returns during certain blocks of time – formed as leads or lags of the NBER recession indicator – to their mean outside these periods. This can be accomplished by running regressions of excess returns on a constant and leads and lags of the recession indicator:

$$\rho_t = \mu + \beta_{-j}\, NBER_{t-j} + \varepsilon_{t,j} \tag{11.1}$$

where $\varepsilon_{t,j}$ is a residual term. Volatility of excess returns may also depend on the stage of the business cycle. We adopt the following specification, similar to the one proposed by Whitelaw (1994), to extract business cycle variations in the volatility of excess returns:

$$\sqrt{\frac{\pi}{2}}\left|\widehat{\varepsilon}_{t,j}\right| = \alpha + \gamma_{-j}\, NBER_{t-j} + u_{t,j} \tag{11.2}$$

where $\widehat{\varepsilon}_{t,j}$ is a consistent estimate of $\varepsilon_{t,j}$ and $\left|\widehat{\varepsilon}_{t,j}\right|$ is its absolute value. Equation (11.2) can either be interpreted as providing information about the variation in absolute returns or as an approximation to variation in the volatility of returns. In the special case where $\varepsilon_{t,j}$ is normally distributed, the coefficients in (11.2) will provide an exact measure of variations in volatility (explaining the use of the normalizing factor $\sqrt{\pi/2}$). Leads and lags of these recession 'windows' correspond to different stages of the business cycle. Leading (lagging) the contemporaneous recession window by one month will both add (remove) a pre-recession month and remove (add) a pre-expansion month in the estimation of β_{-j}. If the coming of a recession is interpreted by the stock market as 'bad' news while an expansion is interpreted as 'good' news, both effects should pull down (up) β_{-j}, and (11.1) is thus designed to give a picture of the timing and magnitude of business cycle variation in excess returns. Of course, β_{-j} measures the differential mean excess return, while $\mu + \beta_{-j}$ measures the total mean excess return,[2] during (leads and lags of) a recession. By symmetry the differential mean excess return during the same window of time around an expansion is simply given as the negative of β_{-j}. A similar interpretation holds for the volatility parameter γ_{-j}.

Suppose there is no business cycle variation in mean excess returns. Then the estimated coefficients $\widehat{\beta}_{-j}$ should neither be significant nor display any systematic patterns related to the length of the lead or lag of the NBER recession indicator. Two alternative hypotheses are of particular interest. First, it is possible that excess returns will be lower during a recession, but that investors take time to realize that the economy has entered into a recession (or that the recession has finished) and so only respond to the business cycle indicator with a lag. According to this hypothesis the β_{-j} coefficients should become negative with a (positive) lag reflecting the time it takes for the stock market to realize that the economy has entered into (or gone out of) a recession. In particular, if the graph for the estimated coefficients β_{-j} reaches a minimum at $j = 0$, investors would recognize immediately a change in the state of the economy. Alternatively, excess returns may be lower during a recession but investors may anticipate the coming of a recession (as well as the end of the recession) some months ahead and hence the smaller excess returns will appear before the NBER recession indicator. Under this hypothesis we would expect that the graph for the estimates of β_{-j} becomes negative before the contemporaneous NBER recession indicator, i.e. for a negative value of j.

Equations (11.1) and (11.2) were estimated jointly by Hansen's (1982) generalized method-of-moments (GMM) using the moment conditions

$$E\left[\begin{array}{c} (\rho_t - \mu - \beta_{-j} \, NBER_{t-j})\mathbf{Z}_t \\ \left(\sqrt{\frac{\pi}{2}} \, |\rho_t - \mu - \beta_{-j} \, NBER_{t-j}| - \alpha - \gamma_{-j} \, NBER_{t-j} \right) \mathbf{Z}_t \end{array} \right] = 0 \quad (11.3)$$

where $\mathbf{Z}_t$ is an arbitrary set of instruments. Initially we simply used $\mathbf{Z}_t = (1, NBER_{t-j})'$ as our particular choice of instruments although this creates some potential estimation problems: due to the *ex-post* determination of the NBER recession indicator, leads and short lagged values of this variable are not publicly available to investors. So there is a potential bias in GMM estimates of the coefficient β_{-j} (γ_{-j}) based on $\mathbf{Z}_t^*$ because of a possible non-zero correlation between the regressor ($NBER_{t-j}$) and the residual ($\varepsilon_{t,j}$). Of course, this is only a problem if lagged values of returns in the stock market provide an important source of information when the NBER construct their recession indicator. For example, suppose that the NBER determined the value of the recession indicator for a given month based on stock returns in that month. Then even if stock returns truly followed a martingale process, a regression analysis based on the NBER indicator might produce what wrongly appears to be systematic patterns in stock returns. However, according to Moore (1983) this scenario does not accurately reflect the way the NBER decides on their recession indicator. This indicator is based on a pattern of decline in total output, income, employment, and trade (but not stock prices). Furthermore, the potential bias in the GMM estimator of β_{-j} and γ_{-j} based on the instrument vector $\mathbf{Z}_t^*$ can be measured by means of a Hausman test comparing GMM estimates based on $\mathbf{Z}_t^*$ to GMM estimates based exclusively on predetermined instruments. On both counts, the potential bias in the GMM estimates based on the instruments $\mathbf{Z}_t^*$ seems unimportant (c.f. the results in section 11.2.1.1 below) so we first report the results from using $\mathbf{Z}_t^*$ as instruments and then compare these to the GMM estimates based exclusively on predetermined instruments.

Figure 11.1 plots the estimated coefficients $\mu + \beta_{-j}$ and $\alpha + \gamma_{-j}$ as a function of 'recession time' (j). The figure is centred on $j = 0$, aligning excess returns with the concurrent value of the NBER recession indicator. When $j = 1$, the NBER indicator is lagged by one month, while $j = -1$ (a negative lag) corresponds to leading the NBER indicator by a month. Time thus moves from left to right in the figure. For our discussion here we focus on the mean coefficients provided in the windows to the left of the figure which

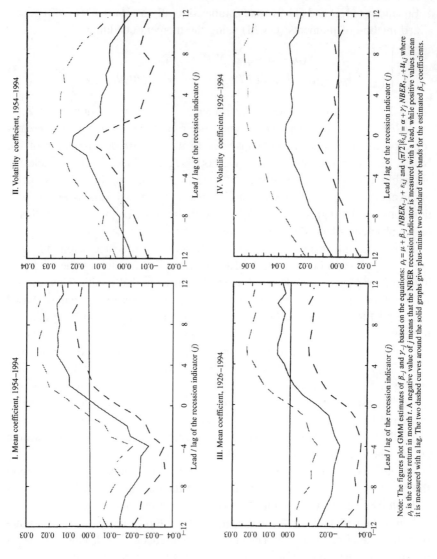

Note: The figures plot GMM estimates of β_{-j} and γ_{-j} based on the equations: $\rho_t = \mu + \beta_{-j} NBER_{t-j} + \varepsilon_{t,j}$ and $\sqrt{\pi/2}|\hat{\varepsilon}_{t,j}| = \alpha + \gamma_j NBER_{t-j} + u_{t,j}$ where ρ_t is the excess return in month t. A negative value of j means that the NBER recession indicator is measured with a lead, while positive values mean it is measured with a lag. The two dashed curves around the solid graphs give plus-minus two standard error bands for the estimated β_{-j} coefficients.

Figure 11.1 *Business cycle variation in monthly excess returns as a function of leads and lags of the NBER indicator*

are based, respectively, on monthly excess returns over the period 1954–1994 and 1926–1994. The post-war sample period was selected to conform with the period after the 'Accord' between the Fed and the Treasury and the presidential election in 1952, after which the Fed stopped pegging interest rates (Mishkin, 1992, p. 453). Results for this sample period facilitate a comparison with the regression results in section 11.3. For both sample periods returns were based on the value-weighted NYSE stock index from the CRSP tapes. A short one-month T-bill rate, obtained from the Fama–Bliss risk-free rates file on the CRSP tapes, was deducted from stock returns to get a measure of excess returns on stocks. Both series were converted into continuously compounded rates.

A surprisingly clear pattern in the business cycle variation in realizations of excess returns emerges from Figure 11.1. The solid curve in the first window shows the mean value of stock returns for leads and lags of the recession indicator and around the curve are plots of plus-minus two standard error bands calculated using heteroscedasticity and autocorrelation consistent standard errors under the procedure proposed by Newey and West (1987).[3] A minimum of the graph is reached at $j = -4$, a lead of four months, indicating that excess returns are lowest around the peak of the business cycle.[4,5]

It may seem surprising that when $j = 0$, that is for the case relating stock returns to the contemporaneous value of the NBER recession indicator, the mean value of excess returns does not appear to differ from the mean excess return computed for the remaining sample. But this finding is consistent with a story based on investors' anticipation of future economic activity: periods corresponding to official recessions include not only the first recession months, but also the first few months right before the beginning of the next expansion. If markets anticipate the next expansion, returns are likely to be higher during these last months, possibly cancelling out against the lower returns during the early recession months.[6] Indeed, the larger mean excess returns measured at lagged values of the NBER recession indicator suggest that during this period, which is dominated by the late recession stage, stock prices go up in anticipation of the coming expansion. These anticipatory increases in stock prices prior to an expansion are large enough to dominate the lower excess returns during the preceding recession months.

At their lowest (for the period covering the last four months of the expansion and finishing four months prior to the next expansion), mean excess returns were -1.9 (-22.3%) per month (year) for the post-war sample and -1.6 (-18.7%) for the longer sample 1926–1994. Annualized figures are given in brackets after the monthly percentages. Around economic troughs mean excess returns peak at a level of 1.7% (21.2%) per month for the post-war sample and 1.0% (12.4%) for the longer sample. The most important difference between patterns in mean returns for the two sample periods is that, while highly significant for the post-war sample, the positive mean excess returns recorded for lags of the NBER indicator are not significant for the longer sample 1926–1994. This difference can be attributed to the length of the great depression which, at 43 months, was almost three times longer than any other recession in the sample: lagging the NBER indicator by 12 or fewer months simply does not shift the weight sufficiently towards the late depression stage and hence does not exclude the block of large negative excess returns towards the middle of the great depression. Nevertheless, mean excess returns were large and positive towards the end of the Great Depression, so in this sense events during that episode are in line with the post-war results.

Although the graph of the estimates of β_{-j} suggests that these coefficients increase systematically from the peak ($j = -4$) to the trough ($j = 4$) of the cycle, this may be misleading because of the correlation between the coefficient estimates. To see whether the differential mean coefficients really increase from peak to trough, we estimated the model (1)–(2) jointly for $j = -4, -3, \ldots, 4$, and tested the null hypothesis $H_0 : \beta_{-4} = \cdots = \beta_{+4}$ against the alternative $H_1 :$ $\beta_{-4} < \cdots < \beta_{+4}$. A likelihood ratio test firmly rejected the null hypothesis at conventional significance levels.

11.2.2   Assessing the effect of using *ex-post* information

A non-zero correlation between leads (or short lags) of the NBER indicator and the residuals in equations (11.1)–(11.2) induces a potential bias in the GMM estimates of β_{-j} and γ_{-j} based on the instruments $\mathbf{Z}_t^* = (1, NBER_{t-j})'$. To investigate the significance of this potential bias we compared the GMM estimates reported in the previous section to GMM estimates based on a set of predetermined instruments. As instruments for $NBER_{t-j}$ we used lagged values of changes in industrial production, monetary growth, the one-month T-bill rate, the default premium, the dividend yield, and growth in the Composite Leading Indicator published by the Department of Commerce. Lag lengths were chosen to ensure that the instruments are publicly known at the end of month $t - 1$. To construct a formal test for the difference between the two sets of estimates, while allowing for heteroscedasticity and autocorrelation in the residuals of the estimated regression, we adopted the two-step estimation procedure described in Nakamura and Nakamura (1981). Thus we first ran regressions of $NBER_{t-j}$ on lagged values of the instruments to form estimates $\widehat{NBER}_{t-j}$ and residuals $\widehat{e}_{t,j} = (NBER_{t-j} - \widehat{NBER}_{t-j})$.[7] In the second step, excess returns (ρ_t) and the volatility proxy ($|\widehat{\varepsilon}_{t,j}|$) from equation (11.2) were regressed on a constant, $NBER_{t-j}$ and $\widehat{e}_{t,j}$, using GMM estimation. Under the null that the regressor ($NBER_{t-j}$) and the error terms ($\varepsilon_{t,j}$, $u_{t,j}$) in (11.1) and (11.2) are uncorrelated, the coefficients on $\widehat{e}_{t,j}$ in the second step regression should equal zero.

For linear specifications Nakamura and Nakamura (1981) prove the asymptotic equivalence between a Hausman test of the consistency of the least squares estimator and a test that the coefficient on $\widehat{e}_{t,j}$ in the second step regression equals zero. For non-linear models like ours the test that the coefficients on $\widehat{e}_{t,j}$ equal zero can be viewed as an LM test of the consistency of the estimates of β_{-j} and γ_{-j}.

In Table 11.1 we report both the GMM estimates of the coefficient β_{-j} and γ_{-j} using $\mathbf{Z}_t^*$ or predetermined variables as instruments and the value of the Hausman test of the equality of these two sets of estimates. For lagged values of the NBER indicator there is no evidence of a significant bias in the GMM estimates of either β_{-j} or γ_{-j} based on using $\mathbf{Z}_t^*$ as instruments. The same result holds for leads of up to five months of the NBER indicator, with the exception of the mean coefficient at a lead of three months. For leads longer than five months the instrumental variable estimates based on predetermined instruments are significantly smaller than the estimates based on $\mathbf{Z}_t^*$, and for even longer leads there is a significant difference between the two sets of volatility estimates. We attribute this last finding to the poor correlation between the instruments and the NBER indicator at leads longer than five months. It is simply very difficult to find good instruments for the NBER indicator more than five months ahead in time.[8] Overall, the evidence suggests that the potential bias in the GMM estimates of β_{-j} or γ_{-j} based on the instruments $\mathbf{Z}_t^*$ is a minor concern[9] (for equation (11.1) see Notes at end of chapter).

11.2.3 Business cycle variation in stock market volatility

We next studied how the volatility of stock returns varies around turning points of the business cycle. The windows to the right in Figure 11.1 show graphs of the GMM estimates of the total volatility coefficients $\{\alpha + \gamma_{-j}\}$ based on the moment conditions (11.3). Again the top window presents the results for the sample 1954–1994 while the bottom window is based on the sample 1926–1994. In the post-war sample volatility peaks during the period preceding by one month the official recession. At just below 6%, the volatility during this period is approximately 50% higher than during months further away from a recession (4%). In the longer sample, 1926–1994, there is a similar build-up in total volatility around recessions, now to a level around, but the subsequent decline in total volatility is slower for this sample. Schwert (1989) reports business cycle dependence in monthly volatility of a similar magnitude to what we find, and, using monthly returns data for the period 1965–1993, Hamilton and Lin (1996) also find that variations in the volatility of stock returns are driven by economic recessions. The new result here is that we map out the volatility for different stages of the business cycle and find that, whereas mean excess returns

Table 11.1 Test of consistency of GMM estimates (1954–1994)

The table shows GMM estimates of the mean and volatility parameters of monthly excess returns around recessionary periods of the economy as measured by leads and lags of the NBER recession indicator. The estimated equations were:

$$\rho_t = \mu + \beta_{-j} NBER_{t-j} + \varepsilon_{t,j} \qquad \sqrt{\pi/2}\,|\hat{\varepsilon}_{t,j}| = \alpha + \gamma_{-j} NBER_{t-j} + u_{t,j}$$

where ρ is the monthly excess return and NBER is the recession indicator published by the NBER. The mean and volatility equations were estimated jointly by GMM and the standard errors were calculated using the procedure suggested by Newey and West (1987). All coefficients have been multiplied by a factor of 100. Two sets of instruments were used. The first simply used the regressors as their own instrument while the second used lagged values of the dividend yield, one-month T-bill rate, monetary growth, default premium, growth of industrial production and growth in the Composite Index of Leading indicators. The Hausman test, explained in section 11.2.1.1, compares the GMM estimates based on the simultaneous and predetermined instruments. Under the null that the two set of parameters are identical the test statistic will be asymptotically normally distributed.

Lag of NBER recession indicator	Simultaneous instruments β^I_{-j}	Standard error	Lagged instruments β^{II}_{-j}	Standard error	Hausman test $Ho: \beta^I_{-j} = \beta^{II}_{-j}$	Simultaneous instruments γ^I_{-j}	Standard error	Lagged instruments γ^{II}_{-j}	Standard error	Hausman test $Ho: \gamma^I_{-j} = \gamma^{II}_{-j}$
-12	-1.399	(0.298)	-5.138	(0.943)	4.478	-0.357	(0.316)	0.846	(0.705)	-1.782
-11	-1.424	(0.427)	-4.835	(0.879)	4.183	-0.220	(0.315)	0.937	(0.648)	-2.039
-10	-1.541	(0.416)	-4.645	(0.824)	4.468	-0.046	(0.338)	1.035	(0.627)	-1.889
-9	-1.666	(0.394)	-4.443	(0.796)	4.254	0.142	(0.377)	1.120	(0.638)	-1.717
-8	-2.005	(0.432)	-4.184	(0.768)	3.643	0.157	(0.311)	1.202	(0.633)	-2.145
-7	-2.333	(0.449)	-4.022	(0.776)	3.059	0.504	(0.352)	1.354	(0.638)	-1.818
-6	-2.371	(0.628)	-3.715	(0.768)	2.577	0.805	(0.358)	1.268	(0.606)	-1.425
-5	-2.399	(0.431)	-3.502	(0.780)	1.706	0.988	(0.438)	1.274	(0.581)	-0.957
-4	-2.765	(0.368)	-3.179	(0.693)	0.890	1.178	(0.492)	1.138	(0.579)	-0.090
-3	-1.902	(0.482)	-2.831	(0.649)	2.167	1.405	(0.438)	1.679	(0.627)	-1.183
-2	-1.748	(0.466)	-2.137	(0.603)	0.802	1.546	(0.473)	1.869	(0.677)	-1.250
-1	-1.063	(0.560)	-1.200	(0.604)	0.214	2.159	(0.459)	2.179	(0.650)	-0.210
0	-0.352	(0.518)	-0.381	(0.574)	0.009	2.085	(0.464)	2.224	(0.661)	-0.477
1	0.301	(0.499)	0.433	(0.607)	-0.254	1.505	(0.611)	1.971	(0.671)	-1.476
2	0.985	(0.557)	0.702	(0.518)	0.487	0.969	(0.812)	1.580	(0.765)	-1.641
3	0.983	(0.515)	0.835	(0.481)	0.278	0.978	(0.817)	1.362	(0.716)	-1.037
4	1.239	(0.504)	1.159	(0.501)	0.136	0.893	(0.878)	1.232	(0.773)	-0.846
5	1.551	(0.486)	1.695	(0.525)	-0.306	0.665	(0.869)	0.896	(0.839)	-0.544
6	1.487	(0.515)	2.006	(0.535)	-1.011	0.733	(0.871)	0.661	(0.827)	0.106
7	1.513	(0.441)	2.369	(0.547)	-1.881	0.550	(0.867)	0.353	(0.757)	0.375
8	1.414	(0.402)	2.415	(0.619)	-2.005	0.591	(0.703)	0.397	(0.783)	0.213
9	1.503	(0.335)	2.170	(0.672)	-1.341	0.560	(0.608)	0.104	(0.742)	0.842
10	1.553	(0.464)	1.886	(0.680)	-0.686	0.283	(0.520)	-0.139	(0.671)	0.967
11	1.215	(0.426)	1.582	(0.648)	-0.799	0.046	(0.418)	-0.261	(0.623)	0.805
12	1.270	(0.479)	1.208	(0.684)	0.104	-0.252	(0.402)	-0.435	(0.569)	0.439

reach distinct low/high points at peaks/troughs of the business cycle, the peak in volatility roughly coincides with official recessions.

Part of the higher volatility in excess returns around recessions can be explained by variations in expected excess returns. In fact, computing expected returns according to the model which will be described in Section 11.3, we found a smooth build-up in the volatility of expected returns, a peak appearing for the period coinciding with official recessions. However, we also found that the residuals from the expected return equation still displayed a clear business cycle pattern.

11.2.4 Monte Carlo experiments

Monthly stock returns are characterized by conditional heteroscedasticity and outliers relative to the benchmark of a normal distribution. As a test of the robustness of the significance of our findings on the variation over the business cycle in the mean and volatility of excess returns, we performed Monte Carlo experiments to obtain the distribution of the $\{\beta_{-j}, \gamma_{-j}\}$ coefficient estimates for the differential mean and volatility of excess returns around turning points. Time paths of a recession indicator, I_t, were simulated based upon the following Markov switching process:

$$P(I_{t+1} = 1 \mid I_t = 1) = p$$
$$P(I_{t+1} = 0 \mid I_t = 1) = 1 - p$$
$$P(I_{t+1} = 0 \mid I_t = 0) = q$$
$$P(I_{t+1} = 1 \mid I_t = 0) = 1 - q \tag{11.4}$$

The initial state of the process was drawn using the steady state of the Markov process so that $P(I_t = 1) = (1 - q/2 - p - q)$, c.f. Cox and Miller (1965). This Markov switching process for I_t was chosen to account for the persistence of recessions. For the period 1954–1994 sample estimates of $p = 72/80$ and $q = 428/436$ were used in the simulations. Recessionary spells thus have an average length, $1/(1 - p)$, of 10 periods and the economy spends on average 16% of all periods in the recession state. Suppose the finding that excess returns tend to be systematically lower and more volatile during recessions is not really related to the stage of the business cycle but just a consequence of, say, the persistence and distribution of the returns data. Then we would expect to see estimates of β_{-j} and γ_{-j} in the simulations similar to the ones we obtained using the actual NBER indicator.

Table 11.2 shows results from this Monte Carlo experiment based on 1000 simulations. For each of the experiments we let the lag of the simulated indicator (j) go from -12 to 12 and report significance levels for the GMM estimates of

Table 11.2 *Significance levels for business cycle variation in the mean and volatility of excess returns. Bootstrap experiments*

The table shows significance levels of estimates of the mean and volatility parameters of monthly excess returns around recessionary periods of the economy as measured by leads and lags of the NBER recession indicator. The estimated equations were:

$$\rho_t = \mu + \beta_{-j} NBER_{t-j} + \varepsilon_{t,j} \qquad \sqrt{\pi/2}|\hat{\varepsilon}_{t,j}| = \alpha + \gamma_{-j} NBER_{t-j} + u_{t,j}$$

where ρ is the monthly excess return and NBER is the recession indicator published by the NBER. Recession indicators were generated randomly using the procedure described in section 11.4 and the excess return equation was re-estimated using GMM. For the mean parameters (β_{-j}), the p-values represent the minimum of the number of simulations producing values of β_{-j} above (for leads of the NBER indicator) or below (for lags of the NBER indicator) the originally estimated coefficients divided by the number of iterations (1000). For the volatility parameters (γ_{-j}) are p-values give the proportion of simulations producing a higher estimate of γ_{-j} than the estimate based on the actual NBER indicator.

Lag of NBER recession indicator	Sample 1954–1994				Sample 1926–1994			
	β_{-j}	p-value	γ_{-j}	p-value	β_{-j}	p-value	γ_{-j}	p-value
-12	-1.399	0.011	-0.357	0.304	-1.464	0.007	0.354	0.286
-11	-1.424	0.010	-0.220	0.402	-1.704	0.004	0.755	0.212
-10	-1.541	0.006	-0.046	0.487	-1.923	0.003	1.091	0.155
-9	-1.666	0.003	0.142	0.375	-2.181	0.000	1.245	0.130
-8	-2.005	0.002	0.157	0.370	-2.261	0.000	1.544	0.088
-7	-2.333	0.003	0.504	0.198	-2.273	0.000	1.969	0.044
-6	-2.371	0.002	0.805	0.095	-2.330	0.000	2.186	0.037
-5	-2.399	0.002	0.988	0.065	-2.471	0.001	2.443	0.024
-4	-2.765	0.001	1.178	0.032	-2.606	0.001	2.623	0.017
-3	-1.902	0.003	1.405	0.018	-2.343	0.000	2.992	0.010
-2	-1.748	0.002	1.546	0.007	-2.185	0.000	3.139	0.008
-1	-1.063	0.032	2.159	0.001	-2.025	0.000	3.531	0.003
0	0.352	0.264	2.085	0.001	-1.434	0.009	3.599	0.004
1	0.301	0.288	1.505	0.007	-0.639	0.113	3.526	0.003
2	0.985	0.044	0.969	0.058	-0.154	0.363	3.178	0.006
3	0.983	0.035	0.978	0.056	0.126	0.424	3.120	0.009
4	1.239	0.018	0.893	0.088	0.309	0.268	3.200	0.007
5	1.551	0.011	0.665	0.151	0.675	0.080	3.075	0.006
6	1.487	0.007	0.733	0.129	0.665	0.083	3.134	0.007
7	1.513	0.004	0.550	0.205	0.491	0.172	3.144	0.008
8	1.414	0.008	0.591	0.180	0.436	0.197	3.249	0.008
9	1.503	0.008	0.560	0.192	0.290	0.303	3.315	0.007
10	1.553	0.008	0.283	0.306	0.674	0.096	2.807	0.012
11	1.215	0.017	0.046	0.435	0.267	0.311	2.696	0.013
12	1.270	0.013	-0.252	0.360	0.427	0.196	2.525	0.014

β_{-j} and γ_{-j} from equation (11.3) based on the simulated recession indicator. The simulated significance levels confirm the findings reported in section 11.2.1: mean excess returns are significantly more negative around peaks of the business cycle and significantly more positive around troughs. Volatility of stock returns is also found to be significantly higher around recessions.

A particularly intuitive statistic concerning the significance of the variation in β_{-j} is the proportion of the simulations for which the maximum value of $\widehat{\beta}_{-j}$ (across all values of j) exceeds the maximum estimate obtained with the actual data. For the post-war and full sample, respectively, 5.2 and 49.4% of the simulations generated a maximum value of $\widehat{\beta}_{-j}$ higher than the estimates based on the actual recession indicator. The proportion of simulations generating a value of $\widehat{\beta}_{-j}$ smaller than the estimated minimum value was 0.7 of a per cent for 1954–1994 and 0.2 of a per cent for 1926–1994. In the case of the simulated maximum and minimum statistics for the volatility parameter, the probability value of the maximum volatility estimate was less than 2% for both samples.

11.3 BUSINESS CYCLE VARIATION IN THE CONDITIONAL DISTRIBUTION OF STOCK RETURNS

It is common in studies on the predictability of stock returns to specify the conditional mean of excess returns as a simple linear function of a vector of factors publicly known at the time of the prediction ($\mathbf{X}_{t-1}$) and most of which have an important business cycle component:

$$\rho_t = \beta' \mathbf{X}_{t-1} + \varepsilon_t \tag{11.5}$$

In this section we perform a simple test of whether the coefficients of the factors in the excess return equation vary with the state of the business cycle.

We follow standard practice and obtain an estimate of the expected excess returns according to a simple linear, constant-coefficients model linking excess returns to four commonly used instruments, namely the dividend yield, a one-month T-bill rate, a default premium and the change in the monetary base. The dividend yield variable (*YIELD*) was derived from the value-weighted NYSE returns with and without dividends, and a one-month T-bill rate (*I1*) was obtained from the Fama–Bliss risk-free rates file, in both cases using the CRSP tapes as our data source. The default premium (*DEF*) was defined as the difference between the continuously compounded monthly yields on portfolios of BAA-rated and AAA-rated bonds, both obtained from the Citibase tapes. Finally the monetary base (*M*) used in this study is the series provided by the St Louis Federal Reserve Bank and also available from Citibase. As our measure of monetary growth we used the 12-month rate of change in the monetary base, defined as $\Delta M_t = \log(M_t/M_{t-12})$. Thus the regression equation used to obtain an estimate of expected excess returns was

$$\rho_t = \mu + \gamma_1\,YIELD_{t-1} + \gamma_2 I1_{t-1} + \gamma_3\Delta M_{t-2} + \gamma_4\,DEF_{t-1} + \varepsilon_t \quad (11.6)$$

where the lags reflect publication delays in the time series. For the sample period 1954–1994 we obtained the least-squares estimates reported in the 'full sample' columns in Table 11.3. The coefficient of the one-month T-bill rate is strongly negative, while the coefficients of the dividend yield, monetary growth and the default premium are all positive. The $\bar{R}^2$ for the full sample regression is 0.08. All these results are in line with findings reported in the literature.

As a simple test of whether the conditional distribution of excess returns given these factors is constant over the business cycle, we estimated equation (11.6)

Table 11.3   *Least-squares estimates for excess return and volatility equations (1954–1994)*

$$\rho_t = \mu + \gamma_1\,YIELD_{t-1} + \gamma_2 I1_{t-1} + \gamma_3\Delta M_{t-2} + \gamma_4\,DEF_{t-1} + \varepsilon_t$$

ρ is the monthly excess return, *YIELD* is the dividend yield, *I1* is the one-month T-bill, *DEF* is the default premium, ΔM is the rate of growth of the monetary base and *V* is the measure of volatility based on daily returns data. Standard errors were calculated using the procedure suggested by Newey and West (1987).

	Estimate	S. Error	Estimate	S. Error	Estimate	S. Error
μ	−0.029	(0.008)	−0.047	(0.022)	−0.022	(0.007)
$YIELD_{t-1}$	1.005	(0.150)	1.143	(0.492)	0.885	(0.138)
$I1_{t-1}$	−6.630	(0.650)	−12.717	(1.747)	−4.319	(0.626)
ΔM_{t-2}	0.109	(0.057)	0.602	(0.133)	0.010	(0.059)
DEF_{t-1}	20.736	(3.368)	39.137	(9.940)	13.441	(3.513)
Adjusted R-squared		0.082		0.249		0.039
S.E.		0.002		0.002		0.001
Observations		492		80		412

$$V_t = \mu + \gamma_1 YIELD_{t-1} + \gamma_2 I1_{t-1} + \gamma_3\Delta M_{t-2} + \gamma_4 DEF_{t-1} + \sum_{i=1}^{3}\gamma_{4+i}V_{t-i} + \varepsilon_t$$

	Full sample		Recession		Expansion	
	Estimate	S. Error	Estimate	S. Error	Estimate	S. Error
μ	0.002	(0.001)	0.003	(0.002)	0.022	(0.001)
$YIELD_{t-1}$	0.016	(0.016)	0.024	(0.045)	0.025	(0.021)
$I1_{t-1}$	0.177	(0.087)	0.134	(0.176)	0.058	(0.067)
ΔM_{t-2}	−0.002	(0.003)	0.029	(0.018)	0.001	(0.004)
DEF_{t-1}	0.017	(0.588)	−0.935	(1.032)	0.357	(0.504)
V_{t-1}	0.358	(0.077)	0.407	(0.097)	0.303	(0.054)
V_{t-2}	0.138	(0.036)	0.119	(0.090)	0.117	(0.040)
V_{t-3}	0.059	(0.045)	−0.092	(0.080)	0.068	(0.047)
Adjusted R-squared		0.265		0.333		0.188
S.E. ($\times 1000$)		0.009		0.009		0.009
Observations		492		80		412

separately for recession and expansion months. The results, reported in Table 11.3 in the columns labelled 'recession' and 'expansion', indicate that the regression coefficients vary with the state of the economy: during recessions the coefficients of the lagged T-bill rate, monetary growth and default premium variables are much larger in absolute value than during expansions. They also obtain higher *t*-statistics during recessions, despite the much smaller sample used to estimate the regression for recessions (80 observations versus 412 for expansions). An *F*-test of the hypothesis that the coefficients of the included factors are identical during expansions and recessions produced a *p*-value of 0.015, rejecting the null at conventional levels. Note that the $\bar{R}^2$ of the recession regression is 0.25 while it is only 0.04 for the expansion regression. Stock returns seem to be driven more by time-varying expected returns during the more volatile recessions than during expansions.

11.3.1   Negative expected excess returns around peaks of the business cycle

The results in Table 11.3 suggest that the standard linear time-invariant model for the conditional mean of excess returns is misspecified. To get a measure of the potential economic and statistical significance of such misspecification, we conducted an experiment comparing recursive predictions from the simple linear model (11.6) to recursive predictions from a model which assumes that agents fit separate linear models to recessions and expansions. Forecasts from the second (mixing) model were computed as the weighted averages of the forecasts from the recession and expansion regressions using as weights the *ex-ante* forecasts of the probability of being in a recession next period obtained from the logit model in section 11.2.2, now computed recursively. For the period 1970–1994 Figure 11.2 plots these recursive one-step-ahead predictions surrounded by bands of plus-minus two recursive standard errors. Also shown in square blocks is the contemporaneous value of the NBER recession indicator. First, consider the forecasts from the simple linear model (11.6). For this model Figure 11.2 shows that predicted excess returns often become negative in the late expansion/early recession stages of the business cycle. Negative expected excess returns are also apparent from Figure 11.1 in Whitelaw (1994), the new observation here being that these are statistically significant in 17% of the sample months, clustered in time and appear to be systematically linked to the state of the business cycle. As noted by Fama and French (1988), who did not find a single prediction of a significantly negative value of nominal stock returns in their study, negative expected stock returns are difficult to explain in the context of a general equilibrium model with risk averse investors. Although the result of negative expected *excess* returns is a slightly weaker finding,

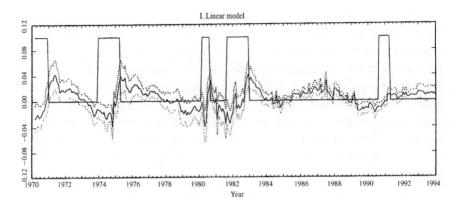

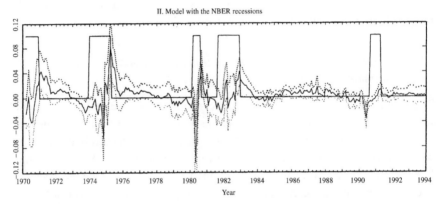

Note: The linear model predicts excess returns by means of a constant and lagged values of the dividend yield, one-month T-bill rate, a default premium and growth in the monetary base. The mixing model uses the same regressors in separate regressions for recession and expansion periods and weights the recursive forecasts by the *ex-ante* estimated probability of being in a recession (expansion) state next period. Around the graphs are drawn plus-minus two standard error bands.

Figure 11.2　*Recursive one-step-ahead predictions from the linear model and the mixing model*

it would still appear to contradict notions of general equilibrium indicating, perhaps, that the simple linear model is misspecified.

A more detailed analysis revealed that the predictions of negative excess returns based on (11.6) are driven by the inclusion of the one-month interest rate and, to a lesser extent, the default premium. Both of these are standard regressors commonly used in the finance literature to predict stock returns. Thus if (11.6) is misspecified, this has strong bearings on the interpretation of many of the existing studies on predictability of stock returns. To see the importance of accounting for the business cycle asymmetry in the excess return equation, consider the recursive predictions from the mixing model in the lower part of Figure 11.2. As one would expect from the parameter estimates in Table 11.3, the predictions generated by the mixing model display more variability than those from the linear model, particularly around recessions.

However, the mixing model also accounts for the much larger standard error of the predictions around recessions and hence fewer of the negative predictions–5% of the total sample–around recessions are statistically significant. This compares with 17% from the simple linear model and suggests that almost all the significantly negative predictions from the linear model can be explained by the use of a misspecified regression model which fails to account for the asymmetry in the return model.[10] By all accounts, the difference between the predictions from the linear and mixing models are very large in economic terms, varying from −6.5 to 4.9% per month. Furthermore, the range for the recursive predictions generated by the linear model, going from −3.98 to 4.22 per month, was less than half the range generated by the mixing model (from −10.22 to 8.22% per month).

11.4 CONCLUSION

Asymmetries linked to turning points of the business cycle appear to be important for understanding the first and second moments of stock returns and for modelling the conditional distribution of monthly stock returns. Our analysis identifies separate peak and trough effects in mean excess returns and quantifies the increase in mean stock returns during recessions. Regression coefficients in the excess return equation of a one-month T-bill rate, monetary growth, and a default premium all appear to depend on the state of the business cycle. Unsurprisingly, the misspecification of the conditional mean of stock returns caused by a failure to account for such asymmetries was shown to be economically and statistically important. Furthermore, the peak in the volatility of monthly stock returns coincides with official recession periods and there is substantial variation in volatility over the economic cycle. These findings are all important to investment strategies aimed at controlling market risk. Such strategies depend mainly on the first and second conditional moments of market returns and hence a proper understanding of systematic patterns in these moments is important. A long-term investor would be well advised to account for predictable components in stock returns during recessions, but would also have to consider the substantially higher volatility associated with holding stocks during recessions.

REFERENCES

Balvers, Ronald J., Cosimano, Thomas F. and McDonald, Bill (1990) Predicting stock returns in an efficient market. *Journal of Finance*, **45**, 1109–1128.
Breen, William, Glosten, Lawrence R. and Jagannathan, Ravi (1990) Predictable variations in stock index returns. *Journal of Finance*, **44**, 1177–1189.

Campbell, John Y. (1987) Stock returns and the term structure, *Journal of Financial Economics*, **18**, 373–399.

Chen, N. (1991) Financial investment opportunities and the macroeconomy, *Journal of Finance*, **46**, 529–554.

Cox, David R. and Miller, H.D. (1965) *The Theory of Stochastic Processes*, Chapman and Hall, London.

Fama, Eugene F. and French, Kenneth R. (1988) Dividend yields and expected stock returns, *Journal of Financial Economics*, **22**, 3–27.

Fama, Eugene F. and French, Kenneth R. (1989) Business conditions and expected returns on stocks and bonds, *Journal of Financial Economics*, **25**, 23–49.

Fama, Eugene F. and Schwert, G. William (1977) Asset returns and inflation, *Journal of Financial Economics*, **5**, 115–146.

Ferson, Wayne E. (1989) Changes in expected security returns, risk, and the level of interest rates, *Journal of Finance*, **44**, 1191–1217.

Ferson, Wayne E. and Harvey, Campbell R. (1991) The variation of economic risk premiums, *Journal of Political Economy*, **99**, 385–415.

Ferson, Wayne E. and Merrick, John J. (1987) Non-stationarity and stage-of-the-business-cycle effects in consumption-based asset pricing relations, *Journal of Financial Economics*, **18**, 127–146.

Glosten, Lawrence R., Jagannathan, Ravi and Runkle, David E. (1993) On the relation between the expected value and the volatility of the nominal excess return on stocks, *Journal of Finance*, **48**, 1779–1802.

Hamilton, James D. and Lin, Gang (1996) Stock market volatility and the business cycle, *Journal of Applied Econometrics*, **11**, 573–593.

Hansen, Lars Peter (1982) Large sample properties of generalized method-of-moments estimators, *Econometrica*, **50**, 1029–1054.

Harvey, Campbell (1991) The specification of conditional expectations, working paper, Fuqua School of Business, Duke University.

Hayashi, Fumio and Sims, Christopher (1983) Nearly efficient estimation of time series models with predetermined, but not exogenous, instruments, *Econometrica*, **51**, 783–798.

Merton, Robert C. (1980) On estimating the expected return on the market: an exploratory investigation, *Journal of Financial Economics*, **8**, 323–361.

Mishkin, Frederick S. (1992) *The Economics of Money, Banking, and Financial Markets*, 3rd ed., Harper Collins Publishers, New York.

Moore, G. (1983) (ed.) *Business Cycles, Inflation and Forecasting*, 2nd ed., NBER/Ballinger Publ. Co., Cambridge M.T.

Nakamura, Alice and Nakamura, Masao (1981) On the relationships among several specification error tests presented by Durbin, Wu, and Hausman, *Econometrica*, **49**, 1583–1588.

Newey, Whitney K. and West, Kenneth D. (1987) A simple, positive semi-definite, heteroscedasticity and autocorrelation consistent covariance matrix, *Econometrica*, **55**, 703–708.

Pesaran, M. Hashem and Timmermann, Allan (1995) Predictability of stock returns: robustness and economic significance, *Journal of Finance*, **50**, 1201–1228.

Schwert, G. William (1989) Why does stock market volatility change over time, *Journal of Finance*, **45**, 1115–1153.

Whitelaw, Robert F. (1994) Time variations and covariations in the expectation and volatility of stock market returns, *Journal of Finance*, **49**, 515–542.

NOTES

1. See, e.g., Balvers, Cosimano and McDonald (1990), Breen, Glosten and Jagannathan (1990), Campbell (1987), Chen (1991), Fama and French (1988, 1989), Fama and Schwert (1977), Ferson (1989), Ferson and Harvey (1991), Ferson and Merrick (1987), Glosten, Jagannathan, and Runkle (1993), Pesaran and Timmermann (1995), Whitelaw (1994).

2. This can best be seen by considering the least-squares estimator of the simple linear equation (11.1) which is given by

$$
\begin{pmatrix} \widehat{\mu} \\ \widehat{\beta}_{-j} \end{pmatrix} = \begin{pmatrix} \dfrac{\sum\limits_{t=1}^{T} \rho_t (1 - NBER_{t-j})}{T - \sum\limits_{t=1}^{T} NBER_{t-j}} \\[2em] \dfrac{\sum\limits_{t=1}^{T} \rho_t\, NBER_{t-j}}{\sum\limits_{t=1}^{T} NBER_{t-j}} - \dfrac{\sum\limits_{t=1}^{T} \rho_t (1 - NBER_{t-j})}{T - \sum\limits_{t=1}^{T} NBER_{t-j}} \end{pmatrix}
$$

Clearly $\widehat{\beta}_{-j}$ measures the difference in mean returns during recessions relative to non-recession periods.

3. Throughout the analysis, Bartlett weights and a window length of 20 were used to calculate the standard errors. The results were found to be robust with respect to changes in the window length.

4. During the post-war sample the average length of a recession is 10 months, so the recession window at a lead of four months covers the four months prior to the official start of the recession, the initial month, and the five months after the beginning of the recession.

5. The *slope* of the graph in Figure 11.1 provides information about mean returns for specific months since, at a lead of j months, the slope measures the difference between the mean excess return j months prior to a recession relative to its value j months prior to an expansion.

6. This may also explain why Ferson and Merrick (1987), in their study of the significance of the contemporaneous value of the NBER indicator in regressions of a short T-bill rate on lagged instruments, obtained a significant coefficient for the recession indicator only for one out of four samples.

7. Logit specifications were used in these regressions because of the binary form of the NBER indicator.

8. For even longer leads of the NBER indicator, the GMM estimates of β_{-j} based on the instruments $\mathbf{Z}_t^*$ were close to zero while the estimates based on the predetermined instruments kept on decreasing, reaching implausibly large negative values. This strengthens our interpretation that, at such long leads, the difference between GMM estimates based on the two sets of instruments is due to the low correlation between the NBER indicator and the predetermined instruments.

9. The potential bias in the least squares estimator of β_{-j} in equation (11.1) is also well understood from the literature on estimation of rational expectations models with unobserved expectations. Equation (11.1) can be rewritten

$$\rho_t = \mu + \beta_{-j}\widehat{NBER}_{t-j} + \beta_{-j}(NBER_{t-j} - \widehat{NBER}_{t-j}) + \varepsilon_{t,j} \qquad (11.1')$$

where $\widehat{NBER}_{t-j}$ is agents' (unobserved) forecast of $NBER_{t-j}$ based on information available at time $t-1$. Using the actual value of NBER in place of its unobserved expectation induces a potential bias in the least-squares estimator of β_{-j} for leads of the NBER indicator and also generates a moving average component of order $(|j| - 1)$ in the residuals of (11.1'). Hayashi and Sims (1983) devise a procedure for overcoming this problem. First, a forward filter is applied to the dependent variable, the regressor and the residuals (but not to the instruments) in (11.1) to transform the data into a form with a diagonal covariance matrix. In the second step instrumental variables estimation is applied to the filtered data to get consistent estimates of β_{-j}. When applied to our data this estimation procedure gave results very similar to those based on the GMM estimator using predetermined instruments.

10. This conclusion is consistent with the study by Harvey (1991) which compares non-parametric and parametric models for expected returns.

Chapter 12

Long memory in stochastic volatility

ANDREW C. HARVEY*

SUMMARY

A long memory stochastic volatility model is proposed. Its dynamic properties are derived and shown to be consistent with empical findings reported in the literature on stock returns. Ways in which the model may be estimated are discussed and it is shown how estimates of the underlying variance may be constructed and predictions made. The model is parsimonious and appears to be a viable alternative to the A-PARCH class proposed by Ding, Granger and Engle (1993) and the FIEGARCH class of Bollerslev and Mikkelsen (1996).

12.1 INTRODUCTION

It is now well established that while financial variables such as stock returns are serially uncorrelated over time, their squares are not. The most common way of modelling this serial correlation in volatility is by means of the GARCH class, introduced by Engle (1982) and Bollerslev (1986), in which it is assumed that the conditional variance of the observations is an exact function of the squares of past observations; see the review by Bollerslev, Chou and Kroner (1992).

The article by Ding, Granger and Engle (1993) analyses the Standard and Poor's 500 stock market daily closing index from 3 January, 1928 to 30 August 1991 and draws attention to two important features. The first is that when the absolute values of stock returns are raised to a power, c, the autocorrelations seem to be highest for values of c around 0.75. The second is that the positive autocorrelations continue to persist for very high lags. This suggests that the conditional variance of stock returns may have a longer memory than is typically

* Faculty of Economics and Politics, University of Cambridge, Sidgwick Avenue, Cambridge CB3 9DD.

captured by a GARCH model and that modelling the conditional variance in terms of squares may be unduly restrictive. They therefore propose the following generalization of GARCH:

$$y_t = \sigma_t \varepsilon_t, \quad \varepsilon_t \sim \text{IID}(0, 1), \quad t = 1, \dots, T \tag{12.1}$$

where

$$\sigma_t^\delta = \alpha_0 + \sum_{1=1}^{p} \alpha_i (|y_{t-i}| - \gamma_i y_{t-i})^\delta + \sum_{j=1}^{q} \beta_j \sigma_{t-i}^\delta \tag{12.2}$$

and $\alpha_0 > 0$, $\delta > 0$, $\alpha_i \geq 0$, $i = 1, \dots, p$, $\beta_j \geq 0$, $j = 1, \dots, q$ and $|\gamma_i| < 1$, $i = 1, \dots, p$. They call this an Asymmetric Power ARCH model, or A-PARCH. When the γ_i's are zero, this reduces to a standard GARCH model when $\delta = 2$ and to the variant of the GARCH model proposed by Taylor (1986) when $d = 1$. When the α_i's and β_i's sum to one, the model is no longer covariance stationary, and is said to be persistent. Non-zero γ_i's allow asymmetric effects of the kind captured by the EGARCH model of Nelson (1991). They fit the model to stock returns by maximum likelihood (ML), assuming ε_t to be normally distributed, choosing $p = q = 1$ and estimating δ to be 1.43.

Baillie, Bollerslev and Mikkelsen (1996) propose a different way of extending the GARCH class to account for long memory. They call their models Fractionally Integrated GARCH (FIGARCH), and the key feature is the inclusion of the fractional difference operator, $(1 - L)^d$, where L is the lag operator, in the lag structure of past squared observations in the conditional variance equation. However, this model can only be stationary when $d = 0$ and it reduces to GARCH. In a later paper, Bollerslev and Mikkelsen (1996) consider a generalization of the EGARCH model of Nelson (1991) in which $\log \sigma_t^2$ is modelled as a distributed lag of past ε_t's involving the fractional difference operator. This FIEGARCH model is stationary and invertible if $|d| < 0.5$.

An alternative way of modelling movements in volatility is to assume that the logarithm of σ_t^2 in (12.1) is generated by a linear stochastic process, such as a first-order autoregression (AR(1)). Thus

$$\sigma_t^2 = \sigma^2 \exp(h_t) \tag{12.3}$$

where

$$h_{t+1} = \phi h_t + \eta_t, \quad \eta_t \sim \text{NID}(0, \sigma_\eta^2), \quad 0 \leq \phi \leq 1 \tag{12.4}$$

where σ^2 is a scale factor, ϕ is a parameter, and η_t is a disturbance term which may or may not be correlated with ε_t. This *stochastic volatility* (SV) model has been studied by a number of researchers, including Taylor (1986), Harvey, Ruiz and Shephard (1994), Melino and Turnbull (1990) and Jacquier, Polson and Rossi (1994). It has two attractions. The first is that it is the natural discrete time analogue of the continuous time model used in work on option pricing; see Hull and White (1987). The second is that its statistical properties are easy to determine. The disadvantage with respect to the conditional variance models of the GARCH class is that exact maximum likelihood can only be carried out by a computer intensive technique such as that described in Kim, Shephard and Chib (1998) or Sandmann and Koopman (1998). However, a quasi-maximum likelihood (QML) method is relatively easy to apply and, even though it is not efficient, it provides a reasonable alternative if the sample size is not too small. This method is based on transforming the observations to give

$$\log y_t^2 = \kappa + h_t + \xi_t, \quad t = 1, \ldots, T \tag{12.5}$$

where

$$\xi_t = \log \varepsilon_t^2 - E(\log \varepsilon_t^2)$$

and

$$\kappa = \log \sigma^2 + E(\log \varepsilon_t^2) \tag{12.6}$$

As shown in Harvey, Ruiz and Shephard (1994), the statespace form given by equations (12.4) and (12.5) provides the basis for QML estimation via the Kalman filter and also enables smoothed estimates of the variance component, h_t, to be constructed and predictions made.

Most of the applications of the SV model have found ϕ close to one. In such cases the fit is similar to that of a GARCH(1,1) model with the sum of the co-efficients close to one. Similarly when ϕ is one, so that h_t is a random walk, the fit is similar to that of the simple IGARCH(1,1) model. Taken together with the evidence on the slowness with which the correlogram of squared observations dies away to zero, this suggests that it is worth exploring long memory models[1] for h_t. In particular, we might take h_t to be generated by fractional noise

$$h_t = \eta_t/(1 - L)^d, \quad \eta_t \sim \mathrm{NID}(0, \sigma_\eta^2), 0 \le d \le 1 \tag{12.7}$$

Like the AR(1) model in (12.4), this process reduces to white noise and a random walk at the boundary of the parameter space, that is $d = 0$ and 1, respectively. However, it is only stationary if $d < 0.5$. Thus the transition from stationarity to non-stationarity proceeds in a different way to the AR(1). As in (12.4) it is reasonable to constrain the autocorrelations in (12.7) to be positive. However, a negative value of d is quite legitimate and indeed differencing h_t when it is non-stationary gives a stationary 'intermediate memory' process in which $-0.5 \le d \le 0$.

The properties of the fractional noise in (12.7) have been studied extensively in the statistical literature, and in section 12.2 it is shown how these properties can be used to determine the dynamic characteristics of $|y_t|^c$. This provides some interesting insights into the stylized facts reported in Ding, Granger and Engle (1993) and Bollerslev and Mikkelsen (1996). Sections 12.3 and 12.4 discuss how to estimate the model by QML and how to carry out signal extraction and prediction. The difficulty here is that the statespace form is cumbersome to apply and is only approximate. The viability of the procedures examined is illustrated with an application involving exchange rates. Section 12.5 considers some extensions, such as the inclusion of explanatory variables.

12.2 DYNAMIC PROPERTIES

The properties of the long memory SV model are as follows. First, as in the autoregressive-stochastic volatility (AR-SV) model, y_t is a martingale difference. Second, stationarity of h_t implies stationarity of y_t, and in this case it follows from the properties of the lognormal distribution that the variance of y_t is given by

$$\text{Var}(y_t) = \sigma^2 \exp(\sigma_h^2/2) \tag{12.8}$$

where σ_h^2 is the variance of h_t, that is

$$\sigma_h^2 = \sigma_\eta^2 \Gamma(1 - 2d)/\{\Gamma(1 - d)\}^2, \quad d < 0.5$$

The kurtosis is $\kappa \exp(\sigma_h^2)$, where κ is the kurtosis of ε_t.

If we assume that the disturbances ε_t and η_t are mutually independent, the autocorrelation function (ACF) of the absolute values of the observations raised to the power c is given by

$$\rho_c(\tau) = \frac{\exp\left(\dfrac{c^2}{4}\sigma_h^2 \rho_\tau\right) - 1}{\kappa_c \exp\left(\dfrac{c^2}{4}\sigma_h^2\right) - 1}, \quad \tau \geq 1 \tag{12.9}$$

where κ_c is

$$\kappa_c = E(|\varepsilon_t|^{2c})/\{E(|\varepsilon_t|^c)\}^2 \tag{12.10}$$

where ρ_τ, $\tau = 0, 1, 2, \ldots$ denotes the ACF of h_t. Taylor (1986, p. 75) gives this expression for c equal to one and two and ε_t normally distributed. When $c = 2$, κ_c is the kurtosis and this is three for a normal distribution. More generally, using formulae given in the appendix

$$\kappa_c = \Gamma\left(c + \frac{1}{2}\right)\Gamma\left(\frac{1}{2}\right) \Bigg/ \left\{\Gamma\left(\frac{c}{2} + \frac{1}{2}\right)\right\}^2$$

Assuming it exists, expression (12.10) may be evaluated for other distributions including Student-t and the general error distribution. For the t-distribution

$$\kappa_c = \frac{\Gamma\left(c + \frac{1}{2}\right)\Gamma\left(-c + \frac{v}{2}\right)\Gamma\left(\frac{1}{2}\right)\Gamma\left(\frac{v}{2}\right)}{\left\{\Gamma\left(\frac{c}{2} + \frac{1}{2}\right)\Gamma\left(-\frac{c}{2} + \frac{v}{2}\right)\right\}^2}, \quad |c| < v/2 \tag{12.11}$$

Note that v must be at least five if c is two.

The ACF, $\rho_c(\tau)$, has the following features. First, if σ_h^2 is small and/or ρ_τ is close to one:

$$\rho_c(\tau) \simeq \rho_\tau \frac{\exp\left(\frac{c^2}{4}\sigma_h^2\right) - 1}{\kappa_c \exp\left(\frac{c^2}{4}\sigma_h^2\right) - 1}, \quad \tau \geq 1 \tag{12.12}$$

compare Taylor (1994). Thus the shape of the ACF of h_t is approximately carried over to $\rho_c(\tau)$ except that it is multiplied by a factor of proportionality, which must be less than one as κ_c is greater than one if the variance of ε_t is positive. Second, for the t-distribution, κ_c declines as v goes to infinity. Thus $\rho_c(\tau)$ is a maximum for a normal distribution. On the other hand, a distribution with less kurtosis than the normal will give rise to higher values of $\rho_c(\tau)$.

Although (12.9) gives an explicit relationship between $\rho_c(\tau)$ and c, it does not appear possible to make any general statements regarding $\rho_c(\tau)$ being maximized for certain values of c. Indeed different values of σ_h^2 lead to different values of c maximizing $\rho_c(\tau)$ with higher values of σ_h^2 associated with lower maximizing values of c. It is important to note that (12.9) does not depend on the kind of volatility process in the model, so long memory is irrelevant, except insofar as it may be associated with high values of σ_h^2. If σ_h^2 is chosen so as to give values of $\rho_c(\tau)$ of a similar size to those reported in Ding, Granger and Engle (1993, p. 89) then the maximum appears to be attained for c slightly less than one. Figure 12.1 shows the relationship between c and $\rho_c(\tau)$ for $\sigma_h^2 = 2$ and ε_t assumed to be normal. The top curve is for $\tau = 1$ while the bottom one is for $\tau = 10$, the values of ρ_1 and ρ_{10} having been set to 0.82 and 0.65, respectively, which happen to correspond to a long memory SV process with $d = 0.45$. The shape is similar to the empirical relationships reported in Ding, Granger and Engle (1993). They do not derive a theoretical expression for the ACF in the PARCH model. It should be noted that a value of σ_h^2 equal to two is much higher than the variances which are typically reported in AR-SV models; see, for example, Jacquier, Polson, and Rossi (1994). If σ_h^2 is set to 0.5, then $\rho_c(\tau)$ is maximized for c between 1.2 and 1.4 when ρ_τ is between 0.8 and 0.99; the values of $\rho_c(\tau)$ are about half the size of those obtained with $\sigma_h^2 = 2$.

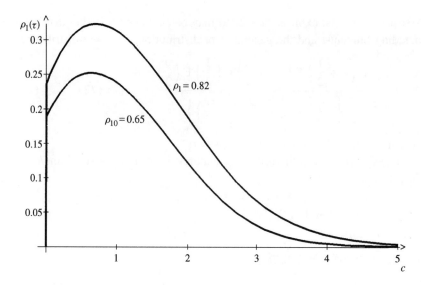

Figure 12.1 *ACF of $|y_t|^c$ against c*

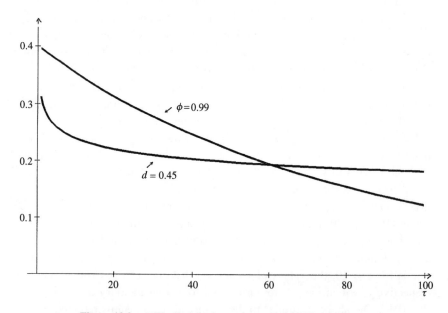

Figure 12.2 *ACF of $|y_t|$ for long memory and AR(1) volatility*

Figure 12.2 compares $\rho_1(\tau)$ for h_t following a long memory process with $d = 0.45$ and $\sigma_h^2 = 2$ with the corresponding ACF when h_t is AR(1) with $\phi = 0.99$. The slower decline in the long memory model is very clear and, in fact, for $\tau = 1000$, the long memory autocorrelation is still 0.14, whereas in the AR case it is only 0.000013. The long memory shape closely matches that in Ding, Granger and Engle (1993, pp. 86–88).

Finally note that the dynamic structure of the SV model also appears in the ACF of log y_t^2, denoted $\rho_{\log}(\tau)$. It is straightforward to see from (12.5) that

$$\rho_{\log}(\tau) = \rho_\tau / \{1 + \sigma_\xi^2 / \sigma_h^2\} \tag{12.13}$$

where σ_ξ^2 is the variance of log ε_t^2; this variance can be evaluated for normal, t, and general error distributions as shown in Harvey, Ruiz and Shephard (1994). Thus as in (12.12), $\rho_c(\tau)$ is proportional to ρ_τ, but in the case of (12.13) the relationship is exact. Furthermore, it holds even if ε_t and η_t are correlated, since as shown in Harvey, Ruiz and Shephard, log ε_t^2 and η_t are uncorrelated if the joint distribution of ε_t and η_t is symmetric.

12.3   ESTIMATION AND TESTING

For a long memory SV model, QML estimation in the time domain becomes relatively less attractive because the statespace form (SSF) can only be used by expressing h_t as an autoregressive or moving average process and truncating at a suitably high lag. Thus the approach is cumbersome, though the initial state covariance matrix is easily constructed, and the truncation does not affect the asymptotic properties of the estimators. An exact ML approach based on simulation is also possible in principle. If the SSF is not used, time domain QML requires the repeated construction and inversion of the $T \times T$ covariance matrix of the log y_t^2's; see section 12.4 and Sowell (1992). On the other hand, QML estimation in the frequency domain is no more difficult than it is in the AR-SV case. Cheung and Diebold (1993) present simulation evidence which suggests that although time domain estimation is more efficient in small samples, the difference is less marked when a mean has to be estimated.

The frequency domain (quasi) log-likelihood function is, neglecting constants,

$$\log L = -\frac{1}{2} \sum_{j=1}^{T-1} \log g_j - \pi \sum_{j=1}^{T-1} \frac{I(\lambda_j)}{g_j} \tag{12.14}$$

where $I(\lambda_j)$ is the sample spectrum of the log y_t^2's and g_j is the spectral generating function (SGF), which for (12.5) is

$$g_j = \sigma_\eta^2 [2(1 - \cos \lambda_j)]^{-d} + \sigma_\xi^2$$

Note that the summation in (12.14) is from $j = 1$ rather than $j = 0$. This is because g_0 cannot be evaluated for positive d. However, the omission of the zero frequency does remove the mean. The unknown parameters are σ_η^2, σ_ξ^2 and d, but if σ_ξ^2 may be concentrated out of the likelihood function by a reparameterization in which σ_η^2 is replaced by the signal-noise ratio $q = \sigma_\eta^2/\sigma_\xi^2$. On the other hand, if a distribution is assumed for ε_t, then σ_ξ^2 is known.

When d lies between 0.5 and one, h_t is non-stationary, but differencing the log y_t^2's yields a zero mean stationary process, the SGF of which is

$$g_j = \sigma_\eta^2[2(1 - \cos\lambda_j)]^{1-d} + 2(1 - \cos\lambda_j)\sigma_\xi^2$$

This quasi-likelihood is not directly comparable with the one for stationary log y_t^2's. Nevertheless if separate maximization is carried out, it is usually apparent that one is preferable, because the other tends to reach a maximum at $d = 0.5$. An alternative approach is to transform the observations by half-differencing, $(1 - L)^{1/2}$, as suggested by Robinson (1994). This yields a stationary process except when the original d is one. Note that half-differencing is based on an autoregressive expansion which must be truncated at some point.

Example

Harvey, Ruiz and Shephard (1994) fitted the AR-SV model to data on the first differences of the logarithms of daily exchange rates over the period 1 October 1981 to 28 June 1985. The estimates of ϕ were all close to zero and it was observed that unit root tests are unreliable in this situation because the reduced form for the differenced log y_t^2's is close to being non-invertible. Estimating the long memory SV model for the dollar–Deutschemark rate using the frequency domain method described above, and assuming ε_t to be normally distributed, gave $\tilde{\sigma}_\eta^2 = 0.04$ and $\tilde{d} = 0.868$.

12.4 SIGNAL EXTRACTION AND PREDICTION

In the AR-SV model, the minimum mean square linear estimator (MMSLE) of h_t based on the full sample can be calculated easily using a statespace smoothing algorithm. An estimator of the corresponding σ_t^2 can then be formed. Predictions of future volatility can be made in a similar fashion; see Harvey and Shephard (1993). For the long memory SV model, the statespace approach is approximate because of the truncation involved and is relatively cumbersome because of the length of the state vector.

Exact smoothing can be carried out by a direct approach based on equation (12.5), which can be written in matrix notation as

$$\mathbf{w} = \kappa\mathbf{i} + \mathbf{h} + \xi \tag{12.15}$$

where $\mathbf{w}$ is a $T \times 1$ vector containing the observations, the log y_t^2's, and i is a $T \times 1$ vector of ones. Suppose that h_t is stationary. If $\mathbf{V}_h$ and $\mathbf{V}_\xi$ denote the covariance matrices of h_t and ξ_t, respectively, and h_t and ξ_t are uncorrelated, the covariance matrix of the observations is $\mathbf{V} = \mathbf{V}_h + \mathbf{V}_\xi$. The MMSLE of h_t

is then

$$\tilde{\mathbf{h}} = \mathbf{V}_h \mathbf{V}^{-1}(\mathbf{w} - \kappa \mathbf{i}) + \kappa \mathbf{i} = \mathbf{V}_h \mathbf{V}^{-1}\mathbf{w} + (\mathbf{I} - \mathbf{V}_h \mathbf{V}^{-1})\mathbf{i}\kappa \qquad (12.16)$$

The ijth element of $\mathbf{V}_h$ is $\sigma_\eta^2 \rho_\tau$ where $\tau = |i - j|$ and ρ_τ is obtained recursively as

$$\rho_\tau = \{(\tau - 1 + d)/(\tau - d)\}\rho_{\tau-1},$$

$$\tau = 1, 2, 3, \ldots$$

The ξ_t's are serially uncorrelated, $\mathbf{V}_\varepsilon = \sigma_\xi^2 \mathbf{I}$ and so

$$\tilde{\mathbf{h}} = (\mathbf{I} - \sigma_\xi^2 \mathbf{V}^{-1})\mathbf{w} + \sigma_\xi^2 \mathbf{V}^{-1}\mathbf{i}\kappa \qquad (12.17)$$

Since κ is unknown, it must be estimated by the sample mean or by GLS. These estimators are not identical, even in large samples, for a long memory model, although as shown in Yajima (1988) there is only a small loss in efficiency if the mean is used. Note that because $\mathbf{V}$ is a Toeplitz matrix the number of multiplications required to invert it is of $O(T^2)$, and there exist algorithms in which the order of magnitude is only $T(\log T)^2$.

When h_t is non-stationary, (12.15) is differenced. Smoothed estimators of the first differences of h_t, denoted h_t^*, $t = 2, \ldots, T$, are then calculated from an expression of the form (12.16) with d replaced by $d - 1$ in the calculation of ρ_τ and $\mathbf{V}_\xi$ redefined so as to have 2's on the leading diagonal and minus ones on the off-diagonals on either side. The term involving κ disappears. Estimators of the h_t's are computed from the recursion

$$\tilde{h}_t = \tilde{h}_{t-1} + h_t^*, \quad t = 2, \ldots, T \qquad (12.18)$$

with $\tilde{h}_1 = 0$.

The implied weights for $\tilde{h}_t$ in the centre of a sample of size 100 are shown in Figure 12.3 for $d = 0.45$ and 0.8. In both cases most of the weight is on the nearest observations but the weights given to more remote observations are slow to die away. This contrasts to the weights in the AR-SV model which die away exponentially; see Whittle (1983, p. 59). Nevertheless, the small weight given to remote observations suggests that if the sample is too large to enable $\mathbf{V}$ to be constructed and inverted, little accuracy would be lost by using weights worked out for a smaller sample size.

Another way of approaching the problem is to use the classical formulae. These are valid even for non-stationary models, as shown in Bell (1984). For a doubly-infinite sample, the required weights may be obtained from the lag polynomial given by the expression

$$w(L) = \frac{\sigma_\eta^2 / |1 - L|^{2d}}{\sigma_\eta^2 / |1 - L|^{2d} + \sigma_\xi^2} = \frac{1}{1 + (\sigma_\xi^2/\sigma_\eta^2)|1 - L|^{2d}}$$

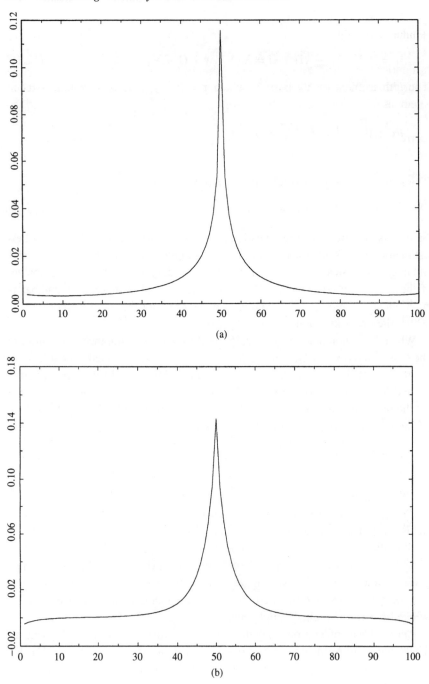

Figure 12.3   *(a) Smoothing weights for d = 0.45, (b) Smoothing weights for d = 0.8*

Finding the weights requires expanding $1 - L$ and $1 - L^{-1}$ and equating powers of L. Alternatively L may be replaced by $\exp(i\lambda)$ and the weights obtained by a Fourier transform. Smoothed estimators near the ends of the sample can be constructed by first extending the sample in both directions using the classical prediction (semi-infinite sample) formula.

Given estimates of h_t throughout the sample, the next problem is to construct corresponding estimates of the σ_t^2's, the variances of the y_t's conditional on the h_t's. To do this we need to estimate the scale factor σ^2. The analysis in Harvey and Shephard (1993) suggests that the sample variance of the heteroscedasticity corrected observations, $\tilde{y}_t$, will provide an estimator which has a relatively small bias. That is

$$\tilde{\sigma}^2 = T^{-1} \sum_{t=1}^{T} \tilde{y}_t^2, \quad \tilde{y}_t = y_t \exp(-\tilde{h}_t/2) \tag{12.19}$$

This can be combined with $\tilde{h}_t$ to produce an estimator of the underlying variance, $\sigma^2 \exp(h_t)$, which does not depend on an assumed distribution for ε_t. On the other hand, constructing an estimator from the estimator of κ, $\hat{\kappa}$, requires an assumption about the distribution of ε_t, since (12.5) implies

$$\hat{\sigma}^2 = \exp(\hat{\kappa} - E(\log \varepsilon_t^2))$$

Given a correct assumption about the distribution of ε_t, $\hat{\sigma}^2$ is a consistent estimator of σ^2 if κ is consistent. However, it is argued in Harvey and Shephard (1993) that the inconsistency of $\tilde{\sigma}^2$ is not necessarily a drawback when the aim is to estimate the underlying variance, σ_t^2, and furthermore $\hat{\sigma}^2$ will tend to have a larger mean square error than $\tilde{\sigma}^2$. Figure 12.4 shows the absolute values of the logged and differenced dollar–Deutschemark exchange rate together with estimates of σ_t calculated from (12.17) and (12.19) for the first 300 observations using the estimated parameters reported at the end of section 12.3.

Now consider predicting the observations on $\log y_t^2$ for $t = T + 1, \ldots, T + l$. If these are denoted by the $l \times 1$ vector $\mathbf{w}_l$, the corresponding MMSLEs in the stationary case are given by

$$\tilde{\mathbf{w}}_l = \mathbf{R}\mathbf{V}^{-1}\mathbf{w} + (\mathbf{I} - \mathbf{R}\mathbf{V}^{-1})\mathbf{i}\kappa \tag{12.20}$$

where $\mathbf{R}$ is the $l \times T$ matrix of covariances between $\mathbf{w}_l$ and $\mathbf{w}$. The corresponding predictions of σ_{T+j}^2, $j = 1, \ldots, l$ are given by exponentiating the elements of $\mathbf{w}_l$ and multiplying by $\tilde{\sigma}^2$.

12.5 EXTENSIONS

We now consider some extensions to the model. The first concerns correlation between ε_t and η_t. Although the methods described above are valid in this case,

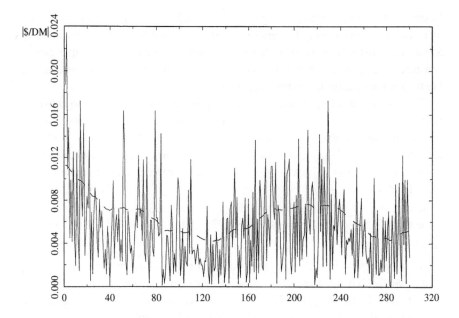

Figure 12.4 *Smoothed estimates of dollar/Deutschemark volatility and values of observations*

more efficient estimators may be obtained for AR-SV models by conditioning on the signs of the y_t's as suggested in Harvey and Shephard (1996). In the present context, this suggestion is not easy to implement. The frequency domain estimator cannot be formed and the **V** matrix is no longer Toeplitz (although it is symmetric) so multiplications of $O(T^3)$ are needed to invert it.

The second extension is to add explanatory variables, x_t, to the right hand side of (12.1) so that

$$y_t = x_t'\beta + \sigma_t\varepsilon_t, \quad t = 1, \ldots, T$$

The approach suggested by Harvey and Shephard (1993) can be applied when $d < 0.5$. Thus it is possible to carry out QML estimation on the OLS residuals and then to construct a feasible GLS estimator of the parameters of the explanatory variables together with a consistent estimator of its asymptotic covariance matrix.

A third extension is to generalize the fractional noise process for h_t. This can be done by letting η_t be an ARMA process, so that h_t is ARFIMA, or by adding other components, including long memory seasonals and cycles.

12.6 CONCLUSIONS

Ding, Granger and Engle (1993) reported two sets of stylized facts for daily stock market data. The first is that the autocorrelations of absolute values of returns tend to be maximized when raised to a power slightly less than one. However, analysis for a stochastic volatility model shows that the maximizing power depends on the strength of the volatility process as measured by its variance and so is not to be taken as an indication of the type of volatility process which is appropriate. The second stylized fact is the tendency of autocorrelations to die away slowly. This feature can be nicely captured by a long memory SV model.

Estimation of the long memory SV model is not as easy as the AR-SV model because the linear statespace form is difficult to use. Generalized method-of-moments (GMM) is possible, but is likely to have very poor properties because of the difficulty of capturing the long memory by a small number of autocovariances. One method that is relatively straightforward to apply is QML in the frequency domain and this may be a reasonable option if the sample size is large.

12.7 APPENDIX

If X_v is distributed as chi-square with v degrees of freedom then

$$EX_v^a = 2^a \Gamma(a + v/2)/\Gamma(v/2), \quad a > -v/2 \tag{12.21}$$

Now if Y is a standard normal variable, (12.21) can be used to evaluate its absolute moments since

$$E|Y|^b = EX_1^{b/2} \tag{12.22}$$

Furthermore if t_v denotes a t-variable with v degrees of freedom, we can write it as $t_v = Y v^{0.5} X_v^{-0.5}$, where Y and X_v are independent, and so

$$E|t_v|^b = v^{b/2} E|Y|^b EX_v^{-b/2}, \quad -1 < b < v \tag{12.23}$$

REFERENCES

Baillie, R.T., Bollerslev, T. and Mikkelsen, H.O. (1996) Fractionally integrated gener-alized autoregressive conditional heteroscedasticity, *Journal of Econometrics*, **74**, 3–30.

Breidt, F.J., Crato, N. and deLima, P. (1998) The detection and estimation of long memory in stochastic volatility, *Journal of Econometrics*, **83**, 325–348.

Bell, W.R. (1984) Signal extraction for nonstationary time series, *Annals of Statistics*, **13**, 646–664.

Bollerslev, T. (1986), Generalized autoregressive conditional heteroscedasticity, *Journal of Econometrics*, **31**, 307–327.

Bollerslev, T., Chou, R.Y. and Kroner, K.F. (1992) ARCH modeling in finance: a review of the theory and empirical evidence, *Journal of Econometrics*, **52**, 5–59.

Bollerslev, T.F. and Mikkelsen, H.O. (1996) Modeling and pricing long-memory in stock market volatility, *Journal of Econometrics*, **73**, 151–184.

Cheung, Y-W. and Diebold, F.X. (1994) On maximum likelihood estimation of the differencing parameter of fractionally integrated noise with unknown mean, *Journal of Econometrics*, **62**, 301–306.

Ding, Z., Granger, C.W.J. and Engle, R.F. (1993) A long memory model of stock market returns and a new model, *Journal of Empirical Finance*, **1**, 107–131.

Engle, R.F. (1982) Autoregressive conditional heteroscedasticity with estimates of the variance of U.K. inflation, *Econometrica*, **50**, 987–1007.

Harvey, A.C. (1989) *Forecasting, Structural Time Series Models and the Kalman Filter*, Cambridge: Cambridge University Press.

Harvey, A.C. and Shephard, N. (1993) Estimation and testing of stochastic variance models, LSE Econometrics discussion paper EM/93/268.

Harvey, A.C. and Shephard, N. (1996) Estimation of an asymmetric stochastic volatility model for asset returns, *Journal of Business and Economic Statistics*, **14**, 429–434.

Harvey, A.C., Ruiz, E. and Shephard, N. (1994) Multivariate stochastic variance models, *Review of Economic Studies*, **61**, 247–264.

Hull, J. and White, A. (1987) The pricing of options on assets with stochastic volatilities, *Journal of Finance*, **42**, 281–300.

Jacquier, E., Polson, N.G. and Rossi, P.E. (1994), Bayesian analysis of stochastic volatility models (with discussion), *Journal of Business and Economic Statistics*, **12**, 371–347.

Kim, S., Shephard, N. and Chib, S. (1998) Stochastic volatility: likelihood inference and comparison with ARCH models, *Review of Economic Studies*, (to appear).

Melino, A. and Turnbull, S. (1990) Pricing foreign currency options with stochastic volatility, *Journal of Econometrics*, **45**, 239–265.

Nelson, D.B. (1991) Conditional heteroscedasticity in asset returns: a new approach, *Econometrica*, **59**, 347–370.

Robinson, P. (1994) Efficient tests of nonstationary hypotheses, *Journal of the American Statistical Association*, **89**, 1420–1437.

Sandmann, G. and Koopman, S.J. (1998) Estimation of stochastic volatility models via Monte Carlo maximum likelihood, *Journal of Econometrics*, (to appear)

Sowell, F. (1992), Maximum likelihood estimation of stationary univariate fractionally integrated time series models, *Journal of Econometrics*, **53**, 165–188.

Yajima, Y. (1988) On estimation of a regression model with long-memory stationary errors, *Annals of Statistics*, **16**, 791–807.

Taylor, S. (1986) *Modelling Financial Time Series*, Chichester: John Wiley.

Taylor, S. (1994) Modelling stochastic volatility, *Mathematical Finance*, **4**, 183–204.

Whittle, P. (1983) *Prediction and Regulation*, 2nd ed., Oxford: Basil Blackwell.

NOTES

1. The original draft of this chapter was written in 1993. At the same time, Breidt, Crato and deLima (1998) independently proposed the same model.

Chapter 13

GARCH processes – some exact results, some difficulties and a suggested remedy

JOHN L. KNIGHT*[†] AND STEPHEN E. SATCHELL*[‡]

SUMMARY

This chapter examines both log and levels models of volatility and determines, where possible, the exact properties of the volatility process and the stochastic process itself. The basic conclusion is that there is little possibility of deriving analytic results except for moments. A simple modification of the GARCH(1,1) process is suggested which is equivalent to an approximation of the original process and leads to much more tractable analysis. An analysis of some typical UK data using both the regular GARCH model and the suggested alternative does not lead to a clear preference of one specification over the other. Finally, we show how stochastic volatility models arise naturally in a world with stochastic information flows.

13.1 INTRODUCTION

The families of ARCH models initiated by Engle (1982) have enjoyed a deserved popularity among applied economists. The success of these models as a way of describing time-varying risk premia in financial models has led to an analysis of the conditional variance as a separate entity, rather like the modelling of the autocorrelation function in the time series work of the 1970s. Thus a

* The first author acknowledges financial support from the Natural Sciences and Engineering Research Council of Canada and Trinity College, Cambridge. Both authors would also like to thank Birkbeck College. For their helpful comments we thank Neil Shepherd, and members of the LSE Econometrics Seminar. The usual disclaimer applies.
[†] Department of Economics, University of Western Ontario.
[‡] Trinity College, Cambridge.

given series of data leads to two series of interest, the series itself, and the series of conditional variances. Findings such as persistence in the conditional variance, see Engle and Bollerslev (1986), suggest that an understanding of the conditional variance density might be of interest. The contribution of this chapter is to present some exact results for the GARCH(1,1) and the multiplicative GARCH(1,1). Our analysis recognizes that GARCH(1,1) models can be represented as stochastic recurrence equations, see Kesten (1973). In this sense, the ARCH/GARCH family have been analysed in applied probability for a considerable period before their discovery in economics. In both cases it is difficult to give results for both the conditional variance *and* the observed variable. For the GARCH(1,1) we can find neither for reasons we present in the text. For the multiplicative GARCH(1,1) we can compute the characteristic function of the conditional variance, the *pdf* can be computed numerically, the *pdf* of the observed variable cannot be calculated, except by Monte Carlo simulation.

To overcome these difficulties, we present an alternative to the regular GARCH(1,1) model by making a minor modification to the specification of the conditional variance. The modification presented allows the distributions of both the conditional variance and the observed variable (unconditionally) to be computed numerically. The parameters can be estimated via maximum likelihood or, as an alternative, from the even moments of the observed variables unconditional distribution.

The standard GARCH(1,1) and multiplicative GARCH(1,1) results are presented in section 13.2. Our new model and its properties are developed in section 13.3. Section 13.4 presents some continuous time models whose exact discretizations are similar to GARCH models. Section 13.5 compares, by way of example, the estimation of our model and that of a GARCH(1,1) using financial data.

13.2   GARCH(1,1) AND MULTIPLICATIVE GARCH(1,1) MODELS

In this section we consider the model

$$X_t = \mu_x + z_t h_t^{1/2} \tag{13.1}$$

where $z_t \sim \text{iid} N(0, 1)$ and $X_t/I_{t-1} \overset{d}{\sim} N(\mu_x, h_t)$ where I_{t-1} is all information up to and including time $t - 1$. This area of econometrics is concerned with the modelling of h_t, our interest is the joint (unconditional) distribution of X_t and h_t. For this reason we shall separate, throughout, the two cases when the process is stationary as opposed to non-stationary; the non-stationary cases being equivalent to conditioning on arbitrary initial values of h_0 and X_0. Given the complexity of the models that have been introduced in this area we shall try and calculate the unconditional moment generating function (mgf) of X_t and h_t.

13.2.1 The GARCH(1,1)

The simplest GARCH process is of course the GARCH(1,1) given by

$$h_t = \alpha_0 + \alpha_1 \varepsilon_{t-1}^2 + \beta_1 h_{t-1}, \quad \alpha_0 > 0, \alpha_1 \geq 0, \beta_1 \geq 0 \tag{13.2}$$

where $\varepsilon_t = h_t^{1/2} z_t$ and $z_t \sim \text{iid}(0, 1)$.

From Bollerslev (1986) we have that $\alpha_1 + \beta_1 < 1$ suffices for wide-sense stationarity and Nelson (1990) shows that this is a necessary and sufficient condition for strong stationarity. Extensions to these results for higher order GARCH systems are discussed in Bougerol and Picard (1992). Straightforward manipulations give

$$h_t = a_0 \sum_{j=0}^{\infty} \prod_{k=1}^{j} (\beta_1 + \alpha_1 z_{t-k}^2) \tag{13.3}$$

If $z_t \sim \text{iid} N(0, 1)$ then we have from Bollerslev (1986) expressions for the $2m$th moment of h_t, and from their appendix the $(2m + 1)$th moments could easily be calculated. However, the non-integral moments of h_t are unknown and thus the properties of ε_t when z_t are non-normal (skewed) will be difficult to find analytically.

While it may be possible to develop a series expansion for the characteristic function of h_t it would be of little use. We are thus left with two alternatives, namely consider some approximation to h_t and analytically examine its distribution or consider the non-stationary case, for fixed h_0, and examine the distribution of h_t. We shall follow the latter in the simplest case of $t = 2$. We note that one can deduce some features of the steady state marginal distribution of X_t by following arguments as in Embrechts *et al.* (1997, Chapter 4).

Before we do, we note that in a recent discussion paper, see Knight and Satchell (1995), the authors derive, for the stationary case, a small $\theta \ (= (\alpha_1/\beta_1))$ approximation to h_t. They also give the characteristic function associated with the approximation and show that approximate moments, to order $0(\theta)$, are equal to those derived by Bollerslev (1986) for h_t. The characteristic function for X_i (unconditional) is also derived leading to the conclusion that the variable X_t behaves like an infinite weighted sum of the difference of two iid $\chi_{(1)}^2$ random variables plus an independent normal variable. As we shall see in section 13.3, the alternative GARCH(1,1) we propose generates a similar distribution for X_t the only difference being in the weights in the linear combination of iid $\chi_{(1)}^2$'s.

Returning now to the non-stationary case we have, for fixed h_0 and $t = 2$

$$h_2 = \alpha_0 + \alpha_1 h_1 z_1^2 + \beta_1 h_1$$

$$= \alpha_0 + (\beta_1 + \alpha_1 z_1^2) h_1$$

$$= \alpha_0 + (\beta_1 + \alpha_1 z_1^2)(\alpha_0 + (\beta_1 + \alpha_1 z_0^2) h_0) \tag{13.4}$$

$$h_2 = \alpha_0(1 + \beta_1 + \alpha_1 z_1^2) + (\beta_1 + \alpha_1 z_1^2)(\beta_1 + \alpha_1 z_0^2)h_0 \tag{13.5}$$

with

$$h_1 = \alpha_0 + (\beta_1 + \alpha_1 z_0^2)h_0$$

Now since $z_0^2 \sim \chi_{(1)}^2$ the $pdf\,(h_1)$ is given by

$$pdf\,(h_1) = \frac{1}{\sqrt{2\pi a_1 h_0}}(h_1 - \alpha_0\beta_1 h_0)^{-1/2} \exp\left[\frac{-1}{2\alpha_1 h_0}(h_1 - \alpha_0 - \beta_1 h_0)\right]$$
$$\times\ \alpha_0 + \beta_1 h_0 < h_1 < \infty \tag{13.6}$$

and the joint $pdf\,(h_1, h_2)$ is given in Theorem 1.

Theorem 1
In the non-stationary case for a GARCH(1,1) model given by (13.2) the joint pdf of the first two conditional variances, i.e. h_1 and h_2 for fixed h_0, is given by

$$pdf\,(h_1, h_2) = \frac{1}{2\pi}[h_0 h_1(h_2 - \alpha_0\beta_1 h_1)(h_1 - \alpha_0 - \beta_1 h_0)]^{-1/2}$$
$$\times \exp\left[-\frac{(h_2 - \alpha_0 0\beta_1 h_1)}{2\alpha_1 h_1} - \frac{(h_1 - \alpha_0 - \beta_1 h_0)}{2\alpha_1 h_0}\right] \tag{13.7}$$
$$\text{for } \alpha_0 + \beta_1 h_0 < h_1 < \infty$$
$$\alpha_0 + \beta_1(\alpha_0 + \beta_1 h_0) < h_2 < \infty$$

Proof   See appendix.

While the joint $pdf\,(h_1, h_2)$ is readily found, the joint cdf, i.e. $P(h_1 < r, h_2 < s)$ cannot be found in closed form; similarly for the marginal distribution of h_2.

However, while for the distribution function results are difficult, moment results are very straightforward and are given in Theorem 2.

Theorem 2
In the non-stationary case with h_t given by (13.2), letting $w_j = \beta_1 + \alpha_1 z_j^2$, $j = 0, 1, 2, \ldots$, we have

$$h_t = \alpha_0 + w_{t-1}h_{t-1}, \quad t \geq 1$$

with h_0 fixed. Consequently, the moments of h_t are given by the recursion

$$E[h_t^m] = E[\alpha_0 + w_{t-1}h_{t-1}]^m$$
$$= \sum_{\ell=0}^{m} \binom{m}{\ell} \alpha_0^{m-\ell} E(w_{t-1}^\ell) E(h_{t-1}^\ell) \tag{13.8}$$

with

$$E(h_1^m) = \sum_{\ell=0}^{m} \binom{m}{\ell} \alpha_0^{m-\ell} h_0^\ell E(w_0^\ell)$$

where

$$E(w_j^\ell) = \beta_1^\ell \sum_{k=0}^{\ell} \binom{\ell}{k} \left(\frac{2\alpha_1}{\beta_1}\right)^k \left(\frac{1}{2}\right)_k \qquad (13.9)$$

Proof   See appendix.

From the results in Theorem 2 we can readily generate *all* the moments. In particular we have

$$E(h_t) = \alpha_0 + E(w_{t-1})E(h_{t-1})$$

and

$$\begin{aligned}
\text{Var}(h_t) &= \text{Var}(w_{t-1})E(h_{t-1}^2) + (E(w_{t-1}))^2 \, \text{Var}(h_{t-1}) \\
&= \text{Var}(w_{t-1})(E(h_{t-1}))^2 + E(w_{t-1}^2) \, \text{Var}(h_{t-1}) \qquad (13.10)
\end{aligned}$$

with

$$\text{Var}(h_1) = h_0^2 \, \text{Var}(w_0)$$

and

$$\text{Var}(w_j) = 2\alpha_1^2$$

Thus in the non-stationary case restrictions on parameters are *not* necessary for the existence of moments.

Consequently, for the GARCH(1,1) model, although the moments are known, it is unlikely that distributional results can be found except for say the small θ case and obviously via Monte Carlo simulation.

We now examine the multiplicative GARCH process proposed by Geweke (1986) in an effort to find a mathematically tractable form. Since there does not appear to be an acronym for this model in an area of econometrics which is very rich in acronyms, see Bollerslev, Chou and Kroner (1992), we offer the following acronym, MULGARCH.

13.2.2   MULGARCH(1,1)

The MULGARCH(1,1) model is basically the GARCH model in logs. Thus

$$\ell n h_t = \omega + \alpha_1 \ell n \varepsilon_{t-1}^2 + \beta_1 \ell n h_{t-1} \qquad (13.11)$$

with $\varepsilon_t = h_t^{1/2} z_t$. This may be written alternatively as:

$$\ell n h_t = \omega + \alpha_1 \ell n z_{t-1}^2 + (\alpha_1 + \beta_1) \ell n h_{t-1}$$

i.e.

$$\ell n h_t = \omega + \alpha_1 \ell n z_{t-1}^2 + \gamma_1 \ell n h_{t-1}; \quad \gamma_1 = \alpha_1 + \beta_1 \qquad (13.12)$$

Simple manipulations lead to

$$h_t = e^{\omega/(1-\gamma_1)} \prod_{j=0}^{\infty} (z_{t-1-j}^2)^{\alpha_1 \gamma_1^j}, \quad \text{for } |\gamma_1| < 1$$

from which, for the stationary case,

$$\ell n h_t = \left(\frac{\omega}{1 - \gamma_1} \right) + \alpha_1 \sum_{j=0}^{\infty} \gamma_1^j \ell n z_{t-1-j}^2$$

In the MULGARCH(1,1) case, we notice that no restrictions are necessary on the parameters α_1 and β_1 to ensure positivity of the conditional variance. However, the restriction $|\alpha_1 + \beta_1| < 1$ is necessary to ensure convergence of $\ell n h_t$ and hence stationarity.

While the characteristic function of h_t seems mathematically intractable all the moments can be easily derived, even the non-integer moments, unlike the GARCH(1,1) model. The characteristic function for $\ell n h_t$, however, is quite straightforward. These results are given in Theorem 3.

Theorem 3

For a MULGARCH(1,1) model given by (13.12) we have, for the stationary solution,

$$E(h_t^{(m+1)/2}) = e^{\omega(m+1)/2(1-\gamma_1)} 2^{\alpha_1(m+1)/2(1-\gamma_1)}$$

$$\times \prod_{j=0}^{\infty} \left[\Gamma((\alpha_1 \gamma_1^j (m+1) + 1)/2) \Big/ \Gamma \left(\frac{1}{2} \right) \right] \qquad (13.13)$$

and in particular

$$\text{Var}(h_t) = e^{2\omega/(1-\gamma_1)} 2^{2\alpha_1/(1-\gamma_1)} \left\{ \prod_{j=0}^{\infty} \left(\Gamma \left(2\alpha_1 \gamma_1^j + \frac{1}{2} \right) \Big/ \Gamma \left(\frac{1}{2} \right) \right) \right.$$

$$\left. - \prod_{j=0}^{\infty} \left[\Gamma \left(\alpha_1 \gamma_1^j + \frac{1}{2} \right) \Big/ \Gamma \left(\frac{1}{2} \right) \right]^2 \right\} \qquad (13.14)$$

The characteristic function of $\ell n h_t$ is given by

$$\phi_{\ell n h_t}(s) = \exp(is\,\omega/(1-\gamma_1))2^{is\,\alpha_1/(1-\gamma_1)}\prod_{j=0}^{\infty}\Gamma\left(is\,\alpha_1\gamma_1^j + \frac{1}{2}\right)\Big/\Gamma\left(\frac{1}{2}\right)$$

(13.15)

Proof See appendix.

Corollary 3
The cumulants for $\ell n h_t$ are given by

$$\kappa_1 = \left[\alpha_1\left(\ell n 2 + \psi\left(\tfrac{1}{2}\right)\right) + \omega\right]/(1-\gamma_1)$$
$$\kappa_m = \alpha_1^m \psi^{m-1}\left(\tfrac{1}{2}\right)/(1-\gamma_1^m); \quad m \geq 2$$

(13.16)

where $\psi^n(\cdot)$ is the polygamma function – see Abramowitz and Stegum (1972, p. 260).

In particular,

$$\mathrm{Var}(\ell n h_t) = \alpha_1^2\pi^2/2(1-\gamma_1^2)$$

Proof See appendix.

We now consider the non-stationary case for the MULGARCH(1,1) where we now introduce a new set of random variables given by

$$q_j = w + \alpha_1 \ell n z_j^2, \quad j = 0, 1, 2, \ldots$$

which results in

$$\ell n h_t = q_{t-1} + \gamma_1 \ell n h_{t-1}$$

(13.17)

giving

$$\ell n h_t = \sum_{j=0}^{t-1}\gamma_1^j q_{t-1-j} + \gamma_1^t \ell n h_0$$

$$\ell n h_t = \omega\sum_{j=0}^{t-1}\gamma_1^j + \alpha_1\sum_{j=0}^{t-1}\alpha_1^j \ell n z_{t-1-j}^2 + \gamma_1^t \ell n h_0$$

(13.18)

Exponentiating (13.18) we have

$$h_t = h_0^{\gamma_1^t}\exp\left(\omega\sum_{j=0}^{t-1}\gamma_1^j\right)\prod_{j=0}^{t-1}(z_{t-1-j}^2)^{\alpha_1\gamma_1^j}$$

(13.19)

While distribution results associated with (13.18) and (13.19) seem out of the question, moment results are straightforward and are presented in the next theorem.

Theorem 4

For the non-stationary case of the MULGARCH(1,1) the moments associated with h_t are given by

$$E[h_t^{(m+1)/2}] = \exp\left(\omega\frac{(m+1)}{2}\sum_{j=0}^{t-1}\gamma_1^j\right)\exp\left(\frac{(m+1)}{2}\alpha_1\ell n2\sum_{j=0}^{t-1}\gamma_1^j\right)$$

$$\times \exp\left(\frac{(m+1)}{2}\gamma_1^t\ell nh_0\right)$$

$$\times \prod_{j=0}^{t-1}\Gamma\left(\frac{(m+1)}{2}\alpha_1\gamma_1^j+\frac{1}{2}\right)\Big/\Gamma\left(\frac{1}{2}\right)$$

with

$$\mathrm{Var}(h_t) = \exp\left(2\omega\sum_{j=0}^{t-1}\gamma_1^j\right)\exp\left(2\alpha_1\ell n2\sum_{j=0}^{t-1}\gamma_1^j\right)\cdot h_0^{2\gamma_1^t}$$

$$\times \left\{\prod_{j=0}^{t-1}\left(\Gamma\left(2\alpha_1\gamma_1^j+\frac{1}{2}\right)\Big/\Gamma\left(\frac{1}{2}\right)\right)\right.$$

$$\left.-\prod_{j=0}^{t-1}\left(\Gamma\left(\alpha_1\gamma_1^j+\frac{1}{2}\right)\Big/\Gamma\left(\frac{1}{2}\right)\right)^2\right\}$$

For the ℓnh_t process we have the characteristic function given by

$$\phi_{\ell nh_t}(s) = \exp(is\gamma_1^t\ell nh_0)\exp\left(is\omega\sum_{j=0}^{t-1}\gamma_1^j\right)\exp\left(is\alpha_1\ell n2\sum_{j=0}^{t-1}\gamma_1^j\right)$$

$$\times \prod_{j=0}^{t-1}\Gamma\left(is\alpha_1\gamma_1^j+\frac{1}{2}\right)\Big/\Gamma\left(\frac{1}{2}\right)$$

Proof   See appendix.

Corollary 4

For the non-stationary case the cumulants for ℓnh_t are given by

$$\kappa_1 = \gamma_1^t\ell nh_0 + \left(\omega+\alpha_1\left(\ell n2+\psi\left(\frac{1}{2}\right)\right)\right)\sum_{j=0}^{t-1}\gamma_1^j$$

$$\kappa_m = \alpha_1^m \psi^{m-1} \left(\frac{1}{2}\right) \sum_{j=0}^{t-1} \gamma_1^{mj}, \quad m \geq 2$$

where $\psi^n(\bullet)$ is the polygamma function referred to earlier.

In particular

$$\mathrm{Var}(\ell n h_t) = \frac{\alpha_1^2 \pi^2}{2} \sum_{j=0}^{t-1} \gamma_1^{2j}$$

Proof   See appendix.

Remark 4.1

From the results in Theorem 4 and the corollary it is clear why, for stationarity, we require $|\gamma_1| < 1$. Since the limit as $t \to \infty$ of the results in Theorem 4 are given by those in Theorem 3, the infinite sums require $|\gamma_1| < 1$ for their convergence.

Remark 4.2

From the results in Theorems 3 and 4 and the associated discussion it is clear that distribution results in the MULGARCH(1,1) case can only be obtained for $\ell n h_t$. For the conditional variance h_t, only moment results are available as is the case for the observed variable X_t given by (13.1).

13.3   AN ALTERNATIVE GARCH(1,1)

In the previous sections we have seen the difficulties, associated with standard GARCH(1,1) and multiplicative GARCH(1,1), in obtaining distributional results for either the conditional variance h_t or the observed variable X_t. For the GARCH(1,1) we can find neither for reasons presented in section 13.2. For the multiplicative GARCH(1,1) the characteristic function for the $\ell n h_t$ was derived, its *pdf* could be found via numerical inversion. However, we cannot find the *pdf* for either the conditional variance h_t or the observed variable X_t.

To overcome the aforementioned difficulties, we now present an alternative to the regular GARCH(1,1) model by making a minor modification to the specification of the conditional variance. The modification presented will be shown to be equivalent to a small θ approximation to GARCH(1,1) as discussed in section 13.2. Consequently, as for the small θ approximation, the distributions for both the conditional variance, h_t, and the observed variable, X_t (unconditionally) can be computed by numerically inverting their characteristic functions.

Returning to (13.1) and (13.2) we now make a change to (13.2) by merely replacing ε_{t-1}^2 by z_{t-1}^2, where $z_t \sim$ iid $N(0, 1)$, resulting in

$$h_t = \alpha_0 + \alpha_1 z_{t-1}^2 + \beta_1 h_{t-1} \tag{13.20}$$

In a recent paper Yang and Bewley (1993) propose the moving average conditional heteroscedastic process and refer to the specification (13.20) as linear autoregressive moving average conditional heteroscedasticity. They do not develop any theoretical properties of h_t or X_t associated with this specification nor do they show the link between this specification and standard GARCH(1,1).

Since z_{t-1}^2 in (13.20) is an iid $\chi_{(1)}^2$ random variable, equation (13.20) can be thought of as an autoregression with a $\chi_{(1)}^2$ innovation. The stationary solution of (13.20) is given by

$$h_t = \frac{\alpha_0}{1 - \beta_1} + \alpha_1 \sum_{j=0}^{\infty} \beta_1^j z_{t-1-j}^2 \tag{13.21}$$

for $\alpha_0 > 0$, $\alpha_1 \geq 0$ and $0 \leq \beta_1 \leq 1$.

From (13.21) we see immediately that h_t will be distributed as an infinite weighted sum of $\chi_{(1)}^2$ random variables. The next theorem states this result explicitly and also gives the unconditional characteristic function of X_t. The remarks which follow the theorem refer to some additional properties of h_t and X_t and comment on the estimation, of this alternative model, via maximum likelihood techniques.

Theorem 5

For the alternative GARCH(1,1) specification given by (13.1) along with (13.20), with $z_j \sim$ iid $N(0, 1)$, using (13.21), we have the characteristic function of h_t, in the stationary case, is given by

$$\phi_{h_t}(s) = \exp(is\alpha_0/(1 - \beta_1)) \prod_{j=0}^{\infty} (1 - 2is\alpha_1 \beta_1^j)^{-1/2}$$

For the observed variable, X_t, given by (13.1), with $\mu_x = 0$, we have

$$\phi_{x_t}(s) = E[E(\exp(ish_t^{1/2} z_t) \mid h_t)]$$

$$= E[\exp(-s^2 h_t/2)]$$

$$= \exp(-s^2 \alpha_0/(2(1 - \beta_1))) \prod_{j=0}^{\infty} (1 + s^2 \alpha_1 \beta_1^j)^{-1/2}$$

Proof See appendix.

Corollary 5

From the characteristic function for h_t and X_t given in Theorem 5 we can readily derive the cumulants, which are given by the following:

For h_t

$$\kappa_1 = (\alpha_0 + \alpha_1)/(1 - \beta_1)$$

$$\kappa_m = (2\alpha_1)^m(m-1)!/2(1 - \beta_1^m), \quad m \geq 2$$

For X_t

$$\kappa_{2m-1} = 0, \quad m \geq 1$$

$$\kappa_{2m} = \alpha_1^m(2m-1)!/(1 - \beta_1^m), \quad m \geq 1$$

Proof   See appendix.

Remark 5.1

Rewriting the characteristic function $\phi_{x_t}(s)$ given in Theorem 5 we have

$$\phi_{x_t}(s) = \exp(-s^2\alpha_0/2(1-\beta)) \prod_{j=0}^{\infty}(1 - is\alpha^{1/2}\beta_1^{j/2})^{-1/2}(1 + is\alpha_1^{j/2})^{-1/2}$$

from which we note that the unconditional distribution of X_t is equivalent to an independent normal plus an infinite weighted sum of the difference of two iid $\chi_{(1)}^2$'s, i.e.

$$X_t \equiv N(0, \alpha_0/(1-\beta)) + \frac{1}{2}\alpha_1^{1/2}\sum_{j=0}^{\infty}\beta_1^{j/2}(G_{1j} - G_{2j})$$

where $G_{k_j} \sim$ iid $\chi_{(1)}^2$ for all j and $k = 1, 2$.

Remark 5.2

In the early part of section 13.2 we referred to results of Knight and Satchell (1995) on the small $\theta = (\alpha_1/\beta_1)$ approximation to the standard GARCH(1,1) given in (13.2). This small θ approximation results in an approximation to h_t given by

$$h_t = \left(\frac{\alpha_0}{1-\beta_1}\right) + \left(\frac{\alpha_0\theta\beta_1}{1-\beta_1}\right)\sum_{j=0}^{\infty}\beta_1^j z_{t-j-1}^2 + 0(\theta^2)$$

Comparing this expression with (13.21) we see that our alternative GARCH(1,1) given by (13.20) can be thought of as an approximation to GARCH(1,1) given by (13.2).

Remark 5.3

One of the reasons that has been put to the authors as to why GARCH is pre-eminent is that $E(h_t \mid I_{t-2})$ is a linear function in h_{t-1}. We note that our alternative GARCH(1,1) given by (13.20) results in

$$E(h_t \mid I_{t-2}) = (\alpha_0 + \alpha_1) + \beta_1 h_{t-1}$$

whereas standard GARCH(1,1) from (13.2) gives

$$E(h_t \mid I_{t-2}) = \alpha_0 + (\alpha_1 + \beta_1) h_{t-1}$$

Consequently, our model (13.20) enjoys the linear conditional h_{t-1} property seen as a virtue by some disciples of GARCH.

Remark 5.4

Under normality, maximum likelihood estimation could be used to estimate our alternative GARCH(1,1) model. In this case we have, for example,

$$X_t = u_t = z_t h_t^{1/2}$$
$$X_t \mid h_t \sim N(0, h_t)$$

and

$$h_t = \alpha_0 + \alpha_1 X_{t-1}^2 / h_{t-1} + \beta_1 h_{t-1}$$

The non-linearity in the specification of h_t presents little additional complication to the standard GARCH(1,1).

Alternatively, since the moment generating function and characteristic function of X_t (unconditional) are known we could estimate the parameters via the even moments of X_t or apply the empirical characteristic function technique (see Feuerverger and McDunnough, 1981). A comparison of our model with standard GARCH(1,1), both being estimated by ML with financial data, is presented in the next section.

13.4   GARCH(1,1) VIA A HETEROGENEOUS POISSON PROCESS

In this section we give a continuous time interpretation of a GARCH(1,1) model. Our starting point is to assume that $P(t)$, which can be thought of as an asset price, follows a stochastic differential equation

$$dP(t) = P(t)(\alpha \, dt + \sigma \, dW(t) + (\exp(Q) - 1) \, dN(t)) \tag{13.22}$$

where $W(t)$ is a Brownian motion, $N(t)$ is a non-homogeneous Poisson process with intensity $\lambda(t)$ and the jump size is $(\exp(Q) - 1)$ where Q is normally distributed $N(\mu_Q, \sigma_Q^2)$. We assume that Q and $W(t)$ are independent. We also assume that $\Delta N(t)$, the increment to $W(t)$ in the interval $(t-1, t]$, has a fixed $\lambda(t) = \lambda_t$ in that interval. The motivation for this is the idea that the flow of information in the day's trading is conditioned by the news known at the close of trading at day $t-1$ or prior to opening at day t.[1] A more realistic model might involve $\lambda(t)$ changing continuously in a stochastic manner, this could be investigated.

In particular, we shall assume that λ_t is day $(t-1)$ measurable and that we only observe end-of-day 'prices' $\{Y_t\}$. In particular, we assume that

$$\lambda_t = \sum_{i=1}^{q} \alpha_i \Delta W^2(t-i) + \sum_{i=1}^{p} \beta_i V(X_{t-i} \mid g_{t-i-1}) \tag{13.23}$$

where all random variables are 'end-of-day' values, $X_t = \ell n(Y_t/Y_{t-1})$, and $V(X_{t-i} \mid g_{t-i-1})$ is the conditional variance of X_{t-i}, conditional on information available at time $t-i-1$.

We can solve equation (13.22) by an application of Ito calculus to mixed stochastic Poisson processes, see Gihman and Skorohod (1972, page 276). The result is[2]

$$Y(t) = Y(t-1)\exp\left[\left(\alpha - \frac{1}{2}\sigma^2\right) + \sigma(W(t) - W(t-1)) + \sum_{i=1}^{\Delta N(i)} Q_i\right] \tag{13.24}$$

where the last term corresponds to the sum of the $\Delta N(t)$ jumps in the day. If we take logarithms our exact discrete time solution is

$$X_t = \left(\alpha - \tfrac{1}{2}\sigma^2\right) + \varepsilon_t + v_t \tag{13.25}$$

where $\varepsilon_t \sim N(0, \sigma^2)$ and $v_t \mid g_{t-1}$ is normal compound Poisson with intensity λ_t given by equation (13.23).

In particular

$$E(X_t \mid g_{t-1}) = \alpha - \tfrac{1}{2}\sigma^2 + \mu_Q \lambda_t$$

and

$$V(X_t \mid g_{t-1}) = \sigma^2 + (\mu_Q + \sigma_Q^2)\lambda_t$$

$$= \sigma^2 + (\mu_Q + \sigma_Q^2)\left(\sum_{i=1}^{q} \alpha_1 \Delta W^2(t-i)\right.$$

$$\left. + \sum_{i=1}^{p} \beta_i V(X_{t-i} \mid g_{t-i-1})\right) \tag{13.26}$$

This shows that equation (13.26) gives us a GARCH in mean model if $\mu_Q \neq 0$ and it is GARCH (p,q) if $\mu_Q = 0$. Furthermore, the conditional density of X_t is compound normal Poisson.[3] That is, the probability density of X_t conditional on g_{t-1} is

$$pdf(X_t \mid g_{t-1}) = \sum_{j=0}^{\infty} \frac{\exp(-\lambda_t)\lambda_t^j \, n(\delta + j\mu_Q, \sigma^2 + j\sigma_Q^2)}{j!} \qquad (13.27)$$

where $n(\cdot, \cdot)$ is the normal density and $\delta = \alpha - \sigma^2/2$.

In what follows, we shall first calculate the moment generating functions of X_t and λ_t in the non-stationary case, conditional on $W(0)$ and λ_1.

We now derive the density of $V(X_t \mid g_{t-1})$. From (13.26) and (13.23), we see that

$$V(X_t \mid g_{t-1}) = \sigma^2 + (\mu_Q + \sigma_Q^2)\left(\sum_{i=1}^{q} \alpha_1 \Delta W^2(t-i)\right)$$

$$+ \sum_{i=1}^{p} \beta_i(\sigma^2 + (\mu_Q^2 + \sigma_Q^2)\lambda_{t-i})$$

Using (13.26) again

$$\lambda_t = \sum_{i=1}^{q} \alpha_i \Delta W^2(t-i) + \sum_{i=1}^{p} \beta_i(\sigma^2 + (\mu_Q^2 + \sigma_Q^2)\lambda_{t-i}) \qquad (13.28)$$

To ease algebraic suffering, we shall restrict ourselves to the GARCH(1,1) case. This means that

$$\lambda_t = \theta\lambda_{t-1} + \alpha_1 \Delta W^2(t-1) + \beta_1\sigma^2 \qquad (13.29)$$

where $\theta = \beta_1(\mu_Q^2 + \sigma_Q^2)$.

The solution to (13.29) is

$$\lambda_t = \alpha_1 \sum_{j=0}^{t-2} \theta^j \Delta W^2(t-1-j) + \theta^{t-1}\lambda_1 + \beta_1\sigma^2 \sum_{j=0}^{t-2} \theta^j \qquad (13.30)$$

where we take λ_1 and $W(0)$ as given. If we set $W(0) = 0$ and treat λ_1 as a constant, the distribution of λ_t can be seen by inspection to be a constant plus a weighted sum of chi-squared ones. Let $\{z_i\}$ denote a sequence of independent chi-squared ones, then

$$\lambda_t \stackrel{d}{=} \theta^{t-1}\lambda_1 + \alpha_1 \sum_{j=0}^{t-2} \theta^j z_{t-1-j} + \beta_1\sigma^2 \sum_{j=0}^{t-2} \theta^j \qquad (13.31)$$

and denoting the (unconditional) moment generating function (*mgf*) of λ_t by $mgf_\lambda(s)$

$$mgf_\lambda(s) = \exp\left[\left(\theta^{t-1}\lambda_1 + \beta_1\sigma^2\sum_{j=0}^{t-2}\theta^j\right)s\right]\prod_{j=0}^{t-2}(1 - 2\alpha_1\theta^js)^{-1/2} \quad (13.32)$$

Now derive the *mgf* of X_t conditional on g_{t-1} from equation (13.25), we call this $mgf_{X_{t-1}}(s)$.

$$\begin{aligned}
mgf_{X_{t-1}} &= \exp\left(\left(\alpha - \tfrac{1}{2}\sigma^2\right)s + \tfrac{1}{2}\sigma^2s^2\right)E(\exp(v_t) \mid g_{t-1})\\
&- \exp\left(\left(\alpha - \tfrac{1}{2}\sigma^2\right)s + \tfrac{1}{2}\sigma^2s^2\right)E_{\Delta N_t}\\
&\times \left(\exp\left(\Delta N_t\mu_Q s + \tfrac{1}{2}\Delta N_t\sigma_Q^2 s^2\right) \mid g_{t-1}\right)\\
&= \exp\left(\left(\alpha\tfrac{1}{2}\sigma^2\right)s + \tfrac{1}{2}\sigma^2s^2\right)\exp\left(\lambda_t\left(\exp\left(\mu_Q s + \tfrac{1}{2}\sigma_Q^2 s^2\right) - 1\right)\right)
\end{aligned}$$
$$(13.33)$$

We now combine our results which are presented as Theorem 6.

Theorem 6
Under the assumption that X_t is generated by equations (13.22) and (13.23), the unconditional time t marginal characteristic functions of the intensity and the time t one-period log return for the GARCH(1,1) model as given by equation (13.25) are

$$mgf_\lambda(s) = \exp\left[\left(\theta^{t-1}\lambda_1 + \beta_1\sigma^2\sum_{j=0}^{t-2}\theta^j\right)s\right]\prod_{j=0}^{t-2}(1 - 2\alpha_1\theta^js)^{-1/2} \quad (13.34)$$

and

$$mgf_X(s) = \exp\left(\left(\alpha - \frac{1}{2}\sigma^2\right)s + \frac{1}{2}\sigma^2s^2\right)$$
$$\times \exp\left[\left(\theta^{t-1}\lambda_1 + \beta_1\sigma^2\sum_{j=0}^{t-2}\theta^j\right)\tilde{\theta}(s)\right]\cdot\prod_{j=0}^{t-2}(1 - 2\alpha_1\theta_j\tilde{\theta}(s))^{-1/2}$$
$$(13.35)$$

where $\tilde{\theta}(s) = \exp\left(\mu_Q s + \tfrac{1}{2}\sigma_Q^2 s^2\right) - 1$, $\theta = \beta_1(\mu_Q^2 + \sigma_Q^2)$ and λ_1 is some constant.

Proof   We take $mgf_X(s)$ as given by equation (13.33). It then follows that

$$\begin{aligned}
mgf_X(s) &= E\left[\exp(\lambda_t\left(\exp(\mu_Q s + \tfrac{1}{2}\sigma_Q^2 s^2) - 1)\right)\right]\cdot\left(\exp(\alpha - \tfrac{1}{2}\sigma^2)s + \tfrac{1}{2}\sigma^2s^2\right)\\
&= \exp\left(\left(\alpha - \tfrac{1}{2}\sigma^2\right)s + \tfrac{1}{2}\sigma^2s^2\right)E(\exp(\lambda_t\tilde{\theta}(s)))
\end{aligned}$$

Substituting from equation (13.32) gives us the result.

Corollary 6

The joint *mgf* of λ_t and X_t, $\phi(s, v) = E(\exp(v\lambda_t + sX_t)) = mgf_X(s)$ in (13.35) with $\tilde{\theta}(s)$ replaced by $\tilde{\theta}(s) + v$.

Proof

$$E(\exp(v\lambda_t + sX_t)) = E(E(\exp(v\lambda_t + sX_t) \mid g_{t-1}))$$

$$= E\left[(\exp v\lambda_t \exp\left[(\alpha - \tfrac{1}{2}\sigma^2) s + \tfrac{1}{2}\sigma^2 s^2\right]\right.$$

$$\left. \times \exp\left(\lambda_t \left(\exp\left(\mu_Q s + \tfrac{1}{2}\sigma_Q^2 s^2\right) - 1\right)\right)\right)]$$

Therefore

$$\phi(s, v) = \exp\left((\alpha - \tfrac{1}{2}\sigma^2) s + \tfrac{1}{2}\sigma^2 s^2\right) \exp(\lambda_t(v + \tilde{\theta}(s)))$$

$$= \exp\left((\alpha - \tfrac{1}{2}\sigma^2) s + \tfrac{1}{2}\sigma^2 s^2\right)$$

$$\times \exp\left[\left(\theta^{t-1}\lambda_1 + \beta_1\sigma^2 \sum_{j=0}^{t-2} \theta^j\right)(\tilde{\theta}(s) + v)\right]$$

$$\times \prod_{j=0}^{t-2}(1 - 2\alpha_1\theta^j(v + \tilde{\theta}(s)))^{-1/2} \tag{13.36}$$

Although Theorem 6 has calculated the unconditional characteristic functions of X_t and λ_t, it follows from equation (13.26) that $V(X_t \mid g_{t-1})$ is a linear transformation of λ_t so that one can easily recalculate our results in terms of $V_t = V(X_t \mid g_{t-1})$ since

$$mgf_{v_t}(s) = \exp(\sigma^2 s)mgf_\lambda((\mu_Q^2 + \sigma_Q^2)s) \tag{13.37}$$

we leave the further calculations to interested readers.

Explicit calculation of moments follows from equation (13.36). If we consider $k(s, v) = \ell n \phi(s, v)$

$$k(s, v) = \left(\alpha - \frac{1}{2}\sigma^2\right) s + \frac{1}{2}\sigma^2 s^2 + \left(\theta^{t-1}\lambda_1 + \beta_1\sigma^2 \sum_{j=0}^{t-2} \theta^j\right)(\tilde{\theta}(s) + v)$$

$$- \frac{1}{2} \sum_{j=0}^{t-2} \ell n(1 - 2\alpha\theta^j(v + \tilde{\theta}(s))), \quad t > 2 \tag{13.38}$$

However, it is simpler to calculate the moments directly from (13.26) and (13.30). Since

$$E(\lambda_t) = \theta^{t-1}\lambda_1 + (\alpha_1 + \beta_1\sigma^2) \sum_{j=0}^{t-2} \theta^j$$

$$E(X_t) = E(E(X_t \mid g_{t-1})) = \alpha - \tfrac{1}{2}\sigma^2 + \mu_Q E(\lambda_t)$$

$$= \alpha - \frac{1}{2}\sigma^2 + \mu_Q \left[(\alpha_1 + \beta_1\sigma^2) \sum_{j=0}^{t-2} (\theta^j + \theta^{t-1}\lambda_1) \right] \qquad (13.39)$$

and

$$V(X_t) = E(V(X_t \mid g_{t-1})) + V(E(X_t \mid g_{t-1}))$$

$$= \sigma^2 + (\mu_Q^2 + \sigma_Q^2) \left[(\alpha_1 + \beta_1\sigma^2) \sum_{j=0}^{t-2} (\theta^j + \theta^{t-1}\lambda_1) \right] + \mu_Q^2 V(\lambda_t)$$

$$= \sigma^2 + (\mu_Q^2 + \sigma_Q^2) \left[(\alpha_1 + \beta_1\sigma^2) \sum_{j=0}^{t-2} (\theta^j + \theta^{t-1}\lambda_1) \right] + 2\mu_Q^2\alpha_1^2 \sum_{j=0}^{t-2} \theta^{2j}$$

$$(13.40)$$

Higher moments may be calculated, we do not do this. Instead, we turn to a discussion of whether X_t will converge to a weakly stationary distribution as t tends to infinity. From a perusal of conditions (13.39) and (13.40) we see that the requirement for convergence in mean-square error is that $|\theta| < 1$. Since $\theta = \beta_1(\mu_Q^2 + \sigma_Q^2)$, this implies that $0 < \beta_1 < 1/(\mu_Q^2 + \sigma_Q^2)$.

In turn

$$\lim_{t\to\infty} E(X_t) = \alpha - \tfrac{1}{2}\sigma^2 + \mu_Q(\alpha_1 + \beta_1\sigma^2)/(1 - \theta)$$

$$\lim_{t\to\infty} V(X_t) = \sigma^2 + (\mu_Q^2 + \sigma_Q^2)(\alpha_1 + \beta_1\sigma^2)/(1 - \theta) + 2\mu_Q^2\alpha_1^2/(1 - \theta^2)$$

We present our stationarity results in Theorem 7.

Theorem 7
(i) The necessary conditions for the GARCH(1,1) model to be weakly stationary are that $\alpha_1 > 0$, $0 < \beta_1 < 1/(\mu_Q^2 + \sigma_Q^2)$.
(ii) If $\alpha_1 > 0, 0 < \beta_1 < 1/(\mu_Q^2 + \sigma_Q^2)$ then (X_t, λ_t) converges in distribution to $(X_\infty, \lambda_\infty)$ with joint *mgf* $\phi(s, v) = E(\exp(\lambda_\infty v + X_\infty s))$ is given by

$$\phi(s, v) = \exp\left((\alpha - \tfrac{1}{2}\sigma^2)s + \tfrac{1}{2}\sigma^2 s^2\right)\exp[(\beta\sigma^2/(1 - \theta))(\tilde{\theta}(s) + v)]$$

$$\times \prod_{j=0}^{\infty}(1 - 2\alpha\theta^j(\bar{\theta}(s) + v))^{-1/2}$$

Proof   We have already proved (i) in the discussion leading up to Theorem 6. For (ii) we use the result that if the limit of a characteristic function exists and is continuous at the origin then the limit is the characteristic function of the limiting distribution, see Cramer (1946, p. 102). If we take v and s fixed and choose ν so that $0 < \nu + \tilde{\theta}(s) < 1$, the result follows on allowing t to tend to infinity in the *mgf* given in the corollary of Theorem 6.

13.5   AN EMPIRICAL COMPARISON

In this section we model the logarithmic daily return, i.e. $X_t = \ln(P_t/P_{t-1})$, $P_t = $ stock price, using both the standard GARCH(1,1) and our alternative GARCH, henceforth denoted ALT-GARCH developed in the previous section. The data consists of 491 daily observations from 1 November 1989 to 11 October 1991 for five UK companies: ASDA Group, British Telecom (BT), Grand Metropolitan (GMET), ICI and Thorn-EMI (THN).

The accompanying Table 13.1 presents the results of maximum likelihood estimation of the four parameters in the specifications:

$$X_t = \mu + h_t^{1/2} z_t, \quad z_t \sim \text{iid} N(0, 1)$$

where for:

$$\text{GARCH(1,1)}: \quad h_t = \alpha_0 + \alpha_1 h_{t-1} z_{t-1}^2 + \beta_1 h_{t-1} \tag{13.41}$$

and for:

$$\text{ALT-GARCH(1,1)}: \quad h_t = \alpha_0 + \alpha_1 z_{t-1}^2 + \beta_1 h_{t-1} \tag{13.42}$$

Table 13.1 *Maximum likelihood estimation*

	ASDA	BT	GMET	ICI	THN
GARCH					
μ	−0.0001	0.0009	0.001	0.005	0.0002
	(−0.13)	(1.57)	(1.72)	(0.89)	(0.39)
σ	0.0003	0.000001	0.000001	0.000018	0.000003
	(2.23)	(15.6)	(3.33)	(7.99)	(8.09)
α	0.662	−0.0	0.033	0.097	0.017
	(6.36)	(−0.0)	(2.59)	(2.80)	(1.42)
β	0.165	0.993	0.961	0.797	0.964
	(2.22)	(0.04)	(52.51)	(12.45)	(29.41)
Value of ML	3.245	3.824	3.817	3.881	3.902
ALT-GARCH					
μ	−0.00055	0.0009	0.001	0.0005	0.00021
	(−0.02)	(0.003)	(0.08)	(0.04)	(3.78)
σ	0.0002	0.000002	−0.000004	0.00001	0.0
	(7.75)	(0.41)	(−2.54)	(1.86)	(0.0)
α	0.00034	−0.0	0.000005	0.000013	0.000002
	(5.70)	(0.0)	(2.76)	(2.77)	(3.27)
β	0.257	0.993	0.9922	0.871	0.979
	(3.76)	(85.46)	(186.7)	(17.97)	(134.9)
Value of ML	3.208	3.837	3.818	3.880	3.899

The numbers in the parentheses are *t*-statistics.

From the table it is very difficult to tell which model has a better fit to the empirical data. Both models have significant estimates of α and β. In terms of magnitude, α is larger in a GARCH model while β is larger in the ALT-GARCH model. Comparing the likelihood value at the maximum in each case we note there is very little difference indicating, albeit roughly, that the two models contain the same amount of information. One could, in principle, throw the whole battery of non-nested test statistics at this problem. Equations (13.41) and (13.42) could be encompassed by an appropriate equation in h_{t-1}, z_{t-1}^2 and $h_{t-1}z_{t-1}^2$, we leave such a task to those better equipped both in technique and spiritual affiliation.

13.6 APPENDIX

Theorem 1 Proof.

From (13.2) we have

$$h_1 = \alpha_0 + (\beta_1 + \alpha_1 z_0^2)h_0$$

and

$$h_2 = \alpha_0 + (\beta_1 + \alpha_1 z_1^2)h_1$$

Since $z_j^2 \sim$ iid $\chi_{(1)}^2$, $j = 0, 1$ and letting $\omega_j = \beta_1 + \alpha_1 z_j^2$ we have that ω_j are independently distributed with joint *pdf*:

$$pdf(\omega_0, \omega_1) = \frac{1}{2\pi}((\omega_0 - \beta_1)(\omega_1 - \beta_1))^{-1/2}$$

$$\times \exp\left[-\frac{1}{2\alpha_1}((\omega_0 - \beta_1) + (\omega_1 - \beta_1))\right], \quad \beta_1 < \omega_0 < \infty$$

$$\beta_1 < \omega_1 < \infty$$

We now transform $(\omega_0, \omega_1) \to (u_0, u_1)$ where $u_0 = \alpha_0 + \omega_0 h_0$ and $u_1 = \omega_1$. The Jacobian of the transformation is $1/h_0$ and again the new variables u_0 and u_1 are independently distributed with joint *pdf*:

$$pdf(u_0, u_1) = \frac{1}{2\pi}(h_0(u_0 - \beta_1)(u_1 - \alpha_0 - \beta_1 h_0))^{-1/2}$$

$$\times \exp\left[-\frac{1}{2\alpha_1 h_0}\{h_0(u_1 - \beta_1)\right.$$

$$\left. +(u_1 - \alpha_1 - \beta_1 h_0)\}\right], \quad \alpha_0 + \beta_1 h_0 < u_0 < \infty$$

$$\beta_1 < u_1 < \infty$$

Finally we transform $(u_0, u_1) \to (h_0, h_1)$ where

$$h_1 = u_0 \quad \text{and} \quad h_2 = \alpha_0 + u_0 u_1$$

with Jacobian $1/h_1$.

Thus the joint *pdf* of (h_1, h_2) is given by (13.7).

Theorem 2 Proof

First we note that

$$E(w_j^\ell) = E[\beta_1 + \alpha_1 z_j^2]^\ell$$

$$= E\left[\sum_{k=0}^{\ell} \binom{\ell}{k} \beta_1^{\ell-k}(\alpha_1 z_j^2)^k\right]$$

$$= \beta_1^\ell \sum_{k=0}^{\ell} \binom{\ell}{k} (\alpha_1/\beta_1)^k E(z_j^2)^k$$

and since $z_j^2 \sim$ iid $\chi_{(1)}^2$ we have $E(z_j^2)^k = 2^k \dfrac{\Gamma\left(k+\frac{1}{2}\right)}{\Gamma\left(\frac{1}{2}\right)}$. Thus

$$E(w_j^\ell) = \beta_1^\ell \sum_{k=0}^{\ell} \binom{\ell}{k} (2\alpha_1/\beta_1)^k \left(\frac{1}{2}\right)_k, \qquad \text{for all } j$$

Next we note that ω_j and h_j are independent. Hence from (13.2) we have

$$E(h_t^m) = E[\alpha_0 + w_{t-1}h_{t-1}]^m$$

$$= \sum_{k=0}^{m} \binom{m}{k} \alpha_0^{m-k} E[w_{t-1}^k h_{t-1}^k]$$

$$= \sum_{k=0}^{m} \binom{m}{k} \alpha_0^{m-k} E(w_{t-1}^k) E(h_{t-1})^k$$

For $t = 1$, we have

$$E(h_1^m) = \sum_{k=0}^{m} \binom{m}{k} \alpha_0^{m-k} h_0^k E(w_0^k), \qquad \text{for } h_0 \text{ fixed}$$

Thus the mth moments of h_t may be derived recursively.

Theorem 3 Proof

Since

$$h_t = e^{\omega/(1-\gamma_1)} \prod_{j=0}^{\infty} (z_{t-1-j}^2)^{\alpha_1 \gamma_1^j} \quad \text{and} \quad z_t^2 \sim \text{iid } \chi_{(1)}^2$$

we have

$$h_t^{(m+1)/2} = e^{\omega(m+1)/2(1-\gamma_1)} \prod_{j=0}^{\infty} (z_{t-1-j}^2)^{\alpha_1 \gamma_1^j (m+1)/2}$$

and thus

$$E(h_t^{(m+1)/2}) = e^{\omega(m+1)/2(1-\gamma_1)} \prod_{j=0}^{\infty} E\left[(z_{t-1-j}^2)^{\alpha_1 \gamma_1^j (m+1)/2}\right]$$

Further, with

$$E[z_{t-1-j}^2]^{\delta} = 2^{\delta}\Gamma\left(\delta + \tfrac{1}{2}\right)/\Gamma\left(\tfrac{1}{2}\right)$$

Then

$$E(h_t^{(m+1)/2}) = e^{\omega(m+1)/2(1-\gamma_1)} 2^{\alpha_1(m+1)/2(1-\gamma_1)}$$

$$\times \prod_{j=0}^{\infty} \Gamma[(\alpha_1 \gamma_1^j (m+1)+1)/2]/\Gamma\left(\tfrac{1}{2}\right)$$

For the Var(h_t) we have:

$$\mathrm{Var}(h_t) = e^{2\omega/(1-\gamma_1)} \, \mathrm{Var} \left[\prod_{j=0}^{\infty}(z_{t-j-1}^2)^{\alpha_1 \gamma_1^j}\right]$$

$$= e^{2\omega/(1-\gamma_1)} \left\{ \prod_{j=0}^{\infty} E[z_{t-j-1}^2]^{2\alpha_1 \gamma_1^j} - \prod_{j=0}^{\infty}\left[E\left(z_{t-j-1}^{2\alpha_1 \gamma_1^j}\right)\right]^2 \right\}$$

$$= e^{2\omega/(1-\gamma_1)} \left\{ 2^{2\alpha_1/(1-\gamma_1)} \prod_{j=0}^{\infty} \Gamma\left(2\alpha_1 \gamma_1^j + \tfrac{1}{2}\right) \Big/ \Gamma\left(\tfrac{1}{2}\right) \right.$$

$$\left. -2^{2\alpha_1/(1-\gamma_1)} \prod_{j=0}^{\infty}\left[\Gamma\left(\alpha_1 \gamma_1^j + \tfrac{1}{2}\right)\Big/\Gamma\left(\tfrac{1}{2}\right)\right]^2 \right\}$$

For the characteristic function of $\ell n h_t$ we require

$$E[\exp(is\ell n h_t)] = E[h_t^{is}] = e^{is\omega/(1-\gamma_1)} 2^{is\alpha_1/(1-\gamma_1)}$$

$$\times \prod_{j=0}^{\infty} \Gamma\left(is\alpha_1 \gamma_1^j + \tfrac{1}{2}\right) \Big/ \Gamma\left(\tfrac{1}{2}\right)$$

Corollary 3 Proof
From Theorem 3 we have the *cgf* of $\ell n h_t$ given by

$$Q(s) = \ell n \phi_{\ell n h_t}(-is)$$

$$= s\omega/(1-\gamma_1) + (s\alpha_1/(1-\gamma_1))\ell n 2$$

$$+ \sum_{j=0}^{\infty}\left[\ell n \Gamma\left(s\alpha_1 \gamma_1^j + \tfrac{1}{2}\right) - \ell n \Gamma\left(\tfrac{1}{2}\right)\right]$$

Thus

$$Q'(s) = \omega/(1 - \gamma_1) + (\alpha_1/(1 - \gamma_1))\ell n 2 + \sum_{j=0}^{\infty} \alpha_1 \gamma_1^j \psi \left(s\alpha_1 \gamma_1^j + \left(\frac{1}{2}\right) \right)$$

and

$$Q^m(s) = \sum_{j=0}^{\infty} \alpha_1^m \gamma_1^{mj} \psi^{m-1} \left(s\alpha_1 \gamma_1^j + \left(\frac{1}{2}\right) \right), \quad m \geq 2$$

Evaluating $Q'(s)$ and $Q^m(s)$ at $s = 0$ gives the cumulants.
   Since

$$\text{Var}(h_t) = Q''(0)$$
$$= \alpha_1^2 \psi^1 \left(\frac{1}{2}\right) / (1 - \gamma_1^2)$$

and

$$\psi^1(1/2) = \pi^2/2 \quad \text{(see Abramovitz and Stegum, 1972, p. 260, 6.4.4)}$$

we have

$$\text{Var}(h_t) = \alpha_1^2 \pi^2/2(1 - \gamma_1^2)$$

Theorem 4 Proof
Rewriting (13.19) to ease the notational burden we have

$$h_t = \exp(\gamma_1^t \ell n h_0) \exp \left(\omega \sum_{j=0}^{t-1} \gamma_1^j \right) \prod_{j=0}^{t-1} (z_{t-1-j}^2)^{\alpha_1 \gamma_1^j}$$

hence

$$h_t^{(m+1)/2} = \exp \left(\left(\frac{m+1}{2}\right) \gamma_1^t \ell n h_0 \right) \exp \left(\omega \left(\frac{m+1}{2}\right) \sum_{j=0}^{t-1} \gamma_1^j \right)$$

$$\times \prod_{j=0}^{t-1} (z_{t-1-j}^2)^{((m+1)/2)\alpha_1 \gamma_1^j}$$

Taking expectations we have

$$E\left[h_t^{(m+1)/2}\right] = \exp \left(\left(\frac{m+1}{2}\right) \gamma_1^t \ell n h_0 \right) \exp \left(\omega \left(\frac{m+1}{2}\right) \sum_{j=0}^{t-1} \gamma_1^j \right)$$

$$\times \prod_{j=0}^{t-1} 2^{((m+1)/2)\alpha_1 \gamma_1^j} \cdot \frac{\Gamma\left(\left(\frac{m+1}{2}\right)\alpha_1 \gamma_1^j + \left(\frac{1}{2}\right)\right)}{\Gamma\left(\frac{1}{2}\right)}$$

$$= \exp\left(\left(\frac{m+1}{2}\right)\gamma_1^t \ell n h_0\right) \exp\left(\omega\left(\frac{m+1}{2}\right)\sum_{j=0}^{t-1}\gamma_1^j\right)$$

$$\times \exp\left(\left(\frac{m+1}{2}\right)\alpha_1 \ell n 2 \sum_{j=0}^{t-1}\gamma_1^j\right)$$

$$\times \prod_{j=0}^{t-1}\Gamma\left(\left(\frac{m+1}{2}\right)\alpha_1\gamma_1^j + \frac{1}{2}\right)\bigg/\Gamma\left(\frac{1}{2}\right)$$

For the Var(h_t) we note

$$\text{Var}(h_t) = E[h_t^2] - (E(h_t))^2$$

with

$$E[h_t^2] = \exp(2\gamma_1^t \ell n h_0)\exp\left(2\omega\sum_{j=0}^{t-1}\gamma_1^j\right)\exp\left(2\alpha_1 \ell n 2 \sum_{j=0}^{t-1}\gamma_1^j\right)$$

$$\times \prod_{j=0}^{t-1}\Gamma\left(2\alpha_1\gamma_1^j + \frac{1}{2}\right)\bigg/\Gamma\left(\frac{1}{2}\right)$$

and

$$E[h_t] = \exp(\gamma_1^t \ell n h_0)\exp\left(\omega\sum_{j=0}^{t-1}\gamma_1^j\right)\exp\left(\alpha_1 \ell n 2 \sum_{j=0}^{t-1}\gamma_1^j\right)$$

$$\times \prod_{j=0}^{t-1}\Gamma\left(\alpha_1\gamma_1^j + \frac{1}{2}\right)\bigg/\Gamma\left(\frac{1}{2}\right)$$

Thus

$$\text{Var}(h_t) = \exp(2\gamma_1^t \ell n h_0)\exp\left(2\omega\sum_{j=0}^{t-1}\gamma_1^j\right)\exp\left(2\alpha_1 \ell n 2 \sum_{j=0}^{t-1}\gamma_1^j\right)$$

$$\times \left[\prod_{j=0}^{t-1}\left(\Gamma\left(2\alpha_1\gamma_1^j + \frac{1}{2}\right)\bigg/\Gamma\left(\frac{1}{2}\right)\right)\right.$$

$$\left. - \prod_{j=0}^{t-1}\left(\Gamma\left(\alpha_1\gamma_1^j + \frac{1}{2}\right)\bigg/\Gamma\left(\frac{1}{2}\right)\right)^2\right]$$

For the characteristic function of $\ell n h_t$ we note that $E[\exp(is\ell n h_t)] = E[h_t^{is}]$ and the result follows immediately upon replacing $(m+1)/2$ by is in the moment formula.

Corollary 4 Proof

From the characteristic function of $\ell n h_t$ given in Theorem 4 we have the cumulant generating function:

$$k_{\ell n h_t}(s) = \ell n \phi_{\ell n h_t}(-is)$$

$$= (s\gamma_1^t \ell n h_0) + \left(s\omega \sum_{j=0}^{t-1} \gamma_i^j \right) + \left(s\alpha_1 \ell n 2 \sum_{j=0}^{t-1} \gamma_1^j \right)$$

$$+ \sum_{j=0}^{t-1} \ell n \left[\Gamma \left(s\alpha_1 \gamma_1^j + \frac{1}{2} \right) \middle/ \Gamma \left(\frac{1}{2} \right) \right]$$

Taking derivatives, we have

$$k'_{\ell n h_t}(s) = \gamma_1^t \ell n h_0 + \omega \sum_{j=0}^{t-1} \gamma_i^j + \alpha_1 \ell n 2 \sum_{j=0}^{t-1} \gamma_1^j + \sum_{j=0}^{t-1} \alpha_1 \gamma_1^j \Psi \left(s\alpha_1 \gamma_1^j + \frac{1}{2} \right)$$

$$k^m_{\ell n h_t}(s) = \sum_{j=0}^{t-1} (\alpha_1 \gamma_1^j)^m \Psi^{m-1} \left(s\alpha_1 \gamma_1^j + \frac{1}{2} \right)$$

evaluating these derivatives at $s = 0$ gives the desired results. When $m = 2$, using the fact that $\Psi'(1/2) = \pi^2/2$ we have immediately that

$$\text{Var}(\ell n h_t) = k^2_{\ell n h_t}(0) = \frac{\alpha_1^2 \pi^2}{2} \sum_{j=0}^{t-1} \gamma_1^{2j}$$

Theorem 5 Proof

From (13.21) we have immediately that

$$\phi_{h_t}(s) = E[\exp(is\, h_t)]$$

$$= E \left[\exp(is\, \alpha_0/(1 - \beta_1)) \exp \left(is\, \alpha_1 \sum_{j=0}^{\infty} \beta_i^j z_{t-1-j}^2 \right) \right]$$

$$= \exp(is\, \alpha_0/(1 - \beta_1)) \prod_{j=0}^{\infty} E[\exp(is\, \alpha_1 \beta_1^j z_{t-1-j}^2)]$$

$$= \exp(is\, \alpha_0/(1 - \beta_1)) \prod_{j=0}^{\infty} (1 - 2is\, \alpha_1 \beta_1^j)^{(-1/2)}$$

The last line follows from the characteristic function of $\chi^2_{(1)}$.

To find the characteristic function of χ_t we note that

$$X_t \mid h_t \sim N(0, h_t)$$

so

$$E[\exp(is\,X_t) \mid h_t] = \exp(-s^2 h_t/2)$$

Thus

$$\phi_{x_t}(s) = E[\exp(is\,X_t)] = E[E[\exp(is\,X_t) \mid h_t]]$$
$$= \phi_{h_t}(is/2)$$

and the result follows.

Corollary 5 Proof

For h_t, the cumulant generating function is given by

$$k_{h_t}(s) = \ln\phi_{h_t}(-is)$$

$$= s\alpha_0/(1 - \beta_1) - \frac{1}{2}\sum_{j=0}^{\infty} \ell n(1 - 2s\alpha_1\beta_1^j)$$

Differentiating with respect to s and evaluating at $s = 0$ gives the desired result. For X_t a similar procedure gives

$$k_{x_t}(s) = \ln\phi_{x_t}(-is)$$

$$= s^2\alpha_0/2(1 - \beta_1) - (1/2)\sum_{j=0}^{\infty} \ell n(1 - s^2\alpha_1\beta_1^j)$$

and we notice immediately that all off-order cumulants will be zero, i.e.

$$\kappa_{2m-1} = 0, \quad m \geq 1$$

For even-order cumulants, straightforward differentiation and evaluation at $s = 0$ gives

$$\kappa_{2m} = \alpha_1^m(2m - 1)!/(1 - \beta_1^m), \quad m \geq 1$$

REFERENCES

Abramowitz, M. and Stegum, I.A. (1972) *Handbook of Mathematical Functions,* Dover Publications Inc, New York.

Bollerslev, T. (1986) Generalized autoregressive conditional heteroscedasticity, *Journal of Econometrics,* **31**, 307–327.

346 Forecasting Volatility in the Financial Markets

Bollerslev, T., Chou, R.Y. and Kroner, K.F. (1992) ARCH modeling in finance, *Journal of Econometrics*, **52**, 5–59.

Bookstaber, R.M. and Pomerantz, S. (1989) An information based model of market volatility, *Financial Analysts Journal*, November/December, 37–46.

Bougerol, P. and Picard, N. (1992) Stationarity of GARCH processes and of some nonnegative time series, *Journal of Econometrics*, **52**, 115–127.

Cramer, M. (1946) *Mathematical Methods of Statistics*, Princeton University Press, Princeton.

Embrechts, P. *et al.* (1997) *Modelling Extremal Events*, Springer-Verlag, New York.

Engle, R.F. (1982) Autogressive conditional heteroscedasticity with estimates of the variance of U.K. inflation, *Econometrica*, **50**, 987–1008.

Engle, R.F. and Bollerslev, T. (1986) Modelling the persistence of conditional variances, *Econometric Reviews*, **5**, 1–50, 81–87.

Feuerverger, A. and McDunnough, P. (1981) On the efficiency of the empirical characteristic function procedures, *Journal of the Royal Statistical Society*, **B43**, 20–27.

Geweke, J. (1986) Modeling the persistence of conditional variances: a comment, *Econometric Reviews*, **5**, 57–61.

Gihman, I. and Skorohod, A. (1972) *Stochastic Differential Equations*. Springer-Verlag, New York.

Jorion, P. (1988) On jump processes in the foreign exchange and stock markets, *Review of Financial Studies*, **1**, 427–445.

Kesten, M. (1973) Random difference equations and renewal theory for products of random matrices, *Acta Mathematica*, **131**, 207–248.

Knight, J.L and Satchell, S.E. (1995) An approximation to GARCH, problem 95.13, *Econometric Theory*, **11**, 211–14.

Nelson, D.B. (1990) Stationarity and persistence in the GARCH(1,1) model, *Econometric Theory*, **6**, 318–334.

Yang, M. and Bewley, B. (1993), Moving average conditional heteroscedastic processes, mimeo, University of New South Wales.

NOTES

1. Bookstaber and Pomerantz (1989) model the arrival of information in a similar way. This in turn leads to a compound Poisson volatility model.
2. By convention if $\Delta N(t) = 0$ the last term takes the value zero.
3. See Jorion (1988) where various financial data are modelled by compound normal Poisson processes.

Index

ALSO FROM BUTTERWORTH-HEINEMANN

Advanced Trading Rules

Edited by *Emmanuel Acar*, Proprietary Trader, Dresdner Kleinwort Benson
And *Stephen Satchell,* Trinity College, Cambridge and Birkbeck College, London.

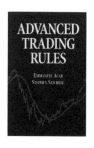

- Complete overview of cutting edge financial markets trading rules
- How to apply econometrics, computer modelling, technical and quantitative analysis to financial markets trading
- Understand how profit by using technical indicators, neural networks, genetic algorithms, quantitative techniques and charts

Advanced Trading Rules is the essential guide to state of the art techniques currently used by the very best financial traders, analysts and fund managers. The editors have brought together the world's leading professional and academic experts to explain how to understand, develop and apply cutting edge trading rules and systems. It is indispensable reading if you are involved in the derivatives, fixed income, foreign exchange and equities markets.

07506 3817 6 Hardback

Fixed Income and Interest Rate Derivative Analysis

Mark Britten-Jones, Assistant Professor of Finance, London Business School

- Crystal clear, up-to-date and thorough coverage of a key topic in finance.
- A comprehensive and accessible explanation of underlying theory, and its practical application. Case studies and worked examples from around the world's capital markets.
- How to use spreadsheet modelling in fixed income and interest rate derivative valuation.

Fixed Income and Interest Rate Derivative Analysis gives a clear and accessible approach to the analytical techniques of debt instrument valuation. Without using complicated mathematical abstractions, this text shows that the fundamentals of fixed income and interest rate derivative analysis can be easily understood when seen as a small number of simple economic concepts.

07506 4012 x Hardback

Strategic Issues in the Life Assurance Industry

Hugh Macmillan, Professor of Business Policy, University of Edinburgh
Mike Christophers, FIA, Partner in KPMG
Foreword by Roy Ranson, Managing Director and Actuary, The Equitable Life
Assurance Society

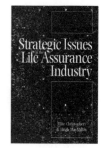

Strategic Issues in the Life Assurance Industry shows:

- how technology, competition and regulation are transforming this market
- how to win the new battles for success in commercial life assurance
- how the leading players are planning to meet the impending challenges

Strategic Issues in the Life Assurance Industry is based upon ground breaking new research that identifies the key strategic issues affecting life assurance over the next five years and beyond.

07506 32801 Hardback